An Introduction to Television Studies

'A wonderfully ambitious and clear introduction to television studies for the undergraduate reader.'
   Gill Branston, University of Cardiff, and co-author of *The Media Student's Book*

'An excellent introduction to television studies, with helpful accounts of key concepts tied to some engaging discussions of recent shows.'
   David Gauntlett, University of Bournemouth and author of
   Media, Gender and Identity

'I have no doubt that this work will become a must for all students wishing to study the new and growing discipline of television studies.'
   Paul Rixon, University of Surrey, Roehampton

'Destined to feature prominently on every television student's preparatory reading wish-list.'
   Deborah Jermyn, University of Surrey, Roehampton and co-editor of
   Understanding Reality Television

In this comprehensive textbook, Jonathan Bignell provides students with a framework for understanding the key concepts and main approaches to Television Studies, including audience research, television history and broadcasting policy, and the analytical study of individual programmes.

Features include a glossary of key terms, key terms defined in margins, suggestions for further reading at the end of each chapter, activities for use in class or as assignments, and case studies discussing advertisements such as the Guinness 'Surfer' ad, approaches to news reporting, and programmes such as *Big Brother*, *The West Wing*, *America's Most Wanted* and *The Cosby Show*.

Individual chapters address: studying television, television histories, television cultures, television texts and narratives, television and genre, television production, postmodern television, television realities, television representation, television you can't see, shaping audiences, television in everyday life.

Jonathan Bignell is Reader in Television and Film at the University of Reading. He is the author of *Media Semiotics: An Introduction* and *Postmodern Media Culture*, editor of *Writing and Cinema*, and joint editor of *British Television Drama: Past, Present and Future*.

An Introduction to Television Studies

Jonathan Bignell

Routledge
Taylor & Francis Group

LONDON AND NEW YORK

First published 2004
by Routledge
11 New Fetter Lane, London EC4P 4EE

Simultaneously published in the USA and Canada
by Routledge
29 West 35th Street, New York, NY 10001

Routledge is an imprint of the Taylor & Francis Group

Designed and typeset in Janson and Akzidenz Grotesk by
Keystroke, Jacaranda Lodge, Wolverhampton
Printed and bound in Great Britain by
TJ International Ltd, Padstow, Cornwall

British Library Cataloguing in Publication Data
A catalogue record for this book is available from the British Library

Library of Congress Cataloging in Publication Data
A catalog record for this book has been requested

ISBN 0–415–26112–0 (hbk)
ISBN 0–415–26113–9 (pbk)

Contents

Illustrations

Acknowledgements

I would like to thank my colleagues at the University of Reading and at Royal Holloway University of London who have assisted in shaping my approach to Television Studies and its teaching. It is difficult to single out individuals to thank, but the work in this book has sometimes benefited from the contributions of particular people. Some of the material on television production in Chapter 6 derives from the excellent teaching of screen drama by Gideon Koppel and Jenny Wilkes, and the exemplary courses on television producing taught by Susanna Capon and Barry Hanson. The wider community of scholars in Television Studies also deserve my thanks, not only for the work explicitly acknowledged and referenced in the text but also for the wealth of ideas that I have encountered over nearly two decades of studying and writing about television. I am grateful to the students I have worked with over the years, and occasionally material in this book derives from their research. In Chapter 6 I draw on an unpublished interview conducted by Helen Quinney for her final-year project, and the discussion of Singaporean television commercials in Chapter 7 draws on a final-year dissertation by Clara Ong. Discussions with past and present postgraduate teaching assistants about teaching Television Studies have been helpful in thinking through the presentation of material in this book, and I am particularly grateful to Christina Adamou, Simone Knox and Sara Steinke in this respect. I also thank the other postgraduate students I have worked with, including Sarah Cardwell, Neil Johnson and Andrew O'Day. Some of these people have already moved on to careers in teaching and research in Television and Film Studies, and have made important contributions of their own to the field. During the preparation of the manuscript I received invaluable feedback from four anonymous readers of draft material. I have also benefited from the expertise and enthusiasm of Christopher Cudmore, Rebecca Barden and their colleagues at Routledge. Pressures of time and other projects have weighed heavily on me during the writing of this book, and I hope that readers will not find too many errors and omissions that have escaped their and my best efforts. Finally, as always, I acknowledge the support and love of Lib Taylor, to whom the book is dedicated.

Introduction

Using this book

This book is an introduction to Television Studies, aimed especially at those who are new to the study of the medium at college and university level. It describes some of the critical approaches to television that have become widely accepted in the subject. It also explains and makes use of key concepts in Television Studies that every student needs to know about. The book re-evaluates the terms and ideas that have been significant in studying television, and tests out their limits, drawing attention to the strengths and weaknesses in the ways in which television has been studied up to now. So the book draws together a collection of concepts and critical languages that are sometimes quite diverse, or even contradictory, and suggests how there are some ways of thinking about television that are more fruitful than others. Television Studies is a new, dynamic and rapidly changing field of work, as the next section explains. This makes the task of the student of television an open-ended and exciting one, and the book also aims to convey some of this energy and diversity in its organisation and layout.

This book outlines significant strands of critical work in the field, and provides worked-though case study examples of how critical approaches can be applied to actual problems, programmes and issues. It encourages active learning by including many Activities which can form the basis of classroom discussion or written assignments. The book is organised around short chapters, suitable for use as preparatory reading for class study, or as follow-up reading to support classroom debate. Significant terms are highlighted in **bold** in the text when they are doing important work in the discussion. A definition of the highlighted term appears in the margin next to its first appearance in a chapter, and these definitions can also be found in alphabetical order in the glossary of key terms at the end of the book. In this Introduction key terms are highlighted in bold though their definitions do not appear in the margin. The terms I have highlighted in this way are those that seem to require a specific definition. Some of them are part of the critical terminology of the academic discipline of Television Studies or one of the areas of research that has fed into the field. Some of them are terms used in the television industry in Britain or the USA, to describe an aspect of how television technology works, or how programme-making and **broadcasting** are carried out. Some terms are more widely known and are part of non-professional language, but seem to me to need a precise definition so that they can be understood and used accurately by readers and students of television. For readers of this book there will be some terms they already know, some they have heard and not understood before, and some completely new vocabulary that I hope will enrich their capacity to talk and write about television.

Each chapter ends with a short list of suggested further reading. The books, essays and articles chosen are often those I have quoted from, but there are also some other books listed that deal with the topics covered in the chapter. There is great insight to be gained from noting how other voices have expressed ideas that I have written about here, and especially so if another writer has an alternative or even opposed attitude to a subject. Like any academic subject, Television Studies is diverse and evolving, and there are strongly held and articulately presented points of view within it that differ greatly in aims, assumptions, emphases and conclusions. Approaches to Television Studies are not a set of tools, but more like a group of different languages. They do not translate neatly one into another, and each defines its world in rather different ways. The book is concerned with the most commonly studied theoretical issues in television courses. The major differences between courses of study are in their focus on one or two of the following areas:

- analytical study of television programmes as **texts**
- the television industry as an institution and its production practices and organisation
- television in contemporary culture and the **sociological** study of audiences
- television history and developments in broadcasting policy.

This book provides introductory explanation, evaluation and routes for further study in each of these areas. I aim to show why these approaches have a significant role in Television Studies, to encourage students to participate in debates within and between these approaches, and to gain an understanding of the strengths and weaknesses of particular theoretical models for studying television.

In each chapter the reader will discover references to work by others who have contributed to Television Studies, and these references can be followed up in the Select Bibliography at the end of the book. Indeed, the Select Bibliography can itself be a useful tool for looking at the range of the subject, and exploring sources for independent work. In a single volume it is impossible for me to note all of the significant ideas in the sources I have used, and readers have many opportunities to build on the brief discussions of existing research that I have included here, by reading the source texts that I have cited. Indeed, the many directions that such further work can take indicate the comparative newness and potential of Television Studies, and I hope that readers of this book will be encouraged to make their own contributions to the subject by identifying the gaps, new directions and even contradictions opened up in these pages.

Television Studies

The academic study of television has had little interest in valuing one programme or kind of television over another. Yet in the ways people talk about television, these evaluative issues are high on the agenda. What might it mean to say that a programme (or a channel, or an evening's viewing) is 'good'? **Quality**, or 'good', television is an informal category that often separates plays and art films, **adaptations** and authored **serials** from the rest, from 'popular' television. Attaching the label 'quality' involves assigning cultural importance to programmes or kinds of television that have acquired a valued position in **culture**, rather like theatre's distinctions between serious theatre and musicals or pantomime. There is a social and cultural framework which enables the study of some television to carry value, and the programmes or kinds of television labelled as 'quality' to carry value in a way that popular television does not. The academic subject of Television Studies has taken popular television seriously, because it is the television most people watch the most. This is despite the common criticism in the press, and sometimes in the television industry itself, that popular television is unimportant, 'just' commercial, and lacking in artistic value.

Television Studies has tried to define how the medium communicates, and this has involved distinguishing between television communication and the media of cinema or radio, for example. But it has used methodologies for describing and analysing television texts that come from disciplines including Film Studies (see Chapter 4), methods of discussing audiences and television institutions that come from sociology, and ways of describing the development of television that amount to different histories of the medium. Charlotte Brunsdon (1998b: 96) has summarised this by explaining that

> much of the literature of television studies could be characterised as attempting to formulate accounts of the specificity of television, often using comparison with, on the one hand, radio (broadcast, liveness, civic address), and on the other, cinema (moving pictures, fantasy), with particular attention . . . to debate about the nature of the television text and the television audience.

Because television includes so many different programmes, channels and ways of addressing its audiences even at one point in time in a single geographical region, it has proved very difficult for critics and commentators to produce useful general insights into the medium. This is even more the case once the history of the medium and its regional variations across countries and regions of the world are considered (see Chapter 2).

Early predictions (in the 1930s for instance) of what television would be emphasised its liveness, its ability to present to a mass audience images of what was happening in the real world. Commentators remarked on television's inability to compete with cinema as entertainment and therefore expected the medium to focus on information and **actuality**. These early thoughts condition the ways in which **realism**, connection to the contemporary and the uneasiness about bringing controversial visions into the home were played out. The connection of television technology to immediacy (television as a means of relaying something that would have happened anyway) predisposes it to linear real-time progress, and the claim to report the real world (see Chapter 8). Film has been theorised in terms of space (what can be seen on the space of the screen), and this has led to theories about how individual film spectators **identify** with the usually fictional characters and **points of view** offered for spectators to see. Some of these ways of thinking from studying film have been deployed in Television Studies to explain how viewers make sense of the television medium. On the other hand, television has also been theorised in terms of time. Television consists of a **flow** of audio-visual material that, although divided up into programmes, runs on across a period of time without empty gaps in between. Brunsdon has noted that: 'Television is, for the most part, made as programmes or runs of programmes: series, serials and mini-series. However this is not necessarily how television is watched. . . . It is precisely this possible "drifting" through an evening's viewing that has come to seem . . . one of the unique features of television watching' (C. Brunsdon 1998b: 105–6). Rather than anticipating and wishing for the end of an individual film **narrative**, the television viewer is usually drawn into and out of a flow of material that does not come to a decisive end.

The experience of watching television occurs in a dimension of time where little end-points (like the ends of programmes) keep occurring, but where viewers are always aware that something new is about to take the place of what they have just been watching. Television Studies has tried to address this situation by looking not only at individual programmes but also at the ways they link together. These links might be in terms of the similarities of one programme with another, where shared features of a **genre** tell us something about the persistence of some kinds of storytelling, sets of issues or ideas being explored or the **conventions** that the makers of programmes adhere to (see Chapter 5). The links might also be in the planning and organisation of a period of viewing, for example an evening's television **schedule** on a certain channel. Planning a schedule to include variety, yet also a continuity of interest that can keep a viewer tuned to a single channel, can tell us a lot about how an idea of the viewing audience and its interests drives the organisation of television and assumptions about how television is used and enjoyed. The links between programmes in a schedule are the responsibility of the institutions that broadcast them, and looking at how television institutions work has been important to Television Studies' understanding of the medium's role as an industrial product (see Chapter 6), made and organised in different ways in different parts of the world.

Television has no dominant **global** form, and is always local. Even though television programmes and formats are distributed globally, its local forms are different (see Chapter 3). This can be seen immediately in the difference between **commercial television** in the USA and the British tradition, which has a strong civic, '**public service**' character. In Britain there has always been a tension between taking television's responsibility to society seriously and regarding television as entertainment for a consumer. So although television has been regarded as the medium most appropriate to the way we live now in Western societies, to the extent that television has been described as '**postmodern**' (see Chapter 7), it is not all the same everywhere across the world; nor does it lack a history that has shaped its present form in each society. The contexts that the organisation of television in particular places offers to Television Studies are important because they draw attention to the fact that television does not have to take the form that it does in the places we might be familiar with. There is no necessity about the fact that in Britain, for example, there are television channels funded by advertising and **sponsorship**, and others funded by a **licence fee** that is in effect a tax on the ownership of television sets.

The ways in which television connects with the character of the society where it is watched raise the issue of the social significance of what television represents. The questions of what is represented, in what ways and with what possible effects have been considered in Television Studies with particular attention to the representation of groups who are relatively lacking in social power (see Chapter 9). This kind of study can illuminate the active contribution of television to the ways that viewers understand and experience their social environments, as well as how television reflects that environment to them. As well as looking at what can be seen and heard in the medium of television, how it is organised in different parts of the world and its relationship with the ways of thinking and experiencing the world in social contexts, Television Studies pays attention to the audiences of television and how they interact with the medium. This involves noting which programmes and kinds of programme are watched the most, using information that television institutions themselves collect in statistical form (see Chapter 11). But it also involves undertaking independent studies where groups of viewers are asked by Television Studies researchers about their attitudes to what they watch, and how their television viewing fits into their life experience and their sense of who they are (see Chapter 12). Research on audiences attempts to engage with how viewers make sense of television, and how it is important (or perhaps unimportant) to them. In this way Television Studies aims to break down the boundaries between the academic agendas that it has developed for specialised work on the medium and the place of watching television in the lives of non-specialist viewers for whom television can function in a range of ways among other routines and everyday experiences.

The organisation of chapters

Studying Television

The first chapter sketches out the topics of study and critical approaches which can be found in academic Television Studies, noting its significant emphases and exclusions. Television Studies in Britain and the USA, for example, most usually addresses **broadcast** television in the English-speaking world. One dominant strand is the detailed **textual analysis** of programmes, with a preference for popular programmes in **serial** and **series** form, concentrating on dramatic, **documentary** and news programmes. This derives from the tradition in academic work of studying content and form in detail. It also reflects the dominance of English-language programmes in the world television market. There are other kinds of television to mention, however, which stimulate thinking about what television can include: trailers, commercials and channel **idents**, for instance. Television can now be viewed on computer screens, competing with games or text, and is viewed in a different position and often in a different room from the traditional household television set. This chapter considers different understandings of what television is, and how Television Studies approaches are based on assumptions about the television text, the form of its transmission and who is watching where and when. The chapter includes a case study comparing and contrasting representations of television viewing in the 1950s and the 1990s, showing how the medium has been thought about in different ways at different times.

Television Histories

This chapter describes and analyses the different approaches to the evolution of television from the 1930s to the 1980s in Britain, comparing and contrasting these with historical approaches to television in other countries, especially the USA. This involves discussion of state **regulation** of television, the increasing proliferation of channels and the introduction of non-**terrestrial** satellite broadcasting systems, competition and commerce. Part of the different historical shape of television around the world comes from distinct and different understandings of the television audience, perceived as a market of consumers or as a public whose needs television should serve. The chapter aims to introduce the subject of television history, with regard to the changing social place of television in society, changes in television institutions and changing conceptions of the television audience and the nature of television viewing. The range of approaches to television history in the chapter provides different selections of landmark developments and landmark programmes, for example according to whether the focus is on technology, institutions or audience issues. The chapter explains a range of historical approaches, in order to show how television history can be written in many different ways. The case study at the end of the chapter explores one aspect of television's likely future, as new technologies allow viewers to compose their own viewing **schedules** and selections of programmes from huge databases from which viewers can download their choices, or have their personal video recorders make choices for them.

Television Cultures

This chapter looks at the competing ways of analysing television institutions, and the significance of national and international **cultures** of television broadcasting. It explains and discusses patterns of commercial and **public service** broadcasting, and debates about whether television contributes to **media imperialism**. This leads to a discussion of television **globalisation**, comparing and contrasting ways of thinking about television as a market and an industry with political implications. Television in the developed world is still largely organised on national lines, but the increasing significance of international flows from West to East and North to South has been hotly debated. The chapter refers to inequalities in production funding and the role of imported programming in national television cultures. The focus of the chapter is on the theories which propose that television institutions both embody and transmit **ideologies** because of their ownership, and their relationships with national broadcasting cultures. The chapter finishes with a case study on the ways in which popular Brazilian drama serials, the telenovelas, have been used as an example in debates about the politics of global television.

Television Texts and Television Narratives

This chapter evaluates the theoretical approaches that have considered television programmes as 'texts' that can be studied in close detail to reveal how their meanings are made. The techniques for undertaking this kind of close analysis, deriving from the methodologies of **semiotics**, are explained. This includes methodologies for analysing **narrative**, the relationships between programmes across a period of television viewing, and ways of thinking about the relations between image and sound. While this way of working can be very powerful, the chapter also considers what it leaves out, such as television's institutional context and history, and the relationships between actual viewers and programmes. The question of who or what is the maker of television's meanings, in other words the question of **authorship**, is also considered in the chapter, and it explores different **genres** of television and how they can be studied. The case study in this chapter takes a single television commercial and conducts a close analysis of its images and sounds, showing how textual and narrative approaches to television can be used in practice.

Television and Genre

The chapter focuses on the significance of **genre** in television, showing how genres are relatively stable, but also how genres mix and change over time. It addresses the distinctions made by academics and broadcasting companies between, for example, fact and fiction, drama and documentary, series and serial. The chapter explains theories of genre, and tests them out in relation to a range of programmes, some of them having mixed or uncertain genre. The effects of the **flow** of television viewing for audiences, and channel hopping, are introduced since understandings of genre depend not only on how programmes themselves work but also on how they are watched. The chapter ends with a case study in which programmes of apparently similar topic, but in different genres and television forms, are compared and contrasted. The related but different examples of the television police series and the true crime **actuality** programme are used to discuss this question.

Television Production

This chapter discusses the production practices and technologies which are used in bringing programmes to the screen, including the **pitching**, production planning, production scheduling, shooting and post-production of programmes. It gives an account of the professional culture of television production in different kinds of broadcasting environment and in different **genres** and forms of programme. The chapter aims to provide a critical understanding of the television industry as a profession. This includes such issues as the **conventions** of lighting, camerawork and editing, and the significance of sound, music and graphics. Attention is paid to developments in technology such as non-linear editing, and the different kinds of equipment used in programme-making. The chapter discusses the institutional organisation and technology of television, and encourages readers to gain an understanding of the production process. The chapter includes a case study of the Avid editing system, noting how the design and operation of the system carries assumptions about the role of the programme-maker, and discussing the opportunities and constraints which the system allows or imposes.

Postmodern Television

Postmodernism has been an important concept in Television Studies in recent years, and the several meanings of the term are discussed and explained in this chapter. Postmodernism can refer to the interrelationships between one programme or television form and others, and the **pastiche** or imitation of existing television forms. Theories of postmodernism also deal with how the television of the present represents a break with the past, or, on the other hand, an irreverent return to past forms. In some of the work in postmodernist theory, the present is regarded as a distinctive new phase in human culture, and this related meaning of the term is also explained in the chapter. As a mass medium, addressed to a broad popular audience, television has been regarded by some theorists as a postmodern medium, and the politics of postmodernism, as a way of describing the media **cultures** of developed societies, are explored. The global and local characteristics of contemporary television are also part of describing television as postmodern, and the chapter ends with a case study on MTV, which has been claimed as postmodern both in its style and form and in its global organisation.

Television Realities

This chapter focuses on the ways that questions of **realism** can be addressed in Television Studies. This includes looking at what realism might mean in different programme genres, and the conventions used in various kinds of **documentary** and factual programmes. Television has a strong tradition of showing its viewers images of reality, using live footage and **actuality** in such diverse forms as news, documentary, **docusoap** and public access television. The chapter debates the different understandings of reality and realism in television, and how kinds of realism are achieved. As well as dealing with television forms which are centred on representations of reality, the chapter considers the realist conventions in fictional programmes, and the crossovers between documentary modes and other television forms (such as docusoap and '**reality TV**'). The chapter contains a case study on the use of actuality footage in news coverage, and the conventions for representing immediate live events.

Television Representation

This chapter looks at how television criticism has dealt with the representation of certain groups in society. In particular it discusses the significance of representations of people belonging to different races, and the issue of **gender** representation on television. The chapter outlines the different methods adopted in Television Studies for approaching these issues, including content analysis, identifying stereotypes and debates over bias and objectivity. Television broadcasting is closely connected to the worlds of public affairs and democratic debate, where creating fair and accurate representations of different kinds of people has been a matter of concern for a long time. In this context television has participated in setting up and also changing the cultural norms that underlie how members of society think about themselves and about people who seem different to them. The portrayal of particular groups is discussed in the chapter, with attention to differences across television forms and genres. The chapter concludes with a case study on the representation of black people in the popular situation comedy *The Cosby Show*, and some of the critical arguments advanced about this programme.

Television You Can't See

This chapter is about **censorship** and **regulation**, with particular attention to broadcasters' assumptions about the audience and what viewers should not see or would like not to see on television. This includes an account of the main principles of broadcasting regulation in Britain, with brief references to other television cultures. The chapter discusses the assumptions about the protection of vulnerable groups (such as children) which are embedded in broadcasting regulations, and the attitudes to such issues as nudity and homosexuality which are focused on in television regulations. A significant aspect of the issue of what can and cannot be shown is the way that television institutions and programme-makers censor themselves, and why and how they do this. The chapter also explains the regulation of programme content at moments of political and military tension, and the effect of a perception by broadcasters of public concern. The chapter ends with a case study on the British television coverage of the Gulf War in the early 1990s, focusing on the problems posed by images of war and death that could be considered disturbing, and the cancellation of programmes which were thought to be in poor **taste** in time of war.

Shaping Audiences

This chapter analyses the methods of understanding audiences, and of seeking to control their television viewing behaviour, which are used by television institutions. The methods used by British and US broadcasters to gather information about television viewers are explained in the context of a discussion of the underlying assumptions about viewers and the television medium which accompany them. The chapter introduces the diifferent industry and academic approaches to audiences, and their implications. The identification of **niche audiences** in today's multi-channel environment, and the ever-increasing drive for reliable information in order to predict audience behaviour, have led to a greater interest by broadcasters in frag-mented, specific viewing groups and viewing practices. This mirrors the emphasis in academic audience research on highly specific studies of audience behaviour and people's responses to television. The discussion of understandings of audience is placed in the context of how broadcasters try to attract and hold audiences, especially through the ways they **schedule** programmes. The chapter concludes with a case study on television scheduling which develops these issues in more specific detail.

Television in Everyday Life

This chapter discusses the different kinds of academic audience research, referring to important studies conducted in the 1980s and 1990s, and debating their critical significance. Much of this work is concerned with highly individual responses to popular programmes. This kind of work represents a significant shift from thinking of the audience as something shaped by the ways a programme addresses its viewers, and has been very important in changing the ways television is studied.

But working with small samples of viewers and focusing on popular television (such as **soap opera**) raise questions about how to apply the conclusions of this recent audience research to other television **genres**. The chapter addresses issues connected with the activity or 'agency' of viewers, the role of academic television audience researchers and the ways that audiences make and **resist** the meanings of television programmes. The relationship of television to other aspects of media interaction and everyday life is also discussed. The chapter ends with a case study on academic work on soap opera, discussing the shifts in methodology and critical stance which have been adopted in this field, and explaining the changing relationships between **feminist** Television Studies and conceptions of the viewer.

Further reading

Allen, R. (ed.), *Channels of Discourse, Reassembled: Television and Contemporary Criticism* (London: Routledge, 1992).

Brunsdon, C., 'What is the television of television studies?', in C. Geraghty and D. Lusted (eds), *The Television Studies Book* (London: Arnold, 1998), pp. 95–113.

Burton, G., *Talking Television: An Introduction to the Study of Television* (London: Arnold, 2000).

Corner, J., *Critical Ideas in Television Studies* (Oxford: Clarendon, 1999).

Fiske, J., *Television Culture* (London: Routledge, 1992).

Geraghty, C. and D. Lusted (eds), *The Television Studies Book* (London: Arnold, 1998).

Goodwin, A. and G. Whannel (eds), *Understanding Television* (London: Routledge, 1990).

McQueen, D., *Television: A Media Student's Guide* (London: Arnold, 1998).

Mullan, B., *Consuming Television* (Oxford: Blackwell, 1997).

Selby, K. and R. Cowdery, *How to Study Television* (Basingstoke: Macmillan, 1995)

Studying Television

Studying Television

Introduction

This chapter briefly maps out the topics of study and introduces some of the critical approaches which can be found in academic Television Studies today, with emphasis on the approaches used in Britain and the United States. By doing this the chapter aims to provide an overview of the kinds of questions which students of television should carry with them as they use this book. Each of the chapters in the remainder of this book focuses on a particular aspect of the study of television, picking up the concerns and ways of thinking about television which are introduced here. The discipline of Television Studies is a relatively new academic subject, and in its short history the questions which have been asked about television, and the answers which researchers have discovered, have changed in interesting ways. Television Studies, like all academic subjects, is in a continual process of development. This is partly because researchers discover new information and respond to changes in what is happening in television in the present. Television Studies also changes because, as ways of thinking about television are discussed and their strengths and weaknesses discovered, new questions and problems in understanding television are found. One of the aims of this book is to involve readers in the debates and disagreements about television which animate Television Studies.

ACTIVITY 1.1

What is it about television that might make it seem unworthy of serious study? How would you respond to such criticisms?

Broadcast television

broadcasting the transmission of signals from a central source which can be received by dispersed receivers over a large geographical area.

Television Studies focuses on **broadcast** television. Both television and radio are broadcast by sending out signals either over the air which are received by aerials or receiving dishes, or along cables embedded in the ground. Many different signals may be available to be received at any one time, like the signals which carry the programmes of several different television channels. But all the television receivers tuned into a signal will receive the same programme at the same time.

The emphasis on broadcasting means that some of the material which we might see on a television screen is not part of the topic of Television Studies because it is not broadcast. Non-broadcast television includes surveillance video made by retailers and police, for example. This material is not designed for broadcast, though it is sometimes included in broadcast programmes. For instance *Crimewatch* might broadcast extracts from surveillance video in order to show a crime being committed and to identify the perpetrator so that television viewers can provide information to help catch the offender. Other non-broadcast material made by members of the public also looks like television, for example wedding videos and video of family holidays. These programmes are often watched on television screens (by plugging the camera into a television set, or by buying the wedding photographer's edited version of the wedding and watching it on television) but they are rarely discussed in Television Studies because they are not broadcast. But some television programmes use extracts from these domestic video programmes for comic purposes (in *America's Funniest Home Videos*, for example). In the case of both surveillance video or domestic video which is broadcast in television programmes, the interesting aspect of using video like this is that it changes its meaning once it is put in a broadcast context. What was private becomes public when it is broadcast. The fascination of '**reality TV**' programmes such as *Big Brother* derives partly from this contrast between the usually private and intrusive material caught by surveillance or amateur cameras and the very public broadcasting of the material on television.

Specialised kinds of non-broadcast television are also made for screening in particular venues, but again they are rarely discussed in Television Studies because of the subject's concentration on material which is transmitted from a central source to a large and unspecified audience. Since the 1960s visual artists have incorporated

reality TV programmes where the unscripted behaviour of 'ordinary people' is the focus of interest.

Figure 1.1 Video surveillance still of James Bulger being led away by a youth in the 'New Strand' shopping centre, Bootle, Liverpool. Reproduced by permission of the Press Association, London.

art video the use of video technology in artistic work intended for gallery exhibition.

avant-garde work aiming to challenge the norms and conventions of its medium, and the group of people making such work.

documentary a form aiming to record actual events, often with an explanatory purpose or to analyse and debate an issue.

schedule the arrangement of programmes, advertisements and other material into a sequential order within a certain period of time, such as an evening, day or week.

connotations the term used in semiotic analysis for the meanings that are associated with a particular sign or combination of signs.

live or recorded video into artworks, to be seen in a gallery space, but the different location of viewing, and the different ways of watching (standing up rather than sitting down, in a gallery rather than in the home), make **art video** different from television. Occasionally these art videos might be screened in a late-night compilation of **avant-garde** works, or as part of a television **documentary**, but like wedding videos these films change their meaning once they are transmitted to a different kind of audience as part of the day's broadcast television **schedule**. At some large public events, such as football matches or rock concerts, live video is shown on big screens, but this is not television because of the specialised venue and non-broadcast transmission of the pictures. But one of the conventions of pop videos such as those shown on the MTV or VH1 broadcast television channels is to recreate the kinds of images which are projected at concerts, by using mist and lighting effects, and footage of the band apparently playing their instruments on a stage. Broadcast television borrows the conventions of non-broadcast video in order to communicate the excitement of being at a live performance.

Studying television nearly always involves studying broadcast television. There are some kinds of material which is live or recorded, seen on screens, captured by television cameras, and shown to an audience, which is not television as Television Studies has come to define it. So Television Studies gets a grip on the things which it studies partly by excluding some kinds of audio-visual material. But even though these other kinds of material, called video, or non-broadcast television, do not fall into the category of television as it is used in this book and in Television Studies, they are sometimes broadcast. Some of the distinguishing features of music television (MTV), or 'reality TV', for example, come from the ways in which they draw on non-broadcast television or video and make use of the **connotations** which they carry, such as

- privacy
- performance, or
- evidence.

'Our' television

subtitle written text appearing on the television screen, normally to translate speech in a foreign language.

dubbing replacing the original speech in a programme, advertisement, etc. with speech added later, often to translate speech in a foreign language.

Almost all the examples of television which are discussed in this book were made and broadcast in the English-speaking world, and most of the books which are used in courses in Television Studies in Britain refer to British and American television. One of the reasons for this is that English-language television programmes are exported around the world to many other countries whose national language is not English, where they are shown either with **subtitled** dialogue or with a **dubbed** soundtrack in a another language, spoken by actors from the country in which the programme is broadcast. This issue is discussed further in Chapter 3, where television around the world is considered. Television advertisements are also sometimes shown in several different countries, with the same visual images but with a soundtrack made in another language. People in Britain are notoriously resistant to watching television programmes in languages other than in English, and are unwilling to read subtitles translating foreign-language dialogue. But this is relatively unusual:

- In Poland imported foreign-language programmes have the dialogue of all the speakers (whether young or old, male or female) read in Polish by a single actor.
- In France British and American programmes are usually shown with dubbed dialogue in French.
- In the Netherlands British and American programmes are shown with Dutch subtitles.

The experience of watching television in Britain is relatively unusual, in that almost all programmes are in English, originating either in Britain or in America or Australia, countries with which Britain has had an historical 'special relationship'. One of the effects of this is that television in Britain nearly always seems familiar and immediately accessible; it feels like 'our' television.

The situation is different in other countries, where imported television from Britain or America is immediately marked as different because of its dubbed or subtitled dialogue. There are also countries where there are several commonly spoken languages and which broadcast television in each of these languages.

- In Singapore there are television channels in English, Chinese and Malay.
- In the United States there are channels in English and Spanish.

The sense of what 'our' television might be is different in these countries, and the experience of familiarity would be different to the experience in Britain. Television has aimed to represent a relatively unified **culture** in Britain, though its division into the nations of England and Scotland, together with the principality of Wales and the province of Northern Ireland, means that television also has a regional character. The further, related division of terrestrial television broadcasting into regional areas (the South-West of England, the Midlands, or East Anglia, for example) which offer some distinctive programmes to their local audiences makes this situation more marked. The issue of belonging to a region, nation or country complicates the assumption that British television can be referred to as a national television culture.

> culture the shared attitudes, ways of life and assumptions of a group of people.

Studying programmes

An important component of many courses in Television Studies is the study of particular television programmes. Particular programmes might be chosen for study in each week of a course, and there are several reasons for this. Television Studies emerged in the 1970s and 1980s out of three ways of writing about television:

- the reviewing of programmes in newspapers and magazines (see Caughie 1984)
- the criticism of programmes as works of art (like literature texts)
- and the **sociology** of culture (see C. Brunsdon 1998b).

> sociology the academic study of society, aiming to describe and explain aspects of life in that society.

Journalists' reviews and literary criticism focus on television programmes as **texts**, where the method of discussing them is to study closely their structure, characters and themes, in similar ways to the study of literature and drama. The advantage for the students and teachers who adopt this way of studying television is that there is

> text an object such as a television programme, film or poem, considered as a network of meaningful signs that can be analysed and interpreted.

an example accessible to the class, who can watch and rewatch the programme, and focus on selected moments in it. By closely analysing a programme it can be discovered how the programme is structured and how it creates its meanings by using images and sound in certain ways; critical arguments about the programme can be tested out and proved by referring back to a concrete example.

Studying television by analysing programmes is useful for setting up categories and making distinctions between programmes. Making distinctions is good way of discovering the rules and **conventions** which the makers of programmes use, and which television viewers learn to recognise, in order to make meaning in the television medium. Even in the 1970s Television Studies books addressing television programmes as texts recognised the significance of the mixed formal and informal **registers** in programmes, and the connections these might have to television's address to its audience and television's relationship with social values. For John Fiske and John Hartley, writing in 1978, the discourse of television was made up of a mixture of what they called 'literate' and 'oral' codes. By this they meant that television programmes have 'literate' components shared with written texts and relatively high-status forms of written communication, since they are 'narrative, sequential, abstract, univocal, "consistent"'. Yet television texts also have features which are more similar to the informal communication of spoken language, in anecdotes, folktales or popular songs, in that they are also 'dramatic, episodic, concrete, social, dialectical' (Fiske and Hartley 1978: 125). The literate codes of television underlie the novelistic narrative structures and linear explanatory forms of programmes, and can be regarded as reflecting the unifying and official language of social power, which imposes an ordered view of the world and a system of values and regulations on society.

On the other hand, Fiske and Hartley saw the 'oral' features of television as deriving from the organic culture of people's own communities and everyday lives, and in some ways as a representation of people's vigorous **popular culture**. In the context of Television Studies' critique of the forces of social control, and its valuation of ordinary people and their world-views, the oral mode of television was regarded as a vital and **progressive** element in the dynamic mixture of the literate and oral modes in television. Television's oral mode seemed to possess radical potential as the vision of a lost social communication, a free speech by the mass audience which restores a lost unity to ordinary people. So although this analysis rests on the interpretation of television texts, it gestures towards Television Studies' increasing desire to validate the ordinary viewer, popular culture and the contribution of television audiences to the meanings apparently fixed immutably in television programmes.

But there are also several drawback to this approach, which mean that the study of programmes as texts misses what seem to be important aspects of television. In broadcasting, television also includes trailers, advertisements and channel **idents**. It can often happen that several minutes in each hour of broadcasting are taken up by these kinds of television, but they are not programmes and are not often studied. Nevertheless, it could be argued that trailers for forthcoming programmes have important functions:

● They inform the audience about what will be available to watch in the future.
● They shape the viewer's expectations about what a future programme will be like.
● They offer suggestions why it might be interesting and enjoyable.

---

conventions the frameworks and procedures used to make or interpret texts.

register a term in the study of language for the kinds of speech or writing used to represent a particular kind of idea or to address a certain audience.

popular culture the texts created by ordinary people (as opposed to an elite group) or created for them, and the ways these are used.

progressive encouraging positive change or progress, usually implying progress towards fairer and more equal ways of organising society.

idents the symbols representing production companies, television channels, etc., often comprising graphics or animations.

Since television advertisements are the means of gaining income for television broadcasters, who charge fees to advertisers to screen them, it could be argued that they are more significant to what television is than the programmes which they interrupt. Television advertisements cost much more per minute of screen-time to make than programmes, and they are often innovative, memorable and amusing. The density and speed of information and meaning in television commercials make them rewarding objects of study, and show the conventions by which images and sounds can be put together in the television medium. Since our society is one where desiring, buying and owning products is important to our sense of identity and our place in society, it is also illuminating to see how products are brought to our attention in television advertisements, so studying them may also tell us much about how our society works. Channel idents are also moments of television which are frequently repeated and familiar, giving a brand identity to television broadcasters, like advertisements for the broadcaster, and they too are worthy of study. So it is not only programmes which can be analysed in Television Studies, though programmes have been the core of syllabuses in the subject for many years.

Studying programmes closely as single texts also has the disadvantage of separating a programme from its place in the schedule of the day in which it was broadcast. Although there are some television programmes which viewers might select and view with special attention ('must see' programmes), this kind of viewing is relatively unusual. Television is most often watched as a sequence of programmes, ads, trailers, etc., and of course viewers also switch channels, sometimes part-way through a programme, and their level of attention may vary considerably from moment to moment and programme to programme. Indeed, within programmes, high-points or turning-points are included by programme-makers where breaks for advertisements are to be included. This is done to encourage viewers to stay on the same channel to find out what the consequences or developments will be once the programme returns after the break. The two consequences of studying programmes as individual units relate to the important Television Studies concept of '**flow**' (Williams 1974). Selecting individual programmes for study means extracting them from the flow of material of which they are a part, and which might have important effects on their meaning. For example, a news programme including items about rising petrol prices might be followed by a commercial break including ads for new cars, and then the film *Gone in 60 Seconds*, in which a gang steals high-performance sports cars. While each programme or ad might be interesting to analyse in itself, more meanings relating to speed, pollution, road safety or **masculine** bravado might arise because of the connections between the programmes and ads in this television flow.

Part of the textual study of television is an interest in **authorship**, in who the authors of television programmes are and what the intended meanings of their work might be. There is an historical context for this approach, which arose in the 1960s when the expansion of the television industry allowed opportunities for younger, working-class university-educated men and women to enter the industry. Rejecting the seemingly staid and conservative values of their predecessors, and picking up on the interest in working people and ordinary lives which were being explored in the film and theatre of the time, these people aimed for a '**committed**' form of television. 'Committed' meant committed to an agenda of social change, where television programmes might be a force to change society in a more equal and tolerant

flow the ways in which programmes, advertisements, etc. follow one another in an unbroken sequence across the day or part of the day, and the experience of watching the sequence of programmes, advertisements, trailers, etc.

masculine having characteristics associated with the cultural role of men and not women.

authorship the question of who an author is, the role of the author as creator and the significance of the author's input into the material being studied.

committed a term used in the study of the politics of culture, implying that a person or a text has a commitment to positive and progressive social change.

direction. Thus the textual analysis of television programmes still carries a legacy of identifying which programmes might be 'progressive' and socially challenging, versus identifying programmes which perpetuate formerly dominant social conventions and support the **status quo**. British television drama has been especially important to Television Studies' discussion of committed and progressive television, because the legacy of cultural value which theatre and literature have has been attached to authored dramatic works on television.

status quo a Latin term meaning the ways that culture and society are currently organised.

In Britain television was established in the 1930s by the same broadcaster, the BBC, which operated all the radio broadcasting. Both radio and television have been required by their legal constitutions to fulfil a **public service** role. Public service television aims to:

public service in television, the provision of a mix of programmes that inform, educate and entertain in ways that encourage the betterment of audiences and society in general.

- provide programmes which are educative or improving
- offer a range of different kinds of programme at different levels of accessibility
- engage audiences in the significant events and issues occuring in the present.

Since literature and drama are also considered to be educative and improving, it is authored dramatic television work which has often featured as the ground for debates about the quality of television in Britain and whether the public service commitment is being fulfilled. Graham Murdoch (1980: 25) wrote, in an early theoretical essay on this subject, 'The promotion of authorship and creativity lies at the heart of the broadcasters' presentation of themselves as guarantors of cultural diversity and patrons of the contemporary arts, elements which are central to their claims to responsibility and public service'. Television drama has been regarded as the most culturally prestigious part of broadcast output, and it is expensive, and often prominently scheduled, trailed and advertised. Its high profile has made it the subject of hype and controversy, orchestrated by the broadcasters themselves, the press, or concerned groups such as the National Viewers' and Listeners' Association (NVALA). Authored drama has also been one of the main forms of television exported to other countries (for example to the *Masterpiece Theatre* strand on US **public television**). There were and still are debates about public service television, seen either as:

public television television funded by government or by private supporters, rather than solely by advertising.

- an old-fashioned and monolithic system which prevents change, or as
- a space in which television which challenges commercial values and aspires to artistic **quality** might find an audience.

quality in television, kinds of programme that are perceived as more expensively produced and, especially, more culturally worthwhile than other programmes.

In this context, the analysis of television programmes provides the grounds for valuing one programme over another, as more or less conducive of social change, or more or less worthy of consideration as a creative statement.

A further reason for this focus on authored television drama and its connection to literary and drama studies is that in the early years of television broadcasting in Britain in the years before and after the Second World War many plays were adaptations of theatre plays or extracts from them, sometimes using the same cast as productions being staged in London's West End playhouses. But a drawback of this concern for television drama as if it were literature or written drama is a neglect of the importance of performers and performances in television. Although Film Studies has for many years had a critical interest in stardom and stars, Television Studies has not often remembered the significance of how actors and television **personalities** affect the meanings which television programmes may have (Caughie 2000).

ACTIVITY 1.2

Look at the articles in current listings magazines. Are any of the articles about the authors of television programmes? If so, what kinds of programmes are these? If not, which personalities are associated with programmes, and why?

The fact that a television play or **serial** can be considered a self-contained text, written by an author, made this television form especially significant for researchers studying television from this perspective. Although there were some early studies of television (Williams 1968, Newcomb 1974) which discussed popular programmes such as **soap opera**, writing about television focused on the high-profile programmes regarded as 'quality television'. But Television Studies has in the last decade or so moved away from the close study of fictional programmes (although this is still an important part of the subject) and considered other problems. Part of the reason for this is that Television Studies has established itself by breaking away from the study of literature and drama, so that the methods of textual criticism increasingly appear to be drawn from subjects outside of Television Studies itself. Rather than studying high-profile television fiction by authors whose names become nationally known (such as Lynda La Plante or Andrew Davies), Television Studies academics have discussed programmes which fall solidly into **genres** (such as soap opera, or police fiction) and whose authors work in teams or groups and are little known outside the television industry. These are also the programmes which attract the largest audiences, and which can be described as 'popular' rather than 'elite' culture.

Television and society

Unlike film, television has always placed emphasis on the witnessing of events in the real world. When television began, all of its programmes were live, because the technology to record television signals had not been invented. The thrill of watching television in its early days, and still occasionally now, is to see and hear representations of events, people and places distant from the viewer. Indeed, the word television literally means 'seeing from afar'. On one hand, television gives viewers access to the world with immediacy and credibility, because television technology appears to transcribe or reproduce faithfully what is seen and heard. The ability of television to disseminate information widely, beyond the local and personal experience of its viewers, can be argued to broaden the experience and awareness of the television audience. The political effects of this might be for television to assist national institutions in involving citizens in social and political debate, so that television enhances public debate and participation in democratic decision-making. Television broadcasting might therefore contribute to the '**public sphere**': to

personalities people appearing on television who are recognised by audiences as celebrities with a media image and public status beyond the role they play in a particular programme.

serial a television form where a developing narrative unfolds across a sequence of separate episodes.

soap opera a continuing drama serial involving a large number of characters in a specific location, focusing on relationships, emotions and reversals of fortune.

genre a kind or type of programme. Programmes of the same genre have shared characteristics.

public sphere the world of politics, economic affairs and national and international events, as opposed to the 'private sphere' of domestic life.

discussion and thought about issues which concern the direction of society as a whole, and have bearing on the lives of most people. On the other hand, television can present only selected images and sounds, chosen by someone else, and present them according to the conventions of storytelling and reporting which are established by television institutions and by legal regulations. In a sense, television takes over the job of relating the viewer to the world around him or her, and separates the viewer from his or her experience of reality. The political consequences of television from this point of view are negative. If television experiences the world on its audience's behalf, and substitutes mediated and partial versions of information and understanding for the authentic experience of people, then its effect is to dissuade people from involvement in discussion and debate. The television viewer might be disempowered and alone, with discussion and participation simulated by television rather than enabled by it. Watching the political question-and-answer programme *Question Time* or the commentaries by experts in current affairs programmes might allow viewers to feel involved in debates when they are not. From this point of view, television viewing reproduces the apparent passivity of consumers and spectators, turning its audience into '**couch potatoes**', and encourages it to continue.

Social science research in Television Studies considers how television has a role in reproducing the patterns of values and the divisions between groups and **classes** of people in society, in other words how television represents and affects the social order. Part of this research concerns how television adopts the 'public speech' of institutions such as:

couch potatoes a derogatory term for television viewers supposedly sitting motionless at home watching television passively and indiscriminately.

class a section of society defined by their relationship to economic activity, whether as workers (the working class) or possessors of economic power (the bourgeoisie), for example.

Figure 1.2 A view of the damage to the area around the World Trade Center following the attack on the Twin Towers on 11 September 2001. Photography by Pablo Ravazzani/Corbis Sygma.

- Parliament
- academia
- the judicial system.

Social science is concerned with how this contrasts with adoptions of 'private speech' such as:

- gossip
- everyday talk
- the language of subcultural groups such as football fans or youth subcultures.

By investigating these aspects of television, it can be seen how television gives different kinds of value and legitimacy to different facets of social life, and separates out or unifies people with each other. Since television is controlled by institutions, and governed by laws, questions of the **regulation** and ownership of television are also addressed by this strand of research. Social science research considers television as a form of mass communication, in relation to sociological and political issues rather than studies of textuality or the form of programmes. Because of their interest in the relations of social groups to each other, and the place of television in communicating social values and attitudes, researchers tend to discuss popular genres such as television sports programmes, or kinds of content (especially violence and social disorder) represented in different kinds of programmes.

> regulation the control of television institutions by laws, codes of practice or guidelines.

The ways in which broadcasting is organised in different nations are surprisingly different, and it is important to study broadcasting cultures in comparison and contrast to each other. Although it might seem that American television is the dominant norm because of the worldwide export of such programmes as the American drama *Baywatch*, about lifeguards, or the pre-school children's programme *Sesame Street*, the conventions, laws and assumptions about television differ in different countries because of the different evolution of television broadcasting and different conceptions of the nature and function of television. In Britain, for instance, broadcasting (first on radio) began as a monopoly business entrusted in 1922 to the British Broadcasting Company (a commercial organisation), paralleling the monopoly control over the supply of water or electricity in the Victorian period. Radio, and television when it appeared in the 1930s, was considered as if it were drinking water, on tap, which could be run by a national company as long as it was kept clean and available to everyone equally (Caughie 2000). Only later did commercial television and competition appear, and even now there is a strong body of opinion in Britain that television must be taken seriously and must fulfil its moral responsibility to an audience of citizens. In America, by contrast, television quickly developed as a form of commercial business, where the requirements of advertisers and the need for local relay stations to make profits from the programmes supplied by programme-makers have driven the development of television. To put this distinction crudely, there is a debate between two sets of assumptions about television:

- television should provide resources to answer people's needs and raise cultural standards, or
- television should give people what the majority seem to want and what makes the most profit.

Television Studies has engaged frequently in this debate, most often by taking the perhaps impossible compromise position that broadcasting should be a public service but that it should not impose the cultural standards of the few upon a majority whose 'popular' tastes should not be sneezed at.

The background to this position in Television Studies is closely bound up with the changes in how broadcasters have conceived of their audiences. The BBC shifted its conception of its role from an initial aim to train its audience to understand and enjoy more and more 'quality' programmes, with 'worthwhile' levels of intellectual content and sophistication, requiring sustained and attentive viewing (Ang 1991). When the arrival of ITV introduced **commercial television** to Britain in 1955, the high **ratings** for the new channel forced the BBC to compete against popular **formats** such as imported American drama series and quizzes. From the 1950s onwards, the conception of the audience as consumers able to exercise a free choice has become increasingly dominant in British broadcasting, and this both reflects and supports the view of society which has come to be familiar and natural today. Rather than thinking of British society as if it were a pyramid with a small cultural elite at the top, with sophisticated tastes, and a broad base of ordinary viewers underneath preferring undemanding entertainment, the image of society has changed to one of overlapping and scattered sets of viewers, or '**niche audiences**', who have changing and diverse preferences across many genres, forms and levels of complexity. Broadcasters no longer attempt to lead the nation to the top of the cultural pyramid, but instead reflect what they believe to be the demands of contemporary society. The audience is conceived as a collection of diverse and autonomous individuals whose viewing habits and interests are hard to discover and predict, and who can be as fickle as the consumers surveyed by **market research**.

commercial television television funded by the sale of advertising time or sponsorship of programmes.

ratings the number of viewers estimated to have watched certain programmes, as compared to the numbers watching other programmes.

format the blueprint for a programme, including its setting, main characters, genre, form and main themes.

niche audiences particular groups of viewers defined by age group, gender or economic status, for example, who may be the target audience for a programme.

market research the collection of information about consumers and their preferences, used to identify products that can be sold to consumers likely to buy them.

Figure 1.3 Watching the television. Photograph courtesy of Powerstock.

ACTIVITY 1.3

Which kinds of television programmes, on which channels, do you think are aimed at a family audience? How do you know?

The role of the academic discipline of Television Studies in political debates about the direction of television in Britain has always been rather peripheral. When the subject focused on making distinctions between progressive or conservative texts in the 1960s and 1970s, and valuing the progressive ones, the highly theoretical arguments about the form and meanings of programmes were largely inaccessible to readerships outside the lecturers and students who engaged in them. Despite the often-repeated claim that programmes could empower audiences to think in challenging and radical ways about their own lives and cultures, Television Studies had little engagement with programme-makers and policy-makers. The discipline of **Cultural Studies**, pioneered in Britain in the 1970s at the University of Birmingham, recognises the significance of popular television and studies how television contributes to assumptions and attitudes of sectors of society, a set of ideas and emotions described as a '**structure of feeling**'. Key work in this field includes the books by Raymond Williams (1974) and John Ellis (1982), whose interest was in the flow of programmes in the television schedule, and how viewers rarely watch programmes singly but instead as part of flow of programmes and commercials over a period of hours. Viewers also switch from one programme or channel to another, composing their own 'text' of television from these segments which does not exhibit the bounded and unified qualities which derive from thinking of television as a series of whole individual texts to be analysed singly. In the 1980s the issue of the progressiveness of particular television texts was overtaken by interests in audiences, and how real viewers gained pleasure from their viewing (Morley 1980). This approach began to transfer to the USA in the 1980s, and is evident in the work of Lawrence Grossberg (Grossberg et al. 1992). While still a political debate, because there could be progressive or conservative kinds of pleasure, this phase in Television Studies refused to identify some programmes as good and some as bad, preferring to value the different kinds of pleasure which different audience groups might gain from programmes. The **commissioners** and **producers** of programmes, let alone actors, politicians or journalists, have always made distinctions between good and bad programmes, in terms of their popularity, cost as compared to profit or the social status of their majority audience.

The sophisticated arguments which led to the refusal to judge quality in Television Studies meant that academic criticism has been largely unable to engage in the debates about television which can be seen expressed in different contexts, including:

- newspapers
- Parliamentary debates
- broadcasters' policy documents.

Cultural Studies the academic discipline devoted to studying culture, involving work on texts, institutions, audiences and economic contexts.

structure of feeling the assumptions, attitudes and ideas prevalent in a society, arising from the ideologies underpinning that society.

commissioning the process by which an idea for a programme is selected to go into production.

producer the person working for a television institution who is responsible for the budget, planning and making of a television programme or series of programmes.

Therefore the issues which still concern viewers and commentators, such as the effects of violence in programmes, whether there is more or less 'quality television' than there was and the standards of **taste and decency** in television, remain absent from the books and articles written and read by Television Studies academics and students. So although Television Studies is crucially about the relationships between television and society, the topic can often seem to be debated in a vacuum.

Television audiences

Because of the variety of the different kinds of programmes and advertisements which television broadcasts, television as a medium appears to offer an almost unlimited range of information and entertainment. The different genres of programme, and the range of factual and fictional output on television channels, appear to offer vast choice and to address the needs and desires of different viewers. This is even more evident in recent years with the emergence of themed channels on **digital television**, which focus, for example, on:

- sport
- films
- science
- drama
- comedy
- shopping
- lifestyle.

Television companies are especially interested in who is watching which kinds of programme, when and why. Television broadcasters have always referred to audiences in order to back up their claims to give the public what it seems to want, to set the level of fees charged to advertisers and as an indication of which forms and genres of programme seem to 'work'. The BBC's two terrestrial channels are funded by a **licence fee** which must be paid by all owners of television sets. The regional television broadcasters using the ITV channel, and the newer terrestrial channels Channel 4 and Channel 5 gain their income from charges made to advertisers to screen their advertisements. The various digital channels available by satellite and cable are funded partly by **subscription** charges and partly by advertising, with the exception of the BBC's digital channels, which are free to their viewers. In each case information about audience size and composition is highly significant to broadcasters. Broadcasters funded by commercial advertising need to attract audiences for their advertisers, and broadcasters funded by licence fee need to justify the compulsory payment of the licence fee by attracting large audiences. The competition between channels is measured by audience size (the ratings, calculated by multiplying the audience sizes in a representative sample of viewers), and by the proportion of the total available audience watching one channel rather than another (**audience share**). The methods of audience research used in the television industry derive from the methods used to identify new markets for consumer products, to survey current users of products and to measure the sales and reactions to products of all kinds, from washing powder to brands of lager.

taste and decency conformity to the standards of good taste and acceptable language and behaviour represented on television, as required by regulations.

digital television television pictures and sound encoded into the ones and zeros of electronic data. Digital signals can also be sent back down cables by viewers, making possible interaction with television programmes.

licence fee an annual payment by all owners of television sets, which is the main source of income for the BBC.

subscription payment to a television broadcaster in exchange for the opportunity to view programmes on certain channels that are otherwise blocked.

audience share the percentage of viewers estimated to have watched one channel as opposed to another channel broadcasting at the same time.

The academic disciplines of the social sciences, such as **sociology** and **anthropology**, have a related interest in television audiences. But rather than finding out about audiences in order to target or maximise audiences in the interests of increasing profits for broadcasters, academic audience researchers seek to understand how television viewing fits into people's cultural life, and how pleasure, knowledge and opportunities for social interaction (but also boredom, anger and dissatisfaction) in television arise. The methods used to gain this information include:

- questionnaires
- interviews
- **focus groups**.

The strand of work in Television Studies called '**uses and gratifications**' research describes the uses and pleasures which audiences derive from television, by focusing on how and why people use television. This approach is in contrast to the study of television's **effects** on its viewers (such as making them more violent, more informed about science or whatever) in that studies of effects regard audiences as passive vessels waiting to be moulded by television messages. Uses and gratifications research shows how television is used as an information source, as entertainment and as a resource for constructing the viewer's sense of identity, often by identifying himself or herself as a member of a group. The drawback of this kind of work, however, is that it can neglect the specificity of the television programmes which viewers actually watch.

Academic audience researchers have been especially interested in understanding the ways television fits into the lives of people whose relatively unequal social position has led the programmes they watch to be denigrated, and their reactions to television belittled. Politics in Television Studies works on programme texts tended to mean 'national issues' such as law and order, work and political viewpoints, associated with the predominantly male spokespersons and leaders in party politics, trade unions and business. The **feminist** movement argued that 'the personal is political', meaning that people's private concerns with family life, shopping or relationships also had political implications, and these areas of life were associated with women. So feminist Television Studies took an interest both in programmes which represented the '**private sphere**' of life, meaning the usually private goings-on in the home, and in the place of television in the lives of ordinary people, especially women. In particular, feminist academics studying television audiences have directed attention to the often despised genre of soap opera, and have explored in detail the ways that women viewers watched television in the real circumstances of their own homes (J. Brunsdon et al. 1997). Indeed the home is an important site of audience research in Television Studies, since television has been associated with domesticity.

One of the shifts which has taken place in television culture over the twentieth and twenty-first centuries has been the massive expansion of television ownership. Just a small proportion of homes in a few areas of the country had television in the 1930-50 period, but the present situation is one in which households may own several televisions, as well as personal computers which can receive broadcast television. From being a collective experience shared with family, friends and neighbours, watching television may take place simultaneously in different rooms

anthropology the study of humankind, including the evolution of humans and the different kinds of human society existing in different times and places.

focus groups small groups of selected people representing larger social groupings such as people of a certain age group, gender or economic status, who take part in discussions about a topic chosen for investigation.

uses and gratifications a theoretical approach that assumes people engage in an activity because it provides them with a benefit of some kind.

effects measurable outcomes produced by watching television, such as becoming more violent or adopting a certain opinion.

feminism the political and theoretical thinking which in different ways considers the roles of women and femininity in society and culture, often with the aim of critiquing current roles and changing them for the better.

private sphere the domestic world of the home, family and personal life.

ACTIVITY 1.4

Feminist television theorists conducted important work on soap opera as a 'women's genre'. Which other television forms might be of interest to feminist television theorists, and why?

---

in the same household, individually by members of the same family. How people of different age groups, genders and daily routines use television in the home is a subject of interest to audience researchers seeking to discover how television integrates into the fabric of present-day life.

ACTIVITY 1.5

In what ways do particular television forms lend themselves to some approaches in Television Studies more than others, for example television news to sociological study? What kinds of television have not appeared in your list of television forms and approaches to them?

The underlying impulse behind these studies of the television audience derives from two related concerns. One is the left-wing political view that the interests and enthusiasms of ordinary people in society have been neglected by always focusing in academic studies on the high-brow cultural products which seem closest to the elite forms of art. The consequence of this view is that programmes sometimes regarded as low brow, trashy and 'mere entertainment' suddenly become the ones which are worthy of study. The second related view is that a great weight of condemnation has been levelled against popular entertainment television by journalistic criticism, professionals within the television industry and earlier generations of academics. Television Studies academics have regarded themselves as rescuing this popular television from its low status and relative invisibility, arguing that what is popular is not unimportant, simply commercial product or lacking in artistic complexity. It had been argued that popular television distracted its audience of 'couch potatoes', offering them 'chewing gum for the eyes'. But Television Studies' interest in audiences and the programmes which most ordinary viewers watch offered to understand the processes of how television engages its audiences in ways which the audience finds satisfying and valuable, rather than simply dismissing ordinary viewers' apparently shallow enthusiasms. With the pendulum of critical interest shifting in the direction of audience studies, popular programmes and relatively inattentive viewing, however, Television Studies unfortunately lost sight of the programmes which are watched with concentration and intensity (such as 'quality drama') until quite recently.

A particular strand of audience research which places special emphasis on what viewers have to say about their relationships with television is the approach called television **ethnography**. Ethnographic studies draw on the methods of the

ethnography the detailed study of how people live, conducted by observing behaviour and talking to selected individuals about their attitudes and activities.

discipline of anthropology, in gathering information through close and often lengthy interactions with small samples of viewers (Lull 1988a). Whereas both mass communications research in Television Studies and the television industry have thought of audiences as homogeneous masses whose reactions and interests are broadly the same, and have investigated them by quantitative methods such as counting audience sizes, ethnographic audience research focuses on smaller-scale groupings, selected by factors such as locality, gender, age group or social class. The problem which ethnography faces is the challenge of selecting some information relevant to the research question while leaving out most of the responses that viewers give to the researcher's questions, and rearranging or 'translating' research information into a wider context which illuminates how television works as a medium (Geraghty 1998). The political project of granting legitimacy to ordinary viewers, their interests and pleasures, as well as involving them directly in Television Studies research as respondents to ethnographic researchers' questions, leads to the claim that audiences are active makers of meaning and negotiators with the television they watch. This celebration of the active audience is most associated with the work of John Fiske (1992, 1994) and with a body of research on television **fan culture**.

fan culture the activities of groups of fans, as distinct from 'ordinary' viewers.

ACTIVITY 1.6

List methods of study which Television Studies might involve. How many of these might appear in studies of another medium? Why is this?

Television fans (such as *Star Trek* fans, or *X Files* fans) use programmes as the central resource for activities including:

- constructing social networks
- setting up social and commercial events (such as conventions)
- creating new texts (such as songs, fanzines or amateur written fiction).

So studies of fan audiences such as the essays in L. Lewis's collection (1991) show how some television viewers take hold of television and transform it into their own cultural text, and it is argued that all television viewers, though to a lesser extent than fans, make their own meanings and social relationships out of television. Fans and audiences in general appear to resist swallowing whole the meanings which television programmes may have, and instead they take and reshape the aspects of television programmes which make sense and offer opportunities to them. However, in the context of Television Studies' continuing interest in the politics of watching television, there is little evidence that these **resistant** and **active audience** practices relate to broader questions of politics in society, around campaigns for a better deal for women or working-class people, for instance (Morris 1988). Nevertheless, the dramatic turn of Television Studies towards the audience can be seen, as David Morley (1992) has argued, as a necessary counter to the hitherto dominant tradition of textual interpretative research.

resistance the ways in which audiences make meaning from television programmes that are counter to the meanings that are thought to be intended, or that are discovered by close analysis.

active audience television audiences regarded not as passive consumers of meanings but as negotiating meanings for themselves that are often resistant to those meanings that are intended or that are discovered by close analysis.

ACTIVITY 1.7

What problems might be associated with ethnographic study of television audience groups different from those which you belong to, children for example? How might you deal with these problems?

Case study: television past and present

Early predictions in the 1930s of what television would be emphasised its liveness, and its consequent ability to present images of what was happening in the real world to a mass audience. There was little sense that the new medium would compete with cinema as an entertainment medium, because of:

- the small size of early television screens
- their poor definition of pictures and sound, and
- the location of the television set in the home.

It seemed that the role of television would be to bring information to its audience, and to relay images and sounds of events actually happening in distant places. These early thoughts conditioned the makers of television to think of the medium in terms of **realism**, since television would reflect society to itself in the present. Television would focus on the contemporary, and as a new technology having a television was associated with being modern and engaged in the growing technological sophistication of Britain's industrial society. At the same time there were concerns about television's intrusiveness, because of the uneasiness or even shock which viewers might feel when the box in the corner had access to their private domestic space.

realism the aim for representations to reproduce reality faithfully, and the ways this is done.

Part of the emphasis on liveness, on seeing things as they happen, made drama and performance important to the first television schedules (Caughie 2000). Plays performed live were fixed points in the BBC's evening television schedules and were very popular, as was a television version of the variety show, where singers, comedians, magicians and other performers from the stage music hall and radio shows of the time did their acts. There were some British films on television, but very few Hollywood films because the Hollywood film studios would not allow television broadcasters to screen them, for fear of competition with the cinema as a dominant medium for entertainment. Plays were performed live in the television studio, and could also be relayed live from a London theatre. So the function of television seemed to be to relay the live occasion of a performance (including one made for television) rather than to find programme forms which were different from what audiences might experience in other media such as radio, music hall or theatre.

British television began broadcasting in 1936 to tiny audiences, but even in 1950 the television audience for the only broadcast channel in Britain, the BBC, was only about 300,000. Television was available only in London and the Midlands, and viewers paid a £2 licence fee covering both television and radio sets. Programmes were broadcast each weekday morning and every afternoon, but stopped in the early evening so that children could be put

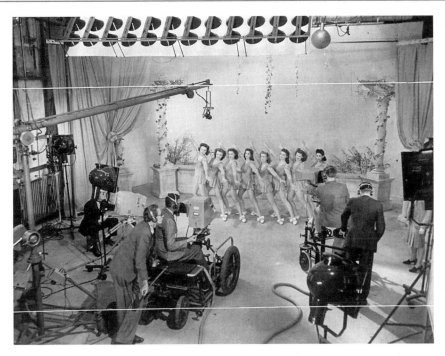

Figure 1.4 Television rehearsals at Alexandra Palace, 1946. Photograph courtesy of the National Museum of Photography, Film & Television/Science and Society Picture Library.

to bed. Programmes began again at 8.00 p.m. (after the closedown period known as 'the toddler's truce' was over) and there was no set closedown time, since **outside broadcasts** could extend the day's viewing hours. On a typical day in 1950, nine hours of television were broadcast altogether.

There was a widespread anxiety that watching television might disrupt family routines and waste people's time, especially if it was too entertaining. Writing in the *BBC Year Book 1951* (an annual collection of reports and essays about the doings of the BBC over the year), Ivor Brown responded to this concern by arguing that 'People who view do not stop going to the play or the films or the cricket-match. Television, at two pounds a year for a whole household and friends, does not, after the initial purchase, seriously affect the family's allotment of cash to fun and games' (p. 17). Brown was somewhat on the defensive, protecting television from the accusation that people had to make a choice between staying in to watch their expensive new television sets or going out and doing something more healthy instead. It is important to notice too that Brown considers the television audience to be 'household and friends', a collective audience rather than a lone viewer in front of the screen.

For most people the experience of watching television was collective, and they gathered in friends' and neighbours' houses to watch television as an event in itself. So rather than being a distraction from other ways of spending time, or a means of filling in dead time, the television set could be a magnet around which social interaction could take place. In the years following the end of the Second World War in 1945 a relatively prosperous middle class was growing up in the expanding suburbs around Britain's major cities, and it was these people who could most easily afford the time and expense of watching television. On one hand, the

outside broadcast the television transmission of outdoor events such as sport or ceremonial occasions, using equipment set up in advance for the purpose. Abbreviated as OB.

continued

new suburban semi-detached houses offered people more private space than they had ever had before (larger rooms, more bedrooms and big gardens, for example), but also potential loneliness in the recently created suburban estates populated by people who were strangers to each other, and intensely conscious of the social status they and those around them possessed. Ivor Brown (p. 17) saw television as a remedy for these problems: 'In the suburb, television is plainly acting as a cohesive force.' Owners of television sets invited people round to watch their televisions, to show them off, to make friends, and to enjoy being an audience for programmes:

> That friends and neighbours should come in to watch makes for better audiences, especially in the case of comedy and light shows . . . The more viewers, in the case of comedy, the more they enjoy themselves, since to be a member of an audience is quite a different thing from sitting aloof at a dress-rehearsal, as all theatre people know. So my guess is that, as television expands, it will begin to collect little group-audiences. So it will become a new factor in social life.
>
> (p. 17)

The television of the 1950s was aimed at community and family. Television replaced the hearth as the place where the family gathered, welcomed visitors and engaged in social talk between themselves and with others. This has to be seen in the context of the BBC's public service ideals, which were to encourage people to expose themselves to a range of programmes, some of them requiring concentration and an aim of self-improvement. Ivor Brown, thinking of watching television as a rather special event, thought that television would support the raising of cultural standards among viewers: 'The BBC has long advocated, I think, selective listening to sound radio, instead of the vague tap-running which is destructive of taste and leaves its public wayward instead of critical. Television curtails the tap, and makes of viewing a planned and intelligent exercise' (p. 19). This conception of television is probably very different from the ways most people think of television viewing now. Brown was concerned about the directions that viewing might take: 'What I most dread for the future is television available at all hours and the coming of the portable plug-in T.V. set which will destroy the isolation and concentration now imposed by the fixing of the mechanism in one corner of the room' (p. 19). His worries about the invention of the portable television were not only that it would lead to more distracted viewing but also that the television would follow viewers around the house to different rooms, breaking up the collectivity and sociability which television involved.

The proliferation of televisions in contemporary homes means that it is common for different age groups and genders within the home to view different programmes in different rooms in different ways. The other domestic technologies such as video games, uses of computers for Internet surfing and email and leisure communication by text messaging and telephone rival the television as the centre of home leisure and the collective experience of television viewing. The current explosion in the number of available channels on **digital television** also means that different individuals or groupings in the household can watch entirely different programmes from each other, on different television sets in different rooms. The nostalgia for family television can be seen in the sitcom *The Royle Family*, where family members and their neighbours gather in front of the television. As in the 1950s, the television forms the focus of a communal experience, though the watching of the programmes is very much secondary to the cohesive force of the television set itself as the centrepiece around which people gather. A major

Figure 1.5 *The Royle Family*. Courtesy of Granada.

question for broadcasters, for Television Studies researchers and for all kinds of commentators on the British media is how digital television will change television culture. But one of the facets of this issue is whether television viewers are actually enthusiastic about this new digital television landscape.

British digital multi-channel television is developing slowly and with an uncertain future. In the first six months of 2000 the rate of increase in digital subscribers was 53 per cent, but in 2001 the increase fell to 10 per cent, suggesting that the 30 per cent of British households now connected are those who are keen on the new technology, and that the mass of the British audience are not attracted by digital services. In a government survey only 25 per cent of British households say they expect to connect to digital television by 2006, the earliest date that the government said it would cease **terrestrial** broadcasts using the existing **analogue** transmission system. In homes connected to digital television, average viewers watch only eight to twelve of the dozens of channels available. The **interactive** services and email through the television set which digital connection offers seem unattractive to households which already have home computers that run these services more quickly and more cheaply.

When dozens or hundreds of channels are available, the size of the audience watching each channel can potentially be a very small fraction of the total. The cost of producing programmes watched by such small audiences, and the cost of providing free **set-top boxes** to receive them, can be supported only by the subsidies provided by the broadcasters which own digital companies, and run into billions of pounds. Some income can be clawed back by the paid channels offering films and sport, but the prospect of paying for content is the main reason why the majority of households have not connected yet. However, the government has committed itself to digital television, primarily so that it can sell the unused analogue frequency spectrums then left over to communications companies. Recent developments have this need to increase digital take-up as their background. In September 2001 the Minister for Culture,

terrestrial
broadcasting from a ground-based transmission system, as opposed to broadcasting via satellite.

analogue
broadcasting signals in waves of varying frequency. Analogue signals require greater space or 'bandwidth' than digital signals, and do not allow interactive response from viewers.

interactive offering the opportunity for viewers to respond to what is broadcast, by sending signals back to the broadcaster (along a cable or phone line, for example).

set-top box
the electronic decoding equipment connected to home television sets that allows access to digital television signals.

continued

budget the money allocated to the making of a particular programme or series of programmes, which is controlled by the producer.

Media and Sport approved BBC plans for two new digital channels, BBC3 and BBC4 (superseding BBC Choice and BBC Knowledge). BBC3 is targeted at under-twenty-fives, including series and serials budgeted at £70,000–230,000 per half-hour, thus matching the **budgets** of BBC2 drama and some cheaper BBC1 programmes. Drama will no longer appear on BBC2 in much proportion, leaving BBC2 to address the over-thirty-five audience with factual and arts programmes, though at the risk of losing audience share to Channel 4, BBC2's major competitor. BBC4 is based around the content provided on BBC2 and also BBC Radios 3 and 4, featuring arts, music and culture programmes. Just as Channel 4 has done with E4 and 4Later, its digital channels, programmes will premiere on digital to attract audiences, and may then migrate to terrestrial channels if successful. But the overall aim is to provide recognisable branded channels from terrestrial broadcasters on non-subscription digital channels, thus increasing the chances of bigger digital audiences.

Television in Britain seems to be at a turning-point which is interestingly similar to that in the early 1950s, when the small audiences and single broadcaster of the time were about to be transformed by new channels, much greater television set ownership and new ways of thinking about audiences. David Liddiment, then head of ITV, spoke at the 2001 Edinburgh Television Festival (his speech was reprinted in Brown and Wells 2001), and said:

> Numbers now seem to be the only universal measure for excellence we have: how many, how much, how often. We are losing sight of the innate value of programmes in our fixation on the successes that can be measured by profit, profile or performance. The relentless quest to find out what viewers want and then give it to them has made for sameness as we all seek to engineer the same schedule.
>
> (Brown and Wells 2001: 3)

The issues of how television is delivered, how it is watched, financed and organised into schedules and channels are a matter of major concern to broadcasters, government and cultural commentators. Studying television in the early twenty-first century is a demanding but important part of understanding culture and society in the past, present and future.

SUMMARY OF KEY POINTS

- Television Studies focuses on broadcast television.
- Television has aimed to represent relatively unified cultures, though it also has regional characteristics.
- British television has an important emphasis on public service functions, and representing society to itself.
- Television Studies has emphasised the study of particular programmes.
- The flow of programming, and audiences' experience of this flow, is a way of distinguishing television viewing from that of other media such as cinema.
- The study of audiences and their response to television has become increasingly significant, both to television institutions and to theorists of television.

Further reading

Ang, I., *Desperately Seeking the Audience* (London: Routledge, 1991).

Brunsdon, J., J. D'Acci and L. Spigel, 'Introduction', in C. Brunsdon, J. D'Acci, and L. Spigel (eds), *Feminist Television Criticism: A Reader* (Oxford: Oxford University Press, 1997), pp. 1–16.

Caughie, J., 'Television criticism: a discourse in search of an object', *Screen*, 25:4–5 (1984), pp. 109–20.

Corner, J., *Critical Ideas in Television Studies* (Oxford: Clarendon, 1999).

Ellis, J., *Visible Fictions: Cinema, Television, Video* (London: Routledge & Kegan Paul, 1982).

Fiske, J., *Media Matters* (Minneapolis Minn.: University of Minnesota Press, 1994).

—— *Television Culture* (London: Routledge, 1992).

Fiske, J. and J. Hartley, *Reading Television* (London: Methuen, 1978).

Geraghty, C., 'Audiences and "ethnography": questions of practice', in C. Geraghty and D. Lusted (eds), *The Television Studies Book* (London: Arnold, 1998), pp. 141–57.

Goodwin, A. and G. Whannel (eds), *Understanding Television* (London: Routledge, 1990).

Grossberg, L., C. Nelson and P. Treichler, with L. Baughman and J. Macgregor Wise (eds), *Cultural Studies* (New York: Routledge, 1992).

Lewis, L. (ed.), *The Adoring Audience: Fan Culture and Popular Media* (London: Routledge, 1991).

Lull, J., 'Critical response: the audience as nuisance', *Critical Studies in Mass Communication*, 5 (1988), pp. 239–43.

Morley, D., *Television, Audiences and Cultural Studies* (London: Routledge, 1992).

—— *The 'Nationwide' Audience* (London: BFI, 1980).

Morris, M., 'Banality in cultural studies', *Block*, 14 (1988), pp. 15–25.

Murdoch, G., 'Authorship and organization', *Screen Education*, 35 (1980), pp. 19–34.

Newcomb, H., *TV: The Most Popular Art* (New York: Anchor, 1974).

Williams, R., *Television, Technology and Cultural Form* (London: Collins, 1974).

Television Histories

Television Histories

Introduction

This chapter discusses ways of approaching the history of television, focusing on Britain but with comparison with and contrast to other countries. Television Studies has historically focused on television in national contexts. But the assumption that programmes would be viewed and discussed by a significant proportion of a national population is now proving less secure than before. The three factors that have given rise to this change in the nature of television are:

- the proliferation of channels
- the presence of several television sets in a single household
- the increasing control of television production and distribution by corporations and institutions whose activities cross national boundaries.

So it is important in thinking about television now to understand that many of the theoretical and critical approaches to the medium derive from a television history that it is undergoing significant change. While the methods of analysis proposed by Television Studies in the past remain significant and useful, it is important to pay attention to the present and the possibilities for television that are being shaped for the future. Although this chapter aims to provide information about some moments in the development and change in television across the period from the 1930s to about 1990, it is concerned less with providing a consistent story and a set of key facts, than with how the history of television can be approached critically. This is because the historical study of any subject involves making assumptions and value judgements about what is important, how links between events and processes are explained, and what the implications of a history might be. History is always a process of narration, which makes sense by including some information and excluding other information, by linking causes and effects and by implying a direction to the ways that events unfold. So this chapter does tell parts of several stories, but tries to suggest that the history of television can be told in many alternative ways.

Collecting the evidence

Histories of television face numerous problems in relation to the evidence on which they are based. Relatively inexpensive video cassette recording only became available in the early 1980s. Until this point, studying television from the past relies on gaining access to the archives of material held by television broadcasting institutions themselves. Only in the last two decades or so could students and academics studying

---

ACTIVITY 2.1

Consider what the following terms might mean in the writing of a history (you could use this chapter and the Further reading at the end to research how the terms could apply to television history, or simply think about the meanings of these terms themselves):

Evolution	Invention
Turning-points	Cultural history
Evidence	National history
Progress	International history

---

television collect examples to work on easily. Even today, when massive libraries of videotape and, increasingly, collections of better-quality DVD can be assembled by interested individuals, by academic institutions or in national archives, it is not easy to know how these resources should be used. When there is plenty of stored television from the past to look at, what principles should be brought to bear in order to decide what to study? Perhaps whole days or even weeks of the output of a particular channel or channels should be studied. Perhaps programmes of a similar **genre** broadcast on different channels should be collected, having decided how the boundaries of a genre should be defined. Perhaps the most popular programmes in a given month or a year should be analysed, on the basis of the audience **ratings** that show which programmes were watched by the most people. Perhaps all the programmes shown by all the channels at a certain time, such as on Friday evenings for example, should be compared and contrasted with each other. Perhaps it is not programmes at all that should be a focus of interest, but instead the different television advertisements, links and trailers that connect them together, since these are the stitches which hold a **flow** of television together as an object for study. Writing a history of television over the last twenty years or so looks easy, since it is not so difficult to gather evidence, but paradoxically this produces the problem that there is simply too much that could be investigated.

To write the history of earlier decades of television is difficult in other ways. Some broadcasting organisations such as the BBC or Granada Television in Britain have maintained archives of programmes on tape or film. But these are far from complete. A few programmes were recorded on film from the 1930s, and more programmes were recorded on videotape after its invention in the late 1950s. But the purpose of recording programmes was not primarily to preserve them for future television students and scholars, but instead:

- to train staff in how to produce, direct and shoot television
- to make recorded repeats possible
- to make programmes available for export.

Often, such practical difficulties as lack of storage space meant that institutions such as the BBC found it too expensive and difficult to keep archives of programmes of any size. Tapes and film copies were simply thrown away, or expensive videotape

genre a kind or type of programme. Programmes of the same genre have shared characteristics.

ratings the number of viewers estimated to have watched certain programmes, as compared to the numbers watching other programmes.

flow the ways that programmes, advertisements, etc. follow one another in an unbroken sequence across the day or part of the day, and the experience of watching the sequence of programmes, advertisements, trailers, etc.

was used again for some immediately useful purpose. The technologies to record programmes on film or videotape were attractive to television institutions because they made it easier to make programmes. Film inserts could be used during live broadcasts, and videotape made special effects much easier to achieve than during a live recording. So the copies of programmes that can be found in broadcasters' archives represent a fragmentary patchwork that was not intended as an objective record or even as a collection of television programmes that could sum up a decade or a channel's output. A further difficulty is that where programmes were preserved they were usually those that had acquired some status and importance. There are few existing copies of light entertainment programmes made before the 1960s, since news programmes, documentaries and some high-profile drama were the only kinds of television thought useful to preserve.

Contemporary Television Studies has focused on the study of programmes in their original audio-visual form. So this section has so far considered the issues of writing the history of television connected to the possibilities of watching television programmes as they were broadcast in some earlier time. Other kinds of history writing can be undertaken by using other kinds of evidence, and some of the recent historical work on television uses written sources to gain an understanding of the television of the past. For example, looking back at the pages of the BBC's listings magazine *Radio Times*, or ITV's *TV Times*, can be instructive in understanding how programmes and programme **schedules** were offered and advertised to their audiences. These magazines also contain features such as interviews with actors and **producers**, and articles by journalistic commentators. They can reveal much about the attitudes to television that were assumed, and the balance between information, education and entertainment that television in particular periods made. These listings publications also contain letters pages with viewers' questions, comments and evaluations of programmes. Although they are hardly representative, these sources give a partial snapshot of the ways that viewers established a relationship with broadcasters, and reveal some of the attitudes to programmes that might have been significant in a particular period.

The archives of broadcasting institutions, especially the BBC, also contain some records of viewer responses to programmes. Some producers kept the letters that viewers wrote to them about programmes, and broadcasters have always engaged in kinds of audience research. The BBC had an Audience Research department, doing similar things to what **focus groups** do now by gathering information by questionnaire and interview in order to gauge what viewers like or dislike, and what they approve of or do not approve of about programmes. As well as raw numerical information about audience sizes, these sources provide another glimpse of how people responded to the television they watched in the past. In broadcasters' archives there are also numerous paper records about the making of programmes. The BBC in particular has maintained extensive archives of letters, memos, reports and policy documents that give insight into how and why programmes were made.

So the issue of evidence in television history is a complex one, since it involves these questions:

- What are the different kinds of evidence available about television in the past?
- How does the selection of evidence make some kinds of history writing possible, and others extremely difficult?

schedule the arrangement of programmes, advertisements and other material into a sequential order within a certain period of time, such as an evening, day or week.

producer the person working for a television institution who is responsible for the budget, planning and making of a television programme or series of programmes.

focus groups small groups of selected people representing larger social groupings such as people of a certain age group, gender or economic status, who take part in discussions about a topic chosen for investigation.

- How does one kind of evidence (such as recordings of programmes) relate to other kinds (such as broadcasters' archives or commercial printed publications)?
- How can the attitudes and responses of audiences be reconstructed, and what do they tell us?
- How have television institutions' attitudes to their programmes shaped the evidence available?

As John Caughie (2000) has argued, the inability to record early television assists the view that television is ephemeral by nature, and in the academic discipline of Television Studies there is still a relative lack of concern with television history. As far as television programming itself is concerned, the versions of television's own past that are aired from time to time (in re-runs of old black-and-white programmes, compilation programmes of old television advertisements or brief clips from old programmes in quiz shows) are almost always presented in a humorous context. Television from the past is used like a family photo album, which invites the audience to be amazed, embarrassed and amused by what television was. Until very recently, television from the past has been something to make fun of rather than to appreciate in its own terms. British television and its audiences are sophisticated and complex, and their awareness of growing up with television can be seen in the programmes which celebrate and deride that history. Programmes such as Channel 4's *Hundred Greatest TV Moments*, or BBC's gameshow *It's Only TV But I Like It*, represent television's memory of itself, and the audience's fondness for programmes of the past.

But the history of television which appears on television is almost exclusively told in terms of memorable programmes, and is often derided and made the subject of

Figure 2.1 *Porridge*. Fulton Mackay, Ronnie Barker and Richard Beckinsale. Courtesy of BBC Photograph Library.

comedy. Television in Britain still seems unable to take its history seriously (in comparison to television coverage of other histories such as those of architecture or cinema). This is despite the increased demand for programme content on the increased number of contemporary channels, which makes the repeating of past programmes a notable feature of the schedules. With the proliferation of new channels, there is some economic value in the archives of old programmes that broadcasters have preserved. The BBC has gained income from its vast library of old programmes, by making business deals with the American cable and satellite company Flextech and the media corporation Pearson in 1995. The pay channel UK Gold, showing repeated programmes, is now joined by a range of BBC cable and satellite channels (BBC3 and BBC4) offering themed types of programmes aimed at certain kinds of audience. The export of BBC programmes, another source of revenue, was also made possible by links with the American Discovery Channel in 1996 and the start of BBC World transmitting programmes internationally. Furthermore, even presenting television from the past as something to laugh at shows how important television is to the shared memories and experiences of generations of viewers, and for **culture** in general. While television as a medium has always placed great emphasis on the moment of the now, partly because live broadcasting has been so significant throughout the development of the medium, both the television industry and the discipline of Television Studies have begun to show an awareness of the significance of television history.

culture the shared attitudes, ways of life and assumptions of a group of people.

Cathy Come Home: the most repeated television play

Cathy Come Home was written by Jeremy Sandford (a journalist and radio and television dramatist), directed by Ken Loach, and produced by Tony Garnett. It was broadcast on BBC1 in the *Wednesday Play* series on 16 November 1966, with an audience of ten million. It is the most frequently repeated television drama ever, having been shown again in 1967, 1968, 1976 and 1993. Rather than aiming for the well-formed studio drama whose conventions derived from the theatre, Garnett and Loach adopted the apparent untidiness and immediacy of documentary. Plays such as *Cathy Come Home* told fictional stories, but used them to make sense of the realistically observed world. Rather than maintaining a consistent relationship of the viewer to the drama, the documentary techniques in *Cathy Come Home* offer the viewer a range of points of view on her story. The drama follows her as she arrives in London from the provinces, meets her husband and starts a family. But things go wrong when her husband is injured at work, and the greater part of the play concerns the family's slide into homelessness, the break-up of the marriage and the inability of welfare services to provide for their needs. Sometimes the camera observes Cathy in a distanced way, or a voice-over will contextualise her situation and provide information. But in other sequences a hand-held camera is close up with Cathy and encourages the viewer to share her experience in emotional terms. The overall effect of the play is to dramatise the separation between officials or institutions and the human experience of being homeless, poor and powerless.

Figure 2.2 *Cathy Come Home*, 1966. Sean King as Sean, Ray Brooks as Reg, Stephen King as Stephen and Carol White as Cathy. Courtesy of BBC Photograph Library.

Inventing television technologies

The history of television can be thought of in terms of the progressive improvement of technology. From the earliest mechanical devices for broadcasting pictures, through the invention of magnetic tape to transmit pre-recorded material, to the invention of **cable television** and **satellite** transmission, it might seem that

cable television originally called Community Antenna Television (CATV). Transmission of television signals along cables in the ground.

satellite television television signals beamed from a ground transmitter to a stationary satellite that broadcasts the signal to a specific area (called the 'footprint') below it.

ACTIVITY 2.2

Analyse the pages of a television listings publication for one day or one week, to find programmes that were made more than a decade ago. On which channels do you find these? What kinds of programmes are they? When are they screened? Who do you think is expected to watch them?

regulation the control of television institutions by laws, codes of practice or guidelines.

the history of television is driven by technological innovation. But technical innovations require the resources of large organisations, and the will to implement technologies in applications which can be sold to a public. They require the stimulation of demand for the technologies, and a framework of **regulation** and law to govern their implementation. So technologies cannot be seen as in themselves the drivers of the development of television. For example, the level of satellite dish ownership rose to five million homes in 1996, largely because of the exclusive rights to football matches which Sky Television had bought using money gained from its majority shareholder Rupert Murdoch's non-television media interests. The recognition of a potential market, and programme content that can be sold to this market, is a precondition for the successful introduction of a new television technology.

The idea of television goes back to the late nineteenth century, when after radio had been invented it seemed a natural next step to transmit pictures to accompany sound. Scientists across the developed world were aware that the way to transmit pictures would be to find a way of breaking down a camera's visual image into tiny areas of black, white or shades of grey. These tiny areas could be reassembled on a television screen in order to reproduce the original image as a series of tiny dots. The principle is the same as the way that newspaper photographs had been transmitted by telephone wires since the beginning of the 1900s, by decomposing an image into clusters of larger or smaller black dots, producing areas of darker or lighter space which together added up to the shades and outlines of a photograph. The discovery of the chemical element selenium enabled this vision of television to seem closer, since a bank of selenium sensors in an electronic camera would turn the different amounts of light falling on them into different strengths of electrical current. If the changing signals for each tiny selenium receptor were sent to a receiver, the changing light and dark of a television picture would result.

Inventors in Britain, Russia and Germany worked on different methods of scanning images with selenium sensors in the years before and after 1900, but without perfecting a workable system. The British inventor John Logie Baird, and engineers at the Marconi EMI company, worked separately on competing systems of television broadcasting in the 1920s, with government and BBC support given to Baird. British television formally began on 2 November 1936, trying out both the Baird and Marconi systems and broadcasting to only about three hundred receivers in the London area.

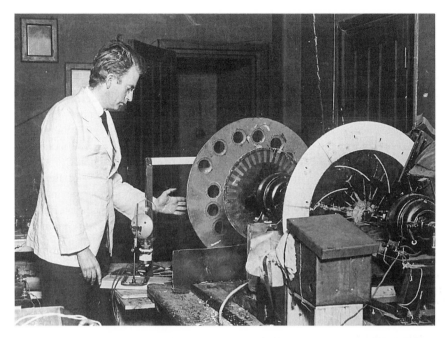

Figure 2.3 John Logie Baird with his experimental television receiver, 1926. Photograph courtesy of the National Museum of Photography, Film & Television/Science and Society Picture Library.

ACTIVITY 2.3

Do some research into what happened when John Logie Baird's and Marconi EMI's television systems were tried out in Britain. What were the strengths and weaknesses of each system? If you think the best system 'won', what made it the best, and for whom?

Television institutions

Television today is a centralised business. Large corporations and institutions own the equipment and facilities to make television programmes, and these are distributed from central transmission sources to the huge number of receiving aerials or cable television ports that serve the homes of the television audience. So production and distribution involve a small number of powerful and centralised organisations, whereas reception is differentiated and distributed across a very broad and relatively powerless constituency of viewers. Television did not need to develop in this way. In the late nineteenth century, commentators speculated about television technologies which would be more like telephone systems (Gripsrud 1998: 20–1). People equipped with small and convenient television recording devices were imagined making and sending pictures and sound to domestic receivers. Television might have been much more personal, unregulated and cheaper to make than it is now. Another way of putting this alternative development of television would be to say that television could have been a popular medium, in the sense that it could have been made and received by people themselves, and the making of television could have been embedded within their own lives. Instead, television became big business, where national governments co-operated to set up technical standards to control the mass-production of television equipment. A professional community of highly trained technicians and production staff undertook the making of programmes.

The government and BBC gave no serious consideration to advertising as a means of support when the work of John Logie Baird was being completed in Britain, and plans for a television service were actively developed. The thinking behind the organisation of the BBC as a semi-autonomous public corporation was inherited from the late Victorian corporations which had **monopolies** to provide services such as gas, electricity and water. Their control of supply and freedom from competition was granted in exchange for a remit to operate for the public good. The BBC took seriously its aims to raise the standards of the entire national audience in terms of sophistication of taste, intellectual appetite and levels of knowledge: television as **public service** broadcasting.

In the United States big corporations such as RCA and General Electric took over the work on the development of television equipment during the 1920s. This was an important development, in that it was not the government, the Hollywood film studios or individual entrepreneurs who took television forward but the industrial combines behind the production of radio equipment. Television in the USA would be modelled on the organisation of radio broadcasting, rather than the cinema industry or the public services, and in the late 1920s experimental television broadcasts were made in New York, Boston and Chicago, backed by electronics manufacturers hoping to sell the television sets to receive them. The radio broadcasters NBC and CBS were promoting television and could supply programmes to broadcast. American television, like radio, would use national **networks** supplying programmes to local stations which paid to broadcast them, gaining income from commercials and the **sponsorship** of programmes. By the time America entered the Second World War in 1941, the regulator, the **Federal Communications Commission** (FCC), had licensed thirty-two commercial television stations, broadcasting to the few thousand owners of television sets in America's largest cities.

In the very different television culture of China, the history, purposes and institutions of television are interesting to compare and contrast with the those of the United States and European countries mentioned in this chapter. Broadcasting in China was established by the ruling Communist Party that took power in 1949 as a means to disseminate government policy, news and entertainment sanctioned by the state. Television began in 1958 with one television station in Beijing, the capital city, but expanded slowly, with only thirty stations in operation by 1970, based in cities and reaching only part of the population. After 1976 television grew faster than any other communications medium in the country, with over six hundred transmitting stations by 1995. In addition to these terrestrial transmitters, eleven million Chinese people could receive satellite television signals, and 1,800 cable systems were operating. The inst itions of television in China have been closely controlled by government, so that the prospect of Chinese people watching programmes and channels made abroad or beamed to them by satellites operated

monopoly control over the provision of a service or product by one institution or business.

public service in television, the provision of a mix of programmes that inform, educate and entertain in ways that encourage the betterment of audiences and society in general.

network a television institution that transmits programmes through local or regional broadcasting stations that are owned by or affiliated to that institution.

sponsorship the funding of programmes or channels by businesses, whose name is usually prominently displayed in the programme or channel as a means of advertising.

Federal Communications Commission (FCC) the government body in the USA which regulates the operations and output of television companies and other broadcasters.

by foreign corporations has led to the licensing of cable television systems and largely unsuccessful attempts to ban the use of satellite dishes. The historical basis of this suspicion of commercial and foreign television in China comes from the principles set out by the revolutionary leader Mao Zedong, who argued that the purposes of broadcasting were:

- to publicise the decisions made by the ruling Communist Party
- to educate the population
- to establish a channel of communication between the Party and the people.

In practice, however, ownership of satellite dishes is common, and services beamed by satellite, notably StarTV, carry channels such as MTV and CNN. The history of television in China can be framed as a gradual movement from state control, with an emphasis on information, political programming and entertainment programmes based in state-approved national values, to increasing commercialisation and diversity. This historical narrative is explored further in the following chapter, where the current state of television around the world in national and international contexts is discussed. But here this brief reference to China shows how the political and cultural histories of a country can take widely different forms as they affect the establishment and development of television.

In Britain the **Annan Committee** report of 1977 put into question the role of television broadcasters as moral and intellectual leaders of society. Instead, television was increasingly considered as a market in which providers of programmes would give their publics what they seemed to want. With three channels and the prospect of a fourth, it no longer seemed necessary for each channel to expose the audience to the full range of both 'accessible' and 'difficult' programmes. The 1970s marked the beginnings of the notion that some channels would direct their resources to some types of programme more than others, leaving viewers to choose for themselves the programmes which catered for their existing tastes. Thus the role of television institutions underwent gradual change across the decades, and conceptions of the purposes of television and its relationship with its audiences developed with different emphases. The history of television involves placing the production and distribution of television in a context informed by the cultural pressures on governments, television institutions and audiences, all of which affect each other.

The setting-up in 1982 of Britain's fourth **terrestrial** channel, Channel 4, was the result of a combination of inherited and traditional views of broadcasting with the new imperatives of the 1979 Conservative government and its allies. From the past came a commitment to **public service**, to educational and cultural programmes, and to programmes for minority audiences. But Conservative policies in the 1980s attempted to introduce the principles of the market into all aspects of British life. So Channel 4 bought programmes from independent programme-makers, who were forced to compete with each other for commissions, and Channel 4 itself made no significant investment in production facilities or training. The channel's funding derived from advertising revenue through a levy on the ITV companies, which sold advertising time on Channel 4 in their regions, and was therefore reliant on the buoyancy of the British economy. The Broadcasting Act of 1980 which established Channel 4 required it to 'encourage innovation and experiment in the form and content of programmes'. The first Chief Executive was Jeremy Isaacs, who led the

Annan Committee
a committee reporting in 1977 to government on the future of broadcasting. It supported public service broadcasting, the funding of the BBC by licence fee, and the planned introduction of a fourth television channel.

terrestrial
broadcasting from a ground-based transmission system, as opposed to broadcasting via satellite.

channel's investment in films for domestic and foreign television screening and cinema release. There were programmes for British Asian viewers, and members of trade unions, while in Wales the companion channel S4C (Sianel Pedwar Cymru) broadcast Welsh-language programmes. Channel 4 was required by the Broadcasting Act to provide 'a distinctive service', but attracted criticism for its 'bad language' and apparent left-wing political bias.

ACTIVITY 2.4

Examine the programme schedules on Channel 4 today. Which programmes do you find that seem to be aimed at minority audiences? Which audiences, and why?

---

soap opera
a continuing drama serial involving a large number of characters in a specific location, focusing on relationships, emotions and reversals of fortune.

independent production companies
businesses making television programmes which can be sold to television networks that transmit and distribute them.

The first night of Channel 4 was on Tuesday, 2 November 1982. The programme schedule ran from 4.45 p.m. to 11.50 p.m., with the two most popular programmes being its new **soap opera**, *Brookside* (4.1 million viewers), and the first specially commissioned television film for the channel, *Film on Four: Walter* (3.75 million viewers), directed by Stephen Frears. These audiences were low by comparison with the traditional channels, with the highest-rated programme in November 1982 being *Coronation Street* on ITV, with 15.7 million viewers. But Channel 4 introduced significant changes to several programme forms, as well as opening up the **independent production** sector in Britain. *Brookside* was the first British soap opera to be made entirely on location, on a new estate in Liverpool. *Channel 4 News* (made by ITN) was Britain's first hour-long news programme, and set standards for news analysis. One of Channel 4's aims was to export programmes in order to maximise revenue, and financing film-length dramas for television which could be sold to foreign broadcasters was one way of achieving this. In the 1980s Channel 4 began to release its films in cinemas, as a way of raising their profile and creating publicity before their television transmission. Channel 4 entered the art cinema market with these films, and the distinction between the television film and the cinema film became increasingly blurred. With the increased cost of making films to cinematic standards (of length, star quality, production value), fewer films could be made.

Professional cultures in a 'Golden Age'

The technology to record television pictures and sound was introduced in Britain slowly in the 1950s and both BBC and ITV made use of it for training purposes, but rarely for transmitting programmes made and recorded on to tape. Instead, the medium of film was the preferred method of recording programmes for preservation, for foreign sale or for brief sequences (such as film shot in exterior locations) that would be played into programmes recorded live in a television studio. It was expensive to transfer programmes shot on film to tape, to buy the tape itself, to store it and to buy and maintain the machines which transcribed from film to tape. This meant that television programmes that used tape were more expensive to make. The people working in television were also required to become expert and professional in new ways once tape and film became as significant as live broadcasting. The mastery of these technologies led to the development of highly trained and specialist personnel with specific tasks to perform in the production process, with fewer of the upper-middle-class attitudes of the enthusiastic amateur which had previously marked many of the personnel in television.

By the 1960s the increase in broadcasting hours and the presence of three television channels in Britain changed the culture of television production, by moving away from the pioneering amateurism which characterised the early years. The first **producers** and **directors** in the 1930s and 1940s had had some of the vision, but also some of the blinkered cosiness of a public school or university drama society as they made up television as they went along. The professionalism and large scale of television in the 1960s and after encouraged programmes to be made more like an industrial product. Professional writers and directors, most of whose working time was spent in television, worked according to consistent schedules and guidelines, and developed skills, professional codes of conduct and shared expectations. In the 1960s and 1970s the producer commissioned programmes, ran the production process, including selecting the directors and technical staff, and oversaw projects to completion. The producer came to have an authorial role, and was also relatively free from the interference of department heads and television executives.

Television's Golden Age in the 1960s has gained this label because it was a period when the **status quo** changed. New values were being put in place, and inherited traditions were confronted by new forms and new pressures. It is important to recognise that professional workers in the television industry do not live in a separate cultural world from the rest of their society, and currents of ideas circulating among people of similar interests, social class and educational background have influences on the ways these people conceive of their role. In Britian popular books of the 1950s and 1960s by left-wing intellectuals such as Richard Hoggart, Raymond Williams, Stuart Hall and E. P. Thompson encouraged the belief that **culture** (television, radio, popular music, home decoration or sport, for example) was significant in shaping people's **class** position and personal identity, and that these cultural activities were connected to the economics of British society. These theories derived in part from **Marxist** thinking, which argues that the forms of everyday life derive from the ways people are positioned as workers in, or owners of, the industries and businesses which produce the wealth of the nation. For these writers the improvement of social structures and people's everyday conditions of existence could come about through changing people's relationships to work and wealth, but also through debate and struggles for change in culture itself. To change television might also change society, and the influence of this view was seen in **realistic** and often pessimistic drama series such as *Z Cars* (a police series), and controversial **satire** programmes such as *That Was the Week that Was*, which challenged conventions of television and also the representations of British society.

These ideas were familiar to the new generation of school leavers and university graduates emerging in the late 1950s and early 1960s, often people from working-class backgrounds who had been given the opportunity to gain a good education through scholarships and the expansion of universities. These people were often resistant to the elitism, conservatism and traditionalism which had dominated the Establishment (the civil service, the BBC, the institutions of the churches, universities and the law) in the past. Television was a young medium, and some of these

director the person responsible for the creative process of turning a script or idea into a finished programme, by working with a technical crew, performers and an editor.

status quo a Latin term meaning the ways that culture and society are currently organised.

class a section of society defined by their relationship to economic activity, whether as workers (the working class) or possessors of economic power (the bourgeoisie), for example.

Marxism the political and economic theories associated with the German nineteenth-century theorist Karl Marx, who described and critiqued capitalist societies and proposed Communism as a revolutionary alternative.

realism the aim for representations to reproduce reality faithfully, and the ways this is done.

satire a mode of critical commentary about society or an aspect of it, using humour to attack people or ideas.

people saw opportunities to carry forward their radical ideas in the television industry. Vigorous and authentic television seemed to entail the bringing on to the screen and into the television business of people from working-class backgrounds, from outside the stodgy south-east of England. In drama a new kind of realism was needed to reflect the lives of ordinary people beyond London and the Home Counties, and television documentary could present the different regions and social classes of the nation to the television audience. Television producers, directors and writers were often resistant to the bureaucracy of the television companies, and rejected the stoical and submissive attitudes to authority which characterised the older generation which had lived through the Second World War.

The attitudes of these people committed to changing society by changing its culture were evident in the programmes being made, but also in ways of thinking and writing about television that would inform the beginnings of Television Studies. In what became known as '**committed** criticism', writers condemned the status quo and sought both to praise radical television (or film or literary works) and to find ways of representing which critiqued the present and offered new and **progressive** ways of thinking. For committed critics it was important to take the **popular culture** enjoyed by ordinary people seriously, but also to discriminate wisely between what was valuable and what was deadening or worthless. One effect of this was to continue the suspicion of American popular culture (rock 'n' roll music, Hollywood cinema or comics, for instance), which had been gaining audiences and making money with the recognition of a new social group – the teenager. In many television fictions of the 1950s and 1960s isolated young outsider figures, often moving between social classes, struggle to find authentic personal meaning in their apparently absurd and empty lives. The independent outsider and rebel was always male, however, and the heroic vigour of the 1960s hero is often opposed to the entrapping seductiveness of marriage and family represented by women.

In more recent times the culture of television professionals in Britain has changed because of the structural changes made to the television industry as a result of new broadcasting regulations imposed by government, and new working practices introduced by television executives. The BBC reduced its staff by seven thousand between 1986 and 1990, for example, and since the 1980s the use of temporary contracts and the **outsourcing** of production to independent producers, and the introduction of an internal market at the BBC, have shifted decision-making powers from programme-makers to schedulers and commissioners and made the career paths of programme-makers much more unstable. The effect of this market-like situation is that the producer, who commissions and oversees the making of television programmes, becomes a powerful figure, to the exclusion of the writer or the director, because the producer is answerable to the demands of the television institution for audiences and cost-effectiveness. When John Birt led the BBC in the 1990s the sweeping changes he introduced weakened the independence of the producer by centralising power in London and giving more control to commissioners, schedulers and controllers. The same process has affected the commercial channels. The BBC sold off many of its programme production and technical facilities in the early 1990s, and increased the proportion of programmes commissioned from **independent producers** rather than made in-house. It increasingly resembles Channel 4 as a commissioning rather than programme-making organisation.

committed a term used in the study of the politics of culture, implying that a person or a text has a commitment to positive and progressive social change.

progressive encouraging positive change or progress, usually implying progress towards fairer and more equal ways of organising society.

popular culture the texts created by ordinary people (as opposed to an elite group) or created for them, and the ways these are used.

outsourcing obtaining services from an independent business rather than from within a television institution, usually as a means of cutting costs.

Reception contexts

Television is now watched in the private space of the home, but in the early days of British broadcasting this was by no means the dominant way that viewers experienced the new medium. Philip Corrigan (1990) has discovered that in 1937, the year after BBC television broadcasting started, there were more than a hundred public venues for watching television. These included railway stations, restaurants and department stores. Audiences sometimes as large as a hundred people could gather to watch television pictures collectively. In the United States a similar situation was evident in the 1930s, and for a short time television looked like a possible competitor with cinema as a medium of public entertainment experienced in buildings set aside for watching (J. Allen 1983). The Nazi government in Germany in the 1930s was interested partly in the propaganda value of television broadcasting, and partly in competing with the large American corporations that were investing in television production and television sets. The fact that the Olympic Games of 1936 took place in Berlin was a stimulus to German television, and broadcasts were received not in individual homes but in viewing rooms established in cities. Once again, television was being thought of as a medium for collective viewing of pictures and sound relayed live from major public events. Some of the buildings in which German television broadcasts were watched could hold audiences as large as four hundred people. But industrial corporations in Germany had considerable political influence during the Nazi era. So the corporations' plans to develop domestic television sets to be watched in individual homes, and thus to develop a consumer market for television sets, meant that these public screenings were to give way to domestic viewing when the Second World War began in 1939 (Uricchio 1989).

When the pattern of centralised production and dispersed individual reception of television stabilised as the norm after the Second World War, the form of television that we know in Western countries today had been established. There are two different and sometimes conflicting results of this pattern. First, central control of production and private individual reception set up a structure that matches the democratic organisation of the developed societies such as those of Europe and the United States. When governments have a direct role in broadcasting, or set up a legal framework of ownership and **regulation** for private autonomous institutions to make television, there is a basis for universal access to information and culture that might promote a fairer society. Mass populations, watching television in their own homes and with members of their families, could be supplied with the information and ideas they need to participate in a national or regional society. Informed viewers would be given the resources to take part in political and social debates, to vote in elections on the basis of a level playing field of information about the issues at stake. The centralised production of television and its dispersed reception suit the concept of **public service** broadcasting quite well as it has developed in Britain and other European countries. Although there is a more questionable side to this issue, since government propaganda and the manipulation of audiences could also be a part of this broadcasting landscape, the structure of broadcasting as we know it is associated with attempts to raise the cultural, educational and social standards of societies.

The second result of centralised production and dispersed reception of television is its connection with the culture of the home. Standards of living and proportions of surplus income available for investment in leisure and entertainment rose steadily through the twentieth century in the industrial nations of the Western world. People's houses were not only places to live but also places where consumer goods could could be accumulated, and new patterns of domestic leisure could develop. Commentators in the 1940s and 1950s in Britain were concerned about how television might prove a disruptive force in the home, disturbing the family routines of eating, conversation and children's bedtimes. To watch could be regarded as a waste of time (compared to reading, doing jobs around the house or engaging in conversation), especially if television was focused on entertainment. However, for most viewers the experience of watching was not the solitary experience it often is today. Because only a small proportion of homes had invested in the new and expensive technology, most viewing was collective as people gathered in friends' and neighbours' houses to watch. Watching television was a social event in its own right, and in some respects helped to form communities. This was especially the case in the newly built suburbs of the major cities where people had chosen to uproot themselves from the close-knit but overcrowded Victorian housing of older towns and city centres. Separated by the hedges and front gardens of their new semi-detached houses, people were able to socialise and display their relative wealth and status by holding informal gatherings around their televisions.

The television set became an important part of the culture of the home, as the prices of television sets fell through the 1950s and they could be acquired not only by the affluent middle class but increasingly by everyone. Television sets became a central feature of the household living room, often positioned next to the fireplace, where families would gather in the evening together both to keep warm (in the age before central heating) and to share the entertainment experiences offered to them by television. As well as experiencing entertainment outside the home, at the cinema for example, or at the pub, television enabled people to take their leisure indoors with their friends and their families. Radio had already fulfilled a similar function, and as the mass ownership of television sets extended in the 1950s in Europe and the United States this continued the drive to make the home the primary site of leisure and consumerism. Overall, then, the pattern of television broadcasting that dominated the twentieth century and continues into the twenty-first century was neither natural nor necessary. But it suited the developing forms of society characterised by these key features:

- the promotion of democracy and citizenship
- participation in a modern consumer society
- the centrality of the home as the location of private leisure and family life
- access by government and industry to private space and private life.

The significance of this narrative of television history is that is a cultural history: it emphasises the ways in which television became embedded in people's lives according to the places they lived, the social classes to which they belonged and the expectations about home, work and leisure that they held.

ACTIVITY 2.5

Look through magazines (such as Sunday newspaper magazines, style magazines or consumer electronics magazines) to find advertisements for recent television equipment such as flat-panel television sets, DVD recorders and players, or digital television receivers. What similarities can you find in the ways these are advertised, and the potential consumers the ads seem to be addressed to?

Programmes and forms

Writing the history of television by choosing significant programmes to exemplify a year, decade or longer period clearly raises difficult problems. The shape of the narrative of television history that this produces is strongly determined by the choice of the examples used to back it up. Since television in Britain has a public service function, one of ways of demonstrating this historical tradition is to note the events that television has covered in order to bring a national audience together as members of a common **culture**. Ceremonies, state occasions and major sporting events are examples that support this view of television history. When the BBC was Britan's only television broadcaster (from 1936 to 1955), it emphasised the live broadcasting of these kinds of events from the start, and set up **outside broadcast** units to cover such public and ceremonial events as the coronation of King George VI in 1937, the annual Wimbledon tennis championships and the Armistice Day ceremony commemorating the end of the First World War. British writers in the 1930s who predicted the future of television emphasised its ability to relay events (such as sporting events, royal events and general elections) live across the country, thus keeping people in touch with what happened beyond their immediate experience and neighbourhood. It was felt that television would not compete with cinema as entertainment because of its domestic setting and lack of a sense of occasion, and would therefore focus on information.

    It was in the 1950s that what we would now describe as mass audiences for television began in Britain. But television sets were still expensive, costing more than £80 in the early 1950s, equivalent to about eight weeks' wages for the average employed man. Between 1952 and 1959 in Britain the number of combined television and radio licences increased from 2.1 million to 10 million. The single television programme with the greatest effect on creating this wider ownership of television sets was the live coverage of the Coronation of Queen Elizabeth II in 1953. Again, a live event relayed by television suits the construction of a certain kind of history. This history regards television as a medium preoccupied with the present, and with live coverage. Furthermore, the Coronation is another example of a television event that addresses a national public (and an international one since in the 1950s Britain still had extensive contacts with and responsibilities for countries that had formed part of its empire). Televised events such as the Coronation connect television viewing with the formation of a national culture defined in part by its relationship with the royal family, heritage, tradition and ceremonial. More than twenty years later the wedding of Princess Anne and Captain Mark Philips in 1974 was broadcast

outside broadcast
the television transmission of outdoor events such as sport or ceremonial occasions, using equipment set up in advance for the purpose. Abbreviated as OB.

live, and seen by an audience of around 25 million, representing about half of the UK population. Television covered the wedding of Prince Charles and Lady Diana Spencer in July 1981, showing five and a half hours of live coverage on BBC and ITV. In the UK 39 million viewers watched live, and it was broadcast live to seventy-four countries. The BBC used about sixty cameras, including twelve in St Paul's Cathedral.

commercial television television funded by the sale of advertising time or sponsorship of programmes.

Independent **commercial television** began broadcasting on 22 September 1955, available first only in the London region but expanding to nearly all the country over the next six years. Many influential figures resisted ITV, including the BBC Director-General John Reith, who compared commercial television to bubonic plague, and concern was fuelled by the American commercial television coverage of the Coronation in 1953, when messages from programme sponsors frequently interrupted the Westminster Abbey service. But the Conservative government was keen to break the BBC monopoly and passed the Television Bill of 1954, which set up the **Independent Television Authority**, though the Bill revealed in its language the concern for the lowering of standards which commercial television might entail. It was to be 'predominantly British in tone and style and of high quality, and nothing was to be included which offended against good taste or decency or which was likely to incite to crime or to lead to disorder or to be offensive to public feeling'. The desire to preserve a national television culture and its protection from the commercialism and triviality associated with another broadcasting culture (of the United States) can be read off from this attitude. In a history of television, this reaction to the start of ITV is evidence of an anxiety about what British television might become.

Independent Television Authority (ITA) the official body set up to regulate commercial television in Britain.

The first night on ITV began with a gala including speeches from the Lord Mayor of London, the **Postmaster General** and Sir Kenneth Clark, chairman of the ITA. The evening was very much in the mould of the BBC: the presenter was Leslie Mitchell, who had worked for the BBC and presented its opening night in 1936. The **variety** performers on the first night, such as Harry Secombe and Billy Cotton, had regularly appeared on the BBC, and subsequent programming that night consisted of extracts from theatre plays and a boxing match, and concluded with a discussion of the latest London fashions shown at the Mayfair Hotel. Each broadcast day ended with the playing of the national anthem.

Postmaster General the person appointed by government to regulate communications institutions such as the Post Office, radio and television.

variety programmes entertainment programmes containing a mix of material such as songs and comedy sketches.

Commercial television was organised in regions, with each part of the country having its own broadcasting provider. The BBC was also divided into regions for television production and broadcasting, just as its radio services had been. Each regional company made programmes specifically for its local audience, and also offered programmes to the national network. Viewers were immediately keen on the new ITV channel, and in 1957 audiences watched ITV two-thirds of the time. In December 1955, for example, 84 per cent of viewers watched the variety programme *Sunday Night at the London Palladium* on ITV. Both ITV and BBC channels used popular formats such as quiz shows, one-off dramas, variety and adventure series to keep their hold on their audiences, with ITV generally catering for more popular tastes. The BBC's audience fell, and it responded by increasing its broadcast hours from forty-one per week to fifty. It introduced its first **soap opera**, *The Grove Family*, in weekly fifteen-minute episodes centring on a suburban middle-class family, resulting in a deluge of approving letters and massive press coverage. Television created the new figure of the television **personality**, familiar figures such

personalities people appearing on television who are recognised by audiences as celebrities with a media image and public status beyond the role they play in a particular programme.

as the on-screen announcers Sylvia Peters, Mary Malcolm and McDonald Hobley on the BBC, and the hosts of popular programmes such as the television cook Philip Harben, gardener Fred Streeter, Annette Mills, with the children's programme *Muffin the Mule*, and Armand and Michela Dennis, featuring in filmed wildlife programmes from around the world.

The reasons that genres of television programmes are created and become significantly popular are varied and complex, so that looking at the selection of programmes with the largest audiences in a particular year can be misleading as well as informative. In the boxes below, the ten most popular programmes in Britian from four different years are listed, measuring popularity according to the size of audience calculated by broadcasters' audience research figures. Some of the critical points that could be made about what these lists reveal are suggested after the lists, together with some issues that complicate possible interpretations of the meaning of the figures.

The ten most popular programmes in March 1958

The ten most popular programmes in March 1958 were all on ITV. At this time audience sizes were measured in millions of homes, though of course the number of viewers in each home could vary widely. *Emergency Ward 10* appears twice in this list because two of its episodes in March made the top ten programmes.

1 *Take Your Pick* (game show, 4.1 million homes)
2 *The Army Game* (sitcom, 4.1m)
3 *Armchair Theatre* (one-off drama, 3.8m)
4 *Emergency Ward 10* (soap opera, 3.8m)
5 *Sunday Night at the London Palladium* (variety show, 3.7m)
6 *Double Your Money* (game show, 3.6m)
7 *TV Playhouse* (one-off drama, 3.6m)
8 *Emergency Ward 10* (3.5m)
9 *Shadow Squad* (thriller series, 3.1m)
10 *Play of the Week* (one-off drama, 3.1m).

The ten most popular programmes in September 1964

The ten most popular programmes in September 1964 were all shown on ITV. Audience sizes were still measured in millions of viewing homes, where of course the number of people viewing could vary considerably. *Coronation Street* and *Emergency Ward 10* appear twice in this list because two episodes from each series made the top ten programmes.

1 *Coronation Street* (soap opera, 8.1 million homes)
2 *Coronation Street* (7.8m)

continued

3 *No Hiding Place* (drama series, 7.8m)
4 *Sunday Palladium* (variety show, 7.4m)
5 *Emergency Ward 10* (soap opera, 7.2m)
6 *Emergency Ward 10* (7.0m)
7 *Take Your Pick* (game show, 6.9m)
8 *Love Story* (drama series, 6.8m)
9 *Drama 64* (one-off drama, 6.8m)
10 *Double Your Money* (game show, 6.7m).

The ten most popular programmes in November 1974

Audience sizes were still measured in millions of homes. Both *Coronation Street* and *Crossroads* appear twice in this list because different episodes of each of them gained large audiences during the month.

1 *Bless this House* (ITV sitcom, 8.6 million homes)
2 *Coronation Street* (ITV soap opera, 7.8m)
3 *Man About the House* (ITV sitcom, 7.8m)
4 *The Generation Game* (BBC game show, 7.5m)
5 *Coronation Street* (ITV soap opera, 7.4m)
6 *Crossroads* (ITV soap opera, 7.4m)
7 *Crossroads* (ITV soap opera, 7.4m)
8 *Upstairs Downstairs* (ITV drama series, 7.3m)
9 *Jennie* (ITV drama series, 7.2m)
10 *Opportunity Knocks* (ITV game show, 7.1m)

The ten most popular programmes in November 1984

Audiences are now measured in millions of viewers.

1 *Coronation Street* (ITV soap opera, 19.0m)
2 *Give Us a Clue* (ITV game show, 15.5m)
3 *Tenko* (BBC drama serial, 15.3m)
4 *Just Good Friends* (BBC sitcom, 15.1m)
5 *Crossroads* (ITV soap opera, 14.8m)
6 *Name That Tune* (ITV game show, 14.6m)
7 *Dallas* (BBC imported US soap opera, 14.6m)
8 *Hi-De-Hi* (BBC sitcom, 14.5m)
9 *Play Your Cards Right* (ITV game show, 14.5m)
10 *Surprise Surprise* (ITV light entertainment, 13.7m).

As Andrew Crisell (1997: 84) has written, 'commercial television was set up as an extension of the public service concept . . . The ITA required the contractors to inform, educate and entertain – to produce programmes of balance, quality and variety'. But, when ITV began broadcasting, the pace and style of British television changed somewhat because in order to compete with the BBC the new channel showed imported American programmes and used American **formats,** as in the action drama series *The Adventures of Robin Hood* and *The Count of Monte Cristo.* In this competitive environment research into audience sizes and preferences became more significant, and television viewers began to be seen as consumers seeking entertainment. Nevertheless, ITV followed the BBC in making **adaptations** of theatre plays, and dramas from Europe translated into English, as well as the populist quizzes and variety shows which ITV is credited with bringing to prominence. Looking at the lists above, though, it seems that ITV had considerable success in attracting large audiences by broadcasting programmes in the forms that are still considered today to be popular entertainment, such as soap opera and game shows. It is important to remember that these programme forms on ITV were designed to deliver audiences to advertisers, who had paid to screen television commercials between programme segments. The formation of large audiences for popular programmes was necessary to the profitability of the ITV companies. On its first night 170,000 sets were able to receive ITV, and, of these, 100,000 were tuned to ITV, while a quarter of households watched BBC instead. The first ITV commercial break was at 8.12 p.m. during the first evening's variety programme, and there were twenty-three commercials that night. Advertisers paid about £1,500 for a slot, a 50 per cent premium above normal rates, and demand led to a ballot to select those ads which would be accommodated. The products advertised were similar to those of today: toothpaste, tyres, drinking chocolate, soap, cars and breakfast cereal. Advertisements were not allowed to concern politics or religion, and had to conform to the standards of good taste overseen by two committees. They could appear only in '**natural breaks**' of up to six minutes per hour, and there had to be a two-minute interval between an advertisement and any appearance by a member of the royal family, state occasion, church service or royal ceremony.

The lists above show that light entertainment programmes such as game shows and sitcoms, as well as long-running **series** and **serials,** have become the mainstay of the output of terrestrial channels. Costs are reduced by using the same crew, performers, sets, costumes and studios for each episode, and series and serials can be sold to overseas broadcasters in ready-made packages of programmes. One of the effects of this is to marginalise programmes which are more unconventional in form, or more challenging in social and political content. The promise that a continuing series or serial has of holding on to an audience for the duration of the programme's run offers the prospect of a consistent audience whose **demographic** appeal and/or large size may be attractive to advertisers.

Genre television (such as soap opera, police or hospital drama, or game shows) is attractive to television executives because a popular generic programme has a brand identity. In the same way as casting a known television **personality** or performer, the recognition and familiarity of the forms and **conventions** of the programmes provide both security and appeal. Generic television also provides a sense of control and ownership to the audience, who have a stake in the programmes rather than simply being offered another new product to consume. As well as being

format the blueprint for a programme, including its setting, main characters, genre, form and main themes.

adaptation transferring a novel, theatre play, poem, etc. from its original medium into another medium such as television.

natural break a vague term meaning a point at which a programme can be interrupted without causing undue disruption to the ongoing flow of the programme.

series a television form where each programme in the series has a different story or topic, though settings, main characters or performers remain the same.

serial a television form where a developing narrative unfolds across a sequence of separate episodes.

demography the study of population, and the groupings of people (demographic groups) within the whole population.

conventions the frameworks and procedures used to make or interpret texts.

constrained by repetition, genre allows for innovation within and between genres, and programmes gain large audiences by manipulating conventions in new ways. Generic categories are no longer separate, and such new formats as **docusoaps**, hospital thrillers and soap-drama feed off the rich history and audience knowledge of television to mix **realism** with **reflexivity**. Thus the BBC's soap opera *EastEnders* continues the British tradition of addressing contemporary social issues, while also casting Barbara Windsor as a Cockney pub landlady to draw on her associations with 1950s and 1960s saucy seaside comedy in the *Carry On* comedy films.

docusoap a television form combining documentary's depiction of non-actors in ordinary situations with soap opera's continuing narratives about selected characters.

reflexivity a text's reflection on its own status as a text, for example drawing attention to generic conventions, or revealing the technologies used to make a programme.

ACTIVITY 2.6

Look in more detail at the lists of the ten most popular programmes presented above. What are the similarities and differences you find between the lists? What might these similarities and differences contribute to a history of British television?

Case study: 'Me TV'

Domestic television technologies cannot in themselves be regarded as the motors of change in the history or future of television, as this chapter has discussed. Technologies become marketable and attractive to purchasers because of the possibilities they offer in extending existing ways of using television, and their ability to lead practices of viewing in new directions. They also have to be integrated into the institutional and structural arrangements which shape how television is made, broadcast and financially supported. This case study considers how the new technology of the digital video recorder might change current ways of watching television and ways that television broadcasters and producers might make it. The introduction of two digital video recorder products occurred in 2000, called TiVo and ReplayTV. These are **set-top boxes** which look rather like video recorders or the decoder boxes used to bring cable and satellite television to the television screen. Both were introduced to the American market first and are now available in Britain, posing a challenge to the extrapolation of trends towards commercially supported television that the history of the medium seems to imply.

set-top box the electronic decoding equipment connected to home television sets that allows access to digital television signals.

The capability of TiVo and ReplayTV is to record digitally and store programmes under the control of the viewer (like a video tape recorder) but also to build up automatically a profile of their user on the basis of the programmes he or she has watched or recorded in the past. The machine will trawl the multiple channels available through digital television broadcasting or cable, and store them selectively according either to the user's instructions or to the machine's expectations of what the viewer might want. This capability has been called the beginning of 'Me TV', in other words the creation of a repertoire of programmes tailored to the desires of the individual viewer. Its implications are significant for both television viewers and broadcasters:

- It is possible to time-shift any programme, in other words to watch it at a different time to its original broadcast, and to record several programmes simultaneously. It is therefore possible never to watch television as it is broadcast at all, but simply to instruct the machine to create a menu of programmes which can be seen at any time.

● The machine can be programmed to omit commercials or to skip through them at high speed. So for channels which gain income from advertising (as almost all channels do in the USA and as the majority of non-BBC channels do in Britain) this threatens to reduce their income dramatically, because advertisers pay fees according to the numbers of viewers expected to watch their ads.

From the perspectives of Television Studies and its accounts of the history of television, this development questions some of the trends identified in this chapter and supports others, changing the possible direction of the history of television in significant ways. This chapter has noted the change from a paternalistic notion of the viewer as a member of a collective national audience to the notion of the viewer as increasingly an individual consumer, offered multiple choices of television content by a proliferating number of channels. Rather than supervising the viewer's cultural education towards 'better' taste and informed citizenship, television institutions increasingly either offer mixed programme schedules which attempt to satisfy perceived desires and capture audiences through entertainment, or diversify their offerings into themed channels which offer related programme types to small **niche audiences**. Digital video recorders promise a future in which the identities of channels and the interest in and loyalty to the programming character of channels become largely irrelevant to television viewers. From among the hundreds of digital channels available in the near future, the digital video recorder would become an agent for the viewer, taking over at least some of the work of programme selection for him or her. The channel on which a programme is broadcast, and the time at which it is broadcast, would become irrelevant since there would be no distinction as far as the viewer is concerned between programmes being broadcast 'live' and those which are recorded. Television would cease to consist of must-see programmes when large audiences view the same live broadcast at the same time, except perhaps in rare times of crisis such as the terrorist attack on the World Trade Center in New York in 2001. The heritage of liveness and the conception of the audience as a mass or series of masses would cease to apply. Viewer choice, along the lines of the almost infinite choice available to online Internet shoppers of today, would be taken to a dramatic extreme.

The response to digital video recorders among American television producers has been one of anxiety or even panic, since American television culture is almost exclusively funded by the advertising which digital recorders can omit for their users. However, virtual digital advertising is one response which is currently being tried, and which may prove widespread in the future. Rather than screening commercials separated from programme content, advertisers are able to buy virtual product placement. This entails the insertion of logos, products or posters created in digital form into the camera shots of programmes. For example, a scene in which characters stand in a city street might have poster hoardings, or a soft-drink dispensing machine, inserted into the background of the shot as an advertisement for the soft drink. This technique was pioneered in the American CBS News programme's coverage of the millennium celebrations in New York's Times Square in 2000, for example, where a large logo for the rival NBC television network was digitally 'pasted out' of the television pictures broadcast by CBS. Virtual hoardings already appear inserted digitally into the images of pitch-side advertising barriers on some American sports coverage. So the distinctions between advertising and programme content, and between 'live' images and virtually enhanced ones are eroded, in order to preserve the links between programme production funding and commercial advertising in American television.

niche audiences particular groups of viewers defined by age group, gender or economic status, for example, who may be the target audience for a programme.

continued

The future of television may involve challenges to the current expectation that television images are records of an environment which actually existed in front of the camera, and the expectation that programme content and advertising are identifiably different. But drawing on the account of television history in this chapter, which stresses the power of television institutions to shape viewing practices at the same time as being attentive in responding to apparent viewer desires, it is also important to note the continuity between present and future which American broadcasters show in their response to the digital video recorder. For rather than considering different ways of organising television along non-advertising-supported lines, the broadcasters attempt to use another aspect of current and future television technology to address the challenge posed by digital video recorders. Just as the digital video recorder uses digital technology to alter viewing habits and television's relationship to the viewer, so advertisers are able to use digital editing technology to insert advertising into programmes in new ways. The economic structure of television in commercially funded systems maintains itself by this means, demonstrating the inertia and power of institutional relationships between programme funding, broadcasting and consumer culture.

ACTIVITY 2.7

How do the issues around the personal video recorder mentioned in the case study rely on ideas about the historical development of television that have been discussed earlier in this chapter and in other sources?

SUMMARY OF KEY POINTS

- The history of television can be told in many different ways, depending on which evidence is selected and how it is approached.
- The evidence for writing television history includes audio-visual records of programmes, and also printed sources and archival documents.
- Television institutions have rarely preserved historical material, though new opportunities for repeating programmes of the past are changing this situation.
- The invention of television, and the development of television institutions, need not have happened in the ways they did.
- The political, economic and cultural conditions in which television developed affect the ways it is made, watched and organised.
- The future of television will be affected by technologies, institutions, regulations and the expectations of audiences.

Further reading

Allen, J., 'The social matrix of television: invention in the United States', in E. A. Kaplan (ed.), *Regarding Television: Critical Approaches – An Anthology* (Los Angeles, Calif.: AFI, 1983), pp. 109–19.

Bignell, J., S. Lacey and M. Macmurraugh-Kavanagh (eds), *British Television Drama: Past, Present and Future* (Basingstoke: Palgrave, 2000).

Brunsdon, C., 'What is the television of television studies?', in C. Geraghty and D. Lusted (eds), *The Television Studies Book* (London: Arnold, 1998), pp. 95–113.

Bruzzi, S., *The New Documentary: A Critical Introduction* (London: Routledge, 2000).

Bryant, S., *The Television Heritage: Television Archiving Now and in an Uncertain Future* (London: BFI, 1989).

Caughie, J., *Television Drama: Realism, Modernism, and British Culture* (Oxford: Oxford University Press, 2000).

Corner, J., *Critical Ideas in Television Studies* (Oxford: Clarendon, 1999).

—— *Popular Television in Britain* (London: BFI, 1991).

Corrigan, P., 'On the difficulty of being sociological (historical materialist) in the study of television: the "moment" of English television, 1936–1939', in T. Syvertsen (ed.), *1992 and After: Nordic Television in Transition* (Bergen: University of Bergen, 1990), pp. 130–60.

Crisell, A., *An Introductory History of British Broadcasting* (London: Routledge, 1997).

Gripsrud, J. 'Television, broadcasting, flow: key metaphors in TV theory', in C. Geraghty and D. Lusted (eds), *The Television Studies Book* (London: Arnold, 1998), pp. 17–32.

Harbord, J. and J. Wright, *Forty Years of British Television* (London: Boxtree, 1992).

Harvey, S., 'Channel 4 television from Annan to Grade', in S. Hood (ed.), *Behind the Screens* (London: Lawrence & Wishart, 1994), pp. 102–29.

Hill, J. and M. McLoone (eds), *Big Picture Small Screen: The Relations between Film and Television* (Luton: University of Luton Press, 1997).

Hood, S. (ed.), *Behind the Screens: The Structure of British Television in the Nineties* (London: Lawrence & Wishart, 1994).

Mackay, H. and T. O'Sullivan (eds), *The Media Reader: Continuity and Transformation* (London: Sage, 1999).

Nichols, B., *Introduction to Documentary* (Bloomington, Ind.: Indiana University Press, 2001).

O'Sullivan, T., 'Television, memories and cultures of viewing 1950–65', in J. Corner (ed.), *Popular Television in Britain: Studies in Cultural History* (London: BFI, 1991), pp. 159–81.

Scannell, P., 'Public service broadcasting; the history of a concept', in A. Goodwin and G. Whannel (eds), *Understanding Television* (London: Routledge, 1990), pp. 11–29.

Smith, A., *Television: An International History*, second edition (Oxford: Oxford University Press, 1998).

Uricchio, W., 'Rituals of reception, patterns of neglect: Nazi television and its postwar representation', *Wide Angle*, 11:1 (1989), pp. 48–66.

Winston, B., *Media Technology and Society: A History* (London: Routledge, 1998).

Television Cultures

Television Cultures

Introduction

This chapter deals with theories of television institutions which analyse how the making and distribution of programmes take place in the present. It looks at British patterns of commercial and **public service** broadcasting, and places these in the context of American and European television. Television in the developed world is still largely organised on national lines, but the increasing significance of international flows from West to East and North to South has been hotly debated, so any discussion of television today needs to take account of the social and political significance of how trans-national and national cultures of broadcasting work in relation to each other. What is at issue is the degree to which the meanings of television are dependent on the kinds of institutions which make and broadcast it, and the conclusions which can be drawn from studying television in terms of its ownership, organisation and spread around the world. There are inequalities in production funding, and different roles of domestic and imported programming in national television cultures, and this chapter refers to television in the less developed world to explain how theorists of television have understood these inequalities.

One of the most significant theories for explaining how television is organised today is that of **globalisation**. Globalisation can refer to the phenomenon whereby some programmes or **genres** of television have spread across different nations and cultures, so that the television schedules of different countries can seem surprisingly familiar. One way of explaining this is to use the concept of **media imperialism**, in which it is argued that 'world patterns of communication flow, both in density and in direction, mirror the system of domination in the economic and political order' (Sinclair et al. 1999: 173). A second meaning of globalisation is to refer to the power of corporations which are relatively independent of nation-states, and which broadcast by satellite into several countries or regions. Theorists of television have debated whether globally broadcast programmes and global television corporations have brought new opportunities and freedoms, or whether they have imposed a deadening sameness on the diverse cultures of the world. An important question which underlies this debate is whether television institutions both embody and transmit **ideological** 'messages' which are the result of their ownership, their relationship to national broadcasting **regulations** and their adoption of particular cultural values. As Chris Barker (1997: 27) notes, the term 'global television' 'implies all the various configurations of public and commercial television which are regulated, funded and viewed within the boundaries of nation-states and/or language communities'. This chapter provides an account of the critical models which can be employed to evaluate these issues, and the divergent conclusions that have been and could be drawn from them.

British television in global contexts

Britain is relatively unusual in global terms because its major broadcasting organisations mainly show programmes made in Britain. In 1999, for example, 82 per cent of the programmes shown on BBC1 and BBC2 were made in Britain. The programmes made by British television broadcasters outnumber those which are bought from other nations, and some British programmes sell to many overseas countries.

- Venezuela has bought the situation comedies *Absolutely Fabulous, Fawlty Towers* and *Blackadder*.
- China has bought the police serial *Prime Suspect*, the drama about fire-fighters *London's Burning* and the detective drama *Poirot*.
- Sweden has bought *EastEnders*.
- Qatar has bought the detective drama *A Touch of Frost*.
- Russia has bought *A Touch of Frost, Coronation Street* and *Absolutely Fabulous*.

The best-selling British television export in 1998 was the BBC nature documentary series *The Living Planet*, sold to eighty-two countries, while the children's programme *Teletubbies* has been sold to Estonia, Portugal, Israel, the USA, Australia

Figure 3.1 *Teletubbies*. Courtesy of Ragdoll Ltd.

and New Zealand. Nevertheless, American television far exceeds British television or television from any other European country in export revenue and coverage. The trade journal *Television Business International* reported in 1996 that the difference between the USA's media trading with Europe and Europe's media trading with the USA amounted to a surplus in the USA's favour of $6.3 billion in the previous year.

ACTIVITY 3.1

How many programmes in this week's British television listings seem to be broadcast with foreign dialogue translated in subtitles? Whom do you think these programmes are aimed at?

ACTIVITY 3.2

Which British programmes do you think are least suitable for foreign sale? Why is this?

---

audience share the percentage of viewers estimated to have watched one channel as opposed to another channel broadcasting at the same time.

subscription payment to a television broadcaster in exchange for the opportunity to view programmes on certain channels that are otherwise blocked.

free-to-air television programming for which viewers make no direct payment.

digital television television pictures and sound encoded into the ones and zeros of electronic data. Digital signals can also be sent back down cables by viewers, making possible interaction with television programmes.

There are nearly twenty-four million households with television in Britain, representing all but a tiny percentage of the total households in the country, and the average British person watches about three and half hours of television per day. When this viewing is divided between channels, BBC1 and ITV have **audience shares** of about 32 per cent each, with BBC2 and Channel 4 gaining equal shares of about 11 per cent each and Channel 5 about 2.5 per cent, leaving about 11.5 per cent of the audience watching cable and satellite channels. In 1997 10 per cent of British homes had cable television, representing fewer than a quarter of the households able to receive it, while 18 per cent of homes were **subscribers** to satellite television services. In comparison to the USA, where cable television has been spectacularly successful, British people seem unwilling to exchange a television culture based on **free-to-air** high-quality programmes for the promise of increased choice which both cable and satellite bring. Whereas the American company Nielsen Media Research predicts that by 2004 thirty million US households will have **digital** satellite television, and a further seventy million households will have digital cable, it seems unlikely that British television culture will move quickly in the same direction.

Cable and satellite television in Britain have continued to grow in significance but at a slow rate. It is very expensive to set up cable networks because of the physical work of wiring up streets and houses across the country, and cable providers borrowed massive sums from banks on the promise of future profits. Since the take-up of cable television is still small, and the introduction of digital television promises hundreds of channels which do not have to be delivered by cable, there are serious questions to be asked about the future profitability of cable in Britain. Satellite television has been more successful at introducing the concept of payment for television channels with mixed content (such as Sky 1) and the concept of direct payment for specific special programmes (such as championship boxing matches). Digital television will enable broadcasters to extend **pay-per-view** television because there will be hundreds of channels available on which to stream programmes that viewers might pay for. However, the availability of hundreds or even thousands of television channels does not mean that there will be very many channels offering mixed programme schedules like those currently offered by **terrestrial** broadcasters. One reason is that the television services will be owned by a small number of large corporations which offer similar services. Owners of the transmission equipment (the satellites and cable networks on which programmes are carried) will make the most profit by providing at least some of the content, so the big firms owning production facilities are also likely to be involved in mergers or joint agreements with the companies which distribute television. The experience of multi-channel television in other countries such as the USA shows that an average viewer watches eight or ten channels with some regularity, and there is little benefit to broadcasters in duplicating services across more channels than this. So the remaining digital capacity will be devoted to pay-per-view movies in which a large range of films or other attractive programmes will be available with staggered start times. It will be possible to pay to view a film starting at 8.00, 8.10, 8.20 and so on, with one channel devoted to each different screening. Channels will also be devoted to shopping services, sports channels and digital data transmission to computers.

The availability of cable and satellite in developed countries such as Britain has the effect of diminishing audiences for the terrestrial channels as hundreds of channels split up the audience. Falling audiences for non-commercial network terrestrial television channels such as Britain's BBC pose a threat to their right to funding, since they cannot expect viewers to pay television **licence fees** if they are rarely watching BBC programmes. But to try to grab audiences back by imitating the programme **formats** and audience address of commercial television programmes causes another problem for such channels since duplicating the programme forms of their rivals means they have no claim to being an essential alternative to commercial television. The BBC and the Australian ABC, for example, have responded to this by capitalizing on their high **brand recognition** internationally to produce global television channels, such as BBC World. BBC World was set up in 1991, and was backed in 1996 by joint deals made with the American TCI subsidiary Flextech and the Discovery Channel to make and distribute BBC World programmes. But the 'objectivity' which is so much a part of BBC news's brand image has been a double-edged sword in some respects. The BBC faced exclusion from the Chinese and Saudi Arabian television markets because its reporting offended their governments. For commercial channels such as ITV and Channel 5, the splitting up of the audience threatens their income from advertisements, since smaller audiences mean less revenue from advertisers unless especially valuable sections of the audience (such as employed childless people in their twenties with surplus income) can be targeted by their programmes.

While the sale of programmes to other national broadcasters and diversification into global channels are useful ways for broadcasters to consolidate their position in the international television marketplace, it is also possible to sell the idea of a programme, its format, rather than the programme itself. The sale of programme formats is similar to the business of selling complete programmes to other national broadcasters. This process involves the sale of a programme idea and its narrative

pay-per-view specific television programmes (such as sports events, or films) offered to subscribers on payment of a fixed one-off fee.

terrestrial broadcasting from a ground-based transmission system, as opposed to broadcasting via satellite.

licence fee an annual payment by all owners of television sets, which is the main source of income for the BBC.

format the blueprint for a programme, including its setting, main characters, genre, form and main themes.

brand recognition the ability of audiences to recognise the distinctive identity of a product, service or institution and the values and meanings associated with it.

ACTIVITY 3.3

Look at the closing credits of a selection of current programmes to see which are co-productions with overseas companies. What are the common features of the co-productions you find?

---

structure, character relationships and setting, often including the scripts for batches of episodes. So rather than buying tapes of the original programme itself, overseas broadcasters acquire the template or set of instructions which enable them to remake the programme using their own facilities, performers and native language and locations. But programmes whose format gained large audiences in one country do not always succeed in another. The US sitcom *The Golden Girls* was tried in Britain (on ITV), using scripts from the US version with small adjustments for British viewers. The idea of remaking the programme must have seemed attractive to producers, since the US version of *The Golden Girls* had been a staple part of Channel 4's prime-time sitcom offering. Although the cast of the remake included well-known British comedy actresses the programme was a commercial and critical failure and was cancelled after six weeks. *Married for Life* was a British version of the US sitcom *Married . . . with Children*, which ran for over two hundred episodes in America and was broadcast in Britain too in a late-evening slot, but the British ITV version ran for only one series. Some television companies specialise in the development and sale of formats, and there have been spectacular successes. The company Action Time specialises in creating formats for quiz programmes, and has sold its formats widely in Britain and abroad, while the Dutch company Endemol developed *Big Brother*, and its vast audiences in Holland were paralleled by the commercial success of the programme when the format was subsequently sold around the world.

Global television

The term globalisation has several possible meanings. It can be used to refer to:

- products of global corporations, whether these are concrete products like shoes or textual products like television programmes.
- the distribution system which circulates these products, like the global network of transmission satellites used by television broadcasters.
- the consumers of products distributed in this way, the global audiences.

Theorists of television have emphasised that at the levels of production, distribution and consumption it is possible for the significance of global television to change, and argue that globalisation is not a natural and unstoppable process. In production, global television corporations can be restrained by national or local laws and regulations which make them operate differently in different places. Global distribution networks may transmit the same television programme over a very wide area, but the ways in which the programme is received (by whom, how, and the significance of receiving global television in a particular society) will be different in different contexts. John Sinclair and his fellow authors (Sinclair et al. 1999: 176) explain that 'Although US programmes might lead the world in their transportability across cultural boundaries, and even manage to dominate schedules on some channels in particular countries, they are rarely the most popular programmes where viewers have a reasonable menu of locally produced programmes to choose from'. So the theory of globalisation in Television Studies is a way of addressing both processes which homogenise television and those which reduce differences, but also a way of addressing processes of differentiation. Furthermore, globalisation theory brings together approaches to television which concern economic, institutional, textual and reception practices.

One of the ways of approaching television globalisation is to consider it as part of **postmodernism**. The American theorist Fredric Jameson uses the term post-modernism to refer to the ways in which cultural products (such as television programmes) as well as physical products (such as bananas) have become part of the global **capitalist** economy. Jameson's political background is in **Marxism**, and therefore he emphasises how the economic basis of capitalism affects television and media culture, and how the production and reception of television carry on the same principles of inequality and consumerism which are found in other aspects of contemporary commerce. When we analyse television programmes, Jameson argues, they turn out to carry the political **ideologies** of contemporary capitalist culture. As an example of how this theory works, consider the background to the children's action series *Mighty Morphin' Power Rangers* (1992), and the meanings which underlie its **narratives**. The series was made by Saban Entertainment, who adapted the scenario from the Japanese television series *Kyoryu Sentai Zyuranger* by inserting live-action sequences filmed in the United States into the effects and model sequences of the Japanese series. So the first points to note are the combination of American- and Japanese-made sequences within the same programme, and the production of the series by a Japanese corporation for a Western television audience. A product which has its origins in the culture of Japan recycles and adds to its antecedents, with an eye to international sales. The inclusion of American teenage actors and English dialogue is especially striking here, because of the predominance of the English language and American racial characteristics as worldwide norms.

In fact *Power Rangers* draws on further borrowings than this, across film and comics as well as television. Since the 1960s Japanese television has produced animated and live-action television which combines traditional martial arts with science fiction (also seen in *anime*, or animated films, and *manga*, comics). *Power Rangers* borrows from the 1979 film and television series *Mobile Suit Gundam*, in which human fighters use armoured robotic body suits, and *Bubblegum Crisis* (1987), which features four female warriors fighting evil in a future Tokyo. *Power Rangers* picks up these narrative elements and adapts them. The series concerns how a group of male and female American teenagers (helping the magician Zordon) who control robot fighting machines (Zords) fight the evil witch Repulsa and her five assistants. Repulsa's henchmen have the combined characteristics of humans, reptiles and machines, and the programme as a whole seems to focus on the differ-ences and similarities between humans, monsters and machines. It is at this point that a **textual analysis** of the programme can illuminate the underlying subtextual

postmodernism the most recent phase of capitalist culture, the aesthetic forms and styles associated with it, and the theoretical approaches developed to understand it.

capitalism the organisation of an economy around the private ownership of accumulated wealth, involving the expoitation of labour to produce profit that creates such wealth.

Marxism the political and economic theories associated with the German nineteenth-century theorist Karl Marx, who described and critiqued capitalist societies and proposed Communism as a revolutionary alternative.

narrative an ordered sequence of images and sound that tells a fictional or factual story.

textual analysis a critical approach which seeks to understand a television text's meanings by undertaking detailed analysis of its image and sound components, and the relationships between those components.

meanings of the series, to show how it might resonate with current concerns and problems which might be unconsciously recognised by its child audience in many developed societies.

It could be argued that *Power Rangers* was successful because it responds to the current cultural concern with the similarities and differences between humanity and technology, an anxiety which may be experienced more by children (whose identities are rapidly developing) than by adults. Control over technology is part of the adult world, and the feeling of mastery which results is represented in the series through mastery over violence, fear and destructiveness by means of technological power over others and the world. So an ideological analysis of *Power Rangers* as a globalised cultural product would emphasise how it engages with questions of power and identity (are humans, machines and animals different, and in what ways, and how can humans deal with a world in which technology and violence seem to disempower us?) and tries to resolve them in a fictional form. At a further level of analysis, the television programme is not independent of other global consumer industries. There were crazes for toys based on *Power Rangers* such as plastic action figures, toy weapons and models of the Zords. As well as being a cult television programme in Britain, *Power Rangers* was used by ninety companies to endorse 350 product lines, from pyjamas to toy figures to snack foods, using the name, logo and imagery of the series in the packaging and design of all kinds of products. The television series was the central node, or knot, from which radiated a whole host of other cultural goods and activities.

Cultural imperialism

One of the problems in conducting an analysis such as that of *Power Rangers* is that it can seem that one programme which is seen by different audiences around the world has the same meanings and significance wherever and by whomever it is watched. In the 1980s, when these questions were taken up by a number of theorists of television, it was particularly striking that American programmes were the ones most exported beyond their own borders, and seen by the largest worldwide audiences. In a famous study, television research by Tamar Liebes and Elihu Katz (1990) found that viewers of the 1980s American soap opera *Dallas* in different national cultures understood it in very different ways. They chose to study viewers of *Dallas* because it had been exported to a large number of nations, and had been seen as an indication that the future of television would be an increasing global homogeneity of programmes dominated by glossy American dramas. But, perhaps surprisingly, *Dallas*'s representation of the 'American dream' of financial success and personal happiness was understood by Jewish members of a kibbutz in Israel as proof that money does not bring happiness. By contrast, members of a North African co-operative thought that *Dallas* proved how money rescues people from everyday problems. Russian Jews who had recently arrived in Israel from the Soviet system believed that *Dallas* was a subtle critique of capitalism which unconsciously exposed its contradictions. So Liebes and Katz's study (1990) showed that, contrary to many people's expectations at the time, the meanings of television programmes are understood in relation to the cultural environment and expectations of viewers, and are not injected like a pernicious drug into the cultures where they are watched.

Sinclair and his fellow authors (Sinclair et al. 1999: 183) noted that 'there tends to be a more distanced realm of "pure entertainment" within which US programmes are processed – as markers of modish modernity, as a "spectacular" world – compared to more culturally specific responses made to domestic and other sources'.

In the 1950s and 1960s the theory of **cultural imperialism** was developed by such theorists as Herbert Schiller, for example, and versions of this theory were used to discuss the global export of Western, and especially American, television. It was this cultural imperialist model of global television that Katz and Liebes's study reacted against. Imperialism refers to the building of empires by European nations, especially during the nineteenth century in Africa and Asia. The purpose of empire was to secure natural resources and trade routes in order to feed the industrialising European nations and to provide markets for the goods produced in their factories, but by the end of the Second World War these empires had been largely dismantled. Cultural imperialism refers to the similar process by which Western nations exercise cultural power over less developed countries, rather than exercising the military, legal and trading power which empire involved. According to this argument, the export of cut-price television programmes (as well as cinema films, pop music and other cultural goods) promotes the commercial interests of Western corporations, especially American ones, and thus supports the political and military interests of the West. By means of the images of affluent Western lifestyles portrayed in television programmes, consumer culture is spread across regions and populations which increasingly aspire to the Western products and expectations which their meagre resources make it difficult for them to acquire.

The crudest forms of this cultural imperialism thesis, which simply proclaim that the world is being Americanised, pay too little attention to the specifics of the local and national organisation of television consumption. They also ignore the flows of television within regions, based for instance on the legacy of the languages of the former empires, which make possible the exchange of programmes in Spanish among the countries of Latin America. There are regional television flows as well as global ones, and sometimes these regional flows allow for reversals of the more common North to South and West to East trade in television, as in the export of Brazilian telenovelas from Latin America to Europe (see the case study at the end of this chapter).

In the late twentieth and the early twenty-first centuries there are some international corporations (such as General Electric, which owns the broadcaster NBC, and Sony) which control the manufacture of television equipment, the making of programmes and related media interests such as film studios and magazine publishing. This **vertical integration** represents not cultural imperialism by a nation but a form of corporate imperialism. Although television and media products may originate in the USA, several of the largest media corporations based there are not US owned. These include:

- Sony (Japanese)
- Seagram (Canadian, owners of Universal)
- Philips (Dutch)
- News Corporation (Australian, owners of the Fox network).

These huge corporations have financial interests in many kinds of products, and also make deals with smaller companies (such as the makers of fast food or toys) to create

cultural imperialism the critical argument that powerful nations and regions (especially those of the Western world) dominate less developed nations and regions by exporting values and ideologies.

vertical integration the control by media institutions of all levels of a business, from the production of products to their distribution and means of reception.

interrelated promotions, advertising and sales opportunities. Although many people are aware of the importance of multinational companies and global business, the sheer extent and interconnectedness of the modern economy, and its dependence on television and other media as channels of communication and trade are often underestimated.

The big seven media corporations

This list shows some of the main holdings of seven of the biggest television-owning corporations (from Boyd-Barrett and Rantanen 1998: 90–1), with emphasis on those operating in Britain.

- Reuters: Reuters TV, Reuters news wire services, minority shareholder in Independent Television News (in Britain), Tele-Noticias news programmes in Spanish, Polish and Russian commercial broadcasting, and minority interests in many programme producers worldwide.
- News Corporation (owned by Rupert Murdoch): Star TV satellite broadcasting in Asia, Sky Television in Britain, Fox network in the USA, Twentieth Century Fox film studios, and minority interests in many programme producers worldwide.
- BBC: BBC1 and BBC2 in Britain, BBC digital services and five British radio channels, BBC World television, BBC News 24.
- Carlton: the largest independent British programme producer, and majority owner of Independent Television News in Britain.
- Disney Capital Cities ABC: ABC television network in the USA, Disney Studios, majority shareholder in WTN news supply network, Scandanavian Broadcasting.
- General Electric: NBC network in the USA and CNBC, NBS SuperChannel, Asian Business Channel, MSNBC.
- Time-Warner: television production, broadcasting and third-largest cable operator in the USA, German-language regional news in Europe, owner of Turner Broadcasting, which controls CNN and CNN International.

ACTIVITY 3.4

How would you find out who owns the television networks or channels you watch? Why is this information difficult to find?

The group of countries with the highest proportion of domestically produced television consists of the United States, Britain, Brazil and Japan, followed by Canada and Australia, which are able to use imports to top up a largely domestic production base. But most of the nations of South America, Africa and Asia have small television industries and insufficient revenue to make many programmes and depend on imports to fill 50 per cent or more of their schedules. The national television networks of Brazil and Mexico, for example, have the funding and facilities to make many of their own programmes, but television broadcasters in the developing world find it much less expensive to buy American or British television than to make their own. In Fiji in 1993, for example, the television schedule included (O'Sullivan et al. 1994: 287):

- *The Bugs Bunny Show* (US animation)
- *My Two Dads* (US sitcom)
- *M*A*S*H* (US sitcom)
- *The Cosby Show* (US sitcom)
- *Highway to Heaven* (US drama)
- *May to December* (British sitcom)
- *BBC News* (British)
- *CBS News* (US)
- *Porridge* (British sitcom)
- *Trainer* (British drama).

Episodes of American television series from several years ago can be acquired by broadcasters in the developing world for just a few hundred dollars, as part of a package of programmes. The production costs of these programmes have of course already been more than covered by showing them in the domestic American market, so that the money made from the export of older series is pure profit for the **networks** which sell them. The much higher production values and the aura of sophistication which often surrounds imported television in non-Western countries means that sectors of the television audience which are attractive to advertisers (such as employed young people with surplus income to spend on consumer goods) may be more likely to watch them. This not only has the effect of marginalising the products of the domestic television industry, reducing its chances of expansion, but also fills the most popular broadcasting slots with Western programmes in which commercials advertising Western consumer products may often appear. Even if crude Americanisation is not the effect of this, consumerisation and the reinforcement of Western values may be.

network
a television institution that transmits programmes through local or regional broadcasting stations that are owned by or affiliated to that institution.

ACTIVITY 3.5

In what ways might television programmes originating in Western television cultures and exported to the developing world, and television advertisements for consumer products associated with affluent Western lifestyles share similar ideologies and ways of addressing audiences?

News, nations and the 'New World Order'

The ways of producing television news are similar in cultures other than Britain because the ways in which professional broadcasters do their work, and the ways

news value
the degree
of significance
attributed to a news
story, where items
with high news value
are deemed most
significant to the
audience.

actuality footage
television pictures
representing an event
that was filmed live.
The term usually
refers to pictures
of news events.

they give **news value** to certain kinds of stories, are held in common by the journalists of many nations and television institutions. Globalisation in television news can be regarded either positively or negatively (Gurevitch 1991). Technologies such as satellite broadcasting allow large and diverse audiences access to television news and live **actuality footage** of events such as the Olympic Games to be made available around the world. This provides possibilities for openness and democratic access to information which have never been available before. On the other hand, footage such as this has to conform to a version of news value which makes these events seem of global importance, and once they have been broadcast these events necessarily acquire global significance. Globalisation can be regarded negatively as the monopoly control of information by a few multinational broadcasters who impose Western news values across the world so that local cultures are drowned out by them. The increase in the quantity of television news which is available makes the activities of news broadcasters in hierarchising and explaining news more significant, because, with more news, the audience is assumed to need increased guidance and support in understanding it. The effect of this is to make the form of news simpler and regularised (reports are short, story structures are simple), so that the difference between the news events reported is diminished. The conventions which organise news stories predominate over the information which the conventions are used to communicate. But even if control of television networks is concentrated in the hands of a few broadcasters, this does not mean that audiences will simply accept the ideological meanings carried in their news programmes. Global television news needs to be analysed also by looking at how global and international news broadcasting is organised, and how it is understood by audiences.

ACTIVITY 3.6

Which kinds of events have been worthy of global broadcasting? What are the common features of these events?

In the modern world the media contribute to new ways of thinking about time, space and people's relationships with the world around them. Since information circulates around the globe across the different time-zones in which people live, the local time and the sense of people's familiar space can be understood as partial and local variations within a global, international time and space. The activities of people in their local area can be seen in the contexts of international and global problems and opportunities, where traditional and historic ways of understanding oneself, one's community or nation are overlaid or even replaced by globally dominant ways of thinking. Television enables its audience to witness events in different places occurring in the local times of different nations and cultures. For

CNN Cable News
Network, the first
international satellite
news channel,
operating from the
United States.

example, international news broadcasts by **CNN** transmitted images of the 1991 Gulf War and the terrorist attacks on New York and Washington in 2001 around the world, images of the apparently comfortable lives and abundant consumer goods were beamed into the countries of the Eastern bloc and aided the populations' desire for political change, and images representing Western culture such as satellite broadcasting of MTV stimulated change in the Soviet Union in the late 1980s. For Chris Barker (1997: 230),

> television on a global scale has the capacity to contribute to democracy (via the principles of diversity and solidarity) through its range of representations, genres, arguments and information. However, the vision of television as a diverse and plural public sphere is seriously compromised by its almost complete penetration by the interest-based messages and images of consumerism.

The international flow of television and its disruption of local cultures can be regarded as politically progressive, though the immediate impact of television has often been to intensify conflicts.

Complete news programmes are broadcast by satellite by the American institution CNN, which broadcasts to about 130 countries with content in major regional languages (such as Spanish in Latin America), and Britain's Sky News and BBC World. The selection of news stories on national television networks around the world, and the structure and form of news broadcasting there are influenced by CNN because its global coverage and broadcasting have the effect of bringing its selection of stories to the attention of national broadcasters. CNN can also affect the events which are being reported as news, since coverage of events almost live on CNN can have the effect of altering the progress of a news event, for example by alerting officials to the perception of their actions abroad, or by attracting demonstrators to attend a protest which CNN is covering. However, it would be mistaken to claim that CNN (or any other global broadcaster such as BBC World) has direct effects on shaping events or attitudes to them. Apart from the important theoretical insight in Television Studies that television's effects need to be considered within institutional, legal and cultural constraints which delimit and redirect them, there are specific restrictions on the gathering of news and the accessibility of global television news. Attempts to manage global news broadcast journalists by national politicians is common, in order to influence the representation of events outside a particular country where a gobal television news broadcaster is gathering news. The influence of global broadcasters is limited also by the fact that their programmes are in English and/or the languages spoken by the affluent elites who are attractive to advertisers, so that only a relatively privileged sector of many societies has access to the global news channels broadcasting via satellite or cable television.

BBC World

BBC World was launched in 1991 as BBC World Service Television. It draws on the global recognition of the BBC's radio World Service and uses the radio service's 250 correspondents and fifty-seven regional bureaux, as well as BBC's television's studios, technicians and reporters already stationed around the world. This scale of operation makes the BBC the world's largest newsgathering organisation. Half of BBC World's twenty-four hours of television consists of news programmes, each half an hour in

continued

length, and the other half is BBC current affairs, factual and entertainment programmes. BBC World is the biggest rival to the American CNN network, and has a contrasting style. Rather than emphasising breaking news and live broadcast of unfolding events, BBC World is based around the journalistic comment on news which its correspondents and reporters can offer, and the very diverse international coverage which it can provide using World Service radio's expert staff. The twenty-four-hour broadcasts began to be beamed by the AsiaSat satellite, through an agreement with Hong Kong's Star TV, and in 1992 the service reached three continents, constituting 80 per cent of the world's population. By the end of 1992 the channel was being watched in 6 million homes and was especially welcomed in Asian countries such as India and Taiwan where broadcasting was dominated by national government-run channels. The Star TV satellite signal also carried an entertainment channel (with mainly American programmes), sports, music video and Mandarin-language programmes, making buying satellite dishes attractive for viewers wanting not only BBC World but also the satellite's other signals. Soon deals had been negotiated for BBC World to be broadcast by satellite to the Middle East, Africa, Europe, Russia, Canada, Japan and Latin America. The channel was the first to offer simultaneous translation of its English-language news programmes into other regional languages, soon followed by its rival CNN. In 1993, however, the global media owner Rupert Murdoch bought a controlling interest in Star TV and challenged BBC World's access to the Middle East, where his own Sky News network planned to begin a news service. In the subsequent arguments China blocked all satellite signals, denying any global broadcaster access to its 4.8 million satellite television households and damaging BBC World's expansion.

Sources of television news are perceived as unequal by television viewers, with some regarded as more reliable than others, and news tends to flow from North to South and from West to East. Such a situation provides fuel for arguments that global television news exacerbates the separation between the West and other regions of the world where news seems to happen, and the insulation of television news from the lives of its viewers. There is a paradox in the increasing quantity and speed of international television news. Television, with its focus on liveness, and the showing of actualities from distant places, draws on Western culture's belief in the power of photographic images to bear witness to real events (the **iconicity** of photography), so that seeing something happen on television news claims the immediacy and veracity of fact. But at the same time the proliferation of representations of realities on television news distances what the viewer sees from his or her own physical everyday experience. It was because of this sense of separation and unreality that the French theorist Jean Baudrillard proclaimed that the 1991 Gulf War was unreal, a **simulation** produced by television news because it was experienced only as images except by the few people who fought in it. Viewers who can afford access to numerous news sources (cable and satellite television channels, for example, but also Internet news and email news services) will enjoy greater diversity and quantity of news, but will be further separated from the experience of news events than people who do not have access to so much information. It has often been claimed that the world is divided not only into the rich and the poor but increasingly into the information-rich and the information-poor. Television contributes to

iconic sign in semiotics, a sign which resembles its referent. Photographs, for example, contain iconic signs resembling the objects they represent.

simulation a representation that mirrors an aspect of reality so perfectly that it takes the place of the reality it aims to reproduce.

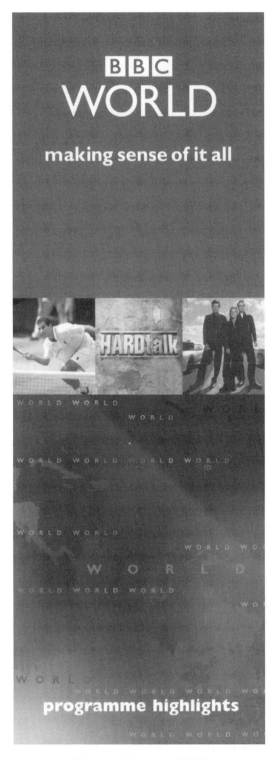

Figure 3.2 Publicity flyer for BBC World. Courtesy of BBC World.

information society
a contemporary
highly developed
culture (especially
Western culture)
where the production
and exchange of
information are more
significant than
conventional
industrial production.

spectacle
a fascinating
image which draws
attention to its
immediate surface
meanings and offers
visual pleasure for
its own sake.

news agency a
media institution that
gathers news reports
and distributes them
to its customers (who
include television
news broadcasters).

the creation of the '**information society**', in which Baudrillard has argued that for the information-rich West there is only **spectacle** in this information and no content. However, such sweeping theories are limited to generalisations about the West and largely to Western television audiences. The blanket coverage of the terrorist attacks on American landmarks in September 2001, when hijacked airliners were flown into the World Trade Center in New York and the Pentagon in Washington, with great loss of life, raises questions about global news and reality. Were these events 'more real' because they were shown almost live around the world to millions of viewers, or 'less real' because the events were so quickly accommodated into the formats and routines of news broadcasting?

Television news broadcasters, it is argued, contain and exchange news in a closed circuit among themselves, producing a global news market which homogenises news. Evidence for this view includes the fact that television news footage is offered to broadcasters by **news agencies** such as Eurovision and Asiavision, and is accessed by British news broadcasters through the European Broadcasting Union (EBU). Six times a day satellite links exchange news footage between Eurovision and Asiavision, for example. As well as using these mechanisms for exchanging news footage, news broadcasters have set up exchange agreements with news broadcasters in other countries. The BBC, for example, has an exchange agreement with the American ABC network. Satellite technology enables the international news agencies such as Visnews and Worldwide Television Network to operate twenty-four hours a day, sending both raw footage and complete news packages to national and regional broadcasters. Because of the different languages of television broadcasting in different nations, the news agencies mainly distribute images without commentary. This makes it more likely that their news footage will be perceived as objective by news editors, and this impression is reinforced by the neutrally phrased written material which the agencies provide with the footage to explain what their pictures denote. The agency footage can have a range of meanings attached to it by the voice-over commentaries which individual news broadcasters add to it for broadcast.

Studies of audience response have tended to show that different audiences are diverse and specific in their response to news, and have capacities for active interpretation. One such study was organised by Klaus Bruhn Jensen in the early 1990s. Contributors to Jensen's study worked on the audience interpretations of national terrestrial television news in households in seven countries watching television news on one day in May 1993. They showed what the content of the news was, how the news was understood and which events were regarded as important. So the project consisted of both observations of people's viewing and conclusions about the place of news in viewers' experience. The study did not focus on trans-national news channels (such as CNN), and instead emphasised the significance of national television institutions and broadcasters' and audiences' perceptions of the seven nations discussed in the book. The countries discussed were:

commercial television
television funded
by the sale
of advertising time
or sponsorship of
programmes.

- Belarus, a former Communist state, now a market economy
- Denmark, which has both **public service** and **commercial television**
- India, with a dominant national state broadcaster experiencing competition from trans-national broadcasters and cable television
- Israel, where at the time there was only one channel
- Italy, where television is closely tied to political parties

- Mexico, which has both state and commercial television
- the USA, the most powerful television culture in the world, with commercial broadcasters.

Researchers interviewed ten families in Bombay, viewing Channel 1 news on Doordarshan, the Indian state TV channel. Of news stories, 57 per cent were about domestic news and 43 per cent about foreign news, though foreign news in over 50 per cent of stories consisted of reports on neighbouring Asian countries such as Pakistan. Indian viewers understood television news in relation to their attitude to the Indian state and their own citizenship of the country. There were 143 news stories on the day that the families were interviewed, of which 60 per cent were about the activities of the government and its agencies, or about foreign relations and terrorism. The Indian viewers saw the state as their representative, and challenges to it by outside forces (such as terrorists) or internal threats to its effectiveness (such as political corruption) concerned them. The majority of news stories concerned the nation-state, and television was controlled by the state. Television news was found to support Indian viewers' sense of citizenship, their faith in the state government, and in television as the representative of themselves and the nation.

There was no television in Israel until 1968, after the Six Day War of 1967, and it was introduced partly to include the newly occupied Palestinian territories and their citizens in an Israeli outlook on the world. More recently a second commercial channel and cable television have been introduced into Israel, after the research was conducted. In 1993 73 per cent of Israel's television news stories were about domestic events, and 27 per cent about foreign news, though over half of the foreign news stories were about neighbouring Arab countries. Israeli citizens serve in the armed forces and feel themselves in a wartime situation, and television news reflected this. Viewers frequently commented that television news should be more patriotic, and did not expect possible threats by Arab nations to be reported objectively. Viewers understood the news by referring each story back to its relationship with Israel and themselves as Israelis, and regarded their nation as beset by problems caused by the opposition political parties, the government itself, religious groups or external enemies. They described their sense of being stuck in insoluble political dilemmas, and viewers identified strongly with television news's representations of the nation-state. Perhaps because of the feeling of being continually at war, there was a strong sense of solidarity with the Israeli nation, and viewers expected television to reinforce this. So the conclusions which can be drawn from this work on local cultures' understandings of news are that people use television in relation to views of their world which they already hold (though they obtain them partly from television), and that they not only accept representations offered to them but also **negotiate** with them and even **resist** them. The ways that this process of negotiation works differ from culture to culture, from place to place and even from person to person. If the conclusions of this research are accurate, they suggest that television news has little direct influence on viewers' outlooks on the world, but on the other hand that viewers use news to reinforce beliefs or prejudices which they already hold.

negotiated reading a viewer interpretation of a television text where the viewer understands meaning in relation to his or her own knowledge and experience, rather than simply accepting the meaning proposed by the text.

resistance the ways in which audiences make meaning from television programmes that is counter to the meanings thought to be intended, or that are discovered by close analysis.

The global and local interrelationship

On an average day in 1990 2.5 billion people in more than 160 countries watched 750 million television sets. Four years later another 100 million households had acquired televisions. The continuing growth in television ownership is happening most quickly in the developing countries of Africa, Asia and Central America. Between 1995 and 2003 there is predicted to be a 50 per cent increase in television ownership in India, 33 per cent in China and Indonesia, and 25 per cent in Thailand and Malaysia. In Asia as whole, television ownership is likely to increase to 500 million television households, making the region three times as large a television region as Europe, with the most lucrative single nation for television advertisers and broadcasters being China, with a population of 1.2 billion and as many as 800 million television viewers even in 1994. Balnaves et al. (2001: 14) divide the world into least developed, developing and developed countries. They compare the number of television sets per thousand people in 1970 to the number of sets per thousand people in 1997. This produces the following figures:

	Least developed countries	*Developing countries*	*Developed countries*
1970	0.5	9.9	263
1997	23.0	157.0	548

Some of these regions have had very low levels of infrastructure (no electricity in rural areas, for example) and average incomes too low for people to buy televisions, so they have been ignored until recently by the global media corporations and the global brands which might support programme content with advertising. In this context it is important to consider not only what people watch, or even which organisations bring television to the viewer, but also what the physical presence of a television within a household means to people in a developing country where television ownership is not universal.

Television viewers' experience of television is partly determined by their social positions in society, and differences between audiences are significant within cultures and nations as well as between them. Research by Leal (1990) on the role of television in the lives of a Brazilian working-class family, for example, showed how the uses of the television in the household, and the programmes watched on it, were affected by and had effects on the family's sense of social identity. The family had recently arrived in the city from a rural background. They kept portrait photographs on top of the television, commemorating previous generations of their family members, and relatives who had migrated to distant parts of Brazil. Tucked into the picture-frames were the passport-size photographs of relatives who had also moved to the city. The assembly of pictures brought together the family's past and its urban present. The **telenovelas** which the family watched on television were dramas set in the city, and the television set, its programmes and the objects around it formed a complex set of negotiations with the family's past and the present, the country and the city, the household's family members and their absent relatives and friends. The television set was a key object among an ensemble of objects which all carried

telenovela a fictional continuing melodrama on television that lasts for a specific number of episodes. Telenovelas are particularly associated with South American television.

meanings for the family. These meanings were in their different ways associated with bridging gaps between past and present, country and city, household and community. The meanings of television in the household Leal studied were clearly different from the meanings of television in the lives of more affluent middle-class Brazilian landowners, for example. The study of television in this **anthropological** sense can show how it is not just programmes which are significant to television's place in global culture but also the embedding of television as a cultural practice, a set of physical objects and a way of understanding one's identity and community.

The global dominance of Western television can easily seem to cover over local and regional differences. Western television theorists are sometimes beguiled by the presence of television familiar to them which is found outside its original cultural contexts. But the fact that Western television seems to be, or seems about to be, everywhere, and appears culturally powerful everywhere, might just reinforce the prejudice that only Western television is worth discussing in arguments about globalisation, whereas it is the interrelations of Western with local and regional cultures which need to be understood. The relationship between place and television culture is complex, and global television and global television corporations make local and regional differences more, not less, important. Local television cultures find their identities alongside or by resisting the globalisation of television, so that the dominance of global television becomes important to the production of local television. Local, in this connection, can also importantly mean regional, in that television cultures cross national boundaries to include speakers of the same language (like Spanish in much of Latin America, but also Spain itself and the USA) or audiences which share similar cultural assumptions and ideologies (like some audiences in the Middle East).

The processes of globalisation are open to regulation by individual nations, rather than being an autonomous and unstoppable process, and global markets are regulated by contracts and by international and national laws. But the world organisations which oversee international television agreements generally support the lowering of national restrictions and **quotas**, because they seek to create a global **free market** economy in communications. The World Trade Organisation, the International Monetary Fund and regional agreements such as the North American Free Trade Agreement and the European Free Trade Association provide support for cross-border television exchanges which are based on the principles of unrestricted commercial exchange. The apparently free and uncontrollable television market is not a natural fact and depends on the taking of political decisions about deregulation and competition in television by nation-states and groupings of states. The European Parliament issued the Television Without Frontiers Directive in 1996, for example, which insists that the majority of programming in member states must originate from within that state. Countries and regional groupings of countries tend both to **deregulate** and to encourage globalisation, but also to introduce further regulation to protect their societies against it.

However, in the global television landscape the concepts of society and nation are diminishing in usefulness. As the philosopher Anthony Giddens (1990) has argued, the concept of society as a unit bounded in time and space loses its force when, for example, live television news or sporting events confuse the sense of time and space by broadcasting across time-zones. Television also brings new ways of understanding space like the notion of a New World Order, for example, which change people's

anthropology the study of humankind, including the evolution of humans and the different kinds of human society existing in different times and places.

quota a proportion of television programming, such as a proportion of programmes made in a particular nation.

free market a television marketplace where factors such as quotas and regulations do not restrict the free operation of economic 'laws' of supply and demand.

deregulation the removal of legal restrictions or guidelines that regulate the economics of the television industry or the standards which programmes must adhere to.

sense of their place in the world. Because television broadcasts such a range of images of culture, like versions of what youth and age, domesticity, work and gender, for example, might mean, global television provides the possibility of reflecting on local cultures. Global television provides resources for people to think about themselves and their social environment, in the same ways that local or national television does. Sinclair and his fellow authors (Sinclair et al. 1999: 187) give this example:

> An Egyptian immigrant in Britain, for example, might think of herself as a Glaswegian when she watches her local Scottish channel, a British resident when she switches over to the BBC, an Islamic Arab expatriate in Europe when she tunes in to the satellite service from the Middle East, and a world citizen when she channel surfs on to CNN.

People around the world **negotiate** their sense of place, time and community in relation to local, regional and global television cultures, and they do this by borrowing from or **resisting** ways of thinking and living shown on the screen.

ACTIVITY 3.7

What are the main arguments for and against the influence of television globalisation? Which side of the debate do you find most persuasive, and why?

Case study: the Brazilian telenovela

There are about 450 million people in Latin America, and 85 per cent of its households had television sets at the end of the 1990s. About 15 per cent of households had cable or satellite television. Because of this growing television market, Western global media corporations have interests in Latin American broadcasting. Brazil itself has a population of over 160 million, and its population's output per person exceeds Poland and Russia, making the country an attractive market for advertisers. But Brazil is something of an exception to the global **media imperialism** thesis, since although its national television networks import nearly 40 per cent of their programmes, its most popular programmes are domestically made continuing dramas, the **telenovelas**. Brazil is a former colony of Portugal, its national language is Portuguese and it retains links with its former European master. The major broadcaster in Brazil is TV Globo, a commercial channel which has a 70 per cent share of the television audience. TV Globo is the fourth largest **commercial television** network in the world (behind the three major US television networks), and in 1993 controlled seventy-nine of Brazil's 247 television stations, which were **affiliated** to it and contracted to broadcast Globo's programmes in their territories. There is minimal public service broadcasting in Brazil such as educational or factual programming, and broadcasters are closely tied to the interests of politicians running the country's political parties. Many of Brazil's politicians are personally wealthy, and have significant financial stakes in broadcasting companies.

    The history of television in Brazil is that it signifies modernity and social status, since the first television stations in the 1950s were set up in the major cities of Rio de Janeiro and São

affiliates local television stations (normally in the USA) that have made agreements (affiliations) with a network to broadcast programmes offered by that network rather than another.

Paulo despite the rural character of much of the country, and the relatively expensive television sets were first owned by the affluent middle class whose lifestyles mimicked those of the United States. This American influence extended to the involvement of the American television technology producers General Electric and RCA, which supplied the broadcasting equipment. The telenovelas on Brazilian television continue this urban and Americanised trend, since they are predominantly set in urban locations, and feature performers drawn from the theatre, film and television elites based in Rio de Janeiro. The programmes themselves must also be considered in relation to the advertisements which are broadcast in and around them, in the **prime-time** evening slots which they occupy. Because of the large audiences which telenovelas attract in comparison to other genres of Brazilian programming, there are a larger number of commercials in them than in other programmes. Furthermore, the setting of telenovela stories among relatively affluent urban families means that consumer culture features as the milieu of the characters, whose costumes, domestic appliances and other possessions mirror the products advertised in commercial breaks.

Telenovelas are structured differently from either conventional Western drama **serials** or **soap operas**. Unlike soap operas, they come to a conclusion after about six months of a slowly unfolding story, though they feature the domestic and emotional narratives and complex complications of relationships which are the focus of soap opera. But telenovelas are often based on popular Brazilian literature, and are therefore somewhat similar to the extended multi-episode adaptations of novels which are seen in British and other Western nations' television. Similarly, telenovela episodes are usually broadcast in one-hour slots, thus aligning them with serial drama in other countries in contrast to the normal half-hour duration of soap opera episodes.

Brazilian television in some ways supports the conclusions of a report for the International Commission for the Study of Communication Problems (1980), which argued for the independence of nations from the global influence of Western communications businesses and the setting up of a 'New World Information and Communications Order' in which cultural imperialism by the Northern and Western nations would be discontinued in the same way that imperialism itself had been largely dismantled. If Brazil could attain a largely independent broadcasting culture, it was argued, then other nations could too. The principle of the New World Information and Communications order was strongly resisted by the USA and Europe, which withdrew their financial support for the United Nations Educational, Scientific and Cultural Organisation (UNESCO), which had sponsored the MacBride Report, in 1985. The argument that cultural imperialism had reached a turning-point was supported by the export of Brazilian telenovelas to the countries of southern Europe, where the related languages and cultures of the Spanish and Portuguese nations offered easier integration of telenovelas with existing television representations and expectations. Similarly, the large Spanish-speaking population of the USA has enabled Mexican television producers to export its Spanish-language programmes to specialist American networks serving Hispanic Americans by cable and satellite.

On the other hand, Brazilian television's dependence on favour from ruling political parties and politicians meant that it was always careful to avoid reporting news which might challenge the authority of government, a government which was carried on during decades of rule by military dictators who terrorised the country's population and tortured dissidents. From this perspective Brazilian television might be independent of Western cultural imperialism but it might nevertheless be considered a form for perpetuating an internal imperialism within Brazil. By providing the population with a diet of entertainment and reassuring propaganda, Brazilian television can be regarded as a block on the development of democratic culture,

prime time the part of a day's television schedule when the greatest number of viewers may be watching, normally the mid-evening period.

serial a television form where a developing narrative unfolds across a sequence of separate episodes.

soap opera a continuing drama serial involving a large number of characters in a specific location, focusing on relationships, emotions and reversals of fortune.

continued

public political debate and improved standards of cultural and educational attainment in the country. Furthermore, since Brazil (and also Mexico) is a much more financially powerful and prodigious producer of programmes than its neighbouring countries in the Latin American region, the export of its programmes to other neighbouring countries is as significant as its export of programmes to Europe and the USA. This regional flow of programmes from Brazil to other Latin American countries complicates the simple arguments both that television flows from Western nations to nations to the East and South and that this flow is being resisted by programmes moving in the opposite direction. Instead, regional television flows seem to represent the building to maturity of television cultures of relative power and powerlessness within continents and linguistic areas.

The legacy of the **media imperialism** argument is that it is not American programmes or American television owners which perpetuate regressive kinds of television organisation. American programmes do not always dominate the schedules of countries with less developed television cultures, and, even if they did, it is not proved that these programmes simply transmit American values to their audiences. Similarly, many American television producers are not owned solely or at all by American individuals or companies, and the ownership of television broadcasting institutions in other parts of the world is more likely to be through a combined deal between global media corporations and local or regional interests. But the aspect of the media imperialism thesis which does remain valid is that the American system of television organisation has been successfully exported to very many of the world's national broadcasters. This trend tends to increase as **deregulation** and liberalisation of television markets advance with the collapse of rigid state broadcasting controls in former authoritarian societies. The financing of television by advertising, as in Brazil, where audiences are targeted by particular types of programmes in order to deliver them to advertisers, is an American model which has become increasingly common. The American model of the competition between broadcasting channels affiliated to major network or cable and satellite providers is adopted also in nations which have their own indigenous television production bases like Brazil. The case of Brazilian telenovelas, therefore, provides evidence against cruder forms of the cultural imperialism thesis, but draws attention to the global spread of Western (and specifically American) forms of television organisation. The example also shows how a distinctive regional television form can develop in response to the history and culture of a particular society, but spread by television export to both relatively similar and also dissimilar television regions. Finally, the case study shows that using examples in Television Studies is a negotiation between choosing a representative instance and choosing an example which suggests that being representative may necessarily entail reducing the complexity of television cultures in order to clarify competing theories of how television culture works.

SUMMARY OF KEY POINTS

- Studying television today involves understanding how national and international television cultures work in relation to each other, in the context of globalisation.
- The media imperialism thesis has argued that political values are communicated

continued

when television programmes and television institutions spread around the world.

● New technologies, especially satellite transmission, have made possible greater exchange of television across the world, mainly from developed countries to less developed ones.

The effects of television globalisation can be both progressive and regressive.

● Local audiences' understanding of global television can be different, so that the meanings of programmes change according to where they are seen.

● Individual viewers understand their identities in relation to the television they watch, and think of themselves in different ways according to the diverse ways that television addresses them.

Further reading

Alleyne, M., *News Revolution: Political and Economic Decisions about Global Information* (Basingstoke: Macmillan, 1997).

Balnaves, M., J. Donald and S. Hemelryk Donald, *The Global Media Atlas* (London: BFI, 2001).

Barker, C., *Global Television: An Introduction* (Oxford: Blackwell, 1997).

Bignell, J., *Postmodern Media Culture* (Edinburgh: Edinburgh University Press, 2000).

Boyd-Barrett, O. and T. Rantanen, *The Globalization of News* (London: Sage, 1998).

Bruhn Jensen, K. (ed.), *News of the World: World Cultures Look at Television News* (London: Routledge, 1998).

Corner, J., *Critical Ideas in Television Studies* (Oxford: Clarendon, 1999).

Dahlgren, P., *Television and the Public Sphere* (London: Sage, 1995).

Dowmunt, T. (ed.), *Channels of Resistance: Global Television and Local Empowerment* (London: BFI, 1993).

Drummond, P. and R. Patterson (eds), *Television and its Audience: International Research Perspectives* (London: BFI, 1988).

Gurevitch, M., 'The globalization of electronic journalism', in J. Curran and M. Gurevitch (eds), *Mass Media and Society* (London: Edward Arnold, 1991), pp. 178–93.

Herman, E. and R. McChesney, *The Global Media: The New Missionaries of Global Capitalism* (London: Cassell, 1997).

Leal, O., 'Popular taste and erudite repertoire: the place and space of television in Brazil', *Cultural Studies*, 4:1 (1990), pp. 19–29.

Liebes, T. and E. Katz, *The Export of Meaning: Cross-cultural Readings of 'Dallas'* (New York: Oxford University Press, 1990).

Lull, J. (ed.), *World Families Watch Television* (London: Sage, 1988).

Mackay, H. and T. O'Sullivan (eds), *The Media Reader: Continuity and Transformation* (London: Sage, 1999).

Sinclair, J., E. Jacka and S. Cunningham, 'New Patterns in Global Television', in P. Marris and S. Thornham (eds), *The Media Reader* (Edinburgh: Edinburgh University Press, 1999), pp.170–90.

—— (eds), *Peripheral Vision: New Patterns in Global Television* (Oxford: Oxford University Press, 1996).

Sreberny-Mohammadi, A. with K. Nordenstreng, R. Stevenson and F. Ugboajah (eds), *Foreign News in the Media: International Reporting in 29 Countries* (Paris: UNESCO, 1985).

Thussu, K. D. (ed.), *Electronic Empires: Global Media and Local Resistance* (London: Arnold, 1998).

Television Texts and
Television Narratives

text an object
such as a television
programme, film or
poem, considered as a
network of meaningful
signs that can
be analysed and
interpreted.

narrative an ordered
sequence of images
and sound that tells a
fictional or factual story.

intertextuality how
one text draws on the
meanings of another
by referring to it, by
allusion, quotation or
parody, for example.

flow the ways
that programmes,
advertisements, etc.
follow one another
in an unbroken
sequence across the
day or part of the day,
and the experience of
watching the sequence
of programmes,
advertisements, trailers,
etc.

semiotics the study
of signs and their
meanings, initially
developed for the study
of spoken language,
and now used also to
study the visual and
aural 'languages'
of other media such
as television.

psychoanalysis the
study of human mental
life, including not only
conscious thoughts,
wishes and fears but
also unconscious ones.
Psychoanalysis is
an analytical and
theoretical set of ideas
as well as a therapeutic
treatment.

sign in semiotics,
something which
communicates
meaning, such as a
word, an image or
a sound.

Television Texts and Television Narratives

Introduction

This chapter evaluates theoretical frameworks for studying television programmes, advertisements, etc. as '**texts**', including methodologies for analysing **narrative**, **intertextual** relations between programmes in a **flow** of different programmes, and **semiotic** approaches to relations between image and sound. These textual approaches are placed in the context of Television Studies in the 1970s and early 1980s, where they developed, which was underpinned by the assemblage of **psychoanalytic**, semiotic and materialist approaches. Rather than being devised specifically for the study of television, these ideas began in the discipline of Film Studies. Textual approaches to television are powerful ways of discussing the meanings made of television by viewers, but they also have some drawbacks. Textual approaches tend to focus on textual detail at the expense of institutional context and history, and to neglect the ways in which television is understood by audiences. The issues to think about here are:

- how meanings can exist 'in' television texts
- how meanings might depend on relationships between viewers and texts
- how knowledge of production context and history 'outside' the text might affect the meanings which television texts have.

The chapter ranges widely across different television genres and forms, showing how textual approaches to television can explain how meanings are made in them, where these meanings come from and how they might be understood critically. There is a case study at the end of the chapter which shows how semiotic and narrative analysis can be used to study a recent television commercial in some detail.

The language of television

Semiotic approaches to television, as to any other kind of meaning-making activity in society, begin by identifying the different kinds of **sign** which convey meaning in the medium. The principle of semiotic analysis is to begin from the assumption that television has a 'language' which producers and audiences of television have learnt to use. The twentieth-century founder of semiotics, the Swiss linguistics professor Ferdinand de Saussure, regarded spoken language as the most fundamental of human meaning-making practices, and argued that all other media could be understood on an analogy with spoken language. He sought to explain the functioning of spoken language at a particular point in time, describing the system of language as *langue* and any instance of language use as *parole* (which means 'speech' in French). The 'language' of television would be the whole body of conventions and rules for conveying meaning in the medium, while any example of a particular shot or sequence of television would be an instance of *parole*, an example of this system in use. The language of television consists of visual and aural signs. Television's visual signs include all the images and graphics which are seen on the screen. Aural signs consist of the speech, sound and music which television produces.

All of the visual signs on the television screen are two-dimensional, appearing on the flat surface of the screen. Many of television's visual signs closely resemble the people, things and places which they represent in both fictional and non-fictional programmes. Signs which resemble their object in this way are called **iconic signs**, to distinguish them from signs which themselves have no necessary relationship to what they signify. The word 'cat', for example, is a **symbolic sign**, meaning that the letters on the page or the sound of the spoken word 'cat' is arbitrarily used in English to signify a particular type of furry four-legged animal. A television image of a cat, however, closely resembles the real cat which it represents, and is thus an iconic sign. The conventions of representation in television most often rely on the iconic nature of television images to convey an impression of **realism** whereby viewers accept that the television image **denotes** people, places or cats, for example, which exist in the real world. But this acceptance of the realism of television's denotative signs is reliant on the conventions of composition, perspective and framing which are so embedded in Western culture that the two-dimensional image seems simply to convey three-dimensional reality. The power of these conventions can be seen when television represents objects which do not exist in the real world, such as the spacecraft in science fiction series such as *Enterprise* or *Babylon 5*. Often the images of these spacecraft are not images of real objects, or models, but are created entirely by **computer generated imaging** (CGI). Yet because the images of them obey the conventions which audiences recognise from the language of television, viewers can both recognise what they are and accept them as if they were real. These conventions include:

- perspective
- proportion
- light and shade
- shot composition.

Semiotics therefore has a particular interest in the conventions such as these, called **codes**, which govern how signs are used in conventional ways to represent or **denote** believable worlds.

Television signs which denote speech, the ambient noises of a represented environment or the music accompanying a visual sequence are also used according to codes in the language of television. The analysis of television using semiotic methods has tended to focus more on image than sound, but sound is important to the viewer's relationship with what is on the screen. Television screens are relatively small, and watching television often competes with other activities in the same room (such as talking, eating or doing the ironing). In order to grab the viewer's attention, sound is used to call the viewer to pay attention. This is very noticeable in television news programmes, which are punctuated with loud brass music to draw the attention

iconic sign in semiotics, a sign which resembles its referent. Photographs, for example, contain iconic signs resembling the objects they represent.

symbolic sign in semiotics, a sign which is connected arbitrarily to its referent rather than because the sign resembles its referent. For example, a photograph of a cat resembles it, whereas the word 'cat' does not: the word is a symbolic sign.

realism the aim for representations to reproduce reality faithfully, and the ways this is done.

denotation in semiotics, the function of signs to portray or refer to something in the real world.

computer generated imaging (CGI) the creation of images by programming computers with mathematical equations that can generate realistic two-dimensional pictures.

code in semiotics, a system or set of rules that shapes how signs can be used, and therefore how meanings can be made and understood.

of the viewer, as well as to connote the importance of news as a programme genre. Music and sound effects in television programmes are signs which direct the viewer how to respond emotionally to the significance of the programme or the action denoted in it. Codes of recording, editing and processing intervene between the sound on the set or in the studio and the sound which emanates from the loud-speakers in the television set. Sound recordists on **location**, or sound mixers in the studio, follow conventional codes in setting the levels of sound, and the relative volume of one sound versus another. The distance of a speaker from the camera, for example, might be signified by the loudness or quietness of her speech, while the relative volumes of background music and speech will nearly always be adjusted to allow speech to have priority. Although television images and sounds are often iconic and denotative, seeming simply to convey what the camera and sound recording equipment have captured, these signs have been processed through the various professional norms, industry practices and conventions of meaning-making that have been consciously or unconsciously adopted by both the makers and audiences of television. These ways of working and ways of understanding are among the codes which structure the language of television.

Connotations and codes

The iconic and arbitrary signs in the language of television are often presented simply as denoting an object, place or person. But signs rarely simply denote something, since signs are produced and understood in a cultural context which enriches them with much more meaning than this. These cultural associations and connections which signs have are called **connotations**. For example, the head-on shots of newsreaders, wearing business clothes, seated behind a desk in news programmes not only denote the newsreader in a studio, but have connotations of authority, seriousness and formality which derive from the connotations of desks, office clothes and head-on address to the camera. These connotations derive partly from social codes which are in circulation in British society, but also from television codes of news programmes which have been conventionalised over time. Newsreaders speak in a neutral and even tone, which is itself a sign connoting the objectivity and authority of both the newsreader and the news organisation which he or she represents. News presenters are usually shot in medium **close-up**, full face, under neutral lighting. This code conventionally positions the newsreader as a mediator of events, who addresses the audience and connects them with the news organisation's reporters, and with the people who are the subjects of the news. The mediator functions as a bridge between the domestic world of the viewer and the public worlds of news. Even though news programmes on Channel 5 have used newsreaders sitting on desks with their scripts in their hands to connote a degree of informality (suitable for the relatively new entertainment-based channel), the desk, the clothes and the head-on address to camera remain because they are so much part of the coding of news programmes.

Television news programmes use music with loud major chords played on brass instruments in their **title sequences**, and these signs carry connotations of impor-tance, dignity and drama. These title sequences also feature computer graphics in fast-moving sequences, **syntagms** in semiotic terminology, connoting technological sophistication. The function of title sequences in television news programmes is to

---

location any place in which television images are shot, except inside a television studio.

connotations the term used in semiotic analysis for the meanings that are associated with a particular sign or combination of signs.

close-up a camera shot where the frame is filled by the face of a person or a detail of a face. Close-ups may also show details of an object or place.

title sequence the sequence at the opening of a television programme in which the programme title and performers' names may appear along with other information, accompanied by images, sound and music introducing the programme.

syntagm in semiotics, a linked sequence of signs existing at a certain point in time. Written or spoken sentences, or television sequences, are examples of syntagms.

Figure 4.1 Peter Sissons on the set of the BBC *Ten O'Clock News*. Photography by Jeff Overs, courtesy of the BBC Photograph Library.

establish the status of news as significant and authoritative, and also to differentiate one channel's news programme from another, providing **'brand recognition'**. The title sequences of news programmes, like the title sequences of all television programmes, share many of the functions of television commercials, in differentiating products which are very similar and endowing them with connotations supporting a familiar identity. Title sequences are sequences of signs which collectively signify boundaries between one part of the continual **flow** of television broadcasting and the rest of it.

It is important to remember that the meanings of television images and sounds are not naturally attached to signs. The pleasure and understanding which viewers gain from television often depend on the significance of how signs relate to each other in a particular context, and it is often misleading to carry over the connotations of a sign in one context into another. In the long-running police drama series *Inspector Morse*, for example, Inspector Morse drove a red Jaguar mark II saloon. In combination with the connotations of Morse's affection for real ale, codes of politeness and love of classical opera, the car had connotations of tradition, 'classic-ness' and Britishness. By contrast, in the police series of the 1970s (such as *The Sweeney*, in which the Morse actor John Thaw was a main character), Jaguar mark II saloons were often driven by gangsters and had connotations of the criminal underworld, the glamour of crime and bravado. In analysing a television programme semiotically, signs gain their meanings in two contrasting ways:

- by their similarity with other signs in the same programme
- by their difference from these surrounding signs.

Television relies on its viewers' often unconscious knowledge of codes and their ability to decode signs and their connotations, and assemble them into meaningful scenes, sequences and stories.

brand recognition
the ability of audiences to recognise the distinctive identity of a product, service or institution and the values and meanings associated with it.

Television broadcasters' aim is to keep the viewer watching by assembling verbal and visual signs in ways which are entertaining or informative, but different kinds of programme achieve this in different ways. In other words, television **genres** have their own codes and conventions which enable viewers to recognise and expect particular kinds of meaning and pleasure. While very many genres of television use extreme **long shots** (ELS) at the beginning of scenes and sequences to establish a physical location, close-up (CU) is very often used to denote emotion signified by performers' facial expressions in soap opera. In general, the greater the genre's emphasis on emotional reaction, the greater the proportion of close-up shots. But while close-up is a signifier of performance in the language of television, and seems highly dramatic, the shot length in soap opera and other emotionally focused dramas is relatively long. Shots are held in order to observe characters' reactions to each other, whereas in action dramas such as police or hospital programmes there is less close-up and shorter shot length. Action dramas also use codes of shot composition differently, since static composition (where the camera is still) allows space to contemplate performance in soap opera versus the dynamic composition (moving camera) in police and hospital dramas such as *NYPD Blue* or *ER*, which focus on disorientation and disorder, and seem to capture action as it is 'naturally' occurring. Even colour can function as a sign in television programmes: for example, the US sitcom *Frasier* connotes the warm and comfortable environment of middle-class Seattle with yellow, red and brown, while other programmes (such as *The X Files*) use the conventionally colder colours of blue, grey and black to signify a more threatening and uncertain environment. The connotations of signs in the codes of shot type, shot length or colour are meaningful because of their use in particular genres of programme, in relation to other signs in the programme.

Narrative structures

Binary oppositions underlie the narrative structures of many television programmes, for example oppositions between **masculine** and **feminine**, or young and old. An example of a narrative structure found in different kinds of television fiction is the use of series of binary oppositions between human and animal, and human and machine. Machines are rigid, in opposition to the flesh and bone of organic creatures. Machines are represented as determined, focused and disciplined, in opposition to human and animal tendencies to appetite and excess. These oppositions are set out and mixed together in the narratives of *Star Trek: The Next Generation*, for example:

● Captain Picard is a human, but his position as captain of the starship Enterprise makes him disciplined, almost machine-like.
● Lieutenant Commander Worf is a Klingon, a race known for its excessive aggression and 'barbarian' behaviour, which aligns him with animal traits of excess and indiscipline that he has to control.
● Lieutenant Commander Data is an android, a machine, but his ambition is to become human, organic and, to some extent, undisciplined.

Storylines in *Star Trek: The Next Generation* often concern these conflicts between opposed animal, human and machine traits in the characters, for example when

genre a kind or type of programme. Programmes of the same genre have shared characteristics.

long shot a camera shot taking in the whole body of a performer, or more generally a shot with a wide field of vision.

binary opposition two contrasting terms, ideas or concepts, such as inside/outside, masculine/feminine or culture/nature.

masculine having characteristics associated with the cultural role of men and not women.

feminine having characteristics associated with the cultural role of women and not men.

BCU
Big close-up

MLS
Medium long shot

CU
Close-up

LS
Long shot

MCU
Medium close-up

VLS
Very long shot

MS
Medium shot or Mid-shot

Figure 4.2 Shot sizes. Photographs courtesy of Jeremy Orlebar.

Captain Picard is captured by the Borg, an aggressive cyborg race who exaggerate Picard's machine-like self-control and insert mechanical technologies into his organic body. Data featured in episodes where he was able to experience human emotions such as anger or humour, and had to cope with these unruly passions. Oppositions like these between human and animal, or human and machine, are the underlying system of relationships and conflicts which give structure and meaning to narratives, though they are often less obvious than those in *Star Trek*.

Thinking of narratives as sets of relations between terms which are opposed or similar is nevertheless useful in understanding how narrative works in television. The tradition in British sitcom, for example, is to oppose:

masculinity	femininity
work	domesticity
rationality	emotionalism
intolerance	tolerance

Humour derives from contrasting these values when they are each embodied in a character, and also from aligning a character who might be expected to represent one side of binary with the other side. For example, Victor Meldrew in *One Foot in the Grave* was masculine and intolerant, but redundant from his work and in an enforced domestic setting that is conventionally regarded as feminine. This offered numerous occasions to create comedy from his sense of being 'out of place' in a situation. *Frasier* adds to this by setting up oppositions between sophistication and crudeness, youth and age, so that Frasier's and his brother Niles's sophistication and relative youth can be contrasted with their father's crudeness and elderliness, for example.

ACTIVITY 4.1

Write down the binary oppositions and structural patterns which underlie a sitcom you have seen. How many other sitcoms can you list which share some or all of these structures?

The simplified character-positions in sitcom are too excessive to be **'realistic'** because it is important to the comedy for a character's place in a system of binary oppositions to be clear in contrast to another character. Sitcom narrative works through setting up oppositions and connections, which by the end of an episode have been laid to rest. The movement of sitcom narrative keeps repeating and developing incompatibilities and compatibilities, playing on the already established position of each character in the system of binaries. But the audience's pleasure partly derives from the anticipation that these conflicts will be resolved satisfactorily. The audience needs to recognise the narrative codes of sitcom and the stakes of the binary oppositions in order to accept the surprising reversals and conflicts which the narrative requires. The interruption of laughter and close-ups held on the performers' facial expressions are important generic signs and narrative turning-points in sitcom. At these points the viewer is invited to recognise the high point of a conflict or reversal among the binary oppositions, and measure its effect on the characters by reading their expressions. The bursts of laughter in the narrative set out the rhythm and pattern in each scene, and punctuate the narrative with stopping-points around which the action turns. This rhythm of stops and starts keeps confirming the position laid out for the viewer to make sense of the narrative and find it funny. The studio audience's laughter confirms the position of the viewer by representing an audience which shares the viewer's expected reaction. The collective audience laughing on the soundtrack is a representative of the viewer at home, and occupies a mediating position between the performance of the sitcom and the television audience watching singly or in small groups, where laughing out loud is often embarrassing. The noisy studio audience allows the viewer access to a kind of excessive response which is itself pleasurable, and which can be enjoyed at second hand by the viewer at home.

Television news consists of narrative reports, and can be analysed as narrative to discover how priorities and assumptions shared by news broadcasters form a code determining which reports have greatest significance within the news bulletin. The reports with the highest **news value** appear near the beginning of the bulletin (in the same way as the front pages of newspapers present some stories as having the highest news value to readers). News bulletins on commercial channels are interspersed with commercials, so that each segment of the programme contains its own hierarchy of news reports. The ranking of reports according to their news value shows how the representation of reality offered by television news is not a **denotation** of events but a narrative mediated by the signs and codes of news television. Binary oppositions, such as those between crime and law, left-wing and right-wing opinions or home and abroad are the basis for news narrative. Television news both shapes and reflects the dominant common-sense assumptions about what is significant, since by definition what is deemed significant is what makes the news.

News narrative contributes to the process of constructing a common-sense climate of opinion through which audiences perceive their reality. Therefore television news shares with other news media (such as newspapers and radio news) the **ideological** function of naturalising the assumption that the day-to-day occurrences in the public arenas of politics, business and international affairs are what is most important about the daily affairs of a society. Within this field of newsworthy aspects of contemporary life, binary oppositions are again an underlying structure which enables broadcasters and viewers to make sense of the news. News programmes seek to connote **balance** and objectivity by giving approximately equal time to conflicting parties and interested groups who comment on the events narrated in news stories. But balance and objectivity are defined in relation to common-sense assumptions held consensually in society, and these common-sense views are naturalised ideological positions. The definition of the norm is a cultural construct and will therefore shift according to the current balance of power. Some decades ago, for example, the social ownership of major industries and institutions such as railways and telephone networks was part of a norm which interviewers and politicians accepted as the usual state of things. After the **privatisation** of these industries and services this view is no longer the norm, and surfaces rarely in television news, as an unlikely possibility. News narrative, despite its commitment to balance and objectivity, measures this

news value
the degree of significance attributed to a news story, where items with high news value are deemed most significant to the audience.

ideology the set of beliefs, attitudes and assumptions arising from the economic and class divisions in a culture, underlying the ways of life accepted as normal in that culture.

balance the requirement in television news and current affairs to present both sides of an argument or issue.

privatisation the policy of placing industries or institutions in the hands of privately owned businesses, rather than state ownership.

balance and objectivity against the currently dominant ideologies in society, which occupy an apparently neutral position.

ACTIVITY 4.2

How do the narratives of news programmes use oppositions between 'us' and 'them', 'powerful' and 'less powerful', to reinforce conceptions of social authority and legitimacy?

ACTIVITY 4.3

Analyses of television news have demonstrated the ideological distortions of news. Would it be possible to create television news which would be free of ideology?

Television news deals with the potentially infinite meanings of events by narrating them in conventional subject-categories, and conventional narrative codes, such as 'foreign news' or 'business news'. These divisions reflect the institutional divisions in news broadcasting organisations, where reporters work in teams of specialist staff. Some news programmes title news stories with captions on the screen next to the news presenter, and these captions connote both the specificity of each news story, which is different to the one before or after it, and also the connection between a particular story and others in the same category. The effect of using this code is to restrict the narrative frameworks which are available for representing the story. Despite the wide-ranging effects and relevance which one news story might have, placing reports in coded categories restricts the viewer's capacity to make connections between one news report and another in a different category, or to bring an alternative narrative structure to bear in understanding the news events.

The significance of the codes which viewers are invited to bring to bear on programmes can be seen in the case of programmes which use codes deriving from more than one form and genre of television narrative. Television fiction is now rarely seen in the form of single one-off programmes, and is increasingly made in episodic forms resembling the serial. **Serials** consist of a developing story divided into several parts, and television soap opera is a special case of the serial form where the end of the story is infinitely deferred. The series form denotes programmes in which the settings and characters do not change or develop, but where new stories involving the continuing characters and setting are presented in each episode. Contemporary television programmes now frequently combine the single setting and new stories in each episode, which are features of the series form, with developing characters and stories episode to episode, as in serials. Robin Nelson (1997) has coined the term 'flexi-narrative' to denote fiction like this which adopts the short sequences of action and rapid editing which occur in television advertisements, along with the developing characters and stories found in television soap opera, and the new stories each

serial a television form where a developing narrative unfolds across a sequence of separate episodes.

episode which are found in television series. The flexi-narrative form is a case of the combination of television forms, but similar mixing and borrowing can be seen within and between television genres.

The hospital drama series *ER* is a flexi-narrative, whose mix of generic components was designed to appeal to American audiences for whom the interruption of commercials into programmes seems to lead to channel-hopping or **zapping** and loss of involvement in ongoing narrative. Bob Mullan (1997: 60) reports that the novelist and creator of *ER* Michael Crichton believed that American viewers 'are incapable of watching television for any length of time unless it is a "news reality" programme like *The Cops* or a courtroom drama like the O. J. Simpson trial. The only way forward, he believes, is to make drama more dramatic than the news and reality programmes'. The narrative of *ER* is patterned to include periodic bursts of rapid action interspersed with more leisurely character development, and the programme as a whole is segmented into a large number of relatively short scenes. The longer and slower scenes of character interaction draw on the conventions of soap opera, in which reaction by one character to events in the life of another is represented by frequent close-up, emotional cues provided by music and an emphasis on the viewer's memory of past events in the characters' lives to enrich what is happening in the narrative present. By contrast, the shorter scenes of rapid activity, usually scenes in which the doctors respond to the arrival of a seriously injured person, use rapid hand-held camera shots, **whip-pans** and rapid editing. In these scenes the dialogue of characters overlaps, and the noises made by medical equipment accompanied by rapid percussion music add to the sense of urgency and confusion. These action sequences use conventions deriving from **observational documentary** or news footage of action caught on the run by the camera, adding to this the uses of dramatic music and complex sound found in action drama series such as police series.

Narrative functions

The theory of narrative has recognised that although the components of narrative are often relatively simple, and organised into binary oppositions and relationships of difference and similarity, there is much in narratives which does not have an obvious functional purpose. Lots of material appears to be redundant. Redundancy consists of the inclusion in the narrative of a number of signs which have a contextual or supporting role. These signs are unremarked, but deepen the consistency and believability of the narrative. They provide texture and tone for the audience. Details of setting, costume, much of the detail of dialogue and some of the narrative action are likely to be redundant from the point of view of getting the story itself across. But in programmes which claim to be **realistic**, redundancy has the crucial effect of embedding the story in a fully realised world. Furthermore, one of the ways that narratives can be most pleasurable and interesting is when the relationship between redundancy and functional narrative components is changed in the course of the story. In detective narratives and whodunits, for example, an apparently redundant detail which seemed simply to lend texture to the fictional world might turn out to be a crucial clue. In science fiction television, redundancy is crucial to establishing a futuristic environment as realistic, in the sense that it has the detail and texture for

zapping hopping rapidly from channel to channel while watching television, using a remote control (a 'zapper').

whip-pan a very rapid panning shot from one point to another.

observational documentary a documentary form in which the programme-maker aims to observe neutrally what would have happened even if he or she had not been present.

it to be believable. News programmes are full of apparently redundant information and visual detail. But here, too, semiotics and narrative theory are useful in showing how redundant information actually fulfils important functions in shaping the meanings of news reports.

Television news has to deal with events which are by definition new in each day's news, and to do this it has powerful codes for giving shape and meaning to news reports. Reports make use of four narrative functions (Hartley 1982: 118–19):

- framing
- focusing
- realising
- closing.

Framing is the activity of establishing the news topic, usually done by the mediating figure of the newsreader, who invokes the narrative code in which the report will be presented. For example, political news is usually coded as adversarial. Although mediators such as news presenters speak in a neutral **register** and establish themselves and the news broadcasting organization as neutral too, the effect of this is to make the setting-up of the narrative code appear invisible to viewers: it seems to arise from the news itself rather than from how it is being presented. Focusing refers to the opening out of the news report into further detail, conveyed by reporters and correspondents who speak for the news broadcasting institution (Hartley (1982: 110–11) calls them 'institutional voices'). The institutional voices develop the narrative by providing background information, explaining what is at stake in the news event, and introducing comment and **actuality footage** which illustrate this. The interviews, film reports and comment by people involved in the news event are part of the function known as realising, whereby authenticity and evidence of the news event and reactions to it from interested individuals and groups are presented. The availability of actuality footage gives important added value to news reports because it is crucial to the narrative function of realising the story. But although actuality footage might seem to be the dominant type of sign in television news programmes, its visual signs never appear without accompanying **voice-over** commentary. While it is possible for visual sequences to narrate on their own, the multiple meanings which images always have can be contained and directed by the reporter's institutional voice on the soundtrack. Realisation therefore tends to confirm the work of the news reporters' framing and focusing activities. Moving out of the news studio to focus and realise news stories allows room for the visual and aural signs in the programme to differ from and affect the news presenter's framing activities. For instance, the connotations of the signs of situation in news programmes have significant empowering or disempowering effects on the meanings of news reports. The authority of the newsreaders and commentators in the studio can contrast with the much less empowering presence of a member of the public in the street, or a reporter struggling to speak over the voices of a crowd, for example. Closing refers to the way that a news report moves towards a condensed encapsulation of the report, likely to be repeated in the closing headlines of the news programme, and which presents the preferred meaning of the report. Closure might involve discounting some of the points of view on the news event which have been represented in the report, or repeating the point of view already connoted by the frame or focus. This movement towards closure is confirmed at the end of reports, but the report as a whole will involve it throughout.

Identification

First of all, television viewers can make sense of television only by taking up a position in relation to it, constituting themselves as an audience. What the audience is watching has to seem to be 'for them', and a relationship can then be constructed with it (whether this relationship to television is marked by pleasure, boredom, anger or frustration). So narrative depends on a shifting pattern of **identification** between the viewer and the programme. Viewers can identify with both fictional and non-fictional performers but also distance themselves from a performer (in order to find him or her funny, for instance). Viewers can also identify with the studio audience denoted by laughter on the soundtrack, taking up a shared position in relation to what the studio audience and home audience have seen. Narrative requires the shifting of the viewer's position into and out of the television programme, and a rhythm of identification and disavowal of identification. But the positioning and repositioning of the viewer as an audience member might succeed or fail for individual viewers in different programmes or parts of the same programme. Narrative lays out positions for its viewers, offering signs and codes which invite the viewers to make sense of and to enjoy what they see and hear, but whether or not viewers actually occupy the position of being-an-audience, and how they inhabit this position, depends on the many variables which compose each viewer's social and psychological identity.

identification
a term deriving from psychoanalytic theories of cinema, which describes the viewer's conscious or unconscious wish to take the place of someone or something in a television text.

ACTIVITY 4.4

In what ways does audience positioning serve to keep viewers watching programmes? What might happen if audience positioning ceases to work for viewers?

Clearly, viewers are not often conscious of the relationships which they take up moment by moment with television, and for this reason television theorists have drawn on **psychoanalytic** models of how people relate to representations. This theory draws on the work of the French psychoanalyst Jacques Lacan, who drew on and modified the insights of Sigmund Freud, the originator of psychoanalysis. Lacan argued that human beings begin to differentiate themselves from the world around them, and to have a sense of self and other people at a stage of development he called the 'Mirror Stage'. Initially, the human infant feels undifferentiated from its surroundings, and its feelings and needs are not located within a self which exists independently. The first moment of difference comes when the infant perceives an image of itself (in a mirror, hence the name 'Mirror Stage'). This image appears more complete, co-ordinated and unified than the reality of its own immature body. Lacan proclaimed that this relationship with the mirror image is the beginning of identification: 'We have only to understand the mirror stage as an identification

. . . namely, the transformation that takes place in the subject when he assumes an image' (Lacan 1977: 2). Because the image is other to the self, the moment of perceiving it separates individual subjectivity and what is outside it, other to it. For ever afterwards, the human subject is defined in relation to what it is not, to further images of itself and others, and to the surrounding world beyond its own body.

The pleasure of seeing images and others brings with it the awareness of absence, that 'I' am not 'you', 'he' or 'she'. Narrative offers numerous images of other people, places and things, and keeps repeating the pleasurable moment of identifying with others which the viewer is not, and the displeasure of recognising otherness forever beyond him or her. Wanting to watch television is part of the viewer's desire for the other, which narrative keeps displacing on to the next moment in the succession of images and sounds which it presents. Television images are always framed, with what the viewer sees always being part of a larger possible view of which only a part can be seen. The movement of the camera to reveal new spaces and the cutting between one point of view and another keep offering new others with which to identify, and offering to satisfy new desires for mirroring relationships between self and other.

This psychoanalytic account of pleasure in watching television has therefore argued that there are several identifications which viewers make from moment to moment. The first of these is an identification with the television medium, as something which delivers images of otherness that promise to satisfy viewers' desire to see and imagine themselves in the place of the other. There are also identifications with all the figures who are presented on the screen, the performers who stand in for the viewer and play out the roles which the viewer might desire to play for himself or herself. There are identifications across narratives with the fictional and non-fictional worlds presented in television, just as in a daydream or fantasy we might imagine worlds where all of the components seem part of a drama where we play all the parts. Narrative texts are constructed from a network of looks: relations between the looks of the figures, the look of the camera and the viewer's look. The movement of television narrative in this way is analogous to the fantasy (particularly close in daydreaming), which allows for mobile patterns of identi-

gender the social and cultural division of people into masculine or feminine individuals. This is different from sex, which refers to the biological difference between male and female bodies.

fication across different **gender** positions. All the possible roles in the narrative are available to the viewing **subject**: he or she can imagine being either the subject or object and can even occupy a position outside the scene, looking on from a spectator's point of view. The importance of an analogy with fantasy is that the disjuncture of looks and positions in its scenarios appears parallel to the procedure in television narrative of cutting and juxtaposing different views to defer complete knowledge and total vision to the viewer, thereby entraining the desire to look again. The desires to look and hear are experienced through the viewer's relations with a set of signs and codes which offer meanings to the viewer. Television narratives work by closing down the many divergent identifications and understandings of the programme, and binding them into coherence. This psychoanalytic model offers a very complex understanding of the processes of watching television, whereby it can be understood in terms of mobile processes of making sense, experiencing pleasure and displeasure, and giving and withholding interest.

subject in psychoanalysis, the term for the individual self whose identity has both conscious and unconscious components.

Nevertheless, there are some difficulties with this psychoanalytic model. The small size of the television screen and its presence as a domestic object among the furnishings of a room may diminish the importance of imagined identifications compared to the experience of watching in a cinema, for example. The psycho-analytic approach described here was developed originally for understanding film spectatorship, where film viewers are much more likely to be immersed in narratives. The dark space of the cinema, the large size of the screen and the choice to place oneself in the position of a viewer among an audience of other viewers all militate in favour of much greater involvement in film than viewers often experience watching television. The television theorist John Ellis (1982: 137) pointed out this distinction by describing the viewer's look at television as a glance, rather than the concentrated gaze of the film spectator:

> The gaze implies a concentration of the spectator's activity into that of looking, the glance implies that no extraordinary effort is being invested in the activity of looking. The very terms we habitually use to designate the person who watches TV or the cinema screen tend to indicate this difference. The cinema-looker is a spectator: caught by the projection yet separate from its illusion. The TV-looker is a viewer, casting a lazy eye over the proceedings, keeping an eye on events, or, as the slightly archaic designation had it, 'looking in'.

In response to this distinction, television theorists have increasingly moved away from psychoanalytic accounts of television viewing, and instead examined how television narratives offer audience positions for viewers who may be often disengaged glancers rather than immersed spectators. Television uses a range of narrating figures to address the viewer directly, audiences within programmes with whom the viewer is invited to identify, and representative figures who take the place of the ordinary viewer at home. Each of these strategies of viewer involvement contributes to hooking the viewer into television narratives and encouraging the kinds of immersive identification that psychoanalytic theory has explained.

Television narrators

A very obvious question to ask about the meanings of television programmes is where they originate from. Are meanings put there by the person responsible for the programme's **authorship**, are they the result of how signs, codes and narrative structures work in a text, or are they constructed through the individual choices of viewers, for example? In earlier decades of British television the promotion of television authors enabled television executives to rebuff the accusation that television is without value, and television writers were compared with theatre dramatists, novelists or poets. But the consequence of this has been the mistaken view that the meanings of television programmes are the result of individual genius and personal vision. The meanings of television are not universal but local (as the differences between, for example, British and American understandings of **quality** and relevance show) and are produced within the conventions and moral and cultural values of their time. Authors always negotiate with the other practitioners in the making of television (**directors**, **producers**, designers and script editors, for instance) and are not free to mastermind a unique vision of their own.

Because of these critiques of authorship, academic studies of television have focused less on drama than other genres in the last couple of decades because of the

authorship the question of who an author is, the role of the author as creator and the significance of the author's input into the material being studied.

quality in television, kinds of programme that are perceived as more expensively produced and, especially, more culturally worthwhile than other programmes.

director the person responsible for the creative process of turning a script or idea into a finished programme, by working with a technical crew, performers and an editor.

producer the person working for a television institution who is responsible for the budget, planning and making of a television programme or series of programmes.

concern that studying drama, with its literary associations with authorship, will entail the celebration of authors. But within the television industry particular authors have been elevated to high status and publicised for reasons of claiming prestige and attracting audiences. An author can function as a brand, a familiar name which alerts the audience to styles and themes that a writer has explored in the past, and distinguishes the programme from the **flow** of the schedule around it. The marketing of authors as brands occurred in the 1980s and 1990s in relation to dramas by Lynda La Plante, for example (*Prime Suspect, Trial and Retribution*), and classic novel **adaptations** by Andrew Davies (*Pride and Prejudice, Emma, Middlemarch*). A few producers have occupied this authorial branding role, such as Tony Garnett (*The Cops, Attachments*) and the American Steven Bochco (*Murder One, NYPD Blue*). More popular generic drama, such as the police series or hospital drama, is often authored in a collaborative way, using a pool of writers, and is rarely offered to audiences attached to the name of an author. But if television, even drama, the most literary form of it, does not consist of 'messages' put there by an author, there is often the sense in watching television that there is an agency communicating with the viewer. As Sarah Kozloff (1992: 78) explains: 'The "implied author" of a television show . . . is not a flesh-and-blood person but rather a textual construct, the viewer's sense of the organizing force behind the world of the show.' This agency behind narrative appears through the various forms of **narration** used in television.

Analysing narrative requires the distinction between story and **discourse**. Story is the set of events which are represented. They could potentially be told in any order (chronologically, or in **flashback**, for example) and with any emphasis. Discourse is the narrating process which puts story events in an order, with a shape and direction. In any medium, someone or something must be doing the storytelling for the audience, on its behalf, and this agency is the narrator, whether it is a voice, an on-screen performer or simply the agency which viewers reconstruct as the force which controls the arrangement of camera shots, sound and music that deliver the story to them. Some fictional and non-fictional programmes have **voice-over** narrators throughout, or in particular sequences. *Star Trek: The Next Generation* begins with the familiar scene-setting narration for the programme as a whole, beginning with the 'Captain's log' where a voice-over narrates the setting and situation at the start of each episode's story, and this is followed by the narration at the start of the **title sequence**, beginning 'Space, the final frontier . . .'. Narration can sometimes be found in the title songs of programmes, as in *Fresh Prince of Bel-Air* and *One Foot in the Grave*. Series such as *ER* may open with voice-over reminding the audience of scenes in a previous programme explained by the phrase 'Previously, on *ER* . . .'. A few drama programmes include a voice-over narrator or an on-screen narrator within scenes, as in *Sex and the City*. Non-fiction programmes such as wildlife programmes, history programmes such as *Time Team*, commercials, cooking programmes and '**reality TV**' programmes such as *Big Brother* or *Survivor* have narrators. In all of these examples the function of the narrator is to establish a link between the audience and the programme narrative, by inviting the viewer to involve himself or herself in the ongoing progress of the story.

Although some programmes make the function of narration explicit in these ways, all television narratives rely on the more complex narration which is made up of camera shots in a narrative progression, often with music helping to link shots together into sequences and to give them an emotional point of view. Sarah Kozloff

adaptation
transferring a novel, theatre play, poem, etc. from its original medium into another medium such as television.

narration
the process of telling a story through image and sound. Narration can also refer to the spoken text accompanying television images.

discourse
a particular use of language for a certain purpose in a certain context (such as academic discourse, or poetic discourse), and similarly in television, a particular usage of television's audio-visual 'language' (news programme discourse, or nature documentary discourse, for instance).

flashback
a television sequence marked as representing events that happened in a time previous to the programme's present.

reality TV
programmes where the unscripted behaviour of 'ordinary people' is the focus of interest.

(1992: 79) notes that 'Music, in film and in television, is a key channel through which the voiceless narrating agency "speaks" to the viewer'. The viewer is aligned with **point of view shots** of characters or performers, alternating with apparently neutral point of view shots which observe the represented space and the figures in it. The performers in television fiction behave as if the viewer is absent, making it more evident that the camera is the agency conveying their actions to the audience, whereas factual programmes perhaps make narration less obvious because the camera appears more to be a neutral observer. But in each case there is an implied narrator composed from the different camera points of view which have been edited together to form the narrative as whole.

The significance of narration is partly that the viewer is necessarily positioned by the changing sequence of camera shots, the words of on-screen or off-screen narrators and the accompanying music in programmes and ads. The position of the viewer is the place to which all of them are directed and from where they can make sense as a coherent whole. Television viewers, when they constitute themselves as an audience and answer television's call to join a community of viewers, are making an **identification** with the audience position laid out for them by the signs, codes and narrative structures of the programme or advertisement. In other words the television viewer has occupied the role laid out for him or her by the broadcaster, which is doing the looking on his or her behalf. It is often hard to specify what this institutional narrator is, whether for instance it is the production team which has designed and made the programme, or the channel on which it is broadcast. Indeed both of these vague collective agencies seem to make claims to be the overall narrators of programmes by virtue of the credits and **copyright** ownership information in the end titles of programmes, and by the channel **idents** and logos which appear between programmes and, in the case of some channels, are superimposed in the corner of the screen throughout them. In any case the most overarching kind of narrator might be the channel on which programmes are broadcast, since the flow of the period of viewing, no matter how diverse the types of programmes and advertisements which it includes, is held together as a unity by the narrating voice of the off-screen announcers who connect programmes with each other. They are also narrators, saying, for example, 'Join us after the break, where Niles is having a bad day in tonight's episode of *Frasier*'. This narrating discourse is striking in the fact that it makes explicit the hailing function of television to call to an individual viewer to constitute himself of herself as part of an audience ('join us') which is given its place by the address made to it.

point of view shot
a camera shot where the camera is placed in, or close to, the position from where a previously seen character might look.

copyright the legal right of ownership over written, visual or aural material, including the prohibition on copying this material without permission from its owner.

idents the symbols representing production companies, television channels, etc., often comprising graphics or animations.

Signs of the viewer

The television medium brings distant events and uncommon sights, such as the exotic animals of wildlife programmes, or distant events recorded for news programmes, into the private arena of the home. Television has always framed its appeal as a medium on its ability to bring what is different, strange and interesting into the viewer's familiar and domestic world. In this sense television seems to bridge the gap between public and private, and outside and inside. The means of connecting the two, such as by using narrators or representatives of the viewer, are therefore particularly significant to gaining a sense of television's image of itself. But the paradox is that the more television programmes use textual means to include viewers in worlds beyond their own experience, the greater the chance of simultaneously revealing the viewer's own disempowerment and non-involvement. Watching a wildlife programme about the imminent extinction of the tiger might raise viewers' awareness and concern, but might also be a substitute for doing anything about the situation. Broadcasters are concerned to provide a sense of activity and involvement for viewers, whether as part of the **public service** function to show and support initiatives in society or as part of a commercial imperative to encourage consumption of products and services. In either case the ways in which programmes address and position viewers are important subjects of study.

Television is a domestic technology, embedded in the home among other technological devices such as radios, microwaves or stereo systems. These technologies, and the activities which come from them, compete for attention. Television calls for viewers to take up membership of an audience sharing an experience with millions of unseen others, and thus join in an imaginary community of viewers watching the same thing. This call to belong, and to share the values and experiences of a particular social group or even a whole nation, is parallel to the way in which the French philosopher Louis Althusser (1971) explained the important media theoretical concept of **ideology**. Ideology is a structure is which people are addressed as particular kinds of subject, and take up a position laid out for them by this call, along with the values inherent in the position to which they are called. People become individual **subjects**, subject to ideological values and constituted as subjects by ideology as the unique destination to which the call is addressed.

> **public service** in television, the provision of a mix of programmes that inform, educate and entertain in ways that encourage the betterment of audiences and society in general.

ACTIVITY 4.5

Can you use an analysis of your own background and experience to explain why you find a particular programme frustrating? What kinds of audience positioning are you resisting?

The inclusion of viewers in programmes, whether literally or by hollowing out a position for the viewer in the discourse of the programme, is complex in daytime talk shows such as *Oprah* or *Rikki Lake*. There is a hierarchy of figures, presided over by the host, including professional 'experts' such as doctors and therapists, guest members of the public, the studio audience and the audience of viewers. The role of the host is to mediate between these categories, by representing the viewer's imagined questions and concerns. Television viewers, along with the studio audience, are invited to evaluate the behaviour and opinions of the speakers, so that the position laid out for the viewer is to identify with any or all the speakers, but especially the studio audience, who are the viewer's representatives. Occasionally television viewers are able to participate in the programme by phoning in, and can adopt a confessional discourse and describe their own experiences, or adopt the position of an expert in order to evaluate other participants in the programme. Although phone-ins appear to empower and involve these viewers, the **codes** and connotations of their appearance have disempowering effects. How long they can speak, being heard but not being seen, and being directed by the host, are all means of controlling who can speak, how and in which discursive code. The discourses adopted by speakers from home or among the studio audience tend to match those of the programme as a whole, for example by appealing to personal experiences as proofs of an opinion, or presenting statistical or institutional information in the discursive code of 'objective' professional advice. Talk-show narrative is a series of confrontations between different discourses, each appealing to one of several kinds of authority and legitimacy. The role of the host is to arrange these different discourses into a sequence, acting as a mediating narrator working on behalf of the audience and claiming to represent its concerns.

Television commercials very often contain characters representing the viewer, often someone addressed by an on-screen or off-screen narrator about a difficulty which can be solved by a product (like a household cleaner which will remove stubborn stains). The use of viewers' representatives enables the relationship of the producer and consumer to be dramatised as a person-to-person relationship, and to provide the product with a concrete setting in the household environment. A variant on this structure is the common use of viewer representatives in car commercials, featuring drivers whose representation attempts both to mirror the viewer and also to include an aspirational element (a younger, richer, more attractive version of the target consumer). The narrative function of viewer representatives, therefore, whether they are studio audiences, talk-show hosts or characters in commercials, is to mediate between the viewer and the representation in the programme or commercial. The viewer is invited to identify with his or her representative, and to take up the position laid out by the signs and codes of the programme or commercial. The viewer is invited to constitute himself or herself as part of an audience, becoming the one to whom the text is addressed.

This becoming-audience for the viewer is enhanced by possibilities for **interaction** with programmes and commercials. Comedy programmes invite laughter, television commercials offer puzzles or jokes which the viewer is invited to figure out, and both commercials and programmes provide telephone numbers and websites which offer further information, special offers or competitions. Television shopping channels are of course entirely predicated on this interaction, since the viewer is explicitly addressed as a potential buyer of the products shown on screen. Television sports coverage is constructed in order to invite the viewer's involvement through offering patterns of reaction to the sport directed by the commentator. Studio comment by invited sports experts (former players, managers, sports journalists, etc.) focuses on discourses of evaluation and prediction, and aims to invite the viewer to engage in speculation and judgement in a similar way. This imaginary dialogue between the viewer and the programme therefore lays out codes in which the viewer's response should take place. In sports television, for example, singing football songs and throwing cans of beer at the screen is not expected, whereas knowledgeable debate and respect for the rules and conduct of the game are expected. The use of slow-motion replays in sports programmes is a further means of presenting and encouraging this kind of rational and evaluative critique.

The discussion of signs, codes, functions and narration in this chapter has focused on how television texts are meaningful to viewers, and how viewers are positioned by texts in order to gain pleasure and understanding from them. One of the assumptions behind this kind of analysis is that television does not usually reveal

interactive offering the opportunity for viewers to respond to what is broadcast, by sending signals back to the broadcaster (along a cable or phone line, for example).

the construction and positioning activities of the text. However, television is an unusual medium in sometimes making its own production, and the failures in its production, a subject for television programmes. But this revealing of behind-the-scenes information and of mistakes in programme production is confined to particular kinds of text. In situation comedy, for instance, it became common in the 1990s for episodes to end with a compilation of **outtakes** and mistakes, or '**bloopers**', from that episode or from several episodes. The animated series *The Simpsons* adopted and made fun of this trend by showing a whole episode supposedly comprised of mistakes, even though animation is made frame by frame and cannot possibly involve these errors. Compilation programmes such as *Auntie's Bloomers* and *It'll Be Alright on the Night* are entirely composed of outtakes and mistakes from all genres of programme. There is an interesting parallel between these programmes and the compilation programmes of viewers' ridiculous home videos (people falling down, pets doing amusing things, etc.). The widespread use of domestic video equipment, and viewers' increasing familiarity with the means by which programmes are made, has led to new kinds of viewer positioning.

The recognition that television programmes play on their own and each other's conventions is one of the components of **postmodernism**. This theoretical term rose to prominence in Television Studies in the 1980s, as a way of distinguishing how programmes since that time appear to be more self-conscious and sophisticated than before. Among the features of television which mark postmodernism are self-consciousness, irony and the **pastiche** or imitation of familiar conventions, formats and structures, like the pastiche of news conventions in *Brass Eye* and *The Day Today*, or the pastiche of television and film conventions in *The Simpsons*. So the term 'postmodern' can be used as a way of describing the textual and narrative characteristics of programmes. The term can also be used to signify a more general shift in television culture, and culture in general. In Chapter 3, for example, it was explained that the **globalisation** of television could be described as postmodern in character. Here the term is used to denote a shift from national broadcasting culture to an increasingly global one, where the ownership of television networks, the international sale of programmes and the worldwide broadcast of some television channels such as CNN or MTV seem to have changed the character of television, at least in Western nations. But in each use of the term 'postmodern' it is used to signify a changed situation. This change is not assumed to be progress from an earlier state of affairs, much less an improvement, but instead a change which puts in question notions of evolution and progress. Indeed, in some formulations of what postmodernism is, it is argued that the very idea of history as a process of development and progressive improvement has ceased to match up to what is happening in culture. The increased awareness on the part of audiences that what they watch are artefacts or textual products (rather than visions of reality) can be adduced as support for this argument.

outtake a shot or sequence which was omitted from a finished programme, because of a mistake during production or an artistic decision.

blooper a mistake by a performer in a programme, or a technical error. The term often refers to humorous mistakes.

postmodernism the most recent phase of capitalist culture, the aesthetic forms and styles associated with it and the theoretical approaches developed to understand it.

pastiche the imitation of forms or conventions in another text. The term can convey a negative view that the imitation is less effective or valuable than the original.

globalisation the process whereby ownership of television institutions in different nations and regions is concentrated in the hands of international corporations, and whereby programmes and formats are traded between institutions around the world.

ACTIVITY 4.6

Are television programmes with the most plural meanings the best programmes? How do standards of value draw on criteria of complexity, plural meaning and innovation?

While television programmes and advertisements offer positions from which pleasure and sense require acceptance of the position laid out by the text, contemporary viewers are increasingly able to recognise, sidestep and reject these positions. Becoming part of the audience is perhaps much more of a conscious choice than some models of television text and narrative might admit. In particular, psychoanalytic models of unconscious positioning need to be supplemented with studies of audiences' conscious and negotiated relationships with television. For just as much of what the audience sees on television is performance, becoming-audience is also a performed role which viewers partly unconsciously and partly consciously adopt. For these reasons studies of television texts and narratives are not a self-sufficient set of approaches in Television Studies. They need to be supplemented by studies of real viewers' relationships with television, to explain how some positions for the viewer are taken up and some are not.

Case study: the Guinness 'Surfer' commercial

This case study begins with a close textual analysis of a television advertisement first shown in 1999, aiming to demonstrate how a **semiotic** and **narrative** analysis works in practice. Because television ads are short, but often take the form of a story told by combinations of image, language and sound, they function well as demonstration pieces for textual analysis. But the later parts of this case study raise some questions about alternative ways of

Figure 4.3 Close-up on the surfer's face. 'He waits. That's what he does. And that's how you want.' Courtesy of Abbott Mead Vickers BBDO.

continued

understanding this commercial. Information about the production of the ad, its historical and commercial context and the intentions of its makers both support and challenge the conclusions of a close textual analysis. So, as well as showing the power of textual analysis itself, this case study aims to draw attention to the exclusions and blind-spots which it involves.

The narrative of the ad can be divided into four segments. First, the surfers wait on the beach, then they ride a huge wave, next they celebrate together and finally an image of a pint of Guinness is connected with this narrative of expectation and fulfilment. The first three segments of the narrative unfold in chronological order, as a story, while the final segment reflects back over the narrative as a whole.

The ad opens in black and white with an unusually long big **close-up** of a man's face, with a brief male **voice-over** and no music. The stillness of the face and the man's upward gaze relay with the narration's introduction the experience of waiting and wanting. The image and the narration work together to set up a narrative structure based on anticipation and desire, which invites the viewer to wonder what the man is waiting for. They begin a story.

The camera's **point of view** reverses, to show surfers entering the water with their surfboards. The wider shots establish a hot foreign location, the beach and the large waves coming on to the shore. Shot length becomes shorter, the camera is hand-held and mobile, speeding up the narrative rhythm of the sequence. The narration continues to elaborate the waiting motif, using the repetition of 'tick' and 'tock' to match the duration of the wait with the duration of a repeated structure of words associated with measuring time. The pounding music connotes the rapid heartbeat associated with excitement and danger, its alternating beats linking

Figure 4.4 Long shot of surfers entering the water. 'Tick followed tock followed tick followed tock followed tick.' Courtesy of Abbott Mead Vickers BBDO.

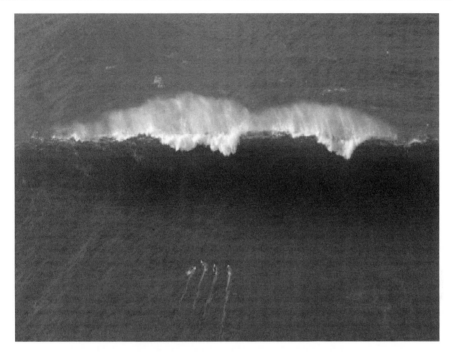

Figure 4.5 The huge wave. 'Ahab says "I don't care who you are, here's to your dream".'
Courtesy of Abbott Mead Vickers BBDO.

with the alternating 'tick' and 'tock' of the voice-over. The sequence increases the momentum of the narrative and suggests that what the surfers are waiting for is about to arrive.

A static long shot from above the beach shows a huge wave approaching, its white top contrasting with the dark water and tiny surfers standing in front of it. The surfers mount their surfboards and move into the wave. The narration links the visual action to the motif of waiting and wanting with the sign 'dream', and introduces Ahab without explaining who he is, though he appears to be situated in a bar making a toast to 'your dream'. The music continues, becoming louder and more fully orchestrated. The 'dream' for which the surfers have been waiting becomes more clearly established as the opportunity to ride this huge wave.

Camera shots become even shorter, and point of view shifts between close-ups of the surfer's face amid the wave, medium shots from the side as he rides the wave and long shots showing several surfers. Many of these shots include large white horses seeming to emerge from the wave, plunging from its top into the space occupied by the surfers. The narration continues to elaborate a scene in a bar, involving 'sailors' toasting Ahab accompanied by a 'drummer'. The narrator exhales, as if having drunk a large gulp. The bar-room scene links with the celebration of a 'dream' and a quest to accomplish something shared by the 'sailors' and 'Ahab', just as the surfers share the experience of riding their dream wave.

The rapid alternation of camera shots ceases, replaced by a still shot of the surfer raising his arms in exaltation. The music stops, and there is no narration. The surfing experience, and the narrator's bar-room toast narrative, seem to have been completed.

Hand-held camera shots follow the surfers back to the shore, and provide different points of view on the group as they collapse on to the sand celebrating and hugging each other. The

continued

Figure 4.6 Surfers and white horses amid the waves. 'The old sailors return to the bar. "Here's to you Ahab". And the fat drummer hit the beat with all his heart.' [Exhalation]. Courtesy of Abbott Mead Vickers BBDO.

Figure 4.7 The surfer raises his arms in exultation. [Music ceases.] Courtesy of Abbott Mead Vickers BBDO.

Figure 4.8 The surfers celebrate together on the beach. 'Here's to waiting'. Courtesy of Abbott Mead Vickers BBDO.

narration reintroduces the toasting motif, connecting the surfers' celebration with the bar-room scene involving the sailors, Ahab and the drummer. The two narratives are parallel to each other.

The still front-on shot of the pint of Guinness (overleaf) shares its static quality and positioning with the opening shot of the surfer's face, creating a cyclical resolution to the ad. The black beer and its white foaming head connect with the dark water and white surf and white horses of the earlier sequences. The drink of beer connects with the toasting motif and bar-room scene in the voice-over. The written signs 'good things' and 'wait' connect with the anticipation of the 'dream' and the surfers' waiting at the start of the ad. The pint of Guinness appears to be equivalent to, or to contain, the various meanings of the action and narration in the ad as a whole.

A close textual analysis of this ad shows that its meanings are developed though **metonymies** and **metaphors**. White rolling surf, white plunging horses and white bubbling Guinness share traits which link them together. Waiting for an exciting surfing experience is parallel to waiting for a delicious drink. The semiotic structure of the ad enables it to correlate seemingly different contents with each other, so they apparently share similar meanings. The exotic, dangerous, masculine achievements of the surfers are correlated with the Guinness brand, giving this product meanings which are attached to it by the quite poetic and self-consciously artistic construction of the ad as a narrative. The analysis of the ad above tried not to explain the constituents of the ad except in the terms which the ad seems to offer unproblematically to its viewers, but some of the ad's ambiguities and puzzles can be explained by historical information, production context and cultural associations. The close

metonymy the substitution of one thing for another, either because one is part of the other or because one is connected with the other. For example, 'the Crown' can be a metonym for the British state.

metaphor the carrying-over from something of some of its meanings on to another thing of an apparently different kind. For example, a television narrative about life aboard ship could be a metaphor for British social life (the ship as metaphor for society).

continued

Figure 4.9 Close-up of a pint of Guinness with the foaming head settling. Courtesy of
Abbott Mead Vickers BBDO.

analysis of the ad is unfinished without introducing some of these factors, which seem to
belong outside the ad itself.

Guinness ads appeared first in newspapers in 1929 with the original slogan 'Guinness is
good for you'. Ads then drew either on variations of this slogan ('Guinless isn't good for you'),
on characteristics of the beer ('Tall dark and have some', 'Not everything in black and white
makes sense'), or on the more generic 'Pure Genius'. Incidentally, a Guinness commercial
was one of the ads shown on the first night of ITV in 1955. The 'Surfer' ad draws on some of
this history. While it does not imply that Guinness is good for you, it does associate the product
with the vigorous outdoor activity of surfing. It is shot in black and white, picking up on the
colours of the product itself, and some of its contents, like the Ahab references and bar-room
toasting **syntagms**, seem at first glance not to make much sense. Certainly the white horses
appearing in the wave are non-realistic, and can be explained as representations of the surfer's
fantasies about his experience.

The production of the ad began with Tom Carty and Walter Campbell of the advertising
agency Abbott Mead Vickers BBDO. They measured that it takes 120 seconds to pour a pint
of Guinness and leave it to settle for serving. The ad's slogan 'Good things come to those
who wait' was a combination of the time and the old 'good for you' slogan. They had created
an earlier ad about an elderly Italian swimmer who crosses a harbour in the time taken to pour
a pint, and the sea connections and waiting time in 'Surfer' sought to connect the ad with its
predecessor. But they were cautious about the connections between surfing and a vintage
Old Spice aftershave ad (1977) featuring a surfer, widely regarded as outdated and naff. They
enriched the surfing motif with references to the climactic sea sequences in the film *Moby*

Dick, where the whaler Captain Ahab obsessively pursues a gigantic white whale, and a painting by Walter Crane which shows white horses mingling with waves. The ad cost about £1 million to make, and its aim was to position Guinness as a sophisticated drink for younger drinkers. So the production context of the ad reveals an awareness of the history of Guinness advertising mentioned above, an attempt to draw on notions of obsession, risk and a history of sea adventure fiction, together with a target market of youthful drinkers who might be expected to respond to its complex narrative structure, and the aspirational theme of the 'dream' of excitement and physical prowess.

ACTIVITY 4.7

Do all television ads address potential buyers of the products they advertise? If not, what function do these other ads serve?

The 'Surfer' ad is in some ways representative of television narrative, especially in ads. It uses dramatic conventions of narrative structure, music and visual effects which could be found in many other ads and television fiction programmes. But it is also unrepresentative, partly because it gained widespread public recognition, and partly because it is longer, more expensive to produce and more self-consciously artistic than many ads. By the age of thirty-five, the average person has seen 150,000 television commercials, amounting to about 75,000 minutes or two months. In this context, an ad which makes a public impact is both unusual and very valuable to the market presence of the product it advertises. The 'Surfer' commercial was the most-voted-for ad in Channel 4's poll of 2000 to select viewers' *100 Greatest TV Ads*. There were 10,000 votes cast in the poll, and the Bank Holiday Monday screening of *100 Greatest TV Ads* drew four million viewers. The final point to make in the context of this case study, therefore, is to note that this ad and the production context and history behind it are unusually accessible compared to the great majority of unremarked and poorly remembered commercials alongside it. A close textual analysis of its narrative is a special form of attention to the making of meanings in television which sets the procedures of Television Studies apart from the more usual kinds of attention which television receives from its viewers.

SUMMARY OF KEY POINTS

- Methods of close analysis deriving from the study of film can show how meanings are constructed in television texts.
- This approach to close analysis relies on analysing the audio-visual 'language' of television.

continued

- The meanings that can be made from television also depend on relationships between viewers and texts.
- Television programmes use conventions and codes to structure their meanings, and television viewers become expert in recognising conventions and decoding meanings.
- Television guides the viewer by using narrative and offering points of identification where viewers can become involved in programmes.
- A knowledge of the production context and history of a television text can affect the meanings which the television text itself may have.
- The meanings of television have ideological significance that shapes relationships between television texts, audiences and society.

Further reading

Bignell, J., *Media Semiotics: An Introduction*, second edition (Manchester: Manchester University Press, 2002).

Corner, J., *Critical Ideas in Television Studies* (Oxford: Clarendon, 1999).

Fairclough, N., *Media Discourse* (London: Arnold, 1995).

Fiske, J., *Television Culture* (London: Routledge, 1992).

—— *Introduction to Communication Studies* (London: Routledge, 1990).

Fiske, J. and J. Hartley, *Reading Television* (London: Methuen, 1978).

Hall, S., 'Encoding/decoding', in S. Hall, D. Hobson, A. Lowe and P. Willis (eds), *Culture, Media, Language* (London: Hutchinson, 1980), pp. 128–38.

Kozloff, S., 'Narrative theory and television', in R. Allen (ed.), *Channels of Discourse, Reassembled: Television and Contemporary Criticism* (London: Routledge, 1992), pp. 67–100.

Lacey, N., *Narrative and Genre: Key Concepts in Media Studies* (Basingstoke: Macmillan, 2000).

Lewis, J., 'Decoding television news', in P. Drummond and R. Paterson (eds), *Television in Transition* (London: BFI, 1985), pp. 205–34.

Masterman, L., *Television Mythologies: Stars, Shows and Signs* (London: Comedia, 1984).

Mullan, B., *Consuming Television* (Oxford: Blackwell, 1997).

Seiter, E., 'Semiotics, structuralism, and television', in R. Allen (ed.), *Channels of Discourse, Reassembled: Television and Contemporary Criticism* (London: Routledge, 1992), pp. 31–66.

Selby, K. and R. Cowdery, *How to Study Television* (Basingstoke: Macmillan, 1995).

Tolson, A., *Mediations: Text and Discourse in Media Studies* (London: Arnold, 1996).

Television and Genre

Television and Genre

Introduction

genre a kind or type of programme. Programmes of the same genre have shared characteristics.

serial a television form where a developing narrative unfolds across a sequence of separate episodes.

news value the degree of significance attributed to a news story, where items with high news value are deemed most significant to the audience.

Genre derives from the French word meaning 'type', and the study of genre has been carried out in relation to television using approaches and terms deriving from the study of genre in film, literature and other cultural forms. This is appropriate since some of the most established television genres derive from types found in other media. For example, the genre of soap opera began in radio broadcasting, where continuing **serials** focusing on the emotional relationships of a group of characters were created to address the mainly female audience during the daytime. These radio programmes were called soap operas because they were sponsored by companies producing domestic products such as detergents and soaps. Drama is of course a form deriving from theatre, and in the early years of television broadcasting many fiction programmes were television adaptations of theatre plays. News and current affairs television share conceptions of **news value** and the institutional structures of reporters and editors with newspapers and news radio broadcasting. Entertainment genres such as sketch shows and situation comedy also have theatrical roots in music hall and variety, which were adapted for radio and later became established in television. The study of genre is based on the identification of the conventions and key features which distinguish one kind of work from another, such as the characteristics of westerns, musicals and thrillers in cinema. The study of genre allows theorists to link the conventions and norms found in a group of texts with the expectations and understandings of audiences. In this respect the study of genre aims to explain how audiences classify what they see and hear on television according to:

● features of the text itself
● generic cues which audiences identify in programme titles
● supporting information in the *Radio Times* or other listings and advertising publications
● the presence of performers associated with a particular genre (in the way that John Thaw was associated with television police drama, for example).

As Steve Neale (Neale and Turner 2001: 1) notes: 'Most theorists of genre argue that generic norms and conventions are recognised and shared not only by theorists themselves, but also by audiences, readers and viewers.'

Theorists working on genre have disagreed about where genre categories come from:

● Do genre forms arise naturally from the properties of texts?
● Are they categories used by the producers of programmes?
● Are they categories brought by audiences to the programmes they watch?

ACTIVITY 5.1

Examine the brief descriptions of terrestrial television programmes included in listings magazines and newspapers. How many programmes are described using a genre designation (such as soap opera, teen drama, thriller, sitcom)? Are there other kinds of designation which seem important (such as featured performers, or the mention of writers, directors or producers)? Why are programmes designated in these ways?

Furthermore, there is disagreement about whether the task of the theorist is to identify genres so that programmes can be evaluated, or whether the task is to describe how actual audiences make use of genre in their understanding of programmes. From an evaluative point of view, both television theorists and television fans might regard some programmes as transgressing the rules of genre and therefore evaluate these programmes as inferior. For example, fans of *Star Trek* regard some episodes as a 'true' *Star Trek* and others as contaminated with extraneous elements such as romance or soap opera. By contrast, some television theorists might argue that programmes which transgress the boundaries of a genre are more valuable because they potentially draw the audience's attention to the conventional rules of television genre and therefore have a critical dimension. This argument derives from the historical perception that genre applies most easily to mass-market **popular culture** texts, so that programmes which are firmly within the boundaries of a genre are regarded as formulaic. Nevertheless, all texts participate in genre to some extent, and often participate in several genres simultaneously. The study of genre is not only a way of pinning programmes down but also a way of explaining how programmes become interesting and pleasurable by working against genre conventions as well as with them.

Identifying programme genre

The **title sequences** of programmes are sequences of signs which signify the boundaries between one part of the **flow** of television and those parts of the flow which precede and follow them. In this respect, title sequences offer cues to viewers which enable them to identify the genre of a programme. There are many different kinds of **sign** that a title sequence might contain, which will enable a viewer to identify the pleasures offered by a programme, and many of these pleasures are connected to genre. For example, the title sequences of news programmes often contain:

- dramatic orchestral music
- images signifying the global coverage of news events
- the immediacy of news signified by a clock face
- signifiers of the institutions such as Parliament that are the producers of newsworthy events.

But it is rare for the components of programmes to belong exclusively to a single genre. In news, for example, there are interviews between presenters and experts or

popular culture the texts created by ordinary people (as opposed to an elite group) or created for them, and the ways these are used.

title sequence the sequence at the opening of a television programme in which the programme title and performers' names may appear along with other information, accompanied by images, sound and music introducing the programme.

flow the ways that programmes, advertisements, etc. follow one another in an unbroken sequence across the day or part of the day, and the experience of watching the sequence of programmes, advertisements, trailers, etc.

sign in semiotics, something which communicates meaning, such as a word, an image or a sound.

officials that are coded in the same ways as interviews in sports programmes. The address to camera found in news programmes can also be seen in sports programmes, or quiz programmes. News programmes contain sequences of **actuality footage** accompanied by a **voice-over**, but similar sequences can be found in **documentary** and current affairs programmes, wildlife programmes and other factual genres. Although the content of news programmes is necessarily different in each programme because, by definition, the events in the news are new, the **format** of news programmes exhibits a strong degree of continuity. The separation of news programmes into separate items, the importance of the news presenter and reporters as a team which appears regularly in programmes, and the consistent use of settings such as the news studio, logos and graphics make today's news programme look very similar to yesterday's and tomorrow's news. Television commercials also use consistent performers who become associated with a product brand, and graphics, logos and music which recur. Television police series personalise law and order in the personas of detectives and policemen, as do other genre programmes such as hospital drama. One of the difficulties in the study of genre in television is identifying which features of programmes are unique to a particular genre, to the extent that these features could form a list enabling the critic to establish the boundaries of a genre.

actuality footage television pictures representing an event that was filmed live. The term usually refers to pictures of news events.

voice-over speech accompanying visual images but not presumed to derive from the same place or time as the images.

documentary a form aiming to record actual events, often with an explanatory purpose or to analyse and debate an issue.

format the blueprint for a programme, including its setting, main characters, genre, form and main themes.

ACTIVITY 5.2

Lacey (2000: 133) proposes that the elements within texts that need to be examined to identify their genre are: character types, setting, iconography, narrative and style. Try applying this list to two programmes within the same genre. Can you find a programme containing similar elements but which seems to belong to a different genre? If so, what do you need to add to your list of elements to maintain the boundaries of the genre you first looked at? How stable are those boundaries?

ideology the set of beliefs, attitudes and assumptions arising from the economic and class divisions in a culture, underlying the ways of life accepted as normal in that culture.

The **ideological** functions of television programmes cross the boundaries between genres. Television police series are structured around the opposition between legality and criminality. Narratives are organised by establishing the central character of the detective or policemen as a personal representative of legality, against whom the otherness of crime and its perpetrators are measured. The television audience is encouraged to identify with the central figure, whereas the criminal is established as an other responsible for disruption. In television news a similar opposition is established between the public, the news presenters and the institution of television news on one hand, and the other nations, public institutions, perpetrators of crime and the impersonal forces of chance, the weather and natural processes which produce the disruptions and disorder reported in the news. Although audiences recognise television news and television police series as different genres, the ideological oppositions between order and disorder, continuity and disruption animate both genres at the level of structure and narrative. Within television news itself, internal boundaries separate news events into different genres. Separate news items and separate teams of reporters and presenters may be devoted to categories of news event such as party politics, economic affairs and sport. These categories are also arranged in a hierarchy, where party politics and economic affairs are generally considered more newsworthy and significant than sport, for instance. The representation of society in television news depends on the use of a principle of categorisation in order to make sense of events. News could potentially include any event, but depends on a basic categorisation which divides those events considered to be of importance, those events which are newsworthy, from those events which are not. There is an unspoken assumption that society is potentially unified, but further categorisations divide the society into groupings based on relative wealth, age, gender, race, institutional power and political outlook.

Just as categorisation is used in television news to make sense of the potentially infinite events occurring each day, genre categories are used in television criticism to make sense of the differences between broadcast material and arrange it into hierarchies and groupings. The study of genre in television criticism has tended to begin from the assumption that what is being studied is complete individual programmes. This is because genre study borrows its methodology from other disciplines such as literary criticism where discrete and complete works are the basic units. As discussed earlier in this book, however, television consists of a flow where programmes are interrupted by ads and **trailers**, and where **teasers** may precede the title sequences that declare the beginnings of programmes. For viewers accustomed to **zapping** between channels and fast-forwarding through videotapes, television is experienced in a much more fragmentary manner. On one hand, whole channels are devoted to one kind of programme, on the Sci-Fi Channel, CNN or the Cartoon Network. On the other, as discussed increasingly through this chapter, programmes borrow **intertextually** from a variety of genres and blur the boundaries between them. As Steve Neale (Neale and Turner 2001: 2) argues, 'The degree of hybridity and overlap among and between genres and areas has all too often been underplayed.' But, on the other hand, Neale goes on to note that 'Underplayed, too, has been the degree to which texts of all kinds necessarily "participate" in genre . . ., and the extent to which they are likely to participate in more than one genre at once'. To make sense of the complexity of the contemporary television landscape, viewers become expert in recognising genre, and also derive pleasure from the manipulation of genre and from the ways that television plays with its boundaries.

trailer a short television sequence advertising a forthcoming programme, usually containing selected 'highlights' from the programme.

teaser a very short television sequence advertising a forthcoming programme, often puzzling or teasing to viewers because it contains little information and encourages curiosity and interest.

zapping hopping rapidly from channel to channel while watching television, using a remote control (a 'zapper').

intertextuality how one text draws on the meanings of another by referring to it, by allusion, quotation or parody, for example.

ACTIVITY 5.3

Examine the listings of cable and satellite programmes in the listings magazines or newspapers. Many channels are named after or based around genres. Which genres are these, and which genres do not have channels based on them? What could be the reasons for this?

The generic space of soap opera

It has been customary in Television Studies to define genres by the content and setting in which programmes take place, but an alternative set of genres could be established by focusing on the representation of fictional space, geographic region or basis in another source text (there could be a genre of literary **adaptation**, for example). It would be possible to divide up television programmes in different ways from the categories customarily used to describe television genres if attention is paid less to the content of programmes and more to their form and ideology. For example, a genre could be constructed of television programmes focusing on community. This could include the communities of people inhabiting a shared space in television soap opera, the communities working together in television hospital drama and television police and detective fiction. Within this large generic category, further distinctions could be made to establish sub-genres in which communities are bound together primarily by family and emotional relationships (as in British soap opera), by an institutional hierarchy (as in hospital and police drama) or by the pressure of an external threat (as in *Buffy the Vampire Slayer*).

The significance of space and setting to the definition of a recognised television genre can be seen in the importance of setting in British soap opera. The titles of *Coronation Street*, *Brookside*, *Emmerdale* and *EastEnders* demonstrate how location functions as a force linking characters with each other, not only as a positive basis for community but also as a boundary which characters find it difficult to transgress. Characters in soap opera are in a sense trapped by their location, and their proximity to each other within the space creates not only alliances but also rivalries and friction. The categorisations which link characters together in soap opera such as:

- family relationship
- working relationship
- age group
- race
- gender

function in a similar way as either a positive ground for connection or a source of rivalry and tension. The overlapping of these categories with each other also produces possible stories in soap opera, since one character is likely to belong to several different categories, perhaps working in the local shop, belonging to a family and pursuing solidarity with other characters of the same age group. Soap opera narrative manipulates these connections and distinctions, changing them over time, thus producing different permutations of connection and distinction, which form the basis of storylines.

In the genre of soap opera the multiple storylines built around a large group of characters living in the same location produce an impression of rapidly recurring events, since the scenes and sequences in any one episode are likely to involve several different combinations of characters. Short scenes involving different combinations of characters follow each other rapidly, producing forward movement in the story-lines. But on the other hand, any one episode of a soap opera usually occurs in a very short space of represented time such as one day or even just a few hours. The exchange of information between characters through gossip and conversation,

---

adaptation transferring a novel, theatre play, poem, etc. from its original medium into another medium such as television.

and the withholding of information which has been revealed to the audience, also encourages the viewer to be aware of developments a long time in the past, to speculate about future events and to experience pleasurable uncertainty about which of the numerous occurrences in any one episode will have effects on the networks of relationships which connect characters with each other. The ways that soap opera works in terms of form have been used as the components to define this genre, but many of the features discussed here are also evident in other programmes which are not in the genre of soap opera but share some of the same elements. For example, hospital drama series such as *Casualty* or *ER* share many of the same features in terms of the relationships between characters, the exploitation of the audience's memory of the past and the encouragement of speculation about future events, as well as taking place in a restricted location where a relatively large group of characters enables the tensions in relationships to be explored. The most significant difference between soap opera and television hospital drama is in the degree of narrative closure in individual episodes. Hospital drama and police drama are characterised by narratives in which transitional characters appear and produce a disruption to the social space represented in the programme, and at the end of an episode this storyline is completed.

ACTIVITY 5.4

Series drama on television has tended to develop towards the serial form. Does this potentially mean that all drama tends towards the genre of soap opera? What features of soap opera make it a special form of continuing drama?

The police genre: us and them

In the BBC police drama series *The Cops* there is a consistent group of main characters who seem at first to be relatively conventional. Indeed, the programme's title is likely to trigger viewers' generic knowledge of other television police series, and set up a pattern of expectations. In the opening episode Mel, a young policewoman working with predominantly male colleagues, was introduced. Viewers also saw a young Asian policeman and a middle-aged veteran beat constable unhappy with the changes to policing, which he regarded with scepticism. These are familiar characters, and it is easy to see how storylines familiar in the police genre can develop around them. There could be tensions between Mel and her male colleagues, explorations of racism within the police institution itself and in the community which the Asian police officer deals with, and conflicts between the middle-aged veteran, his younger colleagues and his superiors responsible for carrying out modern police policies. The members of the public with whom the police characters came most into conflict with were the inhabitants of a local housing estate, and further storylines involving tensions between the police and the community offered conventional stories in the police genre. Problems of poverty, drugs, street crime and burglary, conflicts between older and younger generations in the community, and the difficult

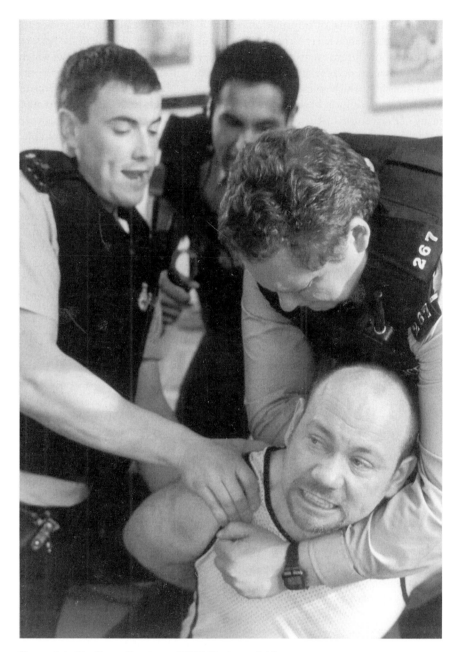

Figure 5.1 *The Cops*. Courtesy of BBC Photograph Library.

task of sustaining relationships between the police and people they grew up with while also enforcing law and order form the basis of the action in the episodes. But *The Cops* not only signalled conventional expectations of the police genre for the audience but also sought to manipulate these. *The Cops* was exciting television because of its negotiation with genre and the audience expectations which it mobilises.

At the opening of the first episode, Mel was introduced in plain clothes, with no indication that she was a policewoman, and was seen snorting cocaine and dancing all night in a nightclub. The distinctions between the upholders of the law and those whose criminal activities make them the object of police attention were being blurred right from the beginning of the series. As the young police officers learned more about the inhabitants of the local housing estate who they were often called upon to search, interrogate and arrest, they developed increasingly caring attitudes to these people and greater understanding of their problems. Again, the distance between the police and the community was reduced, and the easy identification of perpetrators and victims, heroes and villains, was made increasingly difficult for the audience. The television form of the series supported this blurring of genre categories and expectations.

Scenes in *The Cops* were shot with a single camera, always following the police characters into action, rather than establishing a scene before their arrival. The single camera was often hand-held, moving with the police as they moved through the corridors of the police station, through the streets and into houses. Whereas television drama programmes are normally shot using the **shot-reverse shot** convention familiar from cinema, in which scenes are performed several times with the camera positioned differently each time in order to capture the reactions of one character to another and to provide a coherent sense of fictional space, *The Cops* aimed to give the impression of unrehearsed action occurring in real time. This is of course the camera convention used in television documentary, where a single camera operator tries to catch the action as it occurs, and is often forced to **pan** quickly between speakers, and to carry the camera physically as action moves across a space. The effect of this form in *The Cops* was to generate a sense of **realism** in following action as it occurs. It also had the effect of requiring the audience to observe the police and interpret their actions without the camera providing the movements from wider shots to **close-ups**, and dramatic contrasts which usually offer an interpretative point of view on the action. *The Cops* demanded a more active and interpretive viewer than is usual in television drama, with the camera technique implying observation and investigation as much as identification with the characters. The structural and formal qualities of *The Cops* work together both to signal genre conventions and also to blur them. The ideological consequence of this is that *The Cops* put into question any easy distinction between us and them, police and perpetrator, and creatively pushed the boundaries of a very established television genre. The conventions of the police genre with and against which *The Cops* worked are explored further in the case study at the end of this chapter.

Sitcom and the problem of humour

Theorists of television genre have found it very difficult to establish clearly how television comedy programmes, especially sitcoms, work. Obviously the primary characteristic of television sitcom is that it is funny, and this has to do with the relationship between the programme text and the audience. Some components of the programme text can be identified as consistent elements of sitcom, but even these are not exclusive to the genre. Audience laughter, for example, is clearly important to the genre. The moments when laughter breaks into the soundtrack provide cues

shot-reverse shot the convention of alternating a shot of one character and a shot of another character in a scene, producing a back-and-forth movement which represents their interaction visually.

pan a shot where the camera is turned to the left or turned to the right. The term derives from the word 'panorama', suggesting the wide visual field that a pan can reveal.

realism the aim for representations to reproduce reality faithfully, and the ways this is done.

close-up a camera shot where the frame is filled by the face of a person or a detail of a face. Close-ups may also show details of an object or place.

for the audience about what is expected to be funny. At these points the audience is encouraged to join in with the studio audience laughter and recognise the jokes or comic actions. Within the programme text, jokes and comic actions can be identified to some extent as **signs** of comedy. For example, a surprising contrast can be established between what characters say and what they do. Or in a scene involving two or more characters, surprising contrasts between the **discourse** of one and the discourse of another can provide the misunderstanding or conflict of interpretation that becomes comic. Excessive action such as slapstick or pretend violence can also function in this way. Yet sitcom is not the only television genre where each of these textual elements can be found, since shows based on short comic sketches, shows featuring impressionist performers such as Rory Bremner and cartoons can also exhibit several of the same characteristics. The genre of sitcom must be composed of a particular combination of elements such as:

- fictional narrative
- self-conscious performance
- jokes and physical comedy
- the presence of a studio audience denoted by laughter on the soundtrack.

Rather than claiming that sitcom has unique characteristics which define the genre, it is necessary to take account of signs and forms that overlap with other television genres.

Television comedy depends more than most kinds of television on the self-consciousness of performance, and the willingness of the audience to engage with the excessive speech and behaviour of characters that are designed to cue the recognition of a social norm and to surpass it in a manner which becomes funny. Frasier and Niles Crane in *Frasier*, for example, are snobbish and self-involved to the extent that their breaking of norms of behaviour becomes funny. The taping of sitcoms in the television studio using three camera set-ups where the set is open at one side to the studio audience underlines the theatricality and performance aspects of sitcom. The fact that actors will allow pauses in their dialogue for audience laughter, even occasionally acknowledging the audience by building its presence into the format of the series (as in the 'Tool Time' sequences of the American sitcom *Home Improvement*) where a television show is supposedly being recorded), encourages the **identification** of the television audience with the studio audience present at the taping of an episode. Focusing on performance in this way discourages the audience from judging speech and behaviour according to the norms of normality, and instead suspends these norms in order for them to be reacted against for comic purposes. The violence of the BBC sitcom *Bottom*, for example, in which characters attack each other with furniture and domestic objects, is made safe by being performance rather than narrative realism. But these analytical ways of describing how sitcom works are descriptions rather than explanations of how television programmes become funny. What is funny to one viewer may be quite different from what is funny to another, since humour does not only depend on social **codes** and cultural understanding that may be common across a broad age group, nation or region, or **gender**. What is funny also depends on the numerous and largely indiscoverable variables that make up an individual **subject**'s personality. For this reason the only major body of

---

discourse
a particular use of language for a certain purpose in a certain context (such as academic discourse, or poetic discourse), and similarly, in television, a particular usage of television's audio-visual 'language' (news programme discourse, or nature documentary discourse, for instance).

identification a term deriving from psychoanalytic theories of cinema, which describes the viewer's conscious or unconscious wish to take the place of someone or something in a television text.

code in semiotics, a system or set of rules that shapes how signs can be used, and therefore how meanings can be made and understood.

gender the social and cultural division of people into masculine or feminine individuals. This is different from sex, which refers to the biological difference between male and female bodies.

subject in psychoanalysis, the term for the individual self whose identity has both conscious and unconscious components.

analytical work on comedy derives from **psychoanalytic** criticism, and even this is less a theory of comedy than a descriptive account of how conscious and unconscious factors may predispose individuals to find certain kinds of speech and action amusing.

psychoanalysis
the study of human mental life, including not only conscious thoughts, wishes and fears but also unconscious ones. Psychoanalysis is an analytical and theoretical set of ideas as well as a therapeutic treatment.

ACTIVITY 5.5

Repeated programmes are often those which fall into established genres, and are advertised as 'classics' such as (in sitcom) *Dad's Army*, *The Good Life* and *Yes, Minister*. In what ways might audiences' pleasurable nostalgia for these programmes be the pleasure of their familiar generic form? Are 'classic' programmes always solidly generic?

Talk shows and the performance of morality

The genre of the television talk show has undergone significant changes in the past decade. Talk shows can be regarded as television representations of a **public sphere**. The public sphere is a conceptual space in which issues of concern to society as a whole can be debated, using the shared discourses and assumptions which are necessary to rational debate. As discussed earlier in this book, television provides instances of such debate and constitutes a public sphere, at the same time as contemporary broadcasting atomises individuals within their homes and fragments society into smaller and smaller **niche audiences**. Television's public sphere simulates the kind of democratic debate for which the term was first invented, both keeping alive the sense of the public sphere and at the same time standing in for an absent public debate in highly developed societies. American talk shows which rose to prominence in the 1970s, such as the *Oprah Winfrey* show and *Donahue*, conventionally focused on individual guests who represented a larger minority constituency which sought a voice. For example, black single mothers, the disabled or people struggling with drug addictions were able to give voice to an under-represented and stigmatised group, by individualising the problems of that group through the confessional and personal discourse of the guests. This ventilation of personal concerns, connected with the concerns of groups, was itself a mechanism of empowerment and resistance to dominant social values. The contributions of experts on the talk show connected the experiences of the guests to institutional discourses such as medicine, psychoanalysis and civil rights. The translation of personal experience into institutional discourses was also a mechanism of empowerment, though of course it also had the effect of incorporating resistance into society's dominant forms, and converting anger into some more socially acceptable force.

Beginning in the 1980s, however, the genre of the talk show has modulated into a much less liberal form of television with much less focus on empowerment and the valuation of resistant and excluded voices. The reason for this change in the genre is that broadcasters' research into audience preferences led to the creation of new programmes, and the reshaping of old ones, to gain new and larger audiences. Graeme Turner (Neale and Turner 2001: 6) notes that 'the cumulative effect

public sphere
the world of politics, economic affairs and national and international events, as opposed to the 'private sphere' of domestic life.

niche audiences
particular groups of viewers defined by age group, gender or economic status, for example, who may be the target audience for a programme.

of repeated tweaking of the format and content amounts to a change in genre' as 'more finely grained, and more readily available, viewing figures have the effect of influencing content, format and, ultimately, genre'. American television talk shows such as *The Jerry Springer Show* and the *Morton Downey Junior* show had become by the 1990s as internationally successful as *Oprah Winfrey* had been, but with a very different and much more aggressive attitude to their guests. The hosts of these programmes are much more inclined to make accusations against the opinions and behaviour of their guests than to support them in their resistance to a norm. The most commented-upon feature of these programmes is the prevalence of aggressive physical behaviour when guests confront each other in front of the cameras and the audience. For example, heterosexual couples appear as guests and suddenly it is revealed that the secret lover of one of them is also present without their knowledge. The confrontation between one of the partners and the lover has given rise to fist-fights between them, the throwing of furniture across the set, and the necessity for burly security guards to intervene from the edges of the television studio to separate the combatants. The role of the host, who has always functioned both as a representative for social norms signified by the collective audience behind him or her and as a mediator between the guest, the audience and experts, has become instead that of an orchestrator of confrontation and a ringleader encouraging the audience to vent its condemnation of one or more of the studio guests. The prominence of experts has diminished in parallel with this, so that the conversion of social exclusion and violent emotion into the rational terms of institutional discourses is much less the project of the programmes. A remnant of the liberal discourse of empowerment remains at the end of *The Jerry Springer Show*, however, when Jerry delivers his weekly three-minute address direct to camera, containing a more considered homily on the foibles of human nature. Nevertheless the transformation of the talk show genre demonstrates the erosion of these programmes as a public space in which liberal and democratic ideologies of inclusion, empowerment and personal development are enacted in television form. Instead, their ideology has become increasingly focused on the reinforcement of social norms, where audiences (represented by the studio audience) close their ranks against perceived deviance.

A further aspect of this development is the controversial centrality of performance to the talk show genre. There have been celebrated cases (for example in 1999 on the *Vanessa* and *Trisha* shows in Britain) when popular newspapers have revealed that some of the guests have been 'fakes'. Rather than members of the public discovered 'naturally' by programme researchers, these fake guests have been consciously performing their roles in order either simply to appear on television or to make money from appearance fees and **spin-off** newspaper and magazine features. The appetite for new guests on programmes sometimes broadcast every day during the week has led to the scavenging of guests from one show by the researchers on another, and the creation of an informal pool of guests who can be relied on to give dramatic and emotional performances. In the context of this emphasis on performance and the importance to programme **ratings** of guests' extreme emotional responses or violent outbursts, it is not surprising that the line between a 'genuine' and a 'fake' guest becomes blurred. The importance of the public display of guilt, shame and rage in the contemporary talk show further contributes to the blurring of the boundaries of the genre. These factors link the talk show to the dramatic fiction genre of soap opera, for example, where these emotions and their

spin-off
a product, television programme, book, etc. that is created to exploit the reputation, meaning or commercial success of a previous one, often in a different medium from the original.

ratings the number of viewers estimated to have watched certain programmes, as compared to the numbers watching other programmes.

exaggerated display are the focus of the narrative. Of course, it is no accident in this respect that both talk shows and soap opera are conventionally associated with, and scheduled to appeal to, a feminine sensibility and a female audience. For in Western societies it is a conventional attribute of **femininity** to display emotion openly, and to take an interest in the confessional revelations of others. Indeed the movement of many genres of programme mentioned in this chapter, such as documentary and actuality programmes, as well as soap opera and talk shows, towards these conventional attributes of femininity is in itself an interesting development in contemporary television. Programme genres, and their assumed audiences, appear to be moving toward a more generalised social dissemination of femininity.

feminine having characteristics associated with the cultural role of women and not men.

ACTIVITY 5.6

The preceding section suggested that contemporary television has introduced attributes conventionally associated with femininity (such as emotional display, confession and gossip) into a wide range of programmes genres. Are there 'masculine' genres? Which programmes would you include in these genres, and what makes them masculine?

Reality TV and social control

It has become commonplace for television not only to rely on **found footage** supplied by others, such as police camera footage or surveillance footage, but to install covert, hidden surveillance systems in order to generate **actuality** evidence of wrongdoing and criminality. Programmes such as Granada Television's *Rattrap*, *Nannies from Hell* and others in the *from Hell* series such as *Neighbours from Hell* or *Plumbers from Hell* have adopted this technique. There is an assumption behind these programmes that they are engaged in a public service, so that for example the advertisements in *Yellow Pages* and newspapers showing the company names of plumbing companies are shown on screen to inform viewers of exactly which businesses have been exposed as cowboys. Programme narrators provide tips and information on how to spot inferior and overpriced work, and give guide prices for what particular common jobs should cost. But there are several questions to ask about programmes like this. If the cowboy workers exposed by the programme are already known to be operating in dangerous and exorbitant ways, the programme does nothing to change this situation except add evidence. If large numbers of other workers have been shown doing the same work well, this footage would be undramatic and would not be used, though it may be the case that the vast majority of workers are both competent and reasonably priced. These programmes feature only the most disturbing and shocking incidents, and are necessarily unrepresentative.

found footage television or film sequences 'found' in previously made programmes or films, and which can be incorporated unchanged into the programme being made.

The audience for the first programme in the *from Hell* sequence of series, *Neighbours from Hell*, was 11.5 million in 1997. This is a much larger audience than is conventionally gained for documentary programmes in their more traditional forms. The *from Hell* format has been copied by the BBC, and sold by Carlton to America in 1999. By contrast, conventional documentary **strands** such as *World in Action* and *Panorama* have faced declining audiences and **schedule** positions later and later in the evening. The generic markers of documentary in its conventional form include the journalistic structuring of stories, where not only are events denoted but a 'balanced' selection of expert opinion offers opposing views and different contextual frameworks in which to understand them. Conventional documentary narrative hierarchises these elements so that a **hegemonic** discourse is established in which an issue is enfolded by the reliable and responsible discourse of the mediator represented both by the presenter and the television institution. The *from Hell* series and other kinds of quasi-documentary factual programmes focus instead on the dramatic and on barely contextualised actuality. One of the interesting consequences of this is the reduced importance of expertise and the discourse of professionals in making sense of the issues denoted in programmes. A different ideological pattern is being established. The discourses of expert professionals tended to value middle-class virtues:

- specialist knowledge
- rational discourse
- reasoned debate and discussion
- the solution of problems by institutional means.

But new documentary and actuality television formats replace this with something else. Risk, unpredictability and danger are represented as endemic to society, and institutions are represented as impossibly distant and too preoccupied with administrative and bureaucratic issues to deal with these problems. Instead, individuals are expected to monitor their own environments (often by using video technology to gather evidence and record deviance since the police and other authorities are too busy to undertake this themselves) and work out their own balance between accepting crime and nuisance and taking independent action against it. In this ideological framework nothing is certain, individuals are largely on their own and the future is viewed pessimistically. The generic shifts in the television documentary mode both represent and encourage shifts in ideology and the perception and meaning of society.

The grainy images from closed-circuit television which appear in reality segments of television programmes carry powerful political and social **connotations**. The places where **closed-circuit television** cameras are installed are often places where their job is to police the poor and those who are suspected of being socially deviant. Closed-circuit television cameras have become a popular means of controlling public space such as shopping malls and railway stations, in the absence of sufficient police to patrol them. The function of these cameras is to police the boundaries between normal and deviant or criminal behaviour, and sequences shot by closed-circuit television cameras appear in television programmes as evidence of deviance. The very visual style of the footage, grainy, in black and white, with still cameras, has come to be associated with the visible evidence of deviant behaviour and the identification of deviant people. Whereas documentary has a history of representing and arguing for those in society who are the least privileged, the most vulnerable to exploitation, and the most marginalized, the use of documentary footage from

---

strand a linked series of programmes, sharing a common title.

schedule the arrangement of programmes, advertisements and other material into a sequential order within a certain period of time, such as an evening, day or week.

hegemony a term deriving from Marxist theories of society, meaning a situation where different social classes or groups are persuaded to consent to a political order that may be contrary to their benefit.

connotations the term used in semiotic analysis for the meanings that are associated with a particular sign or combination of signs.

closed-circuit television a small-scale television system where the images and sound are not intended for broadcast, for example a network of security cameras.

closed-circuit television in reality television programmes has the opposite force. It is used to reinforce marginalisation, to deprive deviant behaviour and deviant people of the opportunity to explain and provide context for their actions, and to remove their actions from larger social and political contexts. It also generates anxiety for the audience, and potentially exaggerates the divisions between the employers of underpaid care workers and those workers themselves. The television audience is placed in the position of the 'normal' parent and may be encouraged to stigmatise and fear the young and often exploited care workers who appear in the programmes only as the perpetrators of disturbing crimes. In the case of *Nannies from Hell*, the mothers employing the nannies vowed to stay at home and care for their own children, thus also lending weight to conservative definitions of femininity and motherhood. The ideological action of the programme may have been to imply that mothers who work outside the home are both irresponsible and unnatural.

Reality TV is appropriate to a society which is increasingly under surveillance. One effect of this is to separate the scene of crime and deviant behaviour from the process of dealing with it by enforcing the law. Unfortunately, having camera footage of crimes does not guarantee that the criminals can be caught, or charges against them proved. The evidence that criminal behaviour has occurred is only a first stage in a long and complex process of investigation and prosecution. So the fact that television cameras can gather such apparently incontrovertible evidence has the effect of reassuring the audience that criminals can be identified, yet it does not automatically lead to the capture of criminals or the prevention of crime. A second effect of reality crime images like these is that they accustom the audience to the fact of being seen and potentially having images of oneself broadcast and judged. At any time, especially in a city, your movements can be captured by the many surveillance cameras in operation. The knowledge that you are being observed may well affect your behaviour. Not only in the sense that you might be persuaded not to commit a crime (perhaps this is a good thing), but you might also monitor yourself so that nothing you do could be misunderstood as a threatening or criminal activity. Loitering outside a shop, hanging around with a group of strangely dressed young people or approaching strangers to ask them questions might all be activities that could be misunderstood either as criminal behaviour itself or at least as suspicious behaviour. It is footage of activities like these that often appears on reality TV programmes as supporting evidence to show that a particular person had been behaving strangely and it identifies him or her as deviant. Knowing this, often unconsciously, affects the ways people act in public space.

Case study: true crime and fictional crime

This case study compares the generic form of the police series with reality TV programmes that use actuality footage of criminality (such as *Police, Camera, Action* or *America's Most Wanted*). Narratives in the police and detective genre begin with a disturbance in the social world depicted in the programme. A disruption, such as a murder, a robbery or an attack, has taken place, unsettling a family, community or business. It is the task of the police or detective to restore the equilibrium of the social world by:

continued

- finding the explanation for the disturbance
- removing the destructive force (usually a person who has committed the crime)
- providing the conditions for the restoration of order and balance.

The ideological work that the police series does is therefore to provide a means of representing society as a fundamentally ordered and balanced network of relationships, introducing a challenge or threat to society, and dramatising the ways in which this threat can be removed. In order to do this, the central character of the police officer or detective has to be established in the narrative as the representative of law and order. The police officer or detective embodies the values acceptable to the audience as the **consensus** view of right and wrong, and by his or her actions shows how ideological common-sense justice works in practice to keep society on a more or less normal and comfortable track.

consensus a shared and accepted opinion or attitude among a certain group of people.

But the ideology of society is not a single or stable structure. In the police series genre the conflicts within the central character, among the workers in the police institution, and conflicts between the upholders of the law and the criminals they pursue are often equally of interest. Inspector Morse, for example, sometimes overlooked the guilt of a murderer and let him or her go because of his respect or even admiration for the perpetrator of the crime. His sense of fair play, and moral justice, were occasionally at odds with the letter of the law and demonstrated that the character's ideological position could conflict with the normally unquestioned rightness of the law. The work of the narrative, establishing the central character in a complex and realistic way, can produce such a strong identification with the character that he or she appears superior to the system of law which he or she is engaged in supporting. It is commonplace in the police and detective genre for there to be conflicts between the central character and his or her superior within the police institution. The requirement to play by the rules of police procedure can in itself be an obstacle to upholding the law and solving a crime. The characteristics and forms of action used by the perpetrators of crime can be very similar to those of the policemen or detective. Telling lies, casual violence, disrespect for authority and rules are all characteristics which can be found both in the central characters and in the criminals whom they pursue. What distinguishes the police officer or detective from the criminal is the effectiveness of the methods they use, and the aim which justifies their behaviour. John Fiske and John Hartley (1978: 29) have argued that this similarity between police and criminal, and the value placed on efficiency, are symbolic means of presenting ideological conflicts:

commodity a raw material or product whose economic value is established by market price rather than the instrinsic qualities or usefulness of the material or product itself.

> What the police versus criminal conflict may enact symbolically, then, is the everyday conflict of a competitive society in which efficiency is crucial . . . The common concern that television police are becoming more and more like the criminals in their methods and morals, means that the few factors that distinguish them take on crucial significance. Of these distinctive features, efficiency is the most marked.

capitalism the organisation of an economy around the private ownership of accumulated wealth, involving the exploitation of labour to produce profit that creates such wealth.

The aim of a criminal might be to solve an emotional problem, for example by murdering a man with whom his wife is having an affair. Or the aim might be to make money by dealing in illegal **commodities** such as drugs or guns. In the first case the criminal has a misplaced sense of justice, and in the second case the criminal is misusing the **capitalist** system of business and exchange. Narratives in the police and detective genre establish some activities as criminal and excessive, as the misapplication of the principles which underlie a law-abiding society. The representation of crime on television is a means of defining the boundaries between the legal and the illegal in terms of the reasonable versus the excessive, though the desires and motivations behind legal and illegal behaviours may be exactly the same.

The mechanism for identifying the criminal and bringing him or her to justice is the acquisition of information. The process of the narrative is unusually taken up mainly in this process of acquiring different kinds of information, such as:

- the testimony of witnesses
- scientific forensic evidence
- observing the behaviour of suspects.

The task of the police officer or detective is to assemble this information into a narrative of the crime. So the narrative of the programme is occupied with the construction of this other narrative whose events occurred usually either before the beginning of the programme or in its opening few minutes. The closure of the narrative and the resolution of the programme are achieved when the police officer or detective has completed the assembly of the narrative of the crime. This narrative of the crime is presented to the perpetrator, or perhaps to a court or to the detective's superior. The programme can end when this narrative of the crime is confirmed as true, most often by the confession of the criminal. At this point the ideologically correct positions of the characters can be established: the criminal is captured, justice is done for the victims, the police officer or detective has done his or her job and the superior officer is satisfied. The stability of society and the security of the positions occupied by the various characters are confirmed.

The central characters of police and detective series often work in teams of two or more. One reason for this is that it provides opportunities for explaining plot points, evaluating the behaviour of witnesses and suspects and assessing evidence. Conversations between the central characters deal with the difficulty of following the internal cognitive processes by which the police officers or detectives go about solving the crime. In terms of the structure of characters, the difference between one and the other not only serves to create possible tension for the audience but also enables each character to make up for the insufficiencies of the other and supply his or her own special knowledge. Buddy teams in television police series include, for example, a younger and an older man, a man and a woman, a married woman and a single woman, a black man and a white man. The central characters of police series were most often unmarried men until the 1970s, and the work of restoring the ideological values of society, solving the problems represented by crime and embodying the values of justice were associated with heterosexual white masculinity. The introduction of buddy teams of police officers and detectives in more recent years has represented the challenge to the ideological centrality of white masculinity. Single central characters have been personally vulnerable in physical and emotional terms, and the individual members of buddy teams have been unable to function successfully as the vehicles of police genre narrative without the assistance of their partners to provide the knowledge and characteristics which they lack.

The majority of television police series are set in urban environments. The city is a place where people do not know each other, where people are mobile and can be difficult to trace. The plain clothes police officers and detectives are characters who can merge with the locality in which they work, and can work semi-independently of the hierarchy of the police institution. It is possible for the plain clothes police officers to go undercover and simulate the behaviour of the criminals whom they are seeking, and to operate in the same world with the same rules. In the confusing, anonymous and mobile environment of the city, the police officer or detective

continued

needs to take on some of the ambiguity, anonymity and mobility which enable criminals to undertake their crimes. In this environment appearances are deceptive. The narrative has to work hard to establish that, despite the apparent indistinguishability of the detectives and the criminals (in terms of their physical appearance, their behaviour, their attitudes), the police officers are fundamentally supporters of normality and justice, whereas the criminals are forces of violence, disorder and destruction. It is important that the central characters of the police genre are established as having an innate sense of justice. The detectives' success in catching criminals and doing the right thing is proof of their efficiency and the appropriateness of the ideologies which underlie their actions. The satisfying shape of the narrative, moving from an initial problem or disruption through investigation and the gathering of information, to a final resolution where balance and harmony are restored to the represented world, is itself part of the ideological work of the police genre. For the ordered structure of the narrative, its movement from beginning to middle to end, is itself a kind of proof that the assumptions and actions of its central characters are justified. The world of the police genre programme is set up so that the events in that world justify the behaviour of its central characters. The structure of the narrative supports the structure of ideology.

It is interesting to compare the ideological work of fictional police series drama with the ideological implications of programmes in the new genre of reality TV that deal with law and order. Reality TV accustoms the audience to perpetual surveillance and self-surveillance, and contributes to the installation of ideological norms within each subject. Knowing that we are potentially being observed by surveillance cameras, and therefore taking care to monitor our behaviour so that it conforms to the norms expected in our culture, amounts to the internalisation of surveillance. The observing camera has in effect become part of our own mental world. The self-monitoring and self-policing of behaviour are a powerful way of disciplining and controlling society, and eventually might promise that real policemen and real cameras could become no longer necessary. Each person would discipline and police himself or herself. This concept of internalising norms of behaviour is exactly how the concept of ideology has been explained in Media and Cultural Studies. As explained earlier in this book, an ideology is a taken-for-granted set of norms and assumptions which determines how the subject thinks of himself or herself, his or her relations to others and his or her place in society. Ideology is not imposed by force, but is gradually learnt and internalised through the institutions of the family, education, the media and culture in general.

Reality TV programmes customarily use hidden cameras whose images resemble those of the closed-circuit television systems used to gather evidence in police investigations and used in public space to monitor and police deviant behaviour. Those people who are pictured in such images in reality TV programmes are therefore already categorised as potentially deviant. The programme *Nannies from Hell*, for example, showed brief extracts from grainy black-and-white covert surveillance footage that 'proved' that particular nannies were physically abusing children. There is a danger of a rush to judgement in this television form, however, since it is very unusual for the people captured in this covert footage to have a right to defend themselves and reply to the accusations based on the footage. Explanation, justification, background and context are all factors which in a court of law might either excuse or at least explain such actions, but in reality TV the moment of seeing is simultaneously a moment of judging. The pleasure for the audience is in seeing something hidden, seeing the very moment when something shocking and disturbing is happening, and the provision of this pleasure takes much greater precedence than the investigation and exploration of the behaviour which is portrayed.

Police, Camera, Action (ITV) is a factual programme which has connections with both news and police drama. It consists of a collection of extracts from police camera footage linked by the narrating voice of Alastair Stewart. Stewart is a former newsreader, and the programme gains some of its connotations of **public service** from his association with the values of objectivity, seriousness and reliability which derive from television news programmes. The footage in the programme comprises mainly shots from the cameras installed in police cars, as they follow or chase drivers who are either engaged in criminal activities (such as making a getaway from a robbery) or committing dangerous driving errors. Television police series fiction revolves around identifying illegal acts and their perpetrators. What the policeman and detectives do is to discriminate between the innocent and the guilty, creating justice by finding out how crimes have been committed and capturing the people responsible for them. Television is a visual medium, and television drama relies particularly on following the point of view of the protagonist and on providing information through dialogue. The central characters of police series gather evidence by watching and observing. Seeing the scene of the crime and watching the behaviour and body language of suspects enable the central characters to establish the evidence which points to the guilty. Discussions between police officers and detectives give order and structure to the unfolding narrative of the case, while interviews and confrontations with witnesses and victims provide clues by spoken language, and also opportunities to observe the physical signs which might point to the guilty person. These processes in the police and detective genre place the central characters in a similar position to that of the television viewer. Both the viewer and the detective assemble fragments of information, and read clues and signs which promise to solve the case and to bring the narrative to a close.

Programmes using police camera footage sometimes also include closed-circuit television pictures from shops or other premises, and footage from police helicopter cameras used to track suspects who are being pursued. The car chase is of course a conventional element of the police drama series, especially American action police drama, where the chase normally occurs in the third quarter of the drama as a prelude to the capture of the criminal. Car-chase sequences in *Police, Camera, Action* do not have the several camera set-ups available to drama programmes, or the reverse shots showing the drivers of the police car, or of course shots representing the drivers who are being pursued inside their own cars. The visual quality of the police camera footage is less polished than professional television pictures and there is little alternation between points of view or manipulation of narrative time. But despite these important differences between this police camera footage and television narrative fiction, the function of the chase is still as an action sequence as a prelude to the capture of an offender. Dramatic music is used to underscore this excitement and anticipation, and the voice-over narration by Alastair Stewart adopts a point of view which mediates between the pursuing police's commentary and the anticipated reactions of a normative viewer. Stewart points out the stupidity of errors made by drivers, the recklessness of criminals attempting to escape from a chasing police car, the danger posed to other road users by these drivers and the damage and danger caused to the public by them. Since it is customary for police pursuit drivers to give a running commentary on their actions as they pursue an offender, there is also a **diegetic** soundtrack running alongside the pictures which helps to explain the action and provides Stewart's narration with a means of access to the police understanding of events. *Police, Camera, Action* draws connotations of public service and authority from news; it draws music, the narrative functions of the car chase and pursuit from the police drama series, and the visual conventions of the surveillance camera and found actuality footage from

public service
in television, the
provision of a mix
of programmes that
inform, educate and
entertain in ways
that encourage
the betterment
of audiences and
society in general.

diegesis the telling
of events as
narrative. Diegetic
sound is sound
emanating from the
represented
environment, and
extra-diegetic sound
comes from outside
that environment.

continued

documentary. It is a hybrid composed of the codes of several different television genres. Graeme Turner (Neale and Turner 2001: 7) has explained the conflicting forces at work in situations such as this by arguing that

> The "liveness" of television, its investment in immediacy and provisionality, is in direct conflict with the regulated production imperatives implied by genre and format. Further, the cultural richness of the television message, its capacity to carry an excess of meaning for its viewing audience, means that the television message is always difficult to control.

While genre is a way of drawing boundaries between one kind of programme and another, the television industry's perpetual search for new combinations of generic elements and the audience's skill in 'reading' genre in complex ways mean that genre boundaries are always being redrawn by viewers and programme-makers.

ACTIVITY 5.7

This case study has argued that 'true crime' reality footage combines the observational conventions of documentary with the narrative oppositions between 'us' and 'them' in police fiction drama. Do 'true crime' programmes also reassure the audience that order will triumph over deviance, or is this an alibi to protect programme-makers from accusations of exploitation?

SUMMARY OF KEY POINTS

- Genre study is a way of dividing up and classifying groups of television programmes, and also understanding how viewers make use of genre in order to undertand and enjoy programmes.
- Television theorists have debated whether genre is a property of television texts themselves, or a way for viewers and critics to understand them.
- All television texts participate in genre to some extent, and often participate in several genres simultaneously.
- Different genres of television programme address their audiences in different ways, and reveal different assumptions about the interests, pleasures and social meanings of programmes in that genre.
- Comparing and contrasting programmes from different genres can illuminate the similarities and differences in how television deals with related ideas and themes.

Further reading

Allen, R., *Speaking of Soap Operas* (Chapel Hill, S.C.: University of South Carolina Press, 1985).

Ang, I., 'Melodramatic identifications: television fiction and women's fantasy', in C. Brunsdon, J. D'Acci and L. Spigel (eds), *Feminist Television Criticism: A Reader* (Oxford: Oxford University Press, 1997), pp. 155–66.

Brunsdon, C., *The Feminist, the Housewife, and the Soap Opera* (Oxford: Oxford University Press, 2000).

—— 'Structure of anxiety: recent British television crime fiction', *Screen*, 39:3 (1998), pp. 223–43.

Buckingham, D., *Public Secrets: EastEnders and its Audience* (London: BFI, 1987).

Clarke, A., '"You're nicked!": television police series and the fictional representation of law and order', in D. Strinati and S. Wagg (eds), *Come on Down?: Popular Media Culture in Post-war Britain* (London: Routledge, 1992), pp. 232–53.

Corner, J., *Critical Ideas in Television Studies* (Oxford: Clarendon, 1999).

—— *Television Form and Public Address* (London: Edward Arnold, 1995).

Creeber, G. (ed.), *The Television Genre Book* (London: BFI, 2001).

Dahlgren, P., *Television and the Public Sphere* (London: Sage, 1995).

Dovey, J., *Freakshow* (Cambridge: Polity, 2000).

Dyer, R., C. Geraghty, M. Jordan, T. Lovell, R. Paterson and J. Stewart, *Coronation Street* (London: BFI, 1981).

Feuer, J., 'Genre study and television', in R. Allen (ed.), *Channels of Discourse, Reassembled* (London: Routledge, 1992), pp. 138–60.

Geraghty, C., *Women and Soap Opera: A Study of Prime Time Soaps* (Cambridge: Polity Press, 1991).

Kidd-Hewitt, D. and R. Osborne (eds), *Crime and the Media: The Postmodern Spectacle* (London: Pluto, 1995).

Lacey, N., *Narrative and Genre: Key Concepts in Media Studies* (Basingstoke: Macmillan, 2000).

Livingston, S. and P. Lunt, *Talk on Television: Audience Participation and Public Debate* (London: Routledge, 1994).

Neale, S. and F. Krutnik, *Popular Film and Television Comedy* (London: Routledge, 1990).

Neale, S. and G. Turner, 'Introduction: what is genre?', in G. Creeber (ed.), *The Television Genre Book* (London: BFI, 2001), pp. 1–7.

Rose, B. (ed.), *TV Genres: A Handbook and Reference Guide* (Westport, Conn.: Greenwood, 1985).

Shattuc, J., *The Talking Cure: TV Talk Shows and Women* (London: Routledge, 1997).

Sparks, R., *Television and the Drama of Crime* (Buckingham: Open University Press, 1992).

Wagg, S. (ed.), *Because I Tell a Joke or Two: Comedy, Politics and Social Difference* (London: Routledge, 1998).

Television Production

genre a kind or type of programme. Programmes of the same genre have shared characteristics.

slot the position in a television schedule where a programme is shown.

treatment a short written outline for a programme, usually written for a commissioning producer to read, specifying how the programme will tell its story or address its subject.

pitch a very short written or spoken outline for a programme, perhaps only a few sentences, often used to persuade a commissioning producer to commission the programme.

location any place in which television images are shot, except inside a television studio.

storyboard a sequence of drawn images showing the shots to be used in a programme.

director the person responsible for the creative process of turning a script or idea into a finished programme, by working with a technical crew, performers and an editor.

off-line editing the first stage of editing a completed programme, where the sequence of shots, sounds and music is established.

online editing the final stage of editing a completed programme, where effects are added and a high-quality version of the programme is produced.

Television Production

Introduction

The stages in television programme production discussed in this chapter are:

- *development*, where programme ideas are being worked out, researched and planned in an audio-visual form appropriate to a certain television **genre**, **slot** and size of budget, and where the **treatment**, budgets and **pitch** are devised.
- *pre-production*, where after commissioning further research is conducted for **locations** and contributors or performers are selected, the script is written, **storyboards** and production schedules are drawn up, and the design, props, costumes and music are selected.
- *production*, when the shooting takes place, following the plan outlined in the budget and schedule, using the **director**, performers, presenters, contributors and the technical crew that have been selected and organised at the pre-production stage.
- *post-production*, when editing takes place, normally first **off-line** at below broadcast quality, then **online** editing is completed, when effects and sound mixing are achieved. At the end of this process final accounts are prepared.

The chapter discusses the many professional roles involved in making television, with emphasis on the creative and managerial roles of producer, director, screenwriter, editor and camera operator. It is not possible in the space available here to provide as much detailed descriptive information about these roles, or the competences needed to carry them out to professional standards, as can be found in the many 'how-to' books on the market about television production. A few such books are listed in the Further reading section at the end of the chapter. Nevertheless, the chapter considers the different roles in television programme-making and gives an overview of the different stages of the production process, including some of its key terminology. The chapter includes practical exercises which individuals or groups can work on in order to explore these processes for themselves. The aim of this chapter is to develop an analytical understanding of how television production communicates with audiences through the skills and techniques used by professional television-makers. The assumption behind it is that learning about television is not only a critical and theoretical enterprise: television is an industry, a technology and a set of working practices. So the student of television should understand the broad principles of audio-visual composition by learning about the production practices that bring programmes into being, watching a range of television programmes to consider their audio-visual strategies and gaining as much experience as possible of making his or her own short television films in creative and reflective ways.

Television has been for a long time regarded as a producer's medium, meaning that the television producer has the predominant authority over and responsibility for television-making. While there are several other roles that could claim such creative and managerial authority, particularly those of director and scriptwriter, this chapter devotes the greatest space to the key elements of the producer's role. The producer contributes to the process of selecting and working with writers, controls the process of making a programme, and fulfils a responsibility to the television institution that has commissioned the programme by overseeing budgets, personnel, the production schedule and the delivery of the programme. The chapter explains how producers work with a script editor and production assistants in this process, as well as with creative personnel on the production such as the director, performers and designers. As far as possible the chapter offers a discussion that can apply across the genres of factual and fictional television production, but there are specific discussions of genres that have particular patterns of organisation and production, such as the independent documentary in contrast to the big-budget drama. News is not discussed in this chapter (for news production, see Harrison 2000), and nor is the making of television commercials, because the emphasis is on the major contemporary modes of drama and documentary and the ways that their production can be explored in simple practical exercises.

ACTIVITY 6.1

Watch the opening and closing credits of several programmes chosen from different genres (e.g. documentary, news, drama, game show). Compare the total number and different job titles of people listed in the credits. What conclusions can you draw from your analysis about the relative significance of members of the production team (including performers and presenters) in the different genres?

Development

Although the production of television programmes is a linear process from the initial idea to the final broadcast of the programme, making programmes demands anticipation of later stages at every point in the process. An initial idea will need to be shaped so that it will appeal to the audience imagined by the programme-maker. So right from the start the programme-maker will have an audience in mind for the subject, style, genre, aesthetic form and pace of the programme. As the production continues, this sense of the audience may be modified, but it will always be present as a check on the probable effectiveness of each individual decision. At the same time, programmes will have been pitched to producers or commissioning editors, so the idea and the intended process of its realisation will also need to appeal to those people. Although there is potential conflict, then, between the programme-maker's conception of the audience appeal of a programme and the commissioning producer's or editor's conception of the programme's appeal, this degree of difference or similarity may vary considerably. For example, a scriptwriter may be primarily motivated by a sense that his or her documentary or drama production will communicate important messages about gender, ambition, legislation, fear, love, courage or whatever other idea the programme-maker wishes to communicate. The scriptwriter's sense that the audience will be informed, educated or entertained by his or her project may not be shared by the producer or commissioning editor to whom the idea is pitched. In practice there is always a process of negotiation between all of the parties involved in making a television programme, and it is the responsibility of all the parties involved to maintain the integrity of their ideas yet also to be persuaded by the ideas of the others. So tensions, power-struggles and ulterior motives are endemic to television production, as well as the more positive factors of teamwork, creative co-operation and pride in one's expertise.

Whereas cinema has been a medium in which the director has creative control over the film, in television considerably more power is wielded by the producer. Television producers manage all the staff involved in the making of a production, including the director, and have traditionally enjoyed a more secure position in employment. Producers working for large broadcasting institutions will have control over a whole series of programmes, and are likely to employ directors, writers, performers and technical staff on a more ad-hoc basis for individual programmes in a series. Even though broadcasting institutions have contracted out increasing proportions of television production since the 1980s in Britain, independent producers as well as producers working for large institutions remain the central figures in the planning, shooting and post-production of television programmes. Producers are primarily managers, but they also work closely with creative staff and require a broad range of knowledge. Their primary role is to lead the team making a programme, to deliver that programme to a deadline imposed by the institution which has commissioned it and to maintain a standard of quality that will ensure approval from industry colleagues and prospects of further work. The skills needed to achieve this include:

- management skills of wielding authority effectively while maintaining the coherence and harmony of the production team
- commitment to the project
- an ability to understand and evaluate the work of others.

copyright the legal right of ownership over written, visual or aural material, including the prohibition on copying this material without permission from its owner.

Since television programmes are subject to a range of legal considerations such as **copyright**, health and safety, and libel and defamation, the producer needs also to know the basics of these legal frameworks as well as the guidelines provided by broadcasting organisations. Since producers will be managing technical specialists such as camera operators, lighting and sound technicians, graphic artists, designers and editors, they need to know enough about these areas of expertise in order to recruit them and manage and evaluate their work.

In many television genres the producer will need writing skills in order to advise scriptwriters and to edit and sometimes rewrite their work, and an understanding of the visual and sound qualities of television that will be used to realise a programme idea or script. In drama programmes producers work closely with writers and may often have experience and skill in writing themselves. Pitching a programme for commissioning will be done on the basis of a storyline created by a writer, and the episodes of a series, serial or a single television film will be planned, shot and post-produced starting from a script bought from a professional writer. The relationships built up between producers and writers are crucial to the success of television programmes. In factual genres such as **documentary**, even though a programme will not be scripted for performance in the same way as a drama, nevertheless producers are required to have some skill in writing. Documentaries also require scripts, often including written sequences of voice-over, and will be pitched and commissioned on the basis of written outlines. As discussed earlier in this book, documentary is a form of storytelling as well as a genre in which realities are represented, and documentary producers need to be aware of **narrative** structure, structures of argument and the production of dramatic effects, all of which are skills inherited from and connected with the written forms of journalism, drama and literature.

documentary
a form aiming
to record actual
events, often with an
explanatory purpose
or to analyse and
debate an issue.

narrative an
ordered sequence
of images and sound
that tells a fictional or
factual story.

David Chase, writer-producer and creator of *The Sopranos*

David Chase, creator and producer of *The Sopranos*, went to film school and wanted to be an arthouse *auteur*. But he couldn't sell a film of his own so he wrote for television (for the 1970s detective series *The Rockford Files*, for instance). He continued to develop his best film idea, about a tough mobster and his annoying mother. The mobster feels he has to care for her, but she is in some ways tougher than him and even contracts a killer to murder her son. Insight into the mobster's dilemmas about family, violence and power are provided by the device of having him talk to a psychoanalyst. The drama works by the collision and tension between two behavioural codes: the mobster must be tough and secretive, whereas the psychoanalyst expects speech to reveal and unload worrying emotions and weaknesses. The psychological context allows for non-naturalistic forms like dream sequences, in contrast to the naturalistic portrayal of the details of organised crime. Chase's idea became series one of *The Sopranos*. Fox Television commissioned *The Sopranos*, but Chase felt they were trying to smooth out and tame the ideas they had seen in the pilot scripts he showed them. So he took the idea to HBO Original Programming, which supported the tone and ideas of the script. *The Sopranos* contains a mix of genres – family story and mob gangster show – and has achieved the status of 'quality television': aesthetically interesting, psychologically and morally complex, yet sufficiently connected to existing genres and forms to draw large audiences.

ACTIVITY 6.2

Use a few short sentences and simple drawings to create a character on which a short drama can be built. Specify as closely as possible the age, gender, race, history and occupation of the person. Think of a simple activity (cleaning shoes, hanging a picture, talking on the phone) that you could shoot using basic video equipment. Draw seven simple pictures in a sequence (a storyboard) to show how the activity could be shot to reveal the character, using only static wide shots, mid-shots and close-ups.

Figure 6.1 Example of a storyboard. Courtesy of Jeremy Orlebar.

serial a television form where a developing narrative unfolds across a sequence of separate episodes.

series a television form where each programme in the series has a different story or topic, though settings, main characters or performers remain the same.

Pre-production

Producers working in **series** or **serial** television depend heavily on the quality of the scripts they can obtain for their programmes. Production planning will typically begin more than a year before any shooting takes place, and at this stage storylines and scripts need to be commissioned and approved. Maintaining connections with writers, and finding new writers to contribute to the series, are therefore important aspects of the producer's job. During the pre-production process producers will often spend considerable amounts of time outside their office in discussions with writers, seeking ideas and negotiating terms for scripts. For a run of thirteen programmes, for example, producers may need to commission several more scripts than actually get used, to allow for late delivery, refusal of a script by the producer or his or her superior owing to cost implications, unsuitability for the agreed format or conflicts with production guidelines or ethical standards. Even when scripts have been delivered, the producer and the script editor will continue to work on them. Revisions may be required in order to make the script shootable within the agreed budget. Extensive rewriting or polishing of the script can be necessary in order to:

- maintain continuing characters
- adapt scripts to the strengths or weaknesses of performers
- add or remove special design elements or effects.

Because of the numerous other demands on producers, script editors often do much of the detailed work in revising scripts and consulting with writers, and this extensive experience enables script editors to build up expertise and contacts which later enable them to become producers themselves. It is conventionally agreed in the television industry that writers retain credit for the scripts they produce, although in practice the script used during the shooting itself may well have been extensively revised by a script editor and the producer. The authorship of television programmes is there-fore difficult to assign to one person: in practice, authorship is a collective activity involving the whole production team.

In television, the rare single television play and the increasingly common mini-series or low-frequency repeated drama (such as the police drama *Prime Suspect*) are marked by their prominent display of the author's name (Murdoch 1980). The theatrical inheritance in television production leads to the privilege granted within drama to the writer and the notion of creativity. In contrast, all soap operas and high-frequency repeated dramas use a team of writers, either invariant in number or supplemented and exchanged with other writers at intervals. Series are usually commissioned from a single author or an already constituted team of authors, for a contractually agreed number of scripts. Television is regarded by writers as an instrument in which their creative work is distributed to an audience, as well as an occupation that makes them a living. But the script may be altered or drastically changed. It is not simply a transcription of dialogue but also an interrelated set of instructions for all the professional workers involved in production. For the produc-tion team and performers the script directs and restricts their activities. It is the authority to which interpretative and expressive questions are referred, through the figure of the director, who controls the process of realising the written word, such that the script is finally exhausted by being 'translated' into a television programme. In this sense the script is unlike a play text, which not only is performed more than once, but can be transferred between companies and is subject to entirely different interpretations.

Storylines in *Coronation Street*

Coronation Street did not perform too well in 2001. Its stories were driven largely by plot rather than character, despite a cast of more than fifty, and its recently arrived executive producer Carolyn Reynolds decided to concentrate more on the core characters. Reynolds had worked on the programme for over twenty years, as a production assistant, then producer, then as executive producer in the mid-1990s. As executive producer she has a strategic remit to integrate *Coronation Street* with Granada Television's other drama output, with the producer Kieran Roberts (formerly working on *Emmerdale*) running the programme week to week. Granada Television's new director of programmes, John Whiston, explained:

> There are tensions between storyliners, who want a story that gets them logically and clearly to a particular point, and writers, who want to free up enough time for their characters to be what they want them to be. If the balance swings too far to the storyliners, you get a very plot-driven show that is a bit ploppy and for my money there has been too much emphasis on the storyliners.
>
> (Moss 2002: 2)

The background to this shift in power from storyline (plot) to characters (script) is audience ratings: *Coronation Street* was challenged strongly by *EastEnders* in 2001. Partly because *EastEnders* has an omnibus edition at the weekend, *EastEnders'* ratings have almost always exceeded those of *Coronation Street*. Granada TV executives, and the programme's producers, make strategic management decisions about the programme based on their perceptions of audience demands and the balance of power between the staff in their production team.

Although a producer may have the initial idea for a programme in factual genres such as documentary, he or she relies on researchers to flesh out the details of the topic and find contributors. Researchers in factual television are normally young people with a background or interest in journalism, who are often aiming to move up the professional hierarchy into the role of producer or director. Researchers work for producers, who in turn are employed by executive producers contracted to oversee the making of a series of programmes. The sources of programme research are varied, and include not only resources in the control of television institutions but also numerous outside sources, most of which can be accessed free of charge. Researchers will commonly rely on a list of contacts established in earlier projects, such as experts based in academic institutions, government-funded policy units and charities, and a varied collection of people who have contributed to research for previous programmes or appeared in them. These sources do not normally require payment, though researchers can spend a lot of time on the telephone attempting to make contact with them and to shape their contribution into a form useful to a programme. Sources available to researchers within broadcasting institutions are now more accessible with the advent of computer databases, which make possible access to the institution's own archives, previous programmes and libraries of press clippings. However, since programme-making is increasingly contracted out to independent companies who must conduct research at their own expense and using their own facilities, the resources built up by large organisations such as the BBC are not accessible to the researchers working on many contemporary programmes. Research sources such as newspaper archives and libraries can be important to programme research, but the pressure of time and the requirement to travel make it more likely for today's programme researchers to go direct to people they can telephone to request instant information. Working in this way demands various skills from researchers, particularly persistence, diplomacy and persuasion, since information sources will normally see their contribution as an additional unpaid responsibility outside their normal work. But organisations that have a vested interest in providing information to publicise or support their cause can be very helpful: for example charities may be willing to supply packs of information, documents and spokespeople, and may be keen to contribute directly to programmes by providing experts. Clearly, the ulterior motives of research sources and contributors need to be assessed carefully by researchers, and potential problems referred upward to the producer for whom they are working.

New programmes are commissioned on the basis of a **treatment**. This is a short document of one or two pages which organises the ideas on which the programme is based, and provides an indication of its structure, cost and target audience. A treatment normally begins with one or two sentences stating the idea of the programme, followed by an indication of the target audience. Then the style of the production will be outlined, including the creative approach to be taken (for example documentary or drama, location or studio, on-screen narrator or presenter, cinematic or arthouse style, **observational** or narrated documentary). The structure and content section of the treatment is in effect a condensation of the script, where scenes and sequences are briefly described. A storyboard can be used to give a more precise indication of the key visual sequences in the programme. The treatment will specify the level of equipment used to shoot and edit the programme, and provide background information on the creative team and the skills of the technical staff to be used. The budget completes the treatment. Writing production budgets is a skilled and complex task, but the basic principles are to establish the number of days required to shoot the programme and the editing time required to complete it. These facts will determine the cost of employing the people in front of the camera and behind it, who are employed at daily or hourly rates. Shooting days on location are more difficult to estimate because of such factors as travel to and from locations and between locations, and variables such as weather. Editing time is also difficult to estimate, since sequences cut to music can be very complex to edit, whereas interview contributions to a documentary programme can be edited directly into a finished master tape. On average, a programme-maker could expect to edit about ten minutes of a finished programme in one day. Nevertheless, the basic elements of a budget can be listed on a spreadsheet such as the one shown, based on an imaginary two-episode 180-minute medium-to-high-budget drama for the BBC, shot mainly on film on location:

observational documentary
a documentary form in which the programme-maker aims to observe neutrally what would have happened even if he or she had not been present.

Budget category	Estimated cost (£)
Story and script	100,000
Producer's and director's fees	150,000
Main cast	75,000
Sub total	**325,000**
Production management	90,000
Assistant director	40,000
Camera crew	50,000
Sound crew	20,000
Editorial staff	55,000
Stills camera staff	1,500
Wardrobe staff	35,000
Make-up staff	15,000
Casting	25,000
Production accountants	50,000
Art department	70,000
Supporting cast	130,000
Stand-ins, doubles and stunts	30,000
Crowd	55,000
Music	50,000
Costumes and wigs	15,000
Productions stores	7,500
Film and laboratory charges	75,000
Studio rental	90,000
Equipment	100,000
Travel and transport	100,000
Studio and other transport	15,000
Hotels and living expenses	60,000
Studio hotels and living expenses	3,000
Sub total	**1,182,000**
Insurances	15,000
Publicity	5,000
Miscellaneous expenses	20,000
Construction labour	10,000
Construction materials	20,000
Set dressing labour	20,000
Operating labour	30,000
Lighting and spotting labour	40,000
Properties	65,000
Special effects	10,000
Location facilities	80,000
Sub total	**315,000**

Finance and legal	75,000
Total above the line	**325,000**
Total below the line	**1,572,000**
Grand total	**1,897,000**

Figure 6.2 Example of a programme budget.

The categories in this budget should be mainly self-explanatory, and are divided into:

- 'above-the-line' costs relating to the pre-production staff and tasks, and
- 'below-the-line' costs relating to the period of production itself.

The budget would also be broken down into sub-categories under each of the above headings, with each sub-category having an estimated cost attached to it. The 180-minute drama using this budget is of course a quite expensive production, but usefully illustrates the approximate costs of all commonly used categories of staff and service in television production. A low-budget documentary using a small crew, no performers (also known as 'talent') and shooting on digital video cameras would of course be much cheaper.

Because of the very high costs of drama production, for instance, co-production deals with broadcasters or production companies in the United States or Europe are a frequent means of support for British programmes. Co-production is increasingly common in all genres of television production. This is not only the case with major broadcasters such as the BBC, which has a long-standing track record of co-production agreements with the United States (Arts and Entertainment Network, the Discovery Channel, the PBS non-commercial channel) and regional broadcasters in Germany and other European countries. Independent production companies in Britain also seek to finance drama by making agreements with programme financiers in a range of countries, such as Canal Plus in France, the ABC network in Australia and a range of smaller institutions worldwide. In factual television certain genres such as the nature documentary are well-established formats in which co-production contributes significantly to the budget. In the case of nature programmes the key production expense is filming on location, spending large amounts of time and money seeking interesting footage despite difficulties in locating rare animals, coping with difficult weather conditions, working without adequate technical support and recruiting local staff on an ad-hoc basis to support the production. But if good-quality footage can be obtained, the resulting film will be adaptable for translation of its commentary into innumerable languages, and can be sold to a large number of international buyers. Genres in which this kind of translation and suitability to a wide range of markets is more difficult, such as documentaries on British social problems, may be much more difficult to finance by co-production. But even if a co-production deal is forthcoming, producers need considerable expertise in negotiating the legal contractual arrangements. Negotiating with co-production partners for rights to broadcast in particular territories, or for worldwide rights, and making agreements about such potentially lucrative income streams as **merchandising**, and the distribution rights of programmes on video for retail sales, requires specialist legal advice.

Television directors are appointed by the producer. This usually occurs on the basis of the producer's previous contact with the director, or the producer's knowledge of the director's strengths and weaknesses as exhibited in earlier work. A director may be known for work in a particular genre, or work which involves the use of particular television forms. For example, some directors will specialise in working closely with actors, and may be best suited to television drama where there is the budget and time to develop performances and explore the possibilities of the script prior to shooting. On the other hand, some directors may be particularly skilled in working quickly on productions with a limited budget and time, where their effectiveness in getting several pages of script shot in a small number of takes would be the primary reason for the producer to employ them. Television drama such as soap opera clearly needs directors with these skills, since performers and characters are already established and the main requirement is to complete the required number of scenes in only a few days' filming. Yet other directors may be schooled in integrating particular technical processes or services into a production. Integrating effects shots, model shots and post-produced digital effects for science fiction television is a particular directorial skill, while directing in inhospitable locations far from base or working with unpredictable animals may be important for the director of a nature documentary programme. Once appointed, the director will be provided with the script and will engage in extensive discussions with the producer about the choices of lesser performers, members of the technical team and the selection of music and costumes, for example. Because the director is responsible for

merchandising the sale of products associated with a television programme, such as toys, books or clothing.

Figure 6.3 David Attenborough with an iguana in *Living With Dinosaurs*, BBC1, 2000. Photograph by Simon Smith, courtesy of BBC Photograph Library.

the final look of the programme, and the aesthetic style achieved by the use of vision and sound, he or she has considerable input into the production process, though the responsibility and control of the production will ultimately rest with the producer.

ACTIVITY 6.3

Using the storyboard and brief treatment you created in Activity 6.2, decide how you would cast a performer to play the character, and how you would choose a setting and any costume or props needed without spending any money. How would you use a short voice-over narration in the first person ('I') or third person ('he' or 'she') and some music to give tone and meaning to your seven shots? Write the narration and obtain your music.

Production

The five most common types of camera and tape or film stock used in television broadcasting are:

- *VHS, or Super VHS*: the cheapest camera and tape equipment, commonly used for training in non-professional and non-vocational institutions such as schools and many universities. It is not good enough for broadcast.
- *DV*: digital cameras and tape producing higher-quality images than VHS on cameras and tape stock that can be bought from conventional retail outlets, and edited on inexpensive home computer equipment. DV is commonly used in educational institutions and the early stages of vocational training. It is good enough for broadcast in some genres of documentary programming.
- *Beta SP*: digital camera and tape formats available from professional sources, used for a lot of low-budget television production and corporate video-making, and requires editing facilities available through professional facilities houses and broadcasting institutions.
- *Digital Betacam* (DigiBeta): a higher-quality professional format that is more expensive in camera and tape costs, and more expensive to edit. Higher-budget television productions use this format.
- *16 mm or 35 mm* film: a format that has become increasingly rare in television production although it is still used for high-budget drama productions. The cost of this equipment and associated hardware (such as camera **dollies**) as well as the film stock and professional editing of footage are rarely justified for television programme-making now that small lightweight digital cameras have become more accessible and cheaper.

> dolly a wheeled camera platform. A 'dolly shot' is a camera shot where the camera is moved forward or back using this platform.

Human vision is binocular, meaning that having two eyes close to each other but in different positions provides two slightly different images of the world which the brain interprets as a three-dimensional image that has depth and perspective. While cameras are designed to mimic many features of human vision, television pictures are noticeably flatter so that techniques of lighting, sound and shot composition are used to produce the impression of depth and coherence in the space which is shot. Programme-makers have to have in mind the relationships of one shot to another, and when they talk about shots which 'will cut' or shots which 'won't cut' they are describing shots which will connect with the previous and subsequent sequences or not. Shots which will cut are those where the point of view of the camera and the relationships that comprise the shot composition fit the conventions of editing to be used in the programme. Shots which will not cut are those where conventions are not being followed and for the viewer there will appear to be a leap from one represented space to another, from one camera point of view to another, in a way which does not respect the coherence of the narrative or the coherence of the space which has been shot. In drama, for example, the conventions of a shot-reverse shot will allow alternations of point of view between speakers so long as the camera does not break the **180 degree rule**. The position of the camera in individual shots and the use of camera movement have to be planned in advance so that one shot will cut with another. In documentary and other factual genres, relationships between shots also have to respect audience expectations of how figures and spaces are represented. **Noddy shots** and **cutaways** are used to provide bridges between shots, and voice-over, music or other sound are also used to produce the impression of coherence and continuity.

180 degree rule the convention that cameras are positioned only on one side of an imaginary line drawn to connect two performers in a scene. This produces a coherent sense of space for the viewer.

noddy shot in television interviews, shots of the interviewer reacting silently (often by nodding) to the interviewee's responses to questions.

cutaway in fictional dialogue or interviews, shots that do not include people speaking. Cutaways often consist of details of the setting or of interviewees (such as hands).

Camera style in *Attachments*

Attachments is a drama serial based on the workplace lives of staff constructing a website, seethru.co.uk (the website exists, and follows the fictional story of the programme). The camera style of *Attachments* (World Productions for BBC2) evolved from decisions by Simon Heath (the producer) and Tony Garnett (head of World Productions) to match the static environment of the company office with no moving camera work, to emphasise the close attention to details on computer screens that the characters' work involved by using a lot of close-up shots and to allude to the very wide shot size of webcams by including wide shots covering the entire office space. Simon Heath commented in an unpublished interview with Helen Quinney in 2001:

> The energy of the show would come from its cutting style, which itself was a product of having lots of different angles on a scene. We were going for big wide shots which would take in the whole of the office, and then an ordinary close-up, and then a much tighter close-up that would highlight eyes, or mouth – the sort of detail you don't necessarily get on television but that you sometimes get in cinema. And then by fast cutting between different sizes and different angles and different characters in the scene, we'd generate an energy in the same way that a panning camera gave us the energy in *This Life* [World Productions' earlier hit drama serial].

In keeping with the interest in naturalism that Garnett and his collaborators have shown since the 1960s, the filming aesthetic of *Attachments* allows figures to be shot in profile, sometimes with objects masking them, and even shooting through window blinds. By breaking some of the rules of television camera technique, the drama found an aesthetic appropriate to the setting, characters and subject.

ACTIVITY 6.4

Going back to your treatment, storyboard and choices of narration and music from the previous exercises, revise your storyboard to make it conform to broadcast conventions of shot size, cutting for narrative coherence, and integration of image, speech and music. Then make changes to some of these aspects of the sequence to try out more radical strategies. You should end up with plans for two different short films.

The conventional forms of television shooting seemed to centre on sets of three. The three most commonly used shot sizes are **long shot**, **close-up** and a range of medium-long and medium close-ups in between. To create a coherent sense of space, sequences often begin with a long shot to establish the environment, followed by alternations between mid-shot and close-up to follow the action. In studio production for both factual and fiction genres, three camera positions are the standard minimum for covering the studio space and offering the director choices of long shot, mid-shot and close-up from each camera. In location shooting for drama, scenes shot with one camera will normally be played three times, with the camera positioned in three different places: a general view for establishing shots and cutaways, with the remaining two positions used for shot-reverse shot cutting between two points of view on the action. A similar three-position format is used for documentary subjects and interviews, so that mid-shots or close-ups of contributors and presenters can be alternated either with close-ups or with wide shots to be used as cutaways. The reasons for this apparent rule of three are that:

long shot a camera shot taking in the whole body of a performer, or more generally a shot with a wide field of vision.

close-up a camera shot where the frame is filled by the face of a person or a detail of a face. Close-ups may also show details of an object or place.

- a single point of view is conventionally regarded as boring
- alternations between two points of view can appear unrelated if there is not a third shot to bridge them
- more than three shot sizes for cameras can appear confusing to audiences.

Figure 6.4 Shot-reverse shot. Photographs courtesy of Jeremy Orlebar.

Published guides to television production focus almost exclusively on the standard conventions for shooting and develop these conventions in much more detail. But as the boxed text on *Attachments* shows, interesting ways of adapting these rules of three, or even breaking the rules radically, produce the most creative and involving programmes.

Shot composition allows the relationships between people, and between people and things, to be expressed in spatial terms. There are basic conventions of shot composition which enable shots to cut together in the editing process. For example, when one character is looking at or speaking to another, the speaker is usually positioned to one side of the frame with a blank space in front of him or her across which he or she can look towards the other person. Similarly, a person walking normally has space left in front of him or her in the shot, into which the person can walk. Static shots of people should always leave a small amount of space above the head so that the person is framed by the environment behind him or her. These conventions are easy to see and understand when watching broadcast television, and have become conventional norms used unthinkingly by television programme-makers. More interesting uses of shot composition contribute to narrative progression and the tone and meaning of television sequences. The distance between speakers in two-shots, for example, and the relative closeness of each of them to the camera, can be manipulated to signify the quality of their relationship and to generate dramatic tension between them. Similarly, positioning characters in frames within the camera frame (such as doorways, windows or mirrors) can create relationships between spatial areas of the frame that **connote** entrapment, or produce a feeling of distance between the audience and the character. Shot composition is inseparable from the issue of point of view, where the camera's closeness to or separation from the action being shot is extremely influential on the audience's relationship with the action and the people carrying it out. For instance, the sense of being involved in the action or kept separate from it, the sense of being given information transparently by the camera or being denied it, are produced by the interactions between shot composition and point of view, and the dynamics of the relationship between one shot and those before and after it. The tone and meaning of television sequences can be further enhanced by the use of lighting, sound and music. As a matter of principle, no single element of a shot or sequence carries an intrinsic meaning, but attains its meaning by its interaction with the other elements of the programme in the context of a broader interpretation.

connotations the term used in semiotic analysis for the meanings that are associated with a particular sign or combination of signs.

ACTIVITY 6.5

Shoot the two different seven-shot films you have planned, using a single static camera. In what ways do the shots 'work' on their own, and in what ways do the shots require the relationships between shots, and relationships with the speech and music that you have planned in your treatment and storyboard? Why is this?

Lighting for drama works hand in hand with shot composition to direct the audience's attention to significant aspects of the shot or scene, and light gives texture to the image. Harsh lighting produces strong shadow when cast by a dominant key light, and can evoke fear or mystery. Soft or diffused light has a placid tone and can also connote romance. The addition of gels to light can produce warm colours, or cold and foreboding sensations. In factual and entertainment genres frontal lighting is likely to be used for clarity and coverage of the represented space, supported by **back lighting**. It is worth emphasising that the tone and meaning of a shot or sequence can never be designed by mechanically following a set of rules. Tone and meaning depend on all the elements that contribute to *mise-en-scène*: the lighting, music, sound, shot composition, props and objects in frame, costume, and camera movement. The best book about *mise-en-scène* is actually about cinema (Gibbs 2002), but its discussions apply nearly as well to television. The effective direction of television requires the ability to understand and work creatively with all of the elements of *mise-en-scène*.

During a shoot the details of day-to-day and hour-to-hour activities are the responsibility of a production manager. The production manager is responsible to the producer, and works closely with the director. He or she is responsible for the smooth running of travel, accommodation, catering and the hiring of technicians, equipment and facilities, and may assist the producer by doing reconnaissance (recces) for locations and keeping an eye on the production budget. The production manager will also produce a daily progress report on the shoot. The report lists the starting (call) and finishing (wrap) times of the day's work, the locations used and the time in minutes of screen time shot during the day. Similar calculations will show the number of scenes scheduled to be shot, those actually completed and the number of pages of script completed. From these numbers an average screen time per day can be calculated, and the **shooting ratio** worked out. A shooting ratio of 10:1 is usual for television drama, though an effective and lucky production might manage 7:1. The purpose of all this detail is to record the hours worked, facilities used and supplies of film etc. consumed during the day, so that progress in keeping to the budget can be monitored. The role of a production assistant (PA) is to log and update changes to the script, to monitor continuity and to ensure that shots match and will cut. The PA logs takes and matches them with the script. The technical crew is headed by the lighting director, who assists the director to achieve his or her desired aesthetic effect by liaising with the camera operator and lighting electricians. The camera operator works the camera and may be the same person as the lighting director. The sound recordist operates sound equipment, sometimes assisted by a sound assistant who will operate microphones and check equipment. Electricians position and adjust lights, and are known as sparks. If there is more than one electrician, the chief is called the gaffer and his or her assistant is the best boy. A grip is a cover-all term for someone who carries cameras and positions them, and lays the track along which cameras can be moved on location. Shoots conducted in television studios will also involve a vision mixer, who cuts between the output of the different cameras, and a vision controller who is responsible for the picture quality of cameras. The studio sound supervisor operates a sound mixing desk, the floor manager controls activity on the floor of the studio and is the key link person between the director, performers and contributors, and technical staff. Runners are low-paid staff who support the work of others by running errands, making coffee and generally helping out. Being a runner is often the recent graduate's first job in television.

back lighting
lighting the subject of a shot from behind to provide depth by separating the subject from the background.

mise-en-scène
literally meaning 'putting on stage', all the elements of a shot or sequence that contribute to its meanings, such as lighting, camera position and setting.

shooting ratio the number of minutes of film used to film a scene or complete programme as compared to the screen time of the finished scene or programme.

Post-production

The processes of editing, sound dubbing and adding music are the final and crucial steps of television production and are known by the collective term post-production, but they often take place when money is running out and deadlines are approaching. The post-production period is liable to create an overspend on the budget, often due to the interference of the broadcaster or financier attempting to assert control over the progamme to improve it or even 'rescue' it. Another reason why post-production can be a long, complex and expensive business is that modern digital editing technology allows for an extraordinary range of interventions that can be made during post-production. The addition of digital effects for cleaning up footage or importing animated elements and complex graphics, for example, is all done after the production shoot at the editing stage. While on one hand the availability of inexpensive high-quality desktop computer editing systems can enable students and tiny independent producers with tiny budgets to make effective television programmes, on the other hand the expectations of audiences and commissioning broadcasters have increased as the capability of the post-production technology has expanded.

Editing is crucial to television programme-making, just as it is to cinema. Again the producer will be heavily involved in the editing process, working alongside a professional editor who is expert in the use of contemporary digital editing software and hardware. Although directors have a contractual right to the **final cut** of a programme, in the same way as directors in cinema, the fact that the director is normally employed by the producer for a specific programme, rather than having responsibility for the overall look of any serial or series, means that the director is likely to defer to the producer's authority in the editing suite. Editing can be done in analogue ('linear') form, or in digital ('non-linear') form. Linear editing involves re-recording selected shots from the original camera tape, choosing them from the camera tape in the order that they are needed in the finished programme. Picture quality is lost in the re-recording process, and it is time-consuming to change the editing decisions made during the process. Digital tape formats became commonly available in the 1990s, and involve the storage of sound and image information as numerical code stored on the tape, in the same way as data is stored on computer disks. Digital editing involves no loss of picture or sound quality when data is moved from the tape to the editing system and downloaded on to an editing master tape. It is also much easier to revise and rework the programme during editing using digital technology. However, the principles of linear editing are useful for thinking through creative decisions, and for this reason students of television production will often be taught to edit using linear equipment before progressing to digital techniques. The production team will have ensured their familiarity with all the footage prior to editing, logged it and noted ideas to be used in the edit. The factors in the minds of the director, producer and editor will be:

final cut the final edited version of a programme that is delivered to the television institution for broadcast.

- possibilities for creating progression through the programme
- the revelation of dramatic or interesting turning-points
- possibilities for intriguing and holding the audience.

The rhythm and flow of the programme will be dependent on the careful structuring of these elements, referring back to the script and storyboard (in drama) to check that the aims of the programme idea are being effectively achieved.

ACTIVITY 6.6

Using desktop editing software or whatever non-linear editing you have access to, digitise and log the seven shots you have filmed for each of your two mini-dramas. Record the narration and music, and input them into the editing system. Produce a rough cut of each film, leaving blank spaces and gaps if your image and sound and music tracks do not line up perfectly. How would you fill in these gaps, if any? How would you change your films to make the shots 'cut' better?

The editing process begins with viewing rushes from the shoot with burnt-in timecode in vision. The rushes are logged so that particular shots or sequences can be identified later and chosen for editing, and this process also enables the director to remind himself or herself of the various takes and their possible usefulness. Particular shots and sequences are logged along with a label that identifies them descriptively, since this is much easier to remember than numbers or timecode. The next stage is a paper edit, where a provisional order is established for the programme. It is called a paper edit because it is a written list of shots and sequences that will form the material at the first assembly edit stage off-line. The ingredients of the paper edit are always longer than the finished programme, and the editing process in general works by a process of gradual paring down and simplification. It is likely that chosen shots or sequences will be part of a somewhat longer shot or sequence, so the beginning and ending points desired for the next stage are identified by marking the script of the documentary or drama with the words 'In' and 'Out' to specify where the selection from the shot will be made. Next the off-line assembly edit is produced by transferring the sequences identified in the paper edit to the editing software. It is followed by the rough cut stage, where the material from the paper edit is trimmed and ordered more precisely so that it is close to the planned length of the finished programme. The rough cut enables the director to determine the pace and rhythm of the programme, often by cutting on action (where the sequence begins just at the important action rather than including the lead-up to it) and generating interest and suspense (in drama) by cross-cutting between one scene and another. In documentary, voice-over commentary is written at the rough cut stage, when the interaction between image and voice can be tried out.

Sound as well as music will contribute to the world evoked on screen, either emphasising what is already present in the image or contradicting it. Sound adds dramatic perspective to images by providing a 'sound point of view' on the action: action in long shot can be accompanied by sound appearing to bring the action much closer to the audience by its volume and clarity, or on the other hand close-up action can be distanced from the audience by muting or blurring sound. Recorded sound from various locations (seaside, city street, in rooms with different kinds of acoustic tone) or sounds available on CD specifically for use in television productions (sound effects) can be assembled to form a 'library' for use in various projects. In documentary, background sound will be captured by the sound recordist, as well as the speech or other sync sound, for use to cover edits, and provide a background soundscape for the programme. In drama, sound can subtly suggest off-screen intrigue, or provide a rhythmical foundation to the programme, as in the ticking of a clock or approaching footsteps. Contrasting sound and image provoke moods and tones that shape the predominant interpretations of action for the audience, while sound montage opens up a whole range of meanings when running parallel with montages of images. These considerations apply not only to sound in general but also to speech. The factors offering connotations in recorded speech include:

- the apparent acoustic source of speech (within the represented world, or from outside it)
- the gender of the voice
- the accent of the voice
- the relative volume of the voice
- the speed of the speech
- the timbre or tone of the voice.

Broadcast television soundtracks are complex layers of sound edited on to the images in the online edit.

Digital off-line editing systems such as Avid are based on the difference between the digital rushes from the shoot that are stored on the hard disk (known as the 'media') and the control information that the computer uses to determine the order of shots (timeline, timecode and editing instructions, known collectively as the 'project'). While the media require large amounts of hard disk storage space, the project is a small document that can be downloaded on to a floppy disk and used in another computer. As the off-line edit procedure is carried out, the amount of media stored digitally reduces as selections are made from the whole, based on the instructions contained in the project. Eventually the off-line edit will produce a finished tape containing all the right shots and sequences in the right order. The online edit is where this material is fine-tuned, minor repairs can be carried out to unsatisfactory frames, graphics and visual effects are added, and sound and music tracks are attached to images (unless complex sound is being added, where it would be added separately in a dubbing theatre). Online editing effects include transitions between shots such as when one shot is blended seamlessly ('mixed') into another, and three-dimensional effects where moving images can be pasted on to shots and parts of the shot can be shifted around within the frame. All of these online effects can be viewed as soon as they are created, but the computer system needs to render them (process and record them) before the programme can be played back. The resulting programme after online editing is called the fine cut, and at this point the director will review the programme to make minor final changes before the master copy is at last produced.

Making television programmes is extremely gruelling, and it is often hard to tell whether the programme has 'worked' until after it has been completed. The success of a television production is evaluated in several different ways. Newspaper comment on television programmes and the previews of programmes published in listings magazines are available to the public and have important effects in establishing perceptions of the quality of programmes and the attraction of audiences. For the production team, creating good publicity in advance of a programme may be crucial to attracting an audience and establishing a reputation. Gathering a dossier of clippings and reviews can be useful to the scriptwriter, producer or director seeking

Figure 6.5 The Avid Media Composer editing suite. Courtesy of Avid.

ACTIVITY 6.7

How would you evaluate the two simple practical projects you have completed in this chapter using the following different criteria: as training for making conventional genre television programmes? as ways of opening up creative ideas in video production? as mini-dramas that might appeal to viewers (which viewers)? as team-building exercises for the people you worked with? How are these criteria connected or opposed to each other?

---

future employment. But the television industry is a self-enclosed world, with powerful internal hierarchies and codes of shared knowledge, status, competition and gossip. So indicators of success deriving from the industry itself are relatively more significant than indicators deriving from more public sources. The key indicator within the television industry is the response of the audience. This response is determined in terms not only of the total size of the audience but also of the **audience share**. The raw numbers denoting audience size and percentage share are themselves crude, and it is also significant to programme-makers to discover more detailed information, such as the distribution of age groups in the audience of their programme, and the social class distribution of the audience. It is these numbers which are of most concern to the hierarchy within television institutions such as channel controllers, commissioning editors, heads of network programming, department heads and people occupying the other various roles by which those ultimately in control of the employment of programme-makers are known. Professional reputation among fellow workers within a programme-maker's own specialism, along with recognition from more powerful television executives, are at least as important as recognition by the press and public, since these are the fellow professionals and television executives with whom programme-makers compete and from whom they may gain further prospects of employment.

audience share
the percentage of viewers estimated to have watched one channel as opposed to another channel broadcasting at the same time.

Case study: the Avid editing system

The basic principles of the Avid and other digital editing systems involve:

- the transfer of rushes or 'media' to the computer and the logging of their timecode so that they can be identified by the software
- the selection of the desired shots and sequences from the media and their ordering into an Edit Decision List (EDL)
- the manipulation of the chosen shots and sequences using the capabilities of the editing software
- the final assembly of the programme from the shots chosen in the EDL.

Cameras automatically record invisible timecode on to the tapes used during shooting. But since the same timecode numbers could appear on more than one roll of tape, the editing system will remember each shot for a particular production so that each has a unique number that the system can recognise. It is possible to do an off-line edit on a simpler and cheaper system such as a home computer in order to produce an EDL. The EDL can then be loaded into the Avid or other professional system, and the Avid will automatically select the sequences on the EDL for a high-quality online edit. This enables the programme-maker to save expensive editing time by doing preliminary work using an off-line system that may not be much more complex and expensive than a good domestic computer system such as the Apple iMac.

Editing systems treat camera pictures as objects. The picture is treated as though it were a flat two-dimensional surface, such as a piece of paper. This enables the system to appear to move images by flipping them over so that they look back to front, lifting the corners or edges of the picture as though it were the page of a book that can be turned, enlarging or reducing the size of the image so it appears to move towards or away from the viewer, and distorting the image as though it were being turned at an angle to the viewer, folded, squeezed or torn. These effects are different from the importation into television editing of techniques that are already possible with celluloid film, such as cutting, fading, tinting and slow motion. They are possible because the image is stored as a sequence of bits of digital information. Because the image has been decomposed into numbers, and these numbers can be manipulated mathematically by the computer and then turned back into an image, the image is 'plastic', meaning that it can be worked on and transformed. Similar processes are used to record and process sound in digital equipment such as the Avid, so that sound can also be manipulated and transformed by the mathematical operations performed by the computer software. It is possible to smooth out jumps between sound sequences, to adjust the pitch and acoustic quality of sound, and layer different soundtracks in relation to each other. However, very complex sound is likely to be completed in a sound studio or dubbing theatre, where specialist audio equipment is available that surpasses the capabilities of online editing equipment designed to work primarily with images.

The first point to note about the Avid system is the different conception of how editing is done, in comparison to the editing of film that preceded both analogue and digital tape editing systems. A piece of film is a material object that can be handled, cut with scissors and chemically processed to bring out different features of the images recorded on it, and bits of film can be pasted together in any order using sticky tape. The experience of editing film is of a closeness to the material and an ability to perceive it through the senses of sight, touch and smell that is akin to the skills of woodwork or oil painting. Editing images and sound captured on tape is a quite different experience. There is nothing to see on the camera tape, and no moving parts inside the memory chips that hold the media used to edit. Instead of physically cutting pieces of tape and sticking them together (although this was done in the early days of magnetic tape for television programme-making), the process is to re-record selected portions of tape on to another tape. Digital non-linear editing is still based on these principles of re-recording, though it is batches of numerical data that are being moved around and reassembled inside the computer, rather than sequences being physically copied from one tape to the next. But since sequences can be pasted together into any order on the Avid, rather than assembled one after another as on videotape, Avid editing is similar to the cutting and pasting done with cinema film. Non-linear editing is a hybrid of the different approaches to editing in film and analogue video.

One consequence of the Avid's capability to treat images as objects that can be manipulated and transformed in digital form is that the possibilities for transforming images and sounds are startling, and it would be rare for any individual television programme to use more than a few of the great variety of processes that the Avid can perform. Whereas in principle the editing of a piece of film could be done with such simple equipment as reel-to-reel Steenbeck editing tables, a sharp knife and some special sticky tape, the Avid cannot be operated without specialist training to understand the architecture of the software that controls it. While the system is logical in its operation, the accompanying technical manual takes about 1,500 pages to explain all of its functions. Editing systems such as Avid are, however, similar to personal computers in that a few training sessions will enable the user to complete basic processes competently, while professional users will be able to accomplish subtle and individual results by adjusting the numerous parameters that are open to modification. The

Figure 6.6 An example of an Avid Xpress screen. Courtesy of Avid.

continued

capability of the Avid extends the features of professionalisation and hierarchy in the different employment categories in television production. The technical knowledge required to operate it well consists both of systems thinking and organisation that are common in computer technician work, and also of the lateral and creative thinking that characterises direction, lighting camera work and design in television. The non-linear editor is highly professional and competent across different kinds of expertise. He or she is also a specialised worker who operates at a particular level in the hierarchy of a trade group. In general, the computerisation and complexity of digital editing produce extended vertical hierarchies of status in the editing profession, and produce work specialisation that increasingly separates the experience of editors from others in the television industry. This is ironic given that digital technology potentially connects the hardware used to shoot, edit, record sound and display audio-visual media, since it all works on the same principle of translating information into numerical form (digits).

Interestingly, some of the commands on the Avid system refer to one or the other of the cinematic or video editing conventions that preceded digital non-linear systems. The basic command Splice, for example, inserts material selected from the Source Monitor and marked with an In and an Out point. The term Splice derives from the film editing procedure of physi-cally cutting a strip of frames and splicing or joining one to another. The second most basic and useful command on the Avid interface is Overwrite, which lays a selected sequence on top of another, replacing what was previously there at that point on the timeline. Overwrite derives from the video editing process by which an audio-visual sequence from a source tape player is recorded on to the edit master at a point where an existing sequence had previously been recorded. The recording head of the video tape player would write the new material over the top of the previous material, leaving no trace of what was there before. The principles of basic editing on the Avid are a combination of the cutting and joining processes involved in film editing, and the transfer and re-recording processes involved in analogue video editing. In a similar way, the timeline displayed at the bottom of the Avid screen represents the project as a linear strip, like a piece of film or videotape. Representing the project in this way provides a useful graphic representation of the programme as it is edited. Jogging and shuttling using the Avid's keyboard or mouse mimic the freeze-frame (jog) and cue and review (shuttle) functions of a videotape recorder, where the play head moves rapidly across the tape and provides a speeded-up version of the pictures. The Avid's Trim mode allows individual shots to be shortened or lengthened by any number of frames, and is particularly useful to refine cuts on action so that the pace of a sequence can be adjusted. As its name suggests, the effect is what would happen if frames of film were snipped from a sequence using scissors, and joined back on to the preceding or following sequence, slightly shortening or lengthening the complete programme. But again, nothing physical happens to the audio-visual information in the Avid, and frames which have been trimmed out using the control remain virtually and invisibly present so that they can be restored at any time.

The centre of an Avid system is the software program loaded on to the computer. Attached to this are the special keyboard which operates the system via a connecting device called a dongle, a storage device in which the digitised rushes or 'media' are stored on a computer hard disk, two television monitors which display media and the cut which is being worked on, sound input devices such as DAT (digital audio tape) players, speakers for sound output and devices for audio-visual input such as videotape players. The Avid is therefore a concrete example of media **convergence**: it can access a wide variety of analogue and digital infor-mation sources operating in different formats and standards, and integrate and store these

convergence the process whereby previously separate media technologies merge together. For example, computers can now send faxes, show DVD films and play music.

various kinds of input information. By integrating all of these input sources encoded in digital form, it is able to treat them in the same way, manipulate them and produce a new output that can be perceived via the electronic and mechanical devices of the television monitor and loudspeakers. The ways that the Avid separates one project from another in its memory, sets up Bins (like folders on a word processor) containing the digitised rushes or media, and orders the sequences (Clips) manipulated during the edit, all bear no relation to the physical position or arrangement of information in the computer. While the human user requires an interface that separates and categorises these different kinds of information, arranges them in a hierarchy and represents them in understandable ways, the information represented by the interface is virtual. The ability to display representations of media in virtual forms allows the user of the Avid to try out effects, revise and modify the elements of a programme without ever affecting the original form of the media digitised and held in the hard disk drive. It is only at the stage when captions and effects have been added that the Avid editor will declare that he or she has reached the point of Picture Lock. This is where the visual sequences of the programme have been fixed and finalised, and after this is done sound and music will be added until the programme is complete.

SUMMARY OF KEY POINTS

- Studying the professional processes of making television gives a deeper understanding of television institutions, programmes and how meanings are made.
- Development is the stage when programme ideas are being worked out, researched and planned.
- Pre-production is when locations, contributors or performers are selected, scripts are written, storyboards and production schedules are drawn up, and the design, props, costumes and music are selected.
- Production is the shooting stage, when the creative and technical personnel produce the audio-visual raw material for programmes.
- Post-production includes the editing of the material that has been shot, and the inclusion of effects and a sound mix.
- The hierarchy of roles in television production, and the ways that technology is designed to be used, reveal assumptions about the relative status of television professional staff, and how images and sound should be put together.

Further reading

Bayes, S., *The Avid Handbook*, second edition (Woburn, Mass.: Butterworth-Heinemann, 2000).

Dominick, J., B. Sherman and G. Copeland, *Broadcasting/Cable and Beyond: An Introduction to Modern Electronic Media*, third edition (New York: McGraw-Hill, 1996).

Gibbs, J., *Mise-en-Scene: Film Style and Interpretation* (London: Wallflower, 2002).

Harrison, J., *Terrestrial Television News in Britain: The Culture of Production* (Manchester: Manchester University Press, 2000).

Hart, C., *Television Program Making* (Oxford: Focal Press, 1999).

Hood, S. (ed.), *Behind the Screens: The Structure of British Television in the Nineties* (London: Lawrence & Wishart, 1994).

Kauffmann, S., *Avid Editing* (Woburn, Mass.: Butterworth-Heinemann, 2000).

Millerson, G., *Video Production Handbook*, third edition (Oxford: Focal Press, 2001).

Moss, S., 'New kids on the block', *The Guardian* Media section, 28 January 2002, pp. 2–3.

Murdoch, G., 'Authorship and organization', *Screen Education*, 35 (1980), pp. 19–34.

Orlebar, J., *Digital Television Production* (London: Arnold, 2002).

Tunstall, J. *Media Occupations and Professions: A Reader* (Oxford: Oxford University Press, 2001).

—— (ed.), *Television Producers* (London: Routledge, 1993).

Postmodern Television

Postmodern Television

Introduction

The term 'postmodern' or 'postmodernist' is used in relation to television with several related meanings, but taking apart the two component words which make up the term shows that it involves distinguishing between one state of affairs and another. 'Post' means after, while 'modern' means contemporary. Therefore 'postmodernist' or 'postmodern' signifies newness, whether this newness is regarded positively (postmodern television might be experimental, innovative and exciting) or negatively (postmodern television might be shallow, mindless or trivial). Discussing television in relation to postmodernism is a way of analysing how television, and culture in general, has changed.

Postmodernism as a style

When the term is used to describe the form or style of television, 'postmodernist' denotes the self-conscious play with the conventions of television in programmes such as the animated series *The Simpsons* or in the many television ads which refer, often humorously, to other advertisements or advertising conventions. The pleasure of viewing programmes and advertisements such as these derives from the viewer's recognition of this play or '**reflexivity**'. One episode of the sitcom *Father Ted*, for instance, involved the main characters encountering the actor Richard Wilson (Victor Meldrew in the sitcom *One Foot in the Grave*) and pestering him by repeating the character's catchphrase 'I don't believe it!' Much of the comedy in *The Simpsons* comes from the reflexive parody of the conventions of, among others:

reflexivity a text's reflection on its own status as a text, for example drawing attention to generic conventions, or revealing the technologies used to make a programme.

- other animated series
- horror films
- television news
- children's television.

Rather than using these parodic reworkings to criticise the television and other forms which are being referred to, postmodern television involves the celebration and enjoyment of mixing up the conventions of the source texts. It is this lack of critical edge which leads some theorists to attack postmodernism. The richness of meaning which results for the viewer from this postmodern parody might be highly pleasurable, but it has little to offer in terms of the ideological critiques of television forms and conventions which underlie Television Studies' tradition of looking for 'committed', critical and politically progressive programmes. An example of postmodern television which Umberto Eco (1984) gives is when programmes seem to be made in order to celebrate the television-ness of something. So televised awards ceremonies or celebrity chat shows are called 'neo-TV' by Eco. Programmes such as these represent celebrities whose personas have been created on television, for television, and the programmes appear simply to be a vehicle for extending the artificial existence of these figures who seem to exist in the bubble of a television universe. Neo-TV programmes refer to each other and cannibalise each other's formats, celebrities and presenters. They are 'intratextual', meaning that they are parasitic on themselves. Eco is describing an epoch of **simulation** where television becomes divorced from reality, no longer a medium of representation but instead an independently existing virtual world which is both exciting and banal.

The interpretation of texts such as these and the decision to call them postmodern because of the many **intertextual** references which they contain depend on the theorist's and the viewer's ability to identify these references. Postmodern play with allusions to other texts needs to be subtle and to some extent hidden in order for viewers to enjoy the references and to congratulate themselves on their skill at decoding them. As Robin Nelson (1997: 246) suggests: 'Postmodern texts might be summarily characterized by a formal openness, a strategic refusal to close down meaning. They create space for play between discourses allegedly empowering the reader to negotiate or construct her own meanings.' But allusions do not enrich a text if only a very small number of viewers will notice them. In 1995 the film director Quentin Tarantino directed an episode of the hospital drama *ER* entitled 'Motherhood'. The **voice-over** introduction to the programme by Channel 4's continuity announcer informed viewers that Tarantino had directed the episode, newspapers and television listings magazines mentioned the fact and Tarantino's name appeared in the opening credits of the programme. Having been prompted to regard the involvement of Tarantino as significant, many viewers would have noticed the intertextual reference in the episode to Tarantino's film *Reservoir Dogs*. The film famously includes a sequence in which a captured policemen is tortured by having his ear cut off, though the moment of mutilation itself is not seen in the film. The 'Motherhood' episode of *ER* included a patient arriving with a mutilated ear, pouring blood. It was not essential for viewers to make sense of the episode that they recognised the reference to Tarantino's film, and in fact there was no overt reference to Tarantino in the script; nor were individual camera shots direct imitations of those in *Reservoir Dogs*. Instead, the allusion was an enriching aspect of the meaning of the episode for some viewers, a subtle joke which added a self-conscious postmodern playfulness.

simulation a representation that mirrors an aspect of reality so perfectly that it takes the place of the reality it aims to reproduce.

intertextuality how one text draws on the meanings of another by referring to it, by allusion, quotation or parody, for example.

voice-over speech accompanying visual images but not presumed to derive from the same place or time as the images.

ACTIVITY 7.1

Intertextual references are common in television advertisements. Make a note of advertisements you have seen which refer to television programmes, films or other media texts. How might intertextual references serve the needs of advertisers in positioning products and brands, and engaging viewers' interest?

The consequence of identifying postmodern features of style and form in television is that it leads to the argument that television is changing the ways in which subject in psychoanalysis, the term for the individual self whose identity has both conscious and unconscious components.

sign in semiotics, something which communicates meaning, such as a word, an image or a sound.

code in semiotics, a system or set of rules that shapes how signs can be used, and therefore how meanings can be made and understood.

people's **subjectivity** is formed. If television programmes and advertisements are made up of fragmentary moments which often gain their meanings by referring intertextually to other television programmes, advertisements and other media texts, this might mean that the viewer's subjective identity is also fragmented. There is a question, however, about whether it is television which causes a change in subjectivity, or whether television reflects ways of being which are caused by other factors. Nevertheless, emphasising how one television programme is constructed by combining and repeating **signs** and **codes** from other programmes and other media discourses has an effect on the methods of study which are needed to understand and critique it. It would no longer be appropriate to draw on the theories of viewer positioning which have been adapted from theories of classical Hollywood cinema, for example, because the logical unfolding of involving narratives with beginnings, middles and ends, and psychologically realistic characters which are assumed to lay out a secure spectator position, seem inappropriate for the reflexive, intertextual and ironic processes of meaning in much contemporary television. Television viewers construct sense from the diverse fragments of narrative, character, visual pleasure and intertextual reference which postmodern television offers. Indeed, one of the more publicly controversial aspects of irony in postmodern television is that some programmes may be taken at face value by some audiences, and read ironically by others. Debates in the press over Channel 4's light entertainment programmes fronted by the character Ali G are a recent example of this, where the character's apparent racism and sexism can be claimed either to critique these ideologies or to perpetuate them. While there are moments of stability and involvement in television, the role of fragmentary signification, the withholding of resolution and the sense of being suspended in a perpetual middle is what makes the term postmodern useful for describing what watching television is like now. Features of television programmes seem to match descriptions of contemporary culture which focus on how people's identity is mobile and fluid, and composed out of partial fragments.

Intertextuality is essential to television. Programmes and advertisements find their place in the schedules and address their audiences by establishing their similarity to and difference from other programmes and advertisements, and from other media texts. Because of its associations with liveness and with the provision of news and other information to its audience, television is associated with the now. This suggests that television is inherently postmodern in that:

- it forgets the past and history
- it is obsessed with what is new and different.

But on the other hand, there is a strong presence of the past in television since

genre a kind or type of programme. Programmes of the same genre have shared characteristics.

- past programmes are always being repeated
- contemporary programmes communicate about their **genre** and how they should be watched by referring to programmes which viewers already know.

Television classics such as the sitcom *Dad's Army* or *Porridge* return every few years and attract large audiences. On cable and satellite, channels such as UK Gold and Granada Plus have schedules composed entirely of repeated programmes. Channels also repackage television from the past in order to sell it to a new audience.

For example, *Star Trek* is now packaged by BBC2 as a cult classic, with trailers featuring the more outrageous examples of sexist behaviour, **melodramatic** over-acting and laughably low-budget special effects. This ironic repackaging seeks to bring a new younger audience to the programme which was first shown thirty-five years ago. Old television becomes new when watched by a different audience from a different subject position.

melodrama
a form of drama characterised by exaggerated performance, a focus on reversals of fortune and extreme emotional reactions to events.

ACTIVITY 7.2

How might the repackaging of old television programmes as 'cult' programmes, 'classics' or subjects of irony serve the interests of broadcasters with extensive libraries of programmes, seeking to mobilise valuable sections of the audience?

The immersion of subjects in television culture and media culture more generally means that media choices and identities marked out by patterns of television consumption become the co-ordinates which define a person's social role. This is clearly connected with advertising since what advertising does is to associate consumable products with liveable identities. This is not only a positive process of taking on an identity, for example by characterising oneself as a *Newsnight* viewer or a *Neighbours* viewer, but also a negative process of stigmatising those groups of viewers whose difference from oneself enables each person's identity to be constituted. Identities constructed in this way are necessarily temporary as cultural fashions change, and the sense of the individual subject having a continuity of identity across decades and a life becomes more difficult to sustain. Instead, identity is fragmentary, temporary and contingent. In this situation nostalgia is a powerful force which allows viewers to remember a sense of themselves in the past, to connect the present with the past by using memories of television as a way of engaging with who they once were. The popularity of such programmes as *100 Best Kids TV Shows*, *I Love the Seventies*, etc. is a result of this. It is reassuring to share memories of television programmes with others of a similar generation, and because television has until recently been relatively 'scarce' because of the small number of channels and relatively few mass audience programmes, as John Ellis (2000) has recently argued, it is likely that adults will have similar television memories.

Indeed it is not only the programmes which are the focus of nostalgia but also the experience of collective family viewing around a single television set in the home that people reminisce about. The BBC sitcom *The Royle Family* is based on nostalgia for such family viewing, and gently ridicules the notion of the television as the focus of family interaction. The irony of this programme also reminds us that nostalgia is a double-edged emotion, which includes a distance from the experience being remembered in order for sentimentality and regret to be kept at bay. Mastering the past of television by keeping an ironic distance from it allows people to maintain their confidence in the security of their present identity and their control of their uses of television. Television is important to the creation of the past and the creation of the self, and part of this importance can be shown in the ways that television is denied and repudiated by its viewers at the same time as it is celebrated.

Postmodern times

Both of the component words in the term 'postmodern' have to do with time. Since 'post' means after, postmodernism has to be thought of as a stage or moment in time which follows another stage or moment previous to it. For television, using the term postmodern means having to establish what 'modern' television is, the kind of television which precedes the postmodern, and this means constructing a history of television which can be divided up into periods. This problem of identifying what modern television would be is a conceptual issue which affects the term postmodern in general. Modern means what is characteristic of the present period, in distinction to what things were like before in a premodern period. The modern age might refer, for example, to the times after mass communication and industrial society had transformed the nations of the Western world in the late nineteenth century. But as culture moves on, the distinction between what was modern and what is happening in the present tends to break down. New experiences lead commentators to describe their own time as modern, assigning what had been called modern before to being a part of the premodern epoch. Because modern means what is new, the sense of what is modern keeps changing to keep up with new developments, and the premodern period keeps expanding, always ending just before the new times described as modern.

In a similar way the postmodern period must refer to a time when changes occur that react against what is modern or transform it. One of the interesting consequences of this is that the postmodern could be characterised by a return to features which are thought of as premodern. Umberto Eco is a scholar of medieval culture, a **semiotician** and media critic also contributing to media culture by writing novels and journalism and appearing on television. In the medieval period the group with access to knowledge was the Church, which disseminated the religious ideology through which culture was understood. The cathedral's architectural form, frescos, statues and sculpture were the advertisements, television screens and comic strips that explained everything. In postmodernism the elite are those who run media culture: television, advertising and popular culture. So Eco is interested in the similarities between the postmodern epoch and the medieval period. As well as the multinational control of information and culture by a privileged elite, a further similarity is the dominance of visual communication. Today this is the dominance of visual media such as television, print and poster advertising and cinema over written media of communication. In the medieval period Eco notes the importance of physical visual representations such as stained-glass windows, statues and frescos. The parallel between the postmodern and the medieval periods suggests both positive and negative characteristics of contemporary media culture. Like the dominance of the Catholic Church over the Western world during the medieval period, the domination of multinational capitalism in the international media scene could be thought of as oppressive and stifling. Yet also, because of their shared experience of culture, the audiences of postmodern media have a ready-made 'language' in which to speak to each other and to understand their realities, giving them the potential to become a powerful political and cultural force, just as in the Middle Ages the massed peoples of the West could be moulded into a powerful crusading army with shared aims and beliefs.

If postmodernism reacts against the modern, one way of establishing a difference from the modern would be to go back to premodern features of culture and recycle

semiotics the study of signs and their meanings, initially developed for the study of spoken language, and now used also to study the visual and aural 'languages' of other media such as television.

them in new ways. So a further implication of labelling television as postmodern is to suggest that the elements of past culture which it recycles from either modern or premodern epochs are plundered equally. If so, these past elements lose their historical place and significance, and the past is deprived of its 'pastness'. Because of this erasure of pastness, some theorists of the postmodern claim that postmodernism erases history, and produces the sense of a perpetual present. The French philosopher of culture Jean-François Lyotard, in his book *The Postmodern Condition* (1979, translated 1984) has argued that postmodernism entails a loss of confidence in theories which map out historical progress. Such theories as Marx's, which consider that history moves by **dialectical** struggles between the world-views of different social classes and that it is inevitable that the working class will eventually triumph over the **bourgeoisie**, or the liberal theory that humankind evolves towards ever greater understanding between peoples and the betterment of most people's lives by the spread of technology and democracy, are challenged by Lyotard. He regards these and other large-scale historical theories as 'grand narratives' of emancipation and progress that have lost their legitimacy and purchase in postmodern times.

> **dialectic** a term associated especially with Marxist theories, meaning a struggle between two opposing ideas.

> **bourgeoisie** the middle class, who are owners of property and businesses.

ACTIVITY 7.3

If postmodernist theorists such as Lyotard claim that 'grand narratives' have lost their legitimacy, does this claim make postmodernism a 'grand narrative' itself?

Postmodern and avant-garde

Lyotard (1993: 44) argued that something is 'modern only if it is first postmodern'. His version of the term 'postmodern' is that it describes something which we cannot get a handle on, something for which our criteria for

- judging whether it is good or bad
- deciding what category it should fit into
- deciding what kind of approach we should take to it in order to make sense of it

are all impossible to fix on. What we think of as modern, as appropriate to our current state of culture, has to pass through this postmodern state of ambiguity and confusion. So Lyotard thinks of the postmodern as a state which we can recognise only after the event, only after our categories and criteria have been applied and our example has become modern and comprehensible. Once this has happened, and the example is part of the modern, we can look back to that state of confusion in which it first appeared and describe that moment as postmodern. His notion of the postmodern includes these important features:

- The term postmodern is retrospectively attributed to things.
- Being postmodern is a momentary condition which lasts for a short time.

● The postmodern is not an epoch or period but is a characteristic of how cultural products appear and are perceived.

Lyotard approves of the postmodern, because he values things which are hard to categorise and hard to judge. Once something can be explained, judged and categorised Lyotard believes that its creative challenge and artistic interest are lost. Once it is possible to create a narrative or a **discourse** about something which will contain it and make sense of it, the potential for new ideas and experimentation is gone. History is a narrative about the past, which takes control of events by putting them in order and telling stories about them (see Chapter 2), and the fact that the postmodern is something which cannot be controlled and narrated in this way are part of why Lyotard regards the postmodern positively. The postmodern, in Lyotard's definition, cannot be part of a historical narrative because it cannot be controlled and ordered by criteria for judgement and the application of rules and standards which we already know.

Lyotard's argument shows little interest in the groups which have been backed in the past by theorists of society and culture. His interest is in **aesthetics** rather than in the working class, women or people in the Third World. His book *The Postmodern Condition* discusses the state of highly developed Western societies. Other theorists have protested that people in the Third World are still struggling for development and wealth against the former colonial powers, that women are still struggling for economic and social equality in a society dominated by men, that there are still many millions of people in the West who are low paid and socially excluded and therefore unable to experience the luxury of the artistic and cultural experimentation which Lyotard values. His conception of the postmodern does not allow any agency, any possibility of conscious political action for these underprivileged groups. Lyotard's definition of the postmodern applies particularly well to non-referential images such as abstract paintings. In work such as this, it is not clear how to decide whether the painting is good or bad, beautiful or ugly, and what its message might be. Lyotard (1993: 43) argues that work like this, rather than representing something, tries to present what is unpresentable: 'to present the fact that the unpresentable exists. To make visible that there is something which can be conceived and which can neither be seen nor made visible.' It is hard to identify material on television which would fit into Lyotard's category of the postmodern. The American theorist Fredric Jameson (1987) uses the term 'video-text' to refer to commercial television and video art. Jameson argues that video is postmodern, video, 'closely related to the dominant computer and information technology of the late or third stage of capitalism' (1987: 207) is 'a sign-flow which resists meaning, whose fundamental inner logic is the exclusion of the emergence of themes as such in that sense, and which therefore systematically sets out to shortcircuit traditional interpretive temptations' (1987: 219). Because video makes possible the manipulation of time, cutting it up, slowing it down, by using the capabilities of electronic technology, it can contrast with the ordered control of time, pacing and narrative which television and film have customarily used. However, Jameson's conception of video and television is much closer to video art than to network television programmes and the aesthetic conventions and scheduling practices which they involve.

discourse
a particular use of language for a certain purpose in a certain context (like academic discourse, or poetic discourse), and similarly in television, a particular usage of television's audio-visual 'language' (news programme discourse, or nature documentary discourse, for instance).

aesthetic
a specific artistic form. Aesthetics means the study of art and beauty.

ACTIVITY 7.4

How would you use the ability of video recorders or computer editing systems to make 'scratch' videotapes that might qualify as postmodern in Lyotard's and Jameson's sense of the term? In what ways might such texts 'shortcircuit traditional interpretive temptations'?

In the early twentieth century artists such as Picasso, and writers such as Virginia Woolf, were developing ways of representing in images and language that reacted against traditions inherited from the nineteenth century, and found it hard to gain an audience for the experimental and unconventional works they produced. They were part of an **avant-garde**, seemingly ahead of their time (avant-garde can be translated as 'ahead of the pack'). But by the Second World War these various artists, writers, architects and film-makers had been accepted by the highly educated elites of the Western world as a loose grouping of modernists whose work represented important engagements with the ethos of the time. Their paintings appeared in galleries, their books were being taught in universities and their buildings were commissioned by powerful patrons. Modernism became part of the sanctioned official culture, and was considered valuable partly because it was very different from the mass **popular culture** of Hollywood, paperback fiction and popular music. Postmodernism involves mixing the hitherto experimental and innovative methods of the modernists with commercially distributed mass commercial culture, and the theorist Andreas Huyssen wrote (1986: 57), 'it is by the distance we have travelled from this "great divide" between mass culture and modernism that we can measure our own cultural postmodernity'. In other words postmodernism breaks down the division between culture for a small elite group and culture for a mass audience. Television, especially the **public service** television of European nations, has been a crucial contributor to this process.

> **avant-garde** work aiming to challenge the norms and conventions of its medium, and the group of people making such work.

> **popular culture** the texts created by ordinary people (as opposed to an elite group) or created for them, and the ways these are used.

> **public service** in television, the provision of a mix of programmes that inform, educate and entertain in ways that encourage the betterment of audiences and society in general.

Postmodernism and value

An important question which arises from this mixing of 'elite' and 'popular' culture, though, is how to ascribe significance and value to postmodern television. Thinking of an example from earlier in this chapter, it seems quite legitimate to claim that *The Simpsons* is a very important piece of cultural work, at least as important as any contemporary novel, play or painting, because of

- its intertextual complexity
- its self-awareness
- its relevance to the fragmented media landscapes and audiences of the present.

The values of complexity, self-consciousness, and engagement with cultural issues in *The Simpsons* make it fit the criteria for 'art', yet it is obviously part of popular culture, not least because it is a widely distributed television programme.

Figure 7.1 *December 3rd 1998 12.03–1.17 a.m.* by Anthony Discenza, an example of video art work. Courtesy of Video Data Bank.

There are three kinds of answer to this question of value in postmodernist theory. First, theorists such as Fredric Jameson argue that postmodernism is the result of the dominance of powerful global forces of economics and political power centred in the USA and its allies, and, while *The Simpsons* might be interesting and important, it testifies to the success of the Fox television network in producing and distributing a programme which fits the new cultural order of multinational **capitalism**. For Jameson postmodernism is the cultural form which is produced alongside the dominance of global capitalism, a world economic system which is unjust and ripe for criticism. In a second approach to this question the French theorist Jean Baudrillard would argue that the whole issue of value has been made redundant by the postmodern mixing of elite and popular cultural forms. Art has become a commodity (think of the innumerable merchandising opportunities associated with art in today's galleries), while commodities (such as *The Simpsons*, or Madonna's videos) are discussed as if they were art. For Baudrillard the question of value is an amusing and irrelevant hangover from an earlier age. In a third manner of answering this question theorists from the Cultural Studies tradition such as Lawrence Grossberg have argued that value resides in the different ways that audiences use *The Simpsons*. It is enjoyed by children as a cartoon comedy series, by students and young people as sophisticated sitcom and by cultural theorists as a fascinating instance of postmodern theories. For Grossberg value is not absolute, but is a product of the audience's relationship to the programme and the ways that this audience draws the programme into its own discourses. What is perhaps most interesting about each of these three answers is that each of them defers the question of value

capitalism the organisation of an economy around the private ownership of accumulated wealth, involving the exploitation of labour to produce profit that creates such wealth.

by linking *The Simpsons* with another theoretical issue (multinational capitalism, the commodity form, audience cultures). As I have argued elsewhere (Bignell 2000), this very strategy of skidding away from addressing examples on their own terms is part of postmodernist theory, and one reason why some critics find postmodernism so frustrating.

ACTIVITY 7.5

In what ways does the discipline of Television Studies attribute value to some kinds of television and not others? To what extent does studying television require you to justify your work by comparing it to work in more traditional disciplines such as sociology or literary criticism?

An example which has been commonly used to define what postmodern television is like is the American 'cult' drama serial *Twin Peaks*, which began in the United States in April 1990. The advertising for the first episode of the serial in newspapers and magazines promoted the programme as a highly unusual piece of work masterminded by David Lynch, a 'maverick' film-maker responsible for *Eraserhead* and *Blue Velvet*. The television serial was granted the artistic status of being an experimental work that challenged the norms of television, and was attached to the name of an acknowledged cinema director whose work carried prestige among audiences of art cinema. But once *Twin Peaks* had attracted a sizeable audience it began to be promoted as a soap opera that viewers would find addictive, and was advertised in the American magazine *Soap Opera Weekly*. *Twin Peaks* addressed two different audiences, one defined in relation to cinema, art and experimentation and focused on the authorial input of one man, and the other in relation to a mass-audience genre regarded as downmarket and **feminine**. This characteristic is called **multi-accentuality**. *Twin Peaks* producer Mark Frost designed the serial to appeal to audiences of American '**quality** drama', especially the wealthy and discerning viewers of most interest to American television networks. Following the arrival of cable television as a significant force in the United States in the 1980s, network television viewing in evening **prime time** had fallen from 91 per cent of the audience in 1979 to 67 per cent in 1989. *Twin Peaks* was an effort to attract cable viewers back to network television by offering them what appeared to be a prestige 'art' television programme. But the mass audiences associated with network soap opera were also targeted, confusing the boundaries between elite and popular audiences, and blurring the distinctions between 'art television' and popular culture.

Something similar could be seen in the promotional material for the American Second World War serial *Band of Brothers*, screened in Britain in early 2002. This was shown in the prime-time mid-evening slot, and was heavily promoted by television trailers and newspaper and magazine advertising. The promotion focused partly on the fact that the producers were Tom Hanks and Steven Spielberg, known in particular for the war film *Saving Private Ryan* and more generally for such mass-market popular cinema as *Jurassic Park*. Spectacular action sequences, and a focus on the emotional impact of war on the newly trained recruits plunged into combat

feminine having characteristics associated with the cultural role of women and not men.

multi-accentuality the situation where meanings are able to be read in different ways by different groups of viewers because a text offers multiple meanings at the same time.

quality in television, kinds of programme that are perceived as more expensively produced and, especially, more culturally worthwhile than other programmes.

prime time the part of a day's television schedule when the greatest number of viewers may be watching, normally the mid-evening period.

were the two focal points of the advertising. However, aspects of the advertising and the programme itself also addressed a different, more **media-literate** audience. Very detailed reconstructions of actual battles were featured in the programme, whose title sequence began with faded black and white images suggesting historical truth and documentary accuracy. Each programme opened with elderly veterans speaking to camera about their experiences and their knowledge of the real-life characters who were to be fictionally recreated in the episode. These techniques of using reminiscence and documentary conventions had been used in the film *Reds*, about the Russian Revolution, and in Steven Spielberg's production *Schindler's List*, focusing on the Nazi persecution of the Jews. The visual conventions of the serial, some of its subject matter and characteristics of its production such as the use of a large cast of previously little-known actors connected it to epic cinema and 'serious' historical film as well as to popular entertainment.

Audiences and postmodernism

As we have seen, the term postmodernism can be used to discuss the stylistic and formal properties of television programmes, and the distribution of television programmes as part of a global consumer culture, but it is also a way of thinking about how audiences interact with television. Since the 1970s academics working on television have drawn on the theory of **ideology** (deriving from Marxist analysis of society) and the theory of how texts position viewing subjects in order to communicate meanings (originally from the theory of film), and united these approaches to show how television programmes and ads perpetuate dominant ideologies in which consumption is the basis of identity, and class and economic relations between people are obscured. Television programmes become the agents of communicating these ideas, with only minimal opportunities for the viewer to resist their meanings or interpret them in alternative ways. The more recent recognition that different audiences interpret television in different ways, and integrate their use of television into the whole diverse field of their cultural lives, challenges the assumptions of these critical approaches to television, and contributes to postmodernist thinking about the medium.

Work on postmodernism has been part of a shift in discussing television from *structure* to *agency*. Structure refers to the institutions, networks of relationships and professional practices which condition the ways in which television is produced and broadcast. It includes theories of ideology and **globalisation**, for example, which seek to explain audience responses and preferences, and the features of television programme texts, as the result of these structural conditions. Agency refers to a new value attributed to viewer choice, and the ways that audiences engage in negotiations with television texts and media structures in order to define themselves and empower themselves as individuals. The contest and tension between these two approaches are important, however, since neither approach can be correct on its own. Indeed part of postmodern theory is the realisation that explaining television culture requires more than one model, set of critical terms and set of examples.

The arguments about postmodernism are a way of addressing the political impact of the mass media. For some theorists the increased significance of the mass media is part of postmodernism and includes the liberating effects of the wide-

media literacy the skills and competence that viewers learn in order to understand easily the audio-visual 'languages' of media texts.

ideology the set of beliefs, attitudes and assumptions arising from the economic and class divisions in a culture, underlying the ways of life accepted as normal in that culture.

globalisation the process whereby ownership of television institutions in different nations and regions is concentrated in the hands of international corporations, and whereby programmes and formats are traded between institutions around the world.

spread distribution of information and ideas around the globe. On one hand, this can provide people with an unprecedented access to information, ideas and creative possibilities. On the other hand, the global spread of the mass media reduces the uniqueness of each individual and the specific cultures to which individuals belong, so that places and people become virtually the same and are all infected with the same assumptions, desires and fears presented by multinational commercial broadcasters. For much of our knowledge of the world comes through television, especially television news and other factual programmes. At the time of the Gulf War in the early 1990s the French cultural theorist Jean Baudrillard claimed that the almost non-stop coverage of the war smothered the reality of the event, so that the war itself was in effect replaced by the television pictures which claimed to represent it. Only a very small number of people in the West took part in the war, and for almost everyone the war was a media event. The characteristics which allowed this to happen were:

- the simultaneous broadcast of events as they happened
- the global distribution of news pictures
- the use of very simple narrative frameworks (good versus evil, spectacular technology achieving bloodless victories, masculine heroism) to represent it
- the importance of **iconic** images representing complex events
- a global network of interconnected television broadcasting.

iconic sign in semiotics, a sign which resembles its referent. Photographs, for example, contain iconic signs resembling the objects they represent.

In 2001 another similar example happened when terrorists attacked targets in the United States. Complex issues surrounding resistance to the power of the United States in various regions, the several terrorist attacks on 11 September, and questions about what the terrorists intended to achieve and what the proper response should be, were overwhelmed by a small number of brief and dramatic sequences of television pictures. A few seconds of footage of airliners crashing into the World Trade Center, a few seconds of the huge towers collapsing to the ground and a few seconds of reaction to the event from shocked pedestrians in New York became the iconic images which represented this complex of issues and events, and which were repeated innumerable times in television around the world. As in the debates about the Gulf War, television provided the images which encapsulated a complex reality in a few seconds of coverage and enabled this complex reality to be experienced vicariously worldwide. While no one would deny that the events of 11 September happened, their reality was superseded by television representations of their reality.

ACTIVITY 7.6

Baudrillard's arguments about the 1991 Gulf War and their extension to the events of 11 September 2001 are deliberately provocative. How would you defend these ideas against the criticism that they underestimate the emotional impact of television coverage?

Jean Baudrillard is both critical of media culture and also celebrates the triumph of the media over society. Baudrillard does not argue for a political resistance to media culture because political activity would need to stand up for a reality, society or community which he thinks are already absorbed and nullified by the media. He argues (1983a: 108) for conformity and passivity, to make the system collapse on itself: 'the strategic resistance is that of a refusal of meaning.' Baudrillard regards the passive mass audience of television positively, because it absorbs and nullifies the messages of the medium. The process by which he arrives at this conclusion depends on the theory of the sign which was discussed in Chapter 4. It is customary to assume that signs gain their meaning by referring to the conception of real things which we hold in our minds. Television images are signs which are meaningful because they are grounded on the concepts of reality which we understand. What Baudrillard does is to undermine and reverse this relationship between signs and realities.

He argues that the conventions of media representation are so powerful and widespread that it is no longer necessary for conceptions of reality to act as the grounds on which signs rest. The codes and conventions of television stand in the place of conceptions of reality, and render those conceptions of reality either unnecessary or redundant. Our conceptions of reality are shaped by the television conventions and other media forms with which we are so familiar. Baudrillard argues that in fact we do not experience reality at all except in terms of the conventions and codes of television and other media. For example,

- our family relationships are perceived in terms of the melodramatic narrative structures of soap opera and romance.
- our experiences of law and order and crime are perceived in terms of the codes of television police series.

This state of affairs he calls 'the hyperreal', in which the experience of reality has become indistinguishable from the television and media conventions which shape the ways in which we perceive it. The process by which this state of affairs occurs he calls **simulation**, which means the staging of events, feelings and relationships by means of the codes and conventions of television and media culture.

These ideas had already been hinted at in the 1960s by Marshall McLuhan, a charismatic theorist of communication and information who frequently appeared on television programmes about the rapid changes occurring in youth culture and the media during that decade. McLuhan was interested less in what the media communicate than in how the form of media communication shapes what the content can be. He coined the term 'global village' to describe how international flows of information were bringing different cultures together and creating a new global society. He coined the phrase 'the medium is the message' to describe how media such as television were more influential by setting up the role of the television viewer, the expectation of familiar narrative forms and easily available information about distant places and people than in the actual information content which television broadcasts. For McLuhan media extend the capacities of the human mind and body. He regarded television as an extension of the human senses of sight and hearing, by which people could experience exciting, exotic and innovative ways of being. McLuhan regarded television viewing as an active experience, in which the viewer fits together the different visual sequences, sounds and music of television programmes like a child making a collage or a mosaic. This active television viewer could be a creative and artistic figure, more like a poet or painter than a **couch potato**: 'the viewer of the TV mosaic, with technical control of the image, unconsciously reconfigures the dots into an abstract work of art' (McLuhan 1987: 313).

couch potatoes
a derogatory term for television viewers supposedly sitting motionless at home watching television passively and indiscriminately.

Postmodernism and globalisation

Global brands advertise their products in television commercials made specifically for particular national and regional markets. So the global brand L'Oreal exchanged its Western model Andie McDowell for the Chinese film star Gong Li for ads in Chinese-speaking territories. In this case the meanings of elegance, sophistication and beauty which the model signifies can translate relatively well from Western markets to Oriental ones. But in the case of other global commodities there is much more specific local knowledge required for audiences to decode television commercials. Television commercials in Singapore, for example, draw on the specific blend of Western and Oriental histories which have formed the country. Singapore is a wealthy and highly successful capitalist culture situated in the Pacific Rim region, and its neighbours are Japan, China, Hong Kong, South Korea and Taiwan. Members of the large middle class in Singapore are wealthy and have tastes for Western products, and the history of the island is that it was a British colony during the days of the British Empire. The Chinese, Malay and Eurasian people forming its mixed population have different cultural traditions and attitudes which have been retained under the umbrella of Western capitalism and consumerism. Television advertising in Singapore needs to address this complex of cultural histories and identities. Many advertisements are embedded in a cultural context and cannot be interpreted without an awareness of this context. When understood in their local context, ads can reveal a lot about the culture in which they are embedded.

Television commercials in Singapore for McDonald's fast food advertised special offers for the Chinese Lunar New Year 1996. These commercials used culturally specific imagery though they were advertising an American-owned global corporation and were made by Leo Burnett Singapore, a regional office of an international advertising agency. The commercials featured the Disney characters Donald Duck, Goofy and Minnie Mouse, properties owned by the American multimedia conglomerate, but the characters were dressed in the costumes of the Chinese gods of Luck, Wealth and Longevity respectively. Each character held a traditional symbol associated with the god, namely oranges, a gold ingot and a peach. The colours red and orange, which represent good fortune and wealth in Chinese culture, could be paralleled with the red and yellow graphics and logo of McDonald's, and the miniature Disney characters were given away free with McDonald's food as a New Year present. One of the McDonald's New Year commercials showed an elderly woman bringing McDonald's food and the Disney New Year characters home to her grandchildren, and the commercial ended with the granddaughter singing 'Mai Dan Lao zhu nin xin nian hao' ('McDonalds wishes you a Happy New Year'). The connection between the older and younger generation, between traditional Chinese religion and contemporary Disney characters, between a community celebration and fast food was the unifying theme of this commercial. It offered to its audience a **preferred reading** in which McDonald's is a unifying force between the generations of Singaporean society and between its cultural heritage and contemporary consumer culture. The global brand was integrated into local culture, and in many ways the commercial is an example of postmodern television:

- It promotes consumer culture.
- It integrates global and local cultural meanings.
- It addresses multiple audiences across different generations.
- It blurs the boundaries between past and present, the contemporary and the traditional.
- It draws on the audience's intertextual knowledge of other media brands and media texts.

So far in this chapter it has been assumed that postmodern television is something which happens in the Western world, and in theoretical books on postmodern television and postmodernism in general it is usually examples from Western, and more specifically American, television which are used to explain it. Among the reasons for this is postmodernism's relationship to modernity. If modernity consists of the period of industrialism and mass culture, surpassed by postmodernism's post-industrial cultural landscape and fragmentation of mass audiences into **niche audiences**, it is much easier to find evidence for these shifts in the European nations and the USA, where industrial and mass culture first took root. It is much harder to explain postmodernism in terms of these shifts in parts of the world (such as the African nations, or South America) where industrial and cultural development has not taken place in this staged way. It is no accident that these are parts of the world where European nations established colonies and empires, for these now post-colonial societies have very mixed cultures in which there are highly developed media cultures but also deeply traditional and rural cultures at the same time. The theories of fragmented subjectivity and changed senses of space, time and identity, which can work quite well as explanations of how Western culture has changed, fit much less comfortably on to societies where inequalities in access to media, culture and wealth are much more marked. Theories of postmodernism tend to assume that it is a global phenomenon, though it is easy to find examples of nations that are still struggling to become modern industrial mass societies.

Whose postmodernism?

The use of the term postmodern, though it derives from Western intellectual culture, has made possible an alternative to the discourse of hierarchy and super-vision of a 'common' culture which is associated with modernity, and facilitated the entry into the debate of feminist and non-Western critics. Debates in media theory about postmodernism, although they have been conducted mainly from a Western point of view, have provided alternative ways of thinking about culture. The result of this is to produce a discourse in which the certainties of the grand narratives of imperialist Western modernity can be challenged by a focus on difference in media consumption practices. But these practices need also to be placed by their inter-relation with larger-scale determinants, demonstrating that the specific and the local

---

preferred reading
an interpretation of a text that seems to be the one most encouraged by the text, the 'correct' interpretation.

niche audiences
particular groups of viewers defined by age group, gender or economic status, for example, who may be the target audience for a programme.

are articulated in reference to them. Postmodernist theories are alternatives to the notion of culture as a hierarchy of taste with an elite at the top and a mass popular audience at the bottom. They have shown that there is no such thing as a common culture, a national culture or an international culture. Instead there are numerous overlapping and competing cultures at local and regional levels, which co-exist with a multinational and global culture. These ways of recognising differences in terms of place, gender, race, age group and other ways of conceptualising identity have enabled voices representing diverse audiences and identity groups to question the dominant imperial model of media dissemination and consumption that is associated with modernity.

While the other theorists mentioned in this chapter often favour the irrational, the momentary and the ambiguous, the cultural theorist Jürgen Habermas aimed to support the power of rationality and communication to make society better. Improved communication between people, and rational debate about politics and society, would enable people to liberate themselves from the apparently stifling bureaucracy of contemporary societies. In order to achieve such liberation and debate, access to the media and the free exchange of ideas in the media are key priorities for Habermas. The centralisation of ownership and control of the media, and ordinary people's lack of interaction with them, are the main problems which he diagnoses: 'Insofar as mass media one-sidedly channel communication flows in a centralized network – from the center to the periphery or from above to below – they considerably strengthen the efficacy of social controls' (1987: 390). In contrast to this, Habermas calls for individual subjects to speak up and take practical action to gain access to media and to use them for reasoned political debate. Feminist theorists have adopted a similar approach to the postmodern. **Feminism** has always valued the connections between the everyday lives of people and political theories of how to address inequalities in society. It also places a value on active subjectivity, especially of course the subjective experience of being a woman. Feminist postmodernists accept that contemporary experience is bound up with fragmentary identities such as sometimes being:

- a worker
- a mother
- a daughter
- a television viewer
- a fan
- a consumer.

Indeed, one woman could have all of these identities at different times in a single day, for example. What is important for feminist postmodernists is to claim the agency, or activity which allows people to act and create change, that Habermas recommends. Jennifer Wicke and Margaret Ferguson (1994: 1) argue for agency, based on a feminist understanding of the postmodern: 'postmodernism is, indeed, a name for the way we live now, and it needs to be taken account of, put into practice, and even contested within feminist discourses as a way of coming to terms with our lived situations.' Wicke and Ferguson regard postmodern theory and feminism as sharing concerns to multiply discourses and identities.

The fact that television is so closely connected to consumer culture, to the desire for commodities and shopping, to virtual tourism and the representation of exotic

feminism
the political and theoretical thinking which in different ways considers the roles of women and femininity in society and culture, often with the aim of critiquing current roles and changing them for the better.

and foreign places, connects television with the history of consumerism. Whereas in the past, shopping and gazing at exotic sights were experiences which took place outside the home, on tours and cruises and in shopping malls, now these experiences can be indulged in at home, by watching television and interacting via a remote control. Leisure and consumption have always historically been associated with women, with femininity, and television too, as the medium belonging in the home, in domestic space, has also been regarded as feminine. For Andreas Huyssen (1986), postmodernism's celebration of mass culture is a celebration of feminisation. Postmodernism entails feminisation, and means both the distraction and disempowerment which are associated with the feminine, but also the importance of the feminine as the new dominant force in contemporary culture.

But feminist theorists of postmodernism such as Meaghan Morris (1993) have argued that the result of the mass of academic articles and books published on postmodernism is a set of ideas which are worryingly similar to those that the most fashionable postmodern theorists claim to have rejected. There is a group of names of leading thinkers about postmodernism, and all of these are white European or American men (this chapter mentions Jean Baudrillard, Jean-François Lyotard, Umberto Eco and Fredric Jameson, who are the most well known). Despite the argument that postmodernism overthrows the hierarchies of the past, celebrates difference and rejects the dead hand of cultural authority, a select band of male theorists have become the new authorities, at the head of a hierarchy of thinkers, who argue among themselves about the complexities of postmodern theory. Despite the fact that postmodernism and feminism share many emphases, postmodernism can appear to be either a taking over of feminists' theoretical and political efforts, a diversionary sidetrack from feminism or a strategy to deprive feminists of their hard-won academic distinction.

Case Study: MTV as postmodern television

MTV seems to be a perfect example of postmodernism: the material it broadcasts appears to be shallow, based around commodity images with no 'message' except the injunction to buy; it broadcasts a flow of short videos producing an endless present or perpetual flow in which the division between daytime and prime time and the fixed points of conventional terrestrial television schedules are largely absent. It was these characteristics that encouraged the American theorist E. Ann Kaplan to analyse MTV as a postmodern form in one of the first substantial studies of MTV in the 1980s. Kaplan (1987: 41) compared MTV to cinema: 'The main differences between MTV and the classical Hollywood film arise from the structuring of the station as a 24-hour continuous flow with its three- to four-minute texts . . ., and from the song-image format.' One definition of postmodernism is that it describes a society in which images have precedence over reality: where the mediated experiences presented by television and other media are more constitutive of our everyday experience and have a greater role in shaping our assumptions and conceptions of our reality than those experiences which we actually undergo ourselves. MTV provides a twenty-four-hour soundtrack to the lives of its viewers, in which the repeated infusion of music works in combination with a restricted repertoire of imagery presenting celebrities. The Spice Girls, for example, were represented through the adjectives which supposedly described the personalities of each member of the group: Posh,

Scary, Ginger, Sporty and Baby. Such imagery can be easily manipulated, however, showing that the celebrity pop performer on television is a cluster of signs which can mutate, rather than the representation of a real personality which precedes the images seen on MTV. Kaplan (1987: 44) argued that this is a development that matches postmodern versions of identity:

> Perhaps most relevant to our discussion of the postmodernist devices in MTV videos generally is the blurring of distinctions between a 'subject' and an 'image'. What seems to be happening in the play with the image of the various kinds discussed is the reduction of the 'self' to an 'image' merely. Television in this way seems to be at the end of a whole series of changes begun at the turn of the century with the development of modern forms of advertising and the department store window.

Madonna's manipulation of her persona is the most famous example of this, and more recently performers such as Kylie Minogue and Britney Spears have transformed their images from girlish innocence to more sexual personas. MTV is a key part of a much wider culture of celebrity which involves the music industry, the Internet, newspapers, magazines and radio.

Celebrity is the commodification of personality, and not only does MTV further this process but it also advertises itself as a **commodity** which is purchased along with the other channels received by multi-channel audiences. In order to achieve this, MTV needs to present its own personality attractively so that it can be bought by its viewers. This is achieved by simultaneously marketing MTV's global engagement with the global music and entertainment industry, and it is also achieved by addressing local and regional audiences in discourses and languages familiar to them. MTV is a global brand, and therefore exemplifies the global capitalism characteristic of postmodernism, yet it has a local dimension. MTV is programmed differently in each territory to which it is broadcast, though the formats remain largely the same and many of the products advertised on MTV are also global brands appearing in different languages and different territories. The academic writing on MTV rose to prominence in the late 1980s and early 1990s, and MTV has changed considerably since then. Rather than one channel, MTV is four channels (MTV itself, which is a general pop music channel, MTV2, which plays more rock and alternatives to dance music, MTVHits, which is a pop chart channel, and MTVBase, which focuses on rap, rhythm-and-blues and soul), and in Britain there are three widely accessible music channels which compete with it.

commodity a raw material or product whose economic value is established by market price rather than the instrinsic qualities or usefulness of the material or product itself.

MUSIC TELEVISION ®

Figure 7.2 The MTV logo. Courtesy of MTV.

continued

ACTIVITY 7.7

To what extent is the inclusion of 'world music' in MTV a recognition of non-Western local cultures, and to what extent is it an example of the commodification of these cultures for the benefit of the music industry?

MTV originated in the United States, and is owned by an American media corporation. It can be argued that MTV is a vehicle for the global spread of American capitalist values, expressed through the international pop music market, which sells products with no intrinsic value that remain fashionable for a very short time and are part of a wider attempt to extract money from the youth market by selling representations of celebrity identities. In its early years MTV advertising seemed to proclaim this in the slogan 'One world, one image, one channel: MTV', which celebrated the erosion of local differences and diversity by the global spread of the channel. Connections between the MTV channel and wider global consumer culture could be seen in the deals made between pop stars and the soft drinks industry, such as the association of Madonna and Michael Jackson with Pepsi Cola. Commercials featuring the performers and the soft drinks appeared on MTV, making a vicious circle of advertising which encompassed American performers, American television, American soft drinks and American record companies.

But, on the other hand, it is wrong to assume that this field of interconnected media imagery is indifferent to disruption. The arguments about MTV in postmodern theory in the 1980s were also carried through in relation to the performances, especially MTV music video performances, of Madonna. Madonna can also be regarded as a performer who offers radical challenges to conventional norms. She has challenged the representation of femininity by the repeated changes to her celebrity persona, suggesting a freedom of self-expression and pleasure for women. She has been critical of the Catholic Church, especially in its condemnation of sexual pleasure and homosexuality. She has confronted the limits of mass media representation, especially of sexuality, by producing pop videos and other commodities which have generated controversy and occasionally censorship because of their explicit sexual imagery and promotion of sexual pleasure for its own sake. From this point of view, Madonna's economic success as a pop performer frequently appearing on MTV, and the financial assistance for her career provided by her associations with major corporations such as Pepsi Cola, can be seen as ways of using the capitalist media system against itself. For Kaplan (1987: 47) MTV videos had the positive effect of blurring the boundaries between art and commerce, between critique of culture and complicity with consumerism: 'In the case of MTV, video artists are often playing with standard high art and popular culture images in a self-conscious manner, creating a liberating sense by the very defiance of traditional boundaries.' Perhaps by drawing on the global media presence of MTV to get her messages across, and by drawing on connections with other globally recognised brands which keep her own celebrity image to the forefront, Madonna is able to disturb the very structures and ideologies which underlie contemporary television. The most interesting characteristic of postmodern theory, and of postmodern media culture, is the way in which contrasting ideas can be shown to be two sides of the same coin. The complexity and confusion which this produces in theories of television mirror the complexity and confusion that postmodern theorists see around them in television itself.

SUMMARY OF KEY POINTS

● Postmodernism is a critical term that addresses the style and form of television, its place in contemporary culture, and the notion that a new phase of culture has been reached.

● Postmodernist television style includes self-conscious play with the conventions of other television programmes and the pastiche of earlier television forms.

● As a way of describing the contemporary moment, postmodernism means both a break with the past and a new way of engaging in a dialogue with the past.

● The ways that television and other media are deeply embedded in culture and society, at least in developed countries, is evidence of a new postmodern epoch of history.

● Postmodernism can also refer to the sense that our customary ways of judging the value of television, and understanding its significance, may no longer apply.

● Theorists have debated whether postmodern thinking makes possible progressive criticism of television and media culture, or whether it is too accepting of the state of affairs it tries to describe.

Further reading

Alleyne, M., *News Revolution: Political and Economic Decisions about Global Information* (Basingstoke: Macmillan, 1997).

Barker, C., *Global Television: An Introduction* (Oxford: Blackwell, 1997).

Bertens, H., *The Idea of the Postmodern: A History* (London: Routledge, 1995).

Bignell, J., *Postmodern Media Culture* (Edinburgh: Edinburgh University Press, 2000).

Brooker, P. and W. Brooker (eds), *Postmodern After-images: A Reader in Film, Television and Video* (London: Arnold, 1997).

Bruhn Jensen, K. (ed.), *News of the World: World Cultures Look at Television News* (London: Routledge, 1998).

Dahlgren, P., *Television and the Public Sphere* (London: Sage, 1995).

Goodwin, A., 'MTV', in J. Corner and S. Harvey (eds), *Television Times: A Reader* (London: Arnold, 1996), pp. 75–87.

—— *Dancing in the Distraction Factory: Music, Television and Popular Culture* (London: Routledge, 1993).

Herman, E. and R. McChesney, *The Global Media: The New Missionaries of Global Capitalism* (London: Cassell, 1997).

Kaplan, E. A., *Rocking Around the Clock: Music Television, Postmodernism and Consumer Culture* (London: Methuen, 1987).

Kellner, D., *Media Culture: Cultural Studies, Identity and Politics Between the Modern and the Postmodern* (London: Routledge, 1995).

Lewis, L., *Gender Politics and MTV: Voicing the Difference* (Philadelphia, Pa.: Temple University Press, 1990).

McLuhan, M., *Understanding Media: The Extensions of Man* (London: Ark, 1987).

Mundy, J., *Popular Music on Screen: From Hollywood Musical to Music Video* (Manchester: Manchester University Press, 1999).

Nelson, R., *TV Drama in Transition: Forms, Values and Cultural Change* (Basingstoke: Macmillan, 1997).

Wicke, J. and M. Ferguson, 'Introduction: feminism and postmodernism; or, The way we live now', in M. Ferguson and J. Wicke (eds), *Feminism and Postmodernism* (London: Duke University Press, 1994), pp. 1–9.

Woods, T., *Beginning Postmodernism* (Manchester: Manchester University Press, 1999).

Television Realities

8

Television Realities

Introduction

Realism is a particularly ambiguous term in the analysis of television. One meaning focuses on the referent of what is represented: that actual scenes, places and people are represented rather than imagined or fictional ones. A second meaning refers to television's representation of recognisable and often contemporary experience, such as in the representation of characters the audience can believe in, or apparently likely chains of events. This meaning of realism relies on the familiarity of the forms and conventions, the **codes** which represent a reality. But finally, another meaning of realism would reject the conventions of established realistic forms, and look for new and different forms to give access to the real. In each of these meanings, however, realism posits the separation of the text from a real which pre-exists it.

Factual television

For workers in the television industry the kinds of programmes discussed in this chapter fall into the category of 'factual' television. This category includes programmes which feature non-actors on location, in the modes of:

- **documentary**
- drama-documentary
- **docusoap**.

Programmes such as this aim to represent reality, to dramatise events which occurred in the past, or **denote** people living or working in a continuing narrative serial. It might seem that television technology and the conventions of television programme-making are used in these examples as neutral media for representing personalities and situations which already existed or would have existed even if the programme were not being made. Although the representatives of Club 18–30 in Spain might have behaved in similar ways whether or not the docusoap *Club Reps* had been made for ITV, other programmes which appear to be factual cross into the territory of fictional entertainment because they are based in situations designed for television. *Big Brother* is the most well-known example of television like this, a '**reality TV**' programme where the members of the public had been chosen to appear, in a house specifically built for the programme, and were aware that they were being recorded twenty-four hours a day. Similarly, some programmes aim to reconstruct events which actually happened, such as the crimes reconstructed in *Crimewatch UK*, but use actors performing scripted dialogue and action to do this. Some apparently real events in television programmes become performances, and some performances are

Figure 8.1 The contestants from *I'm a Celebrity. . . . Get Me Out of Here!* Courtesy of Granada.

designed to be equivalent to real events. Television realism is a flexible category, containing at one end of the spectrum news footage which claims to document events occurring independently of the fact that they are being recorded, and at the other end of the spectrum drama entertainment programmes which claim to be realistic but are constructed for television. Television realism is a matter both of content and of the conventions or codes which structure the representation seen on the screen. It is the interaction between what is on television and the ways in which an audience understands a programme that is at the heart of television realism. Television has a 'language of realism' which programme-makers and audiences share.

In Television Studies, theorists have tried to establish what makes television different from other media such as cinema or radio.

- Like radio, television is broadcast across a wide area and its viewers receive the same signals simultaneously.
- Like radio, television can broadcast live, and television and radio have a history of addressing nations and regions with public service information as well as entertainment.
- But television is like cinema in its combination of image and sound.
- Like cinema, television addresses its viewers as consumers of entertainment and fiction.

In relation to forms of realism, however, television factual programmes aim to present information about the diverse ways in which people live and to broaden the horizons of understanding for the audience. Television audiences are invited to experience the lives of others through the mediation of television documentary forms, for example, so that television realism carries an assumption of social responsibility.

Television realism aims both to mirror society to itself and to show the diversity which exists within a society which is assumed to have an overall unity. Television realism constructs a sense of an organic and unified culture, partly by exhibiting the complexity and diversity of culture. Television realism consists of a negotiation between ideas of unity and difference, familiar and unfamiliar, and thus performs an **ideological** role in shaping the norms of society.

ideology the set of beliefs, attitudes and assumptions arising from the economic and class divisions in a culture, underlying the ways of life accepted as normal in that culture.

ACTIVITY 8.1

Consider the limits on the ways the term 'realistic' can be used about television: are there ways in which science fiction programmes can be realistic, or fantasy programmes such as *The X Files* or *Xena Warrior Princess*? What criteria are you using to formulate your answers to this question?

Realism and television technologies

Television programmes are coded as transcriptions of the real world, but they are assembled from the different discourses of image and sound which are available in the 'language' of television. Television cameras admit rays of light through a lens on to an electronic grid which registers them as quantities of red, green and blue. These signals are encoded for transmission, and the corresponding colour tubes of the television set resynthesise the signal as a beam scanning across 312.5 lines, twice for each image, producing the effect of a 625-line image. In sound recording, the recording mechanism isolates and intensifies some sounds and not others. It produces an implied perspective on the sound source, representing sound through the hidden electronic processes of recording, transmission and reproduction. Television realism is reinforced by the combination of sound and image, each providing references to and 'evidence' of the smooth unity of the television text as a transcription of reality. There is a separation between the objects or people which are recorded and the recording itself. Since television uses technologies of recording images that seem to transcribe realities 'objectively', or in **semiotic** terminology 'denotatively', television images acquire the status of evidence. But because of this separation, because they are representations of realities rather than realities themselves, television representations are ideological: they encode social points of view which condense, displace or forget social relationships.

semiotics the study of signs and their meanings, initially developed for the study of spoken language, and now used also to study the visual and aural 'languages' of other media such as television.

commodity a raw material or product whose economic value is established by market price rather than the intrinsic qualities or usefulness of the material or product itself.

Programmes often conceal the work of their production, just as other kinds of product made for our mass society (such as tins of soup, cars, newspapers or clothes) are abstracted from the work processes and institutional arrangements which created them. Products like this are called **commodities**, and in the early twentieth century the German theorist Walter Benjamin (1969: 212) argued that mechanical reproduction processes which give rise to the media of photography, cinema and now television substitute 'a plurality of copies for a unique existence'. Television images are 'copies' of reality not in the sense that they are fakes but in that they are the result of a mechanical process and circulate remotely from the physical body of their producer. Television's 'copies' of reality can be distributed widely, and are seen at the same time by mass audiences either on their own or in groups. Media images produced by mechanical reproduction free what has been recorded from its social and historical environment, and free it (to some extent) from control by the state or elite groups. The interpretation of television images is not controlled by these contexts and social relationships either. Three of the effects of this are that:

- television images seem to float free of the frameworks which determine them
- television images circulate in culture as commodities
- television images are separated from the people, places and events which were recorded.

These effects occur despite the **iconic** relationship between those people, places and events and the images themselves.

Contemporary **digital** technologies for recording and editing television, and for transmitting it over networks, pose a potential challenge to the iconic realism of the medium. These digital processes extend the process of unfixing the image from its referent, its maker and its social and historical determinants. Digitisation:

- increases the ease of manipulating images
- allows the transmission of images as electronic units of data along phone cables in the global communications system at high speed and across national boundaries
- permits the digitisation of existing footage into electronic data which can be stored and accessed remotely
- allows the **convergence** of television with interactive systems.

New technologies have modified the realist claims of television, so that digital images, or the grain of video (which is recorded digitally on to the analogue medium of magnetic tape) can connote immediacy, in surveillance video footage for example, in the same way as the visibility of photographic grain produced by chemical recording in film, and apparently proving the simultaneity in time and space of the person who made the recording and the event which has been recorded. The photographic grain of film, which is inseparable from the celluloid on which it is carried, is an iconic sign and physical trace of the object photographed. This separation of the production of the registering material from the activity of making the image by exposing the chemical surface to light underlies film's claim to show reality as it occurred. But we know that post-production effects are used in film to alter images. In digital recording, images and sound are converted into numerical values which can be easily manipulated in the computer. Although they seem like different media, with film seeming to show what was really before the camera more reliably, both technologies' claims to realism are mythical.

There is a correspondence between thinking of realism as a set of codes which document recognisable realities and thinking of society as constituted by the exchanges of speech and expression between individuals. For realist television forms assume the transparency of the television medium, just as society assumes transparent communication between individuals. In the same way that different kinds of people use different **discourses** deriving from their social class, gender, religion or political

iconic sign in semiotics, a sign which resembles its referent. Photographs, for example, contain iconic signs resembling the objects they represent.

digital television television pictures and sound encoded into the ones and zeros of electronic data. Digital signals can also be sent back down cables by viewers, making possible interaction with television programmes.

convergence the process whereby previously separate media technologies merge together. For example, computers can now send faxes, show DVD films and play music.

discourse a particular use of language for a certain purpose in a certain context (such as academic discourse, or poetic discourse), and similarly in television, a particular usage of television's audio-visual 'language' (news programme discourse, or nature documentary discourse, for instance).

ACTIVITY 8.2

Research how 'fake' television pictures have been used in the past. Do contemporary technologies of digital manipulation amount to a significant challenge to the reliability of 'realistic' television images?

---

outlook, so television realisms represent realities in ways which are recognisable to some viewers and not others. If television realism can never match its codes and conventions to the different versions of reality which actual viewers experience, we need to ask how the notion of realism has become such a widely understood and widely used criterion for discussing and evaluating television. The answer to this problem is to understand how some forms of realism have become dominant codes, and why.

The dominant form of realism in television, labelled by theorists 'classic realism', roughly coincides with the epoch of modern industrial society. It can be seen in the majority of television fiction programmes, and also affects the representation of people in television factual programmes and documentary. Individuals' character determines their choices and actions, and human nature is seen as a pattern of character-differences. These differences permit the viewer to share the hopes and fears of a wide range of characters. The comparisons and judgements about identifiable human figures represented on television are reliant on a common code of judgement, a notion of 'normality', which is the terrain on which the viewer's relationships with characters can occur. Classic realism represents a world of psychologically consistent individual **subjects**, and addresses its viewers as the same kind of rational and psychologically consistent individual. The action of the television text is to establish communication and offer involving **identification** with the images it shows. Individual television texts need to be constructed as wholes which promise intelligibility and significance. The realist assumption of the match between the television text and a pre-existing reality underlies this process, by posing the image as equivalent to a real perception of recognisable social space. This depends on the equivalence between what and how the viewing subject might see and be seen, and what and how the television point of view might see and be seen. So the category of the rational perceiving subject is the connecting assumption shared by the viewer and television, and by his or her world and the world represented on television. The viewer's varied and ordered pattern of identifications makes **narrative** crucial to classic realism, for the different kinds of look, point of view, sound and speech in narrative are the forms through which this communication between text and audience is produced.

subject in psychoanalysis, the term for the individual self whose identity has both conscious and unconscious components.

identification a term deriving from psychoanalytic theories of cinema, which describes the viewer's conscious or unconscious wish to take the place of someone or something in a television text.

narrative an ordered sequence of images and sound that tells a fictional or factual story.

British soap opera and realism

The television form of British soap opera exhibits several kinds of realism, for it is a continuing form, flowing onward like our conventional experience of time in reality. British soap opera's social realism derives from the historical circumstances in 1960 when the first regular British soap, *Coronation Street*, was created. The portrayal of Northern working-class life contains the same nostalgia for community which was being dramatised in the cinema films and television and theatre plays of the late 1950s, at a time when this culture was no longer representative of how most British people lived. Community is always already lost, and persists as the impossible dream of binding separated families and groups together. Soaps are multi-character dramas, and their stories, settings and concerns are embedded in the mythologies of community in national popular culture.

Soaps appear to 'reflect' reality, with their fictional worlds functioning as a microcosm of 'ordinary life'. But the condensation and narrative progress which are necessary to television fiction mean that soaps do more than 'reflect'. There are very frequent breaking-points in soap opera families and communities (such as divorce, birth, death, gossip and antagonism between characters), which enable new stories to begin. So while the foundations of soap opera reflect ideological norms in being centred on the family, community and regional identity, it is the lack and disturbance of these structures which drives the narrative. Plots are often based on 'common-sense' wisdom about human nature, like 'pride comes before a fall', or 'a little knowledge is a dangerous thing'. These common-sense axioms are the ideological assumptions which underlie dramatic dilemmas. Charlotte Brunsdon (1981: 35) has explained that 'The coherence of the serial does not come from the subordination of space and time to linear narrativity, as it does in classical narrative cinema, but from the continuities of moral and ideological frameworks which inform the dialogue'.

Brunsdon (1981: 36) argues that

> although soap opera narrative may seem to ask "What will happen next?" as its dominant question, the terrain on which this question is posed is determined by a prior question – "What kind of person is this?" And in the ineluctable posing of this question, of all characters, whatever their social position, soap opera poses a potential moral equality of all individuals.

The action in soaps takes place within a set of values that provide the norms for characters' lives, and, even though characters continually violate these norms, they remain bound by them and have to learn to adjust to them or suffer the consequences. While the narrative of the serial poses these moral questions of its characters, the leakage of these questions out of and back into the realities of the viewer's life, and out of and into other media discourses such as newspaper stories, spreads them across society as a whole. It is soap opera realism which allows this transfer between fiction and reality, and enables soaps to claim social responsibility and **public service** functions. Phil Redmond (quoted in Nelson 1997: 114–15), the creator and producer of Channel 4's soap opera *Brookside*, set in Liverpool, explained that, when the programme began in the early 1980s, 'I wanted to use the twice-weekly form to explore social issues, and, hopefully, contribute to any social debate . . . From the outset one of my main aims was to try and reflect Britain in the 1980s.' Soaps are an arena for the mediated 'debate' about morality and social behaviour in modern societies, and pose television institutions as socially responsible. The proof of this concern is measured by the responses of viewers (in phone-ins, viewers' letters and audience **ratings**) to programmes. But there are no issues without the media to

public service in television, the provision of a mix of programmes that inform, educate and entertain in ways that encourage the betterment of audiences and society in general.

ratings the number of viewers estimated to have watched certain programmes, as compared to the numbers watching other programmes.

ACTIVITY 8.3

In what ways do the realisms of British soap operas depend on the mythologies and stereotypes that represent the regions of Britain in which soaps are set? Does this make them more realistic, or less?

---

represent them and direct them back to their source in society, so the important question for Television Studies becomes how particular forms of address and representational form are used to 'reflect' and respond 'responsibly' to social life.

The realism of soaps depends not only on their construction and form within their television **genre** but also on the discourse generated around them. The stories about soap operas in newspapers and television listings magazines offer information and advertise soaps in ways which support the kinds of realism established by the forms of the programmes themselves. The soaps are represented as entirely familiar: the articles profiling the actors presuppose familiarity with the names, identities and major events in the lives of the characters, and the fascination with what will happen, and with the continuing production of the series, particularly in relation to the changes in personnel among the actors, helps to support the creation of a continuous present in the soaps. The television industry is able to publicise its soaps extensively, while maintaining secrecy about forthcoming events in the narrative and its technical mode of production. But the popular press is also involved in the comparison and testing of the soap narratives against reality, running articles on the 'real' people of the East End of London, and on the lives of the actors in *EastEnders*. The exaggerated **melodramatic** forms of soap opera narrative (its use of comic, grotesque or stereotypical characters, for instance) play against its realism, and the viewer's pleasure must therefore partly depend on his or her recognition of the mediation of realism by television forms and institutions. The back and forth movement between fiction and fact in these discourses both maintains their separation from each other and shows how interdependent they are, testifying to the unstable border between what is considered 'real' and what is a performance or representation of reality.

The television theorist Robert Allen (1985: 85) has argued that 'soap opera trades narrative closure for paradigmatic complexity', meaning that although soaps, like life, never end, the result of this is that very large numbers of narrative strands can be kept going in parallel. For any one character, change and unpredictability are the norm, but in the long run this has no effect on the community as a whole. Yet, at any one moment, a change in any character will affect all the other characters with whom he or she comes into contact. The realism of soap opera refers not only to this apparent unpredictability and change but also to the programme's consistently represented world and fidelity to its own fictional identity.

The shifting relations of characters in soap opera are paralleled by the shifting of the camera's points of view, which give access to the widely differing people and locations that appear in each episode. *EastEnders*, like all soaps, represents a community with a regional identity. It has a residential setting in an urban area, like Coronation Street or Brookside Close. Flows of characters and interaction between them are made in Albert Square, around and through which characters

genre a kind or type of programme. Programmes of the same genre have shared characteristics.

melodrama a form of drama characterised by exaggerated performance, a focus on reversals of fortune and extreme emotional reactions to events.

walk, and the various shops, pubs, houses and the market where characters meet. There is a sense that there is no escape from Albert Square, but the roads into it also lead outwards into Walford and the rest of London, allowing the diffusion of the action towards the edge of the represented space and the invasion of that space from the outside. Within the rooms and other smaller spaces where scenes are set, Sandy Flitterman-Lewis (1992: 224) has argued that the camera does not create a consistent space by alternating establishing shots and **shot-reverse shots** in order to situate the drama securely for the viewer, 'for what the reverse shot accomplishes in the soap opera is something altogether different. The quality of viewer involvement, instead, is one of continual, momentary, and constant visual repositioning, in keeping with television's characteristic "glance".' The movement of the narrative point of view allows the sense of incompletion and future necessary to soap opera form. This maintenance of 'the now' is supported by the emphasis in journalistic discourses on each soap's identity and unity.

> **shot-reverse shot**
> the convention of alternating a shot of one character and a shot of another character in a scene, producing a back-and-forth movement which represents their interaction visually.

Realism and ideology

Television realism places the viewer in the position of a unified subject 'interpellated' with, or folded into, the discourses of a dominant ideology (Althusser 1971), subjected (made into a **subject**, and subject to the ideology) to a version of reality in which he or she misrecognises that reality and misrecognises himself or herself. This theory of how ideology in television separates the subject from his or her 'real' self shares its structure with the French psychoanalyst Jacques Lacan's theory of subjectivity. For Lacan the subject is the result of a division between his or her 'real' self and the means (such as words, photographs or other representations) through which the subject comes to know himself or herself. Theorists of television have therefore turned to **psychoanalytic** theory in order to explain how individuals are hailed into ideology and subjectivity by the experience of watching television. One of the consequences of the ideologies of television realism is a contradiction between the viewer's working activity, where he or she is producer, and his or her leisure activity, in which he or she is positioned as a consumer. Althusser makes the very important point in his essay that ideology is not just a question of ideas circulating in people's heads but is inscribed in certain material practices. The reactionary practice of television realism involves the entrapment of the spectator in a position of apparent dominance and control over the represented reality offered by television's discourses about reality. Realist television discourse resolves contradictions by representing a unified and rational world of causes and effects, actions and consequences, moral choices and rewards or punishments. It distances the viewer from the contradictory and ambiguous dynamics of reality and suggests that political action to intervene in the ways that reality is produced from day to day is unnecessary.

> **psychoanalysis**
> the study of human mental life, including not only conscious thoughts, wishes and fears but also unconscious ones. Psychoanalysis is an analytical and theoretical set of ideas as well as a therapeutic treatment.

If television, particularly realist television, is performing ideological work in concealing a more correct vision of social and political realities, the makers of television might be under an obligation to draw the attention of the viewer to the non-equivalence of television and reality. According to this view, television cannot be a 'true' representation, but it may be a medium in which the beginnings of a recognition of the true state of affairs could occur. In this context realism is no longer a reflection of an exterior reality but one of the forms in which representations and audiences connect with each other. The makers of television must draw the viewer's attention to his or her relationship with the medium in order to make him or her recognise the social relations that this relationship involves. So perhaps the strangeness or unrealistic nature of television versions of reality might draw the viewer's attention to the fact that he or she is watching a representation and not a reality. When familiar recognitions and identifications break down, viewers might grasp what it is that the relations between television and audience, and between real and representation, involve. This strategy is known as 'critical realism', and involves recognising a relationship between the television text and material social realities, yet resisting the television text's transcription of reality as if television were a neutral medium, so that the work of the forms through which representation takes place is recognised as not natural but cultural and constructed.

News and liveness

One of the uses of photography has been for military surveillance, first by placing cameras in balloons to observe enemy troops and positions, and modern uses of satellite surveillance and computer enhancement of images continue this aim to provide a superior and powerful vision of space and detail beyond the capacity of the human eye. The broadcasting of such images, however, is controlled by military institutions:

- by allowing or withholding access to the action
- by exercising powers to censor information, or
- by encouraging television crews to self-censor the images they acquire.

In the Gulf War of 1991, for example, television journalists were organised into 'pools' or collective groups called Media Response Teams, where, in exchange for accepting military discipline and following rules on reporting, journalists were provided with transmission facilities that enabled them to send information to London less than an hour after acquiring it. **CNN** was able to broadcast television pictures live, and the CNN reporter Peter Arnett in Iraq's capital Baghdad was able to observe American cruise missiles destroying buildings a few blocks from his location and transmit pictures of the action using a portable satellite dish. Television pictures of air attacks on Baghdad became available worldwide, beamed by the communications satellites which now reach 85 per cent of the world's surface.

CNN Cable News Network, the first international satellite news channel, operating from the United States.

The attraction of television as a medium relies in part on its ability to broadcast events live. The excitement of live television derives not only from the sense of participation and presence at an event which live broadcasting provides, but also from the assumption that what we see and hear in live broadcasting is unmediated, uncontaminated and accurate. When sports events such as the Olympics or the football Cup Final are broadcast live, or when a national event such as a royal wedding or the occurrence and aftermath of disasters are broadcast, it is the accidental detail and unpredictable unfolding of events which are fascinating. And now, because live broadcasting is relatively rare, those things which are broadcast live gain a particular importance. Live events are those which it is assumed have a universal importance for society. Live television gives the audience access to an 'other' space and also to an alternative time: the viewer's present and the present experience of others in a distant place are equivalent but different. The caption 'Live' is significant in itself, for it means 'alive', connoting that a living reality for other people is being shown, and is open to the audience's involvement.

Contemporary networks of electronic mediation allow digital images denoting realities to be circulated around the world from television news crews back to their producers at home, and also to the news agencies which sell packages of news pictures to broadcasters. Television technologies are not neutral, and the capacity to circulate images denoting realities has political effects. One example of this is the perception of the Third World by Western television audiences, where some categories of event are the most frequent versions of reality denoted in news and current affairs television. Large-scale political violence and natural disasters are the predominant form of news image broadcast of Third World countries and developing countries such as China. Media theorists have studied the patterns of regional and global news coverage, and discovered that, although the greater part of news imagery relates to the country in which news is made or to the neighbouring countries, it is the United States and other Western nations which appear in news coverage as the active makers of news, while countries in the developing world are portrayed as the passive suffering objects of news events. These divisions between active makers of the news and passive sufferers of news events are parallel to the division between the rich Western nations which intervene in world affairs and control world institutions such as the World Bank or United Nations, and the relatively impoverished and politically disempowered nations in the rest of the world.

ACTIVITY 8.4

Collect samples of television news stories relating to nations in Africa. What patterns do you find in the kinds of stories about Africa, and the ways in which they are represented in image and sound? What conclusions can you draw from this exercise?

The documentary mode

Factual programmes denote society, and inform and educate the audience about aspects of life with which they are familiar, or aspects signified as unfamiliar. Factual programmes make the 'other' into the familiar, and make the familiar seem 'other' by denoting it in unfamiliar ways. The BBC's 1999–2000 budget gave considerable funding to factual programmes. The digital channels BBC News 24 and BBC Knowledge (broadcasting factual programmes) cost £50 million and £21 million each. Looking at programme categories, 'factual and learning' programmes cost £350 million, 'news' cost £310 million, 'sport' cost £178 million, and music and arts programmes (mainly factual) cost £107 million. The fiction categories of entertainment and drama cost £253 million and £244 million, so, although fiction programmes are prestigious, expensive and important to the BBC, factual programmes are invested in at least equally. This is in part because the denotation of society in factual programmes, especially documentary, is part of television's public service function.

Figure 8.2 Mrs Hymers cooking on *The 1940s House*. Courtesy of Simon Roberts.

British television documentaries often belong to **strands** such as *Cutting Edge* or *Modern Times*, where different teams of programme-makers produce documentaries on different subjects under the shared identity of the series 'brand', whereas documentaries such as *Vets in Practice* follow the same people across a whole series. Documentary series such as this have been very successful. For example, Channel 4 factual programmes drew a high proportion of viewers from the valuable ABC1 social groups (professional, managerial and skilled workers) who are attractive to advertisers: *The Kama Sutra* got a 54 per cent share of ABC1s, and *The 1940s House* 53 per cent. Factual programmes are scheduled in evening prime time partly because they gain large or valuable audiences cheaply. They require few personnel and limited equipment: the Channel 4 documentary series *Undercover Britain*, for instance, needed just one person covertly operating a concealed button-sized camera, and no performers of course. Fiction drama cost about £650,000 per hour to make in the late 1990s, versus about £125,000 per hour for documentary.

In order to produce the impression of realism in television documentary, several very unnatural procedures have to be carried out. The documentary subject will almost always be aware that he or she is being recorded, witnessed or even pursued by the camera operator and often also by a sound recordist. Once the footage has been gathered, the documentary-maker will edit the footage together in order to produce a coherent argument or a narrative. While the finished programme may acknowledge the presence of the documentary-maker, it is often the case that documentaries imply that the subject is behaving 'naturally' or at least representatively. So there is a tension between producing a documentary which is representative and 'accurate' and providing the audience with a programme which conforms to the conventions of argument or storytelling. It is this tension which gives rise to the complaints and occasionally legal cases brought by documentary subjects against documentary-makers, where the subject claims that he or she has been misrepresented or made to look foolish. The assumption of accuracy which always accompanies the documentary mode brings with it the danger of claims of misrepresentation. Techniques such as covert filming, or showing the documentary-maker on screen developing a relationship with the documentary subject, are two different ways of coping with these problems.

> **strand**
> a linked series of programmes, sharing a common title.

ACTIVITY 8.5

Try to find examples of 'spoof' or 'parody' documentary such as *The Office* or *People Like Us*. How do these programmes draw attention to the problems of documentary-making and the codes of documentary? What impact might they have on audiences' attitudes to 'real' documentaries?

It is not only the observation of the documentary subject which provides an impression of reality in documentary television but also the inclusion of supporting **narration**, testimony or expert commentary. These devices make links with other factual genres, where:

> **narration** the process of telling a story through image and sound. Narration can also refer to the spoken text accompanying television images.

- the authority of a narrator provides coherence and continuity
- testimony of members of the public supports the authenticity of the programme
- expert commentary provides backing for the assertions and arguments of the programme-maker or the figures appearing in the programme.

Devices such as these are found in, for example, sports programmes, science programmes, nature programmes and current affairs. It is always the case that television programmes gain their meanings by their similarity to and difference from each other, and the overlap of codes and conventions among programmes. Some documentary conventions connote unmediated reality, such as hand-held camera, 'natural' rather than expressive lighting and imperfect sound, while other conventions connote drama, argument and interpretation, such as voice-over, narrative structure and contrastive editing.

metonymy the substitution of one thing for another, either because one is part of the other or because one is connected with the other. For example, 'the Crown' can be a metonym for the British state.

The device of **metonymy** in documentary enables part of reality to stand for the larger real world which it represents. One day in the life of a hotel metonymically stands for any other day. The work of an inner-city social worker stands metonymically for that of all inner-city social workers. Specific images or sequences, or specific documentary subjects, have metonymic relationships with the reality of which they are a part. This device is one of the unstated assumptions which enables television programmes to claim implicitly that they represent society to itself, and connect the specific subjects of programmes to larger social contexts. But the impression of realism in television depends on the relationship between the codes of the programme and the codes available to the audience for interpreting it. Kilborn and Izod (1997: 39) call 'accommodation' the shaping of documentary programmes to accord with the assumed knowledge of the audience. Documentaries about hotels or social work accommodate themselves to some extent with ideological assumptions about hotels and social workers that circulate in society. Television's claim to present the real rests on the ideologies which shape that reality for the audience.

Television drama-documentary re-tells events, often recent events, in order to review or celebrate them. The key figures and turning-points of the story are often familiar to the audience, though opening statements and captions make clear the factual basis of docudramas, while disclaimers may state that some events and characters have been changed, amalgamated or invented. Derek Paget's (1998: 82) definition of drama-documentary is that it 'uses the sequence of events from a real historical occurrence or situation and the identities of the protagonists to underpin a film script intended to provoke debate . . . The resultant film usually follows a cinematic narrative structure and employs the standard naturalist/realist performance techniques of screen drama.' Drama-documentary offers a single and personalised view of a dramatic situation, in which identification with central figures allows access for the audience but where the documentation of an historical situation 'objectively' sets these identifications into a social and political context. Narrative provides the linkage between the forms of documentary and of drama, as John Caughie (1980: 30) describes: 'If the rhetoric of the drama inscribes the document within narrative and experience, the rhetoric of the documentary establishes the experience as an experience of the real, and places it within a system of guarantees and confirmations.' British docudrama is based in carefully researched journalistic investigation, and follows the conventions of journalistic discourse such as the sequential unfolding of events and the use of captions to identify key figures.

Realism and public service: *Crimewatch UK*

Crimewatch UK both represents recent crimes in realistic ways and also, as John Sears (1995: 51) has argued, performs 'a social function by helping to solve crime, and drawing on the collective responsibilities, experiences and knowledge of the viewing audience in order to do so'. This monthly BBC1 mid-evening programme has been running since 1984, and performs a 'public service' function by informing the audience, involving the audience in solving crime and constituting a community whose boundaries are marked by the criminals outside it. *Crimewatch* often features crimes which have been reported already in television news and newspapers, borrowing **intertextual** meanings from other media such as the brassy and military music used in news and action drama (such as police and medical drama). Fictionalised reconstruction of crimes aims to achieve change by dramatising events, emphasising particular details, sometimes shocking the audience and drawing them into the dramatic narrative of solving crimes.

intertextuality how one text draws on the meanings of another by referring to it, by allusion, quotation, or parody, for example.

Crimewatch reduces its codes and conventions, and the problems it addresses, to a few highly coded images and devices which engage viewer knowledge derived from other genres of television, particularly crime drama. E-fits (images of suspects derived from witnesses' reports), photographs of stolen property, security camera footage and physical clues also appear in television police fiction. These coded images are metonyms, parts of the narrative of the crime which are connected with each other and stand in for the crime. Conversely, reconstructions on *Crimewatch* are **metaphors**: they parallel the facts of the crime but are fiction. Metaphoric reconstructions stand in for the actual crime, and represent it. *Crimewatch* title images in the 1990s signified 'information'. Visual signifiers represented:

metaphor the carrying-over from something of some of its meanings on to another thing of an apparently different kind. For example, a television narrative about life aboard ship could be a metaphor for British social life (the ship as metaphor for society).

- police using computers
- police photographing evidence
- police knocking on doors, and
- members of the public telephoning the police.

The sequence of information-gathering draws attention to audience participation and in the rest of the programme banks of phone operators in the studio metonymically represent police information-gathering. Specific callers' information metonymically signifies all the callers ringing in, and all the information collected. Crucial detailed clues lead to the solving of the crime, and this technique is shared with television detective fiction. This factual programme borrows intertextually from television fiction, and its realism sometimes derives from the mixing of factual and fictional conventions. Victims or witnesses sometimes appear in reconstructions playing themselves. It uses codes from several television genres, including current affairs, crime drama, documentary and phone-ins. *Crimewatch* has been successful in assisting the police to change the reality denoted in it by helping to catch criminals, part of television's public service function.

But although the programme constructs a sense of community, and works on behalf of society in general, it individualises its address to the viewer and the crimes which it features. Despite the fact that television is a mass broadcast medium, viewers are addressed as individuals who might be able to assist in the solving of crime. The individualised notion of address is also evident in such public service formats as

---

ACTIVITY 8.6

How are reconstructions used in programmes other than *Crimewatch*, such as history programmes? Are the reconstructions you find always there for 'public service' informational and educational purposes?

---

telethons or the BBC's annual charity fundraiser *Comic Relief*. The presenters of *Crimewatch* address viewers directly with questions such as 'Were you there that morning? Did you see him? Can you help?' The individual action requested from viewers is represented as a response to crimes perpetrated by individuals against individuals. Abstract and structural problems such as the complex of factors which cause crime, and crimes perpetrated by corporate bodies or government agencies, are never represented in *Crimewatch*. This also leads to the underrepresentation of what are known as 'white collar' crimes such as fraud, since these rarely have direct impacts on individuals who could feature in *Crimewatch* as the victims. White collar crimes are a generally committed within large institutions, against other institutions, and their complexity makes it unlikely that they could be featured in the few minutes available for a *Crimewatch* item.

The 'reality' of crime for *Crimewatch* is that it is committed by a small group of deviant outsiders, against certain unfortunate individuals. The practices of gathering information and solving crimes undertaken by institutions, especially the police force, are not represented either since these are also carried out by collective structures rather than simply by individuals. The consequence of this emphasis on individuation in *Crimewatch*, in common with many other programmes concerned with social problems, is a blindness to the large-scale forces which animate individual action and give it its social meaning. The ways in which individual action is determined by factors of

- social class
- economic position, and
- ideologies of gender or race

cannot be accommodated in this form of television representation. So the realism of *Crimewatch* uses metonymy to connect the individual viewer into the larger collective television audience, to connect particular individual experiences to a social experience of crime that remains vague and to connect representatives of the law to the unseen institutions of law enforcement. The particular is linked to the general in *Crimewatch* by the form of the programme, through the metonymy which it uses.

Docusoap: actuality and drama

Docusoap combines the observation and interpretation of reality found in documentary with the continuing narrative centring on a group of characters in soap

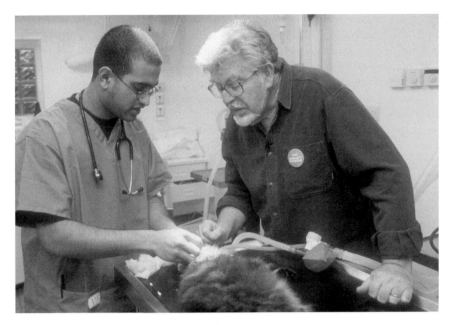

Figure 8.3 Rolf Harris and a vet on *Animal Hospital*. Courtesy of BBC Photograph Library.

opera. Docusoap observes real people and structures this observation into dramatic narrative, both denoting everyday experiences of ordinary people and focusing on performance and narrative. In 1998 the ITV docusoap *Airline* achieved a 50 per cent average audience share, with 11.4 million viewers, while BBC1's *The Cruise* (aboard a cruise liner) and *Animal Hospital* attracted ten million viewers and shares of 40 per cent each. BBC1's first prime-time factual programme, *Airport* (1998), attracted a 44 per cent audience share, and in response ITV moved its competitor, the fire service drama *London's Burning*, to a different place in the schedule. But docusoaps have been criticised for lacking the depth of insight into character or situation that television documentary has conventionally aimed for. Formally, docusoaps use rapid cutting between scenes and characters to maintain audience interest, and do not adopt the sustained focus on the subject which has signified television documentary's quest for understanding. Perhaps the best-known (and most controversial) docusoap of the turn of the twenty-first century was the BBC's *Driving School*, which was scheduled against the popular ITV police drama *The Bill* yet attracted twice as many viewers, peaking at 12 million.

The narrative codes of television fiction structured *Driving School*, and it featured quirky 'characters' experiencing dramatic moments and changes of fortune. Learner driver Maureen and her husband Dave became celebrities, appearing on talk shows and in tabloid newspapers, after Maureen was represented nearly hitting other cars, weeping when she made mistakes and arguing with her husband. The dramatic turning-points, conflicts and moments of comedy were embedded in a narrative provided by voice-over narration. The emphasis on 'real-life drama' in *Driving School* was the subject of controversy when it was alleged that scenes had been 'faked', effectively scripted like drama rather than observed as in documentary. When Maureen was seen waking Dave in the early hours of the morning to go practising, this was a re-enactment, a fictionalised reconstruction. *Driving School* producers were also attacked for selecting subjects such as Maureen who were likely to exaggerate their emotions for the camera and seemed keen to become celebrities. The 'objectivity' of documentary seemed to have been exchanged for 'entertainment', perverting the expectations of realism in factual television genres.

Docusoap is a middle genre between documentary and drama. Docusoap subjects are drawn from the 'middle' of society: neither members of a powerful elite nor powerless and socially excluded. They are typically in service sector jobs – hotel workers, holiday reps, driving instructors or shop assistants – and deal with the public. They are 'like us', as ordinary as their audience, but being on television makes them not 'like us', and they occupy a middle position between ordinariness and celebrity. Docusoaps focus on another kind of middle by documenting their subjects' public working lives as well as their private lives, crossing a boundary between two kinds of experience. For Graeme Burton (2000: 159), docusoap 'stands for a growing use of viewers to entertain the viewers – an approach familiar from the game-show genre and the use of studio audiences. It creates the illusion that television recognises its audience and works for its audience.' In docusoap the divisions between television and ordinary reality, programme and audience, public and private, stardom and anonymity, are crossed.

Changing people

Programmes featuring ordinary people have become commonplace on British television. This movement began in the BBC series *Video Nation*, made between 1995 and 2000. Its producers were keen to bring to television the heritage of collecting the comments and personal accounts collected in the 1930s by the Mass Observation project, where a large number of people kept diaries of their everyday lives and commented on the social and political events of the time. *Video Diaries* continued this interest in ordinary people, and the concept of collecting reports from a wide range of social classes and regions of Britain. But instead of providing a picture of social and political attitudes, it focused on the detail of people's everyday lives, their work and leisure, worries and attitudes. In the last twenty years, in *Video Diaries* and many other programmes featuring ordinary people, the video diary format has been introduced in reality TV and documentary. Participants speak privately to camera about themselves, knowing that this private speech will become public when the programme is broadcast. In contemporary television the boundaries between private and public are blurred by the video confessional.

The 'makeover' genre is factual, and programmes such as *Changing Rooms*, *Looking Good* and *Ground Force* denote the transformation of homes, gardens, meals, clothing, hair, etc. by 'experts'. But these programmes' climax is a dramatic moment of revelation when the transformed house, garden or person is presented to an internal audience in the programme (such as members of a family) and the television audience. The reaction to the transformation highlights the public nature of a normally private process, and the programme presenter manages the turning of the 'ordinary' person he or she has befriended towards the public audience of the programme. In *Stars in Their Eyes* members of the public transform themselves into imitation celebrities, seemingly transformed into public figures. Television combines dramatic and documentary modes, and blurs the boundary between private and public experience, between ordinariness and celebrity.

Pop Idol and *Fat Club* (both ITV 2002) are in effect versions of the makeover show where what is made over is the person. BBC has adopted the same format of the makeover for its programme *Would Like to Meet* (2002). In each of these programmes members of the public are advised, but importantly they are also abused, by a team of experts who guide their transformation. In some cases the objective of the transformation is explicitly public fame and recognition, as in *Pop Idol*, and the narrative progress of the serial is from ordinariness to extra-ordinariness, from alignment with the television audience to separation from the audience as the central figure becomes a star. But even in programmes where the objective is simply to become more attractive by losing weight, or to begin a satisfying relationship with a member of the opposite sex, in all cases the focus is on the often aggressive moulding of the subject. The assumption behind these programmes is that the self is a malleable and transformable object, which can be worked upon with the assistance of experts and with personal self-discipline. There is a persistent injunction for the subject to take control of himself or herself and to embark on a potentially infinite programme of self-improvement. In many of these programmes, though not all of them, the proof of success in the programme of self-improvement has a sexual dimension. Since sexuality is considered to be the prime location for the expression of personal identity, and sexual activity is a test of the subject's integration into the social norms of (hetero)sexual interaction, this aspect of subjective identity is a readily available demonstration of the integration of the subject.

Reality TV: *Big Brother*

The first series of *Big Brother* was shown in the Netherlands in the spring of 1999, produced by Jon deMol's television production company Endemol. The format has been successfully sold around the world, and its value to television companies in attracting audiences is shown by the willingness of CBS in the United States to pay $20 million to Endemol for the rights to the format. Generically, the programme combines material from several different television genres:

- It is a competition in which there is a prize of £70,000.
- It is a real-life soap opera with that genre's emphasis on the expression of emotion and the formation of sub-groups in the community and the exclusion of outsiders from those groups, and the use of bounded physical space as a symbolic representation of a wider society.
- It is a documentary featuring a social experiment that aims to explore the patterns of interaction between people under various kinds of 'natural' and 'artificial' pressures.

This latter form of realism was emphasised in the British version by the prominence of inserted sequences featuring the programme's two resident psychologists analysing and discussing the behaviour of particular participants. This psychological discourse appeared both in the 'serious' form of the commentaries by Professor Beattie and Professor Collett and on the *Big Brother* website, which alluded to psychometric data presentation in its flirting index, its kissing index and its statistics on who had hugged whom.

A significant focus of interest in *Big Brother* for its participants, for its commentators and for the audience was the question of whether any of the participants would begin sexual relationships with each other. Sexuality is of course a common means of attracting audiences to television programmes by promising voyeuristic coverage of sexual behaviour. The nudity of participants early in the first series of *Big Brother* was a prominent part of its visibility as a programme (demonstrated in the popular press), and in the second series the producers installed a hot-tub in the house, thus providing further opportunities for the display of the participants' bodies. Partly because there was little else for them to do, participants spent a lot of time exercising and developing their bodies, at the same time presenting and developing their physicality for the cameras. Sexuality is a particularly intimate aspect of social behaviour; it also corresponds to the programme's emphasis on the construction of identity, and the potential conflicts both within individuals and between individuals over matters of desire and the formation of relationships which include some and exclude others. These questions of internal conflict and conflict between participants over sexual relationships also conform to the pseudo-scientific discourse justifying the programme, where the enforced hothouse situation could be argued to correspond to a laboratory experiment in which sexual behaviour could be observed. The inclusion of gay and lesbian participants in *Big Brother* in Britain places further strains on these individuals and their fellow participants, because of the still prevalent homophobia of British society. The potential for the formation of alliances and the stigmatisation of individuals around their sexuality becomes another possible focus of interest for the audience, which is also invited to support participants on the basis of their sexuality or their potential for sexual activity, and to exclude others from the programme by voting them out.

In *Big Brother* ten volunteers were observed by permanently installed cameras in a specially built house in London for nine weeks. £70,000 was on offer to the contestant who survived weekly nominations for ejection by his or her housemates and the public's votes. The private space of the house became public (even more so on the Internet, where real-time footage was screened), promising access to private space and the opportunity of interaction by phone-in voting. As Vivian Sobchack (1996: 82) has noted, 'While our personal access to the space of others has been appreciably amplified through television and computers, our privacy has been simultaneously reduced'. *Big Brother* gossip was a key pleasure for viewers since the programme's realism encouraged viewers to feel they knew the contestants. The programme consisted largely of sequences of the participants interacting and conversing, with frequent close-ups reinforcing an apparent intimacy between the audience and the contestants. For Graeme Burton (2000: 146): 'The dominance of this way of using and experiencing television gives the illusion of physical closeness, invokes those rules of social interaction which demand attention and which create some sense of social proximity.' Press coverage of *Big Brother* built up a selection of character-types (most famously the manipulative and deceptive 'Nasty Nick' Bateman – the 'villain'), and the producers' selection of outgoing and dominant contestants provoked dramatic conflict and performance comparable to soap opera fiction. The participants attempted to play roles that would stop other participants voting them off, and which would enlist audience support. Just as in docusoap, the realism of 'reality TV' is partly performance, and it is telling that several *Big Brother* contestants have become television presenters.

ACTIVITY 8.7

Perhaps the oddest feature of the *Big Brother* house was its lack of a television set. How was the realism of the programme either increased or reduced by depriving its inhabitants of the chance to watch television?

The genre of the television talk show (see Chapter 5) and 'reality TV' like *Big Brother* exemplify an uneasy shift in the contemporary ideologies of television from a liberal emphasis on personal empowerment and public service concern with social issues to an aggressive surveillance of the individual subject and the engagement of the audience in a process of stigmatisation, competition and risk. It is appropriate that the participants in *Big Brother* were all aged between twenty-two and thirty-eight, and that its audience mainly comprised viewers in the sixteen to thirty-four age group, of whom 75 per cent watched the programme during its first run. This is the audience most attractive to television advertisers, and it is not only the large audiences for *Big Brother* which are attractive to broadcasters, but also the spending power of the audience group dominating its participants and its audience. For this younger generation the dynamic shift between a liberal and a free market indi-vidualist ideology is apposite to their lived experience (student grants have been abolished, low-paid work is common, conspicuous consumption and excessive behaviour are conventional, illegal activity such as drug use is accepted and threats such as sexually transmitted diseases and violence against the person are more likely than for other age groups).

Big Brother's title alludes to George Orwell's novel *Nineteen Eighty-four*, where the citizens of a future totalitarian society were monitored by video surveillance: 'Big Brother is watching you.' The programme's title connotes entrapment, restric-tion and control, and *Big Brother* was marketed at first as an experiment about how human society works, with the contestants like rats trapped in a laboratory maze. As if in a psychological test, the selfishness of desiring the prize of £70,000 conflicted with the contestants' need to gain loyalty from their housemates. Rules were imposed by the production team, and tasks were set through which contestants were rewarded with necessities and rewards, in the way that laboratory animals are trained to undertake tasks to gain food. *Big Brother* set up the tensions between freedom and control, individual and community, work and pleasure, which model social reality. So its realism also consists of its representation of the real conditions of existence in society in a coded form. *Big Brother* showed society to itself, largely unconsciously, by putting key aspects of contemporary ideology into real physical forms.

Case study: actuality in television news

balance
the requirement
in television news
and current affairs to
present both sides of
an argument or issue.

actuality footage
television pictures
representing an event
that was filmed live.
The term usually
refers to pictures of
news events.

electronic
newsgathering
(ENG) the use
of lightweight
cameras and digital
technology such
as portable satellite
transmission dishes
to record and
transmit news
pictures and sound.

news value
the degree
of significance
attributed to a news
story, where items
with high news value
are deemed most
significant to the
audience.

Television has overtaken newspapers as the dominant source of news in Britain and other developed nations. This is partly because broadcasting regulations demanding '**balance**' and 'objectivity' govern television news but not newspaper publishing. But another key consideration, which is the focus of this section, is the value of immediacy in television news deriving from its incorporation of **actuality** pictures and live reporting. Television news programmes can, on rare occasions, incorporate live footage during programmes, although the technological complexity of doing this can make news producers wary of links with news crews in distant locations. News programmes are planned to the second, so the immediacy of live **ENG** footage potentially conflicts with the desire to connote orderliness and authority in news broadcasting. A more common use of ENG footage is therefore to create packages where sequences of actuality pictures have been edited together with a voice-over by the news reporter. The package will be of a known length and can be combined with live studio discussion and other commentary. But since television news attracts its audience with the promise of seeing and hearing news events happen, especially when they are happening live, there is both a professional pride for broadcasters and a hook for potential audiences in using actuality footage. Therefore on-screen captions denoting a live report and the frequent mention of the word 'live' in the pieces to camera by news presenters are a notable feature of television news programmes.

There is a hierarchy of **news value**, in which live actuality pictures are the most attractive to the producers of television news programmes, followed by actuality pictures which have been pre-recorded and finally those stories which cannot be illustrated by actuality footage or other visual forms such as an interview, and which are the stories which are least likely to appear in the producer's running order for a programme. News programmes depend on a mythology in which the television audience can apparently witness directly any significant events occurring anywhere in the world. Television news claims to denote events objectively and immediately, offering a neutral and transparent channel of communication. The iconic quality of television images, which appear simply to record what is unfolding in front of the camera, are key signifiers of this mythology of transparency in television news and in other television factual genres. The word 'television' means seeing at a distance, and television news is a central example of the mythology underlying the medium. For almost everyone in the television audience, the public world of politics, war, business and natural catastrophe is distant, but television news advertises its ability to connect the relatively isolated and disengaged viewer with this more dramatic and apparently important reality. Television news bridges the gap between public space and private space, which has ambivalent ideological effects:

- On one hand, the audience is linked by the medium of television with the wider public world.
- On the other hand, this wider world is shaped according to the codes and conventions of television news, and necessarily remains at a distance from the audience.

The institutional and representational structures of television news simultaneously involve the audience and disempower it.

When two Boeing 767 airliners were flown into the side of the twin towers of the World Trade Center in New York on 11 September 2001, television channels cleared their schedules in order to bring live actuality footage and studio discussion. In the jargon of television production, this is when programmes become 'open ended', meaning that they continue as long as new information is available, rather than finishing at the scheduled fixed point planned by the programme's schedulers. Television news, because of its liveness or potential liveness, is usually the medium that viewers turn to when major news stories are breaking in order to see pictures of the events and discover the most recent developments. On the 11th the maximum audiences for news on terrestrial channels were:

BBC1	9.4 million
BBC2	2.6 million
ITV	7.7 million
Channel 4	1.8 million
Channel 5	0.6 million
Sky News	0.99 million
BBC News 24	0.37 million
ITN News Channel	0.17 million.

Although channels began to cease open-ended coverage of the event in the evening of the first day, news audiences remained high until the end of the week. The BBC adopted the strategy of simultaneous broadcast on its terrestrial BBC1 network and its digital channel BBC News 24. This strategy simplified the management of news broadcasting in a potentially chaotic and highly complex situation, and also functioned as an advertisement for the recently launched BBC rolling news channel. ITN, by contrast, broadcast live news across five different networks: ITV, Channel 4, Channel 5, ITN News and Euronews. This enabled each network to maintain the well-known presenters associated with its programmes and provided different programming to viewers on each of the channels. There was some difference in approach between the BBC and ITN coverage. Although both news organisations often repeated video sequences showing the airliners crashing into the twin towers, the BBC quickly introduced analysis and discussion into their coverage as well as live updates from reporters in the United States. ITN, on the other hand, persisted with live footage (usually of presenters in New York and **vox pop** interviews) rather than analysis. All commercial breaks were dropped from the schedule during ITN news programmes.

vox pop literally meaning 'the voice of the people', short television interviews conducted with members of the public, usually in the street.

Four airliners were hijacked at the same time, one crashing into the Pentagon, another crashing in Pennsylvania en route to another target, and two flown into the towers of the World Trade Center. The television coverage focused primarily on the World Trade Center events, partly because of the larger scale of casualties but also because of the availability of several different points of view on the attack itself filmed by amateur camera users and the comparative ease of access to eyewitnesses, officials, government spokespeople and experts in the New York metropolitan area. News coverage quickly reduced to extracts of a few seconds' duration showing the impact of each airliner into the twin towers, brief soundbites from witnesses close to the scene and a grainy still photograph of Osama bin Laden. Ironically for a news event for which such dramatic pictures were available, and where numerous correspondents were present in New York to provide live coverage of the developing crisis, many of the microwave dishes used to transmit television pictures back to the UK were located on the top of the World Trade Center and were therefore destroyed. Communications between live news studios in London and presenters in New York were fragile during the first day of coverage. Television networks also had to rely on those journalists and presenters who were already

continued

Figure 8.4 The second hijacked plane moments before crashing into the second tower of the World Trade Center, New York, on 11 September 2001. Photograph by Masatomo Kuriya/Corbis Sygma.

present in America at the time, since within hours the United States and Canada closed their airspace to foreign flights. While British television networks wanted their main presenter, their 'anchor', in New York, and hastily chartered aeroplanes and sent their reporters to airports around London in order to fly there immediately, the most well-known news anchors never made it to the city. Programmes remained anchored in London, with live satellite pictures presented by less well-known correspondents in New York. Whereas live broadcast coverage had been developed into a recognised form which could be managed by broadcasting networks, after their experience in covering the Gulf War of 1991 and the Balkan conflicts of the late 1990s, all news broadcasters were dismayed and frustrated that they were unable to broadcast pictures from 'ground zero', the wreckage of the World Trade Center itself, which had been closed to all but emergency personnel. Nevertheless, the days following the attacks were saturated with television coverage. CNN broadcast live to a worldwide audience of almost one billion, in ten languages including English, to 900 affiliated television stations.

But the images broadcast by all Western television sources based all of their coverage on a Western, and particularly American, point of view. Although there were difficulties in gaining access to satellite **uplink** facilities to transmit pictures from the United States to Britain and Europe, these were the result of overloaded facilities and of preference being given to American news crews. The satellite uplinks were the only way of relaying pictures quickly, and had to be booked in advance, with intense competition between broadcasters for access to the available uplink slots. It was very difficult for news broadcasters to provide actuality footage representing the point of view of anti-American individuals or institutions, particularly in Afghanistan, because of the complex restrictions on Western television personnel there. On 11 September 2001 there were very few Western journalists in Afghanistan. There are very

uplink the electronic system which beams television signals from the ground to a satellite for onward transmission to a television institution elsewhere.

few uplink points in Afghanistan, and access to these is strictly controlled. But in any case Afghan government restrictions on Western journalists prevented them from filming in the country in the first place, so, for a complex of reasons, explanation or justification of the attacks on the United States could not be represented. The result was that poor-quality pictures of Osama bin Laden and a few seconds of controversial footage apparently showing Palestinians jubilantly celebrating the attacks on the United States were the primary images representing alternatives to the vengeful and racist discourses emerging from the United States in the aftermath of the attacks. CNN was exceptional in having a reporter in Kabul (the capital of Afghanistan) equipped with a satellite videophone. This technology allowed CNN reporter Nic Robertson to report live from Kabul by unfolding a satellite antenna, connecting the camera to the videophone, and transmitting live pictures. However, the videophone had to be smuggled across the Afghan border and used illegally for short periods in different locations. The efforts made by television news teams to gather images such as these demonstrate the significance of realist television footage to the news genre in particular, but more generally to the television medium and its audiences.

SUMMARY OF KEY POINTS

- Realism in television can refer to an adequate relationship between what television represents and how it is represented.
- The technologies for recording images and sound in television predispose the television medium to realism, but reality can never be captured unproblematically.
- Realism also refers to the conventions used in particular forms of programme to convey the impression that something real is being represented.
- Television audiences are accustomed to realist conventions, and expect realism from some kinds of programme, such as news and documentary, more than others.
- The factual genres of television have a special relationship to realism because they seem to represent something that would have happened anyway.
- Fictional programmes also make use of realist conventions, in their representations of place, character and narrative.

Further reading

Allen, R., 'Audience-oriented criticism and television', in R. Allen (ed.), *Channels of Discourse, Reassembled: Television and Contemporary Criticism* (London: Routledge, 1992), pp. 101–37.

Boyd-Barrett, O. and T. Rantanen, *The Globalization of News* (London: Sage, 1998).

Bruhn Jensen, K. (ed.), *News of the World: World Cultures Look at Television News* (London: Routledge, 1998).

Brunsdon, C., 'Crossroads – notes on soap opera', *Screen*, 22:4 (1981), pp. 32–7.

Bruzzi, S., *The New Documentary: A Critical Introduction* (London: Routledge, 2000).

Buckingham, D., *Public Secrets: EastEnders and its Audience* (London: BFI, 1987).

Caughie, J., 'Progressive television and documentary drama', *Screen*, 21:3 (1980) pp. 9–35.

Corner, J., *The Art of Record: A Critical Introduction to Documentary* (Manchester: Manchester University Press, 1996).

Dovey, J., *Freakshow* (Cambridge: Polity, 2000).

Flitterman-Lewis, S., 'Psychoanalysis, film, and television', in R. Allen (ed.), *Channels of Discourse, Reassembled* (London: Routledge, 1992), pp. 203–46.

Geraghty, C., *Women and Soap Opera: A Study of Prime Time Soaps* (Cambridge: Polity Press, 1991).

Kilborn, R. and J. Izod , *An Introduction to Television Documentary: Confronting Reality* (Manchester: Manchester University Press, 1997).

MacGregor, B., *Live, Direct and Biased? Making Television News in the Satellite Age* (London: HodderHeadline, 1997).

Nelson, R., *TV Drama in Transition: Forms, Values and Cultural Change* (Basingstoke: Macmillan, 1997).

Nichols, B., *Introduction to Documentary* (Bloomington, Ind.: Indiana University Press, 2001).

—— *Blurred Boundaries: Questions of Meaning in Contemporary Culture* (Bloomington, Ind.: Indiana University Press, 1994).

—— *Representing Reality: Issues and Concepts in Documentary* (Bloomington, Ind.: Indiana University Press, 1991).

Paget, D., *No Other Way to Tell It: Dramadoc/Docudrama on Television* (Manchester: Manchester University Press, 1998).

Sreberny-Mohammadi, A. with K. Nordenstreng, R. Stevenson and F. Ugboajah (eds), *Foreign News in the Media: International Reporting in 29 Countries* (Paris: UNESCO, 1985).

Winston, B., *Claiming the Real: The Documentary Film Revisited* (London: BFI, 1995).

Television Representation

Television Representation

Introduction

genre a kind or type of programme. Programmes of the same genre have shared characteristics.

This chapter discusses television representations of particular groups, especially those defined by gender or race, with attention to their differences in different television forms and **genres**. This involves considering the different methodologies that can be used in Television Studies to approach these issues, and the strengths and weaknesses of different means of answering related questions. The chapter includes a case study on the representation of black people in popular situation comedy, noting the significance of work on the long-running American situation comedy *The Cosby Show*, and exploring the critical arguments advanced about this programme. Activities in this chapter include suggestions for applying a range of methodologies to the issue of television representation, and the underlying assumptions about television's role in society that this depends on.

There are three central questions that have informed work in Television Studies on the issue of representation. Each of them stems from an initial assumption that television has connections with the real world of culture and society in which it exists. Earlier chapters have noted that the television medium has a continuing interest in the present moment, in documenting what is happening now, and engaging with the lives lived by its viewers. Connected with this is the historical relationship between television and the present that comes from the fact that television began as a medium of live broadcasting, and still broadcasts both live programmes and programmes that are not live but masquerade as being live. So the question of representation in television is connected to the issue of realism discussed earlier in Chapter 8. The three concerns that Television Studies has addressed about representation are:

- Who is doing the representing? – a question about production.
- What is represented and how is this done? – a question about textuality.
- How are representations understood by audiences? – a question about reception.

Each of these questions draws attention not only to content but also to the forms and processes of representation. In Television Studies television is approached as something that is actively made by someone, using particular textual forms to communicate some meanings and not others, with meanings that are not simply delivered to the audience but that are appropriated and used by them in complex ways.

Quantitative research: content analysis

In contrast to many of the theoretical methodologies discussed in this book, there is a long tradition in the social sciences, including the study of television, that seeks to find empirical data to answer research questions. As John Fiske (1990: 135) explains, the aims of empiricism are to:

- collect and categorise objective facts
- form hypotheses and explain them
- eliminate human bias from the process of investigation
- devise experimental methods to prove or disprove the validity of the data.

Content analysis works by gathering a sample of material to be studied, such as a group of television programmes broadcast on the same day, or programmes that feature representations of a particular gender, economic or ethnic group, and devising a method for subdividing the sample into relevant units that can be counted. While content analysis is sometimes used as a method of television analysis on its own, it is more common for it to be deployed as one of several different methodologies, including, for example, **textual analysis** or audience research. Content analysis is quantitative, in that, rather than making an interpretation of the meanings of selected components of television programmes, it attempts to offer precise information on the relative quantities of one kind of representation or another, so that these can be compared with each other. The method is effective when there is a sufficient quantity of recorded material available to be analysed. Since it is now quite easy to record television and amass a considerable volume of potential research data, content analysis is not difficult to carry out on the medium, though the design of a study and the specific methodology used to answer any particular research question can be difficult to establish.

> **textual analysis**
> a critical approach which seeks to understand a television text's meanings by undertaking detailed analysis of its image and sound components, and the relationships between those components.

There are five steps to take in conducting a content analysis:

- selecting the sample
- defining the categories to analyse
- reviewing and coding the data
- analysing the data
- drawing conclusions based on the results.

Using a term from statistical analysis, the sample of material to be analysed is called a 'population'. The population might be, for example, all of the programmes, advertisements, trailers and other linking material broadcast on Channel 5 between 6.00 a.m. and midnight on a particular day. Or it might be all of the situation comedies broadcast on **terrestrial** channels in the month of October 2003. The sample will be chosen to answer a research question. A research question might be, for example, how many acts of violence involving the use of firearms appeared in programmes, advertisements and other kinds of broadcast during the hours of Channel 5 programming that have been recorded. Clearly, the most productive answers to a research question will depend on having a suitably large sample population to study. The aim of content analysis is often to provide a snapshot that gives a reliable sense of the frequency of representation of a particular chosen type

> **terrestrial**
> broadcasting from a ground-based transmission system, as opposed to broadcasting via satellite.

of content. When television analysts have sought to conduct studies of the representation of particular groups of people on television, they have often adopted content analysis in order to produce representative quantitative figures that may be interesting in themselves or useful to compare and contrast with other samples that have been analysed in the same way.

ACTIVITY 9.1

If you were conducting a content analysis to find out how often black characters have leading roles in television detective fiction series, what kind of sample 'population' of programmes would be representative of television programming? What decisions would you take about how much material to study, and what 'leading role' means?

Once the research question has been decided, and the sample population recorded, the analysis of data usually requires the definition of categories of content. For example, in a content analysis of the representation of disability in television programmes, it might be useful to separate the categories of physical and mental disability, perhaps introducing further sub-categories representing a range of types of disability. It can be a long and frustrating activity to apply all of the categories and sub-categories to the sample population and to record the data. The application of categories to the sample is called coding, since each instance of relevant content will be represented in a numerical form. As the analysis goes on, it may also be necessary to refine the categories or even to reassess the usefulness of the research question. Categories of content may be too vague, and too difficult for the researcher to assign to cases which seem to belong to more than one category. Nevertheless, the end result of the coding and recording process will be a numerical count of the instances in each category, so that these can be displayed in a useful way, in a graph, table or pie chart for example. The next step will be to analyse the data, and computer packages for analysing statistics are now often used for this purpose. Some knowledge of the significance of statistical analysis is necessary at this stage, in order to understand how to use procedures involving standard deviation, means, medians and modal distributions, for instance. Once the data have been analysed by these methods, it will then be possible to draw inferences and make interpretations about the results, and also to relate them to other kinds of research method (such as textual analysis or audience research) that may have been used to address the research question.

An example of how content analysis was supplemented by audience research can show how important criticisms can be made of television conventions in representing conflicts between ethnic groups. The long-established group of media researchers the Glasgow Media Group studied the representation of Israeli and Palestinian Arab conflict currently continuing in the Middle East (Philo 2002). The current conflict between Israelis and Palestinian Arabs on the west bank of the Jordan river arises from a series of historical events. When the state of Israel was established in 1948, Palestinians living in the country were displaced from their land and became refugees. In May 1948, a war between Israel and its Arab neighbours produced more

Figure 9.1 Israeli soldiers at Ramallah on the West Bank, 2002. Photograph by Ricki Rosen/Corbis SABA.

refugees, many of whom moved to the Gaza Strip (then controlled by Egypt) and to the West Bank (controlled by Jordan). In 1967 Israel was at war with its Arab neighbours again and occupied Gaza and the West Bank, bringing the Palestinian refugees there under its control. Eastern Jerusalem (formerly controlled by Jordan) was also occupied by Israel. To cement its control, Israel built settlements in the areas it had occupied. The settlements caused anger among the refugees because of the presence of Israeli citizens in former Arab territories, and also because their farming activities deprived Palestinian farmers of water. The subsequent violence in the Middle East consists of attempts by Israel to maintain its control over occupied territory, and attempts by Palestinians to resist the occupation and regain their land.

The Glasgow Media Group sought to explore the degree of understanding among television viewers of this conflict, by undertaking a content analysis of television news stories on BBC and ITN and interviewing sample viewers. The researchers interviewed twelve groups of viewers, totalling eighty-five people, from a cross-section of ages and social backgrounds. They also interviewed 300 young people aged between seventeen and twenty-two. All of those surveyed were asked what they had understood about the conflict from television news. Of the whole sample 82 per cent named television news as their main source of information, and regarded the main message of the coverage as being that conflict and violence were occurring. The news stories analysed related to the uprising by Palestinians from September 2000 until the middle of October 2000. There were eighty-nine bulletins broadcast, comprising 3,536 lines of transcribed text, of which only seventeen lines explained the history of the conflict. The majority of the people surveyed did not understand who was occupying the occupied territories, or why. Among the sample of 300 young people, 71 per cent did not know that the Israelis were occupying the territory, and 11 per cent believed incorrectly that the Palestinians were occupying it and that the settlers were Palestinian. Although many more Palestinians have been killed in the conflict to date than Israelis, only 30 per cent of the sample of young people recognised this.

Discussing the research in the *Guardian*, Greg Philo (2002) of the Glasgow University Media Group suggested the following reasons for this situation:

- Television journalists did not provide any explanation of the history of the conflict, or referred to it only by brief shorthand phrases that the viewers did not understand.
- Television news programmes focused more on actuality coverage of violence occurring than explanations for the violence.
- The content analysis revealed that Israelis spoke twice as much on television news as Palestinians, thus favouring the Israeli perception of events.
- The close relationships between British politicians and the United States government tends to favour the pro-Israeli position adopted by the United States, and this official position was reflected in television coverage.

ACTIVITY 9.2

Why do you think the Glasgow Media Group wanted to interview viewers as well as conduct their content analysis of Middle East coverage? How did audience research support content analysis in this case?

---

melodrama
a form of drama characterised by exaggerated performance, a focus on reversals of fortune and extreme emotional reactions to events.

code in semiotics, a system or set of rules that shapes how signs can be used, and therefore how meanings can be made and understood.

prime time the part of a day's television schedule when the greatest number of viewers may be watching, normally the mid-evening period.

Feminist work on popular television

Television **melodrama** is marked by its focus on women characters, on the emotional and the psychological and on moments of dramatic intensity. The melodramatic mode supplies the means to interpret dramatic turning-points and crises through a repertoire of stock character-types and familiar **codes** of gesture and expression. As Ien Ang's (1997: 157) research on *Dallas* showed (see Chapter 12), the appeal of **prime-time** soap melodrama in the 1980s rested primarily on the central women characters, especially Sue Ellen Ewing: the viewers who communicated with Ang 'assert that the appeal of Sue Ellen is related to a form of realism (in the sense of psychological believability and recognizability); more importantly, this realism is connected with a somewhat tragic reading of Sue Ellen's life, emphasizing her problems and troubles'. Sue Ellen hated her husband but lacked the strength to leave him. She was a successful businesswoman in a masculine world, but her business (Valentine Lingerie) was set up as a tactic to separate J. R. from his rival, his mistress. While activity in the masculine world of business intrigue was present, its significance lay in its relationship to Sue Ellen's personal dilemmas. In prime-time melodrama, conflict between characters produces emotional drama, and characters also experience conflicts within themselves which are expressed by rapidly alternating and conflicting emotions, often expressed through physical, bodily behaviour. The repertoire of characteristics which define melodrama characters are composed of a restricted repertoire of facial expressions, tones of voice and gestures.

In the other major prime-time melodrama of the 1980s, *Dynasty*, the central woman character was Alexis Colby, whom the audience was invited both to admire and to despise. Jostein Gripsrud (1995) has commented on Alexis's ability to transform traditional feminine weaknesses into the sources of her strength, through her uninhibited use of her (and men's) sexuality in her struggle for power, combined with her own skills at business manoeuvring, previously deemed masculine. Alexis was regarded as the ultimate bitch, aggressive and sexually manipulative, but all because of her untimely separation from her beloved children. In other words, her masculine behaviour was the result of a thwarted and distorted femininity. Alexis in *Dynasty* was fascinating because of the contrast between masculinity as a role and the femininity expected of women. Alexis was determined to control the Colbyco corporation, and manipulated the men around her.

The expression of emotion, as David Lusted (1998) notes, is a marker both of femininity and of working-class culture. While masculine values entail the suppression of emotion in favour of efficiency, achievement and stoicism, feminine values encourage the display of emotion as a way of responding to problems. Similarly, elite class sectors value rational talk and writing as means of expression, versus emotional release. These distinctions, which are of course culturally produced rather than biological or natural, have been important to work in Television Studies on the relationship between **gender** and the different genres of television, where news and current affairs are regarded as masculine, and melodrama as feminine. On the basis of these gender, class and genre distinctions, the role of emotional display takes on increased significance. US prime-time soaps are set in a world controlled predominantly by men, but offer pleasures to the woman viewer by showing that male power can be challenged by moral questioning, and by women's refusal to be controlled. **Patriarchy** was critiqued by women using feminine and masculine gender traits as weapons against male competitors. Melodrama presents characters as simplified types, for example as good mother or bad mother, faithful spouse or unfaithful spouse, conformist or rebel, princess or bitch. Christine Geraghty (1991) and other feminist critics have argued that the world depicted in melodrama is potentially **utopian**, since the suggestion is always there that it could be reorganised in terms sympathetic to women's desires for community, and for openness and honesty of feeling.

gender the social and cultural division of people into masculine or feminine individuals. This is different from sex, which refers to the biological difference between male and female bodies.

patriarchy a social system in which power is held by men rather than women, and masculine values dominate.

utopia an ideal society.

ACTIVITY 9.3

What examples can you find of melodramatic codes in contemporary television? Are these in programmes containing strong women characters, and/or in programmes that appeal to women viewers more than men? Is social class important to the programmes you have listed, and if so how?

Gender representations: *Sex and the City*

discourse
a particular use of language for a certain purpose in a certain context (such as academic discourse, or poetic discourse), and similarly in television, a particular usage of television's audio-visual 'language' (news programme discourse, or nature documentary discourse, for instance).

commodity
a raw material or product whose economic value is established by market price rather than the intrinsic qualities or usefulness of the material or product itself.

Marxism
the political and economic theories associated with the German nineteenth-century theorist Karl Marx, who described and critiqued capitalist societies and proposed Communism as a revolutionary alternative.

semiotics the study of signs and their meanings, initially developed for the study of spoken language, and now used also to study the visual and aural 'languages' of other media such as television.

sign in semiotics, something which communicates meaning, such as a word, an image, or a sound.

The American sitcom *Sex and the City*, made by the US production company Home Box Office (HBO) and shown in Britain on Channel 4, has gained a high profile in the press and among audiences as an example of the representation of women and feminine sexuality in popular television. It focuses on the collective and individual day-to-day activities of four women friends in New York. The four characters are very rarely seen at work, but are wealthy enough to spend much of the on-screen time shopping, going to parties, lunching with each other and dating wealthy professional men. The programme derives from the journalistic writing published originally in a column by Candace Bushnell. Her book *Sex and the City* was a popular bestseller, and derived from the newspaper columns she has published since 1994 in the *New York Observer*. It was in this print context that Bushnell's apparently autobiographical alter ego, the central character of the sitcom, Carrie, was developed. Bushnell initially wrote about the New York party-going elite for the magazine *Beat* before writing freelance for *Self*, *Mademoiselle* and other magazines. The three aspects of the sitcom that this section considers in relation to women's magazine **discourse** are:

- *confession*: episodes always contain voice-over narration in which Carrie presents her self-doubt about her attractiveness, the state of her relationships with friends and lovers, her future and the morality of her behaviour, for example.
- *sexuality as the key to identity*: happiness in sexual relationships, the prospect of sexual pleasure or worry over the unavailability of sex, and a sense that characters' identities are expressed through their sexuality, are fundamental to the four women's sense of themselves.
- **commodity** *fetishism*: this term (deriving from **Marx**'s analysis of capitalist societies) describes a fascination with consumer objects whose value lies in their power to signify as signs of luxury, social power, sexual attractiveness or some other valued meaning in the context of the ideology of Western societies. Examples of fetishised commodities in *Sex and the City* include designer shoes and clothes.

The television sitcom draws on concerns with the components of feminine gender identity that are found in the discourse of women's magazines, and such details as that Carrie's sometime boyfriend Big is based on Ron Galotti, publisher of *Vogue*, lend support to this connection between magazine culture and the television series. Feminist media critics writing about women's magazines have argued that magazines such as *Cosmopolitan* and *Marie Claire* define the concerns of what Janice Winship (1987) calls a 'women's world'. This world is composed of representations that present a set of interests, problems and desires that may sometimes be incoherent and contradictory but nevertheless construct an identity for the feminine. In **semiotic** terms this world is a set of **signs** that define the signified meaning 'feminine' in distinction to the masculine: it is not a representation of the 'natural' reality of being a woman, but instead a structure of meanings that provide significance and social identity to women who buy into it. Magazines are themselves commodity products, whose costs of production are covered not simply by their purchase price but also by the advertisements for products presented to their readers. For Winship and other feminist critics magazines sell to women a representation of femininity that shapes the social place of women. Ellen McCracken (1993: 3) argues that 'women's magazines exert a cultural leadership to shape consensus in which highly pleasurable codes work to naturalise social relations of power'. The pleasure of reading glossy women's magazines, like the pleasure of watching *Sex and the City*, is the medium through which these ideological meanings of femininity are passed on. Magazines provide a location in which a sense of community and shared interest among women can be established, and where certain pleasures are attributed to feminine identity. These pleasures include self-adornment (using cosmetics, adopting a personal style, being fashionable), self-improvement (how to have better sex, better hair, healthier food) and sharing a collective identity (sharing in the same concerns and problems as other women). But as McCracken (1993: 136) argues, 'within this discursive structure, to be beautiful, one must fear being non-beautiful; to be in fashion, one must fear being out of fashion; to be self-confident, one must first feel insecure'. Feminists have argued that the pleasures offered by women's magazines rest on the assumption that women's lives offer relatively few pleasures, and that the aspirations addressed in them (to be beautiful, fashionable and confident, for example) show that women's real lives deserve to be changed, rather than be made temporarily more tolerable by the short-term enjoyment of reading magazines.

From this point of view, the emphases of *Sex and the City* episodes are on the wrong things, and perpetuate the agendas set by the women's magazines that Winship, McCracken and others criticised. Carrie and her friends are almost never seen at work. The ability of Carrie and her friends to live lives of consumption, seeking happiness through relationships and exchanging gossip and insecurities, must depend on a relatively high level of income. Even the fact that they live in comfortable apartments in Manhattan shows that they belong to a small and privileged group of young professionals who can live single, independent lives. From this perspective *Sex and the City* can be argued to render invisible the questions of economic status, work and social power for women. Furthermore, the central characters' fascination with clothes, shoes, hair and personal style is a focus on relatively trivial aspects of women's lives, in contrast to questions of gender equality and the difficulty that real women face in employment and opportunity. But perhaps most significantly for a feminist critique of gender representations in *Sex and the City*, the discourses of confession and self-doubt that occupy so much of Carrie's voice-over and the conversations among the group of friends perpetuate the assumption that feminine identity is a perpetual struggle with dissatisfaction about oneself. As feminist critics have argued in relation to women's magazines, feminine identity is represented in *Sex and the City* as something centred on lack and potential disappointment. The fact that the programme is a comedy is significant here, because, if it were not, the anxieties and struggles of the characters might have a more critical function. As in the sitcom *Ally McBeal*, which concerns a young woman lawyer and her problematic relationships with her colleagues and her attempts to define herself as a woman who is childless and lacking a satisfying sexual relationship, the sitcom format enables *Sex and the City* to engage with questions of feminine identity but also to dissipate them into physical comedy and verbal wit. Indeed, the sophisticated character comedy, the witty phrases, moments of insight and minor revelations that Carrie's voice-over presents distance the viewer from the issues that are the subject of the **narrative** and instead focus attention on the television form

narrative an ordered sequence of images and sound that tells a fictional or factual story.

Figure 9.2 The cast of *Sex and the City*. Photograph by Trapper Frank/Corbis Sygma.

in which they are communicated. Jokes, clever turns of phrase and comic reversals of fortune in *Sex and the City* focus the audience's attention on Carrie and her friends' ability to cope with emotional and social problems rather than their inability to analyse them critically and politically, or to change them.

The *Sex and the City* television series draws on modes of confession that are also found in talk shows, in which individuals represent themselves by airing their problems and by bearing witness to the tribulations of other people. The programme establishes a '**structure of feeling**' that is not unique to *Sex and the City* but that television audiences are already familiar with and in which they are invited to

structure of feeling
the assumptions, attitudes and ideas prevalent in a society, arising from the ideologies underpinning that society.

participate. What marks out *Sex and the City* from this context is its focus on a social elite, rather than the lower-middle-class participants in the majority of television confessional programmes. The television series features millionaires, wealthy men who date models and the fine art scene, and is peopled by characters who are rich, attractive and well connected. So while *Sex and the City* uses television forms that are already significant in programmes such as *The Oprah Winfrey Show*, where the audience is invited to identify with 'problems' and share in discussion of how to improve the lot of participants and themselves, the sitcom transfers these worries about the self and how to live into an elite social group, and places them in the context of comic fictional narrative. The significance of the transfer of the confessional discourse from women's magazines and talk shows into this class and status group is that it enables the programme to address a valuable television audience sector.

The fact that *Sex and the City* was nominated for nine Emmy awards (the American television 'Oscars') in 2001 is not simply a recognition that it is promoted and watched as **'quality'** television in the US broadcasting context and in the international markets where it is sold. It is also a recognition of the programme's success at attracting relatively affluent mainly female audiences, and the consequent profitability of the programme for HBO. For broadcasters funded by advertising revenue, a programme that attracts a large and relatively affluent audience group such as women between eighteen and thirty-five is attractive because it offers a place where advertisements for aspirational products (branded clothes, cars or perfumes, for example) as well as products aimed at women in general can be placed. So there is a connection between the commodification represented narratively in the programme and the commodity status of the programme itself. Carrie and her friends' concern that they are seen in public to best advantage when wearing Manolo Blahnik shoes or Gucci handbags provides a very supportive environment for the commercials that are screened between segments of the programme.

> quality in television, kinds of programme that are perceived as more expensively produced and, especially, more culturally worthwhile than other programmes.

ACTIVITY 9.4

Watch at least one episode of *Sex and the City*. What pleasures are represented as important to the main women characters? In what ways do these correspond to the pleasures attributed to women in an issue of a contemporary women's magazine (such as *Elle* or *Cosmopolitan*), and what does this reveal about cross-media representations of femininity?

Furthermore, the fact that HBO is owned by the media conglomerate Time Warner places it among a group of media properties in print publishing as well as television. Time Warner is a magazine publishing company as well as the owner of the television production company, and, although the publishing and television businesses operate independently, *Sex and the City* is an example of 'synergy', meaning that the interests of one part of the Time Warner conglomerate benefit the interests of another of its component companies. Taking a critical Television Studies position in relation to this programme, *Sex and the City* can be regarded as a commodity in which a gendered discourse of confession and witness becomes commodified itself, as a means of addressing a particular class and gender group in the television audience. Its creator Candace Bushnell has been quoted in magazine interviews as saying that she regards the programme as concerned less with gender than with the dynamics of wealth and power. She meant that, in her view, *Sex and the City* is about people's relationships that have more to do with their social position and status in relation to each other than with whether an individual is male or female. In one sense this is accurate, since, for the production company and its parent company, *Sex and the City* is primarily important as a vehicle to address a specific audience and thus to generate revenue and profit, whether that audience is male or female, and whether the representations of characters in the programme are socially and politically progressive or not. But an analytical approach to the sitcom would be concerned not only with this economic context but also with the detail of how representations of gender and sexuality are constructed in the programme, and how audiences might understand them. From a point of view interested in the representation of femininity and the political impact of those representations, *Sex and the City* can be argued to perpetuate discourses about women's self-absorption, the focus on heterosexual sex as the barometer of personal and social success, and the normalisation of commodity fetishism as the environment in which women exist 'by nature'. For more than thirty years feminist critics have been reacting against these kinds of representation, and aiming to liberate women from their oppressive restrictions on what being female and feminine mean.

Race and ethnicity: *EastEnders* and *Goodness Gracious Me*

British soap operas have a long history of representing working-class characters and communities, but often in anachronistic and insipid ways. When *Coronation Street*, Britain's longest-running and most popular soap opera, began broadcasting in 1960, the overwhelmingly white working-class families represented in the programme, employed in the factories of industrial towns in the North of England and living close together in small terraced houses, were already being swept away in the real world by the redevelopment of towns and cities. But when the BBC soap opera *EastEnders* began broadcasting in 1985, it continued this tradition by focusing on the two extended working-class families of the Beales and the Fowlers, in which middle-aged women were the central characters and possessed the most social power. But *EastEnders* attempted also to represent the social diversity in class and **ethnicity** which were being regarded as the reality of contemporary Britain. In doing this the serial also responded to concerns among executives and policy-makers in broadcasting that popular drama had an obligation not only to represent a 'realistic' cross-section of characters but also to advance public understanding along the lines of the **public service** remit espoused in British television. As David Buckingham (1987: 100) has commented: 'Perhaps the most significant fact about *EastEnders*' black characters is simply that they exist: compared with other British soaps, and indeed with much British television in general, their presence is unusual. Furthermore, the black characters are often given central dramatic roles within the narrative.'

ethnicity
membership of a group with a specific identity based on a sense of belonging, such as British Asian, or Italian-American for example.

public service
in television, the provision of a mix of programmes that inform, educate and entertain in ways that encourage the betterment of audiences and society in general.

ACTIVITY 9.5

Who are the black or Asian characters in EastEnders now? Are there ways in which their ethnicity is important to continuing stories? Why is this?

It has sometimes been the case that black and Asian characters in *EastEnders* can be criticised for occupying stereotyped roles (for example as Asian shopkeepers), but as Buckingham argues (1987: 102): 'The crucial question is not whether *EastEnders*' black characters are "realistic", but how the serial invites its viewers to make sense of questions of ethnicity – and in particular, how it defines ethnic difference and inequality or racism.' It is therefore more important to understand how the narrative discourse of the programme positions its ethnic characters than to conduct a content analysis of their frequency or measure them against stereotypes. It is certainly the case that, when white characters express racist opinions, they are always rebuffed and corrected by other characters. However, racism in *EastEnders* remains a failing of particular individuals, rather than a matter of structural and institutional racism in British society in general. The design of *EastEnders*, in common with the majority of British fiction programmes, adopts a multicultural approach in which it is assumed that all races and ethnicities are equal with each other, and in which matters of colour are incidental. Buckingham (1987: 103) quotes Julia Smith, the producer of *EastEnders*, encapsulating this approach: 'We have got a couple of very nice young Bengali characters whom I think everyone will like, and I hope that people won't even realise they're Bengalis.'

The BBC sketch show *Goodness Gracious Me* was a surprise hit with audiences in the late 1990s. The programme drew on a conscious engagement with the stereotypical representations of black and Asian people on British television, especially in comedy, going back at least as far as the 1970s. Sitcoms in the 1970s such as *Mind Your Language*, *Love Thy Neighbour* and *It Ain't Half Hot, Mum* presented black and Asian characters often as the more competent and successful character in narrative terms, yet drew on exaggerated signs of their cultural difference from the majority white British population. *Goodness Gracious Me* relies on the comic strategies of exaggeration and reversal in order to draw attention to stereotypes in a critical way. For example, in an often-repeated dramatic sketch, younger middle-class Indians were shown 'going for an English' after an evening of heavy drinking in an Indian city, reversing the stereotype that young British people meet for a curry dinner after drinking in Britain. Being rude to the white British waiter, and challenging each other to eat the most exotic food (in this case, the most bland rather than the most spicy), drew attention to the ways in which some British people abuse the staff of Indian curry restaurants and challenge each other to consume the hottest dishes. The sketch ridiculed the behaviour of the Indian diners, but, more significantly, drew attention to the racism and loutishness that British Asians often suffer.

One of the questions that might be asked about *Goodness Gracious Me* is who its intended audience is, and how other audiences might respond to it. In another sketch that became a running motif of episodes of *Goodness Gracious Me*, stereotypical representations of British Asian mothers' attitudes to their sons were exaggerated for comic effect. Two middle-aged Asian women meeting at a social event reported to each other how their sons were succeeding, by running profitable businesses, buying expensive cars or going out with beautiful women. The exchanges between the women gradually escalated to ridiculous heights, claiming increasing achievement for their sons, until eventually the only claim left to make was about the enormous size of their sons' penises. The stereotype of a possessive mother, living out her ambitions through the activities of her children, was exaggerated in a way that critiqued representations of family relationships, and conflict between generations, in the British Asian community. When the programme was devised and first scheduled, both its performers and producers were concerned about whether there was a significant audience that might be drawn to it. Since *Goodness Gracious Me* relies on a degree of cultural competence among the audience not only about a television tradition of racial stereotypes but also about the traditions, religions, family structures and economic positions of British Asians, they were anxious that it might only appeal to British Asian viewers themselves. For this reason, the series was first scheduled on the BBC's minority channel BBC2. However, very quickly, favourable press coverage and word of mouth drew large and diverse audiences to the programme.

It seems likely that there were main two reasons for the success of *Goodness Gracious Me*. One of these is the relatively simple comic strategies employed by the programme, that most often consist of the reversal of stereotypes and exaggeration. A very wide range of viewers are sufficiently literate in the **codes** and conventions of British comedy to find these strategies and structures familiar and entertaining, and the series' engagement with the history of representations of race and ethnicity in television comedy supports this. Secondly, the long history of the integration of Asians into British culture (especially since the late 1960s when many Asians emigrated to Britain from Africa) and their visibility as small-business owners in British towns and cities provide white British television viewers with sufficient understanding of British Asian culture for the jokes about the culture in *Goodness Gracious Me* to be comprehensible. It is also worth noting that the sketch-show format of the programme has a long history reaching back to the programmes featuring performers such as Dick Emery, Benny Hill and Morecambe and Wise. While in some respects *Goodness Gracious Me* was a new departure in British television, it also engages with television **formats** that are deeply embedded in it.

format the blueprint for a programme, including its setting, main characters, genre, form and main themes.

ACTIVITY 9.6

Do you think it is all right for black and Asian performers on television to make jokes about racism and about the stereotypical representations of people of the same ethnic group? What are the main arguments for and against this kind of comedy?

Case study: *The Cosby Show*

The American situation comedy *The Cosby Show* began a significant new development in the representation of black people on television. But, before considering the representations in the programme itself, it is important to be aware of the economic and institutional context of the programme, since its economic success was a precondition for programme-makers to continue to explore the possibilities opened up by it. In the United States *The Cosby Show* was **syndicated** for broadcast to local television stations around the country. It was regarded by local television stations as such a valuable commodity that the programme's distributor, Viacom, was able to set up a bidding war among broadcasters in the same territory who wished to compete for the right to screen it. By the early 1990s *The Cosby Show* was producing revenues of around $600 million for its owners. As Timothy Havens has shown (2000), the success of *The Cosby Show*, not only in the United States but in television markets around the world, persuaded American programme-makers to embark on a string of situation comedies featuring middle-class black families. The importance of syndication revenue in the United States, and foreign sales, provide attractive motivations for programme-makers to exploit the audience that has been discovered by this programme. Of course, one aspect of its international appeal is that it represents a black family. Havens argues that representations of race operate transnationally, and provide a focus for identities that are not simply national but international, and connect audiences in diverse regions and nations together. However, the specific national and regional circumstances in which programmes are shown need to be taken into account in determining the significance of representations.

> **syndication** the sale of programmes for regional television broadcasters to transmit within their territory.

Because of the centuries of movement of populations of different races to nations and regions that they do not consider to be their homelands, modern nations are not homogenous in terms of race. The ancestors of many black Americans first arrived in what is now the United States as slaves captured from locations all around the African continent. In the same way as British Asians (such as those represented in *Goodness Gracious Me*, discussed above) have ancestors who came to Britain from India, Pakistan and African nations to which they had previously emigrated, there are not necessarily shared histories of place, language, history or culture among black people. Racial identities do not primarily derive from a sense of belonging to an original place. Instead, they derive from social and cultural factors that have led a dominant racial group to regard, for example, black people as different and other from a white majority. A consequence of this, in turn, may be that black people have come to identify themselves as different as a defensive strategy that allows them to create a sense of their own collective identity in resistance to a dominant culture. When studying the representations of race in television programmes, it is important to recognise that the racial categories identified by a programme text or by viewers do not have a direct connection to physical, linguistic or psychological facts about a particular group. Instead, the notion of a racial group is culturally produced by the categories and divisions between people that operate in a particular society.

Havens reports that the international popularity of *The Cosby Show* ran from 1985 to 1995, though the programme is still regularly repeated on British television in the early twenty-first century. In those ten years the programme featured in the ten most popular programmes in the Philippines, Australia, Lebanon and Norway, among other countries. The only parts of the world where it was unsuccessful were Central and South America. In countries which import the majority of their programming owing to the lack of financial power to fund the making of television of their own, *The Cosby Show* was particularly successful. Although some of these

continued

ACTIVITY 9.7

Which racial and ethnic group do you belong to? Do you consider that your group is represented correctly on British television, and what might 'correctly' mean? How might television representations of your group affect your sense of who you are?

countries had majority black populations, such as in the Caribbean nations, it was also the case that audiences in the Middle East and Asia were attracted to the programme. Audiences belonging neither to majority white nor to majority black populations, such as in the Lebanon, the Philippines, Indonesia and Hong Kong, watched *The Cosby Show* in sufficient numbers to feature the programme in the top ten highest rated shows. In Britain *The Cosby Show* drew audiences of between two and three million viewers on Channel 4, a relatively small audience compared to British-made situation comedies such as *One Foot in the Grave*, which could regularly attract audiences of around fourteen million. The fact that *The Cosby Show* was broadcast on Channel 4 suggests that its schedulers regarded it as a programme for a minority audience, perhaps primarily a black audience, in line with the channel's remit to provide programming for minority audiences not catered for by the other **terrestrial** channels. With relatively small British audiences, Channel 4 was charged only between £10,000 and £15,000 per episode by Viacom for the programme, thus making *The Cosby Show* an economically viable proposition for Channel 4. The low cost of the programme contrasts dramatically with the prices charged by Viacom to regional broadcasting stations in the United States, where *The Cosby Show* was very popular, and could cost up to $500,000 per episode. Nevertheless, the two or three million viewers in Britain belonged to the AB social group, possessing relatively large disposable incomes and with relatively high social status, thus drawing an audience to *The Cosby Show* that was attractive to the advertisers on Channel 4.

In the years preceding the start of government by the black majority in South Africa, *The Cosby Show* was criticised in the South African Parliament for presenting political messages that were favourable to the African National Congress (ANC), a political movement representing black people's resistance to white South African hegemony. When shown in South Africa, *The Cosby Show* was the most popular television programme among white audiences. Research reported by Havens suggests that the professional occupations, relative wealth and social status, and adherence to middle-class values in the Huxtable family made the characters easily identifiable and sympathetic to the relatively privileged white South Africans. But, interestingly, black South Africans regarded the family as characters who they might aspire to be, representing a future settled and prosperous black community that black South Africans might one day enjoy themselves. These two racial audiences of South Africa appeared to read the programme in ways that confirmed attitudes and aspirations that they currently held, despite the fact that these attitudes and aspirations were different from each other.

In a study of both black and white American audiences for *The Cosby Show*, Jhally and Lewis (1992) argued that the representation of family life for the black characters in the programme excluded the economic hardship and discrimination that are common features of experience for black Americans. They argued that the middle-class status of the Huxtable family, in which the father, Cliff, is a doctor and his wife Claire a lawyer, enabled the programme to give the impression that in the contemporary United States there are no barriers for black

Americans that would prevent them from achieving the same comfort and standard of living as their white counterparts. The effect of this, they argued, was that black audiences would be reassured that the **ideology** of the United States required no significant revision. The rights of the citizen to life, liberty and the pursuit of happiness, which the United States Constitution declares are the possession of all citizens, appear to extend to everyone regardless of their colour or race. In a similar way, white Americans would be absolved of any responsibility to assist in the improvement of conditions for black Americans, and would be reassured that black people shared the same values and aspirations as whites. The relatively minor personal problems and family disagreements that occupy the narrative of episodes of *The Cosby Show* very rarely impinge on political questions of race and opportunity. Instead, they revolve around relatively trivial rivalries between children, conflicts between generations and moral issues of how to behave in a challenging situation. The stability of the family as a whole, and the comfortable living circumstances of the characters, avoided matters that might be more controversial, and that are components of stereotypical representations of black people elsewhere on television and in other media. For example, problems of inner-city housing, drug addiction, violence, crime and dysfunctional family relationships did not appear in *The Cosby Show*. In an earlier study Justin Lewis (1991) found that white American viewers perceived the characters in a 'colour blind' way, as ordinary and middle class, like the many other families who appear in American sitcoms. White viewers decoded *The Cosby Show* as consonant with the American dream of upward mobility, and did not associate it with what the white viewers perceived as 'black people's humour', which they thought was loud and dominated by physical comedy. But the black viewers approved of the programme's positive portrayal of black people, in contrast to a perceived lack of positive images of black people on television. They noted the programme's references to black culture (which the white viewers did not), as represented by the Huxtable family's paintings featuring black people, their anti-apartheid posters and love of jazz music. Black viewers were not 'colour blind' in their understanding of the programme, and although they talked of the lack of 'realism' in the absence of racism and prejudice in *The Cosby Show*, this was more than compensated for by their approval of its representation of their own cultural group. For Lewis this analysis showed how *The Cosby Show* addresses different audiences in different ways.

The focus on sibling rivalry among children, the difficulties of parenthood that the children presented for Cliff Huxtable and his wife Clare, and the romance that infused the parents' relationship despite their day-to-day concerns with work and child rearing, could be understood by a diverse range of international audiences. Indeed, these three components of relationships between children, relationships between adults and children and relationships between adults enabled the programme to address audiences across a broad range of age groups and potentially increase its attractiveness as family viewing. Despite the fact that black American audiences in Lewis's 1991 study did not regard *The Cosby Show* as using elements of the tradition of physical comedy in black culture, the performance of Bill Cosby as Cliff Huxtable in particular does draw on some of these elements. Some episodes contain sequences where Cliff clowns around to amuse his children, where he lip-syncs to popular music, and where exaggerated gestures and facial expressions are embedded in the narrative as Cliff plays with his young children. The physicality of comedy in *The Cosby Show* also makes it more amenable to international audiences, especially since in some export territories the programme would be either **dubbed** or **subtitled** in another language.

The success of *The Cosby Show* in its domestic American market and around the world led to a string of programmes adopting some or all of the same elements. Sitcoms featuring

ideology the set of beliefs, attitudes and assumptions arising from the economic and class divisions in a culture, underlying the ways of life accepted as normal in that culture.

dubbing replacing the original speech in a programme, advertisement, etc. with speech added later, often to translate speech in a foreign language.

subtitle written text appearing on the television screen, normally to translate speech in a foreign language.

continued

black American characters included *A Diff'rent World, The Fresh Prince of Bel-Air, Family Matters* and *Moesha*. Each of these programmes has been shown in Britain, though all of them have appeared on the minority channels BBC2 and Channel 4. As Havens notes, however, a significant difference between these programmes and *The Cosby Show* is the centrality of child and teenage characters to their formats, rather than the emphasis in *The Cosby Show* on the parents and particularly on the father as played by Bill Cosby. Since youth audiences are particularly attractive to broadcasters, despite the fact that they watch relatively few hours of television, it is perhaps not surprising that this shift in focus has occurred.

SUMMARY OF KEY POINTS

- The study of television representation includes the question of who (such as which television institutions) are representing certain groups and for what reasons.
- It also includes the question of who and what is represented, and in what ways.
- Studying representations involves considering how audiences understand and respond to the representations of people they see.
- The methodology of content analysis is a statistically based method for finding out about representation in samples of television.
- Textual analysis has been used by television theorists (such as feminist television theorists) to discuss the meanings of the representations of selected groups on television.
- Representations in television do not exist in isolation but in relation to other television representations and representations in other media.
- The meanings of representations in one context may differ from their meanings in another, such as a different region or country.

Further reading

Ang, I., 'Melodramatic identifications: television fiction and women's fantasy', in C. Brunsdon, J. D'Acci and L. Spigel (eds), *Feminist Television Criticism: A Reader* (Oxford: Oxford University Press, 1997), pp. 155–66.

Buckingham, D., *Public Secrets: EastEnders and its Audience* (London: BFI, 1987).

Dahlgren, P., *Television and the Public Sphere* (London: Sage, 1995).

Fiske, J., *Introduction to Communication Studies* (London: Routledge, 1990).

Geraghty, C., *Women and Soap Opera: A Study of Prime Time Soaps* (Cambridge: Polity Press, 1991).

Gray, H., *Watching Race: Television and the Struggle for 'Blackness'* (Minneapolis, Minn.: University of Minnesota Press, 1995).

Gripsrud, J., *The Dynasty Years: Hollywood Television and Critical Media Studies* (London, Routledge, 1995).

Hall, S. (ed.), *Representation: Cultural Representations and Signifying Practices* (London: Sage, 1997).

—— 'Black and white television', in D. Morley and K. Chen (eds), *Remote Control: Dilemmas of Black Intervention in British Film and TV* (London: BFI, 1996), pp. 13–28.

Havens, T., '"The biggest show in the world": race and the global popularity of *The Cosby Show*', *Media Culture & Society*, 22:4 (2000), pp. 371–91.

Jhally, S. and J. Lewis, *Enlightened Racism: The Cosby Show, Audiences, and the Myth of the American Dream* (San Francisco, Calif.: Westview, 1992).

Livingston, S. and P. Lunt, *Talk on Television: Audience Participation and Public Debate* (London: Routledge, 1994).

Lusted, D., 'The popular culture debate and light entertainment on television', in C. Geraghty and D. Lusted (eds), *The Television Studies Book* (London: Arnold, 1998), pp. 175–90.

Macdonald, M., *Representing Women: Myths of Femininity in the Popular Media*, (London: Arnold, 1995).

Modleski, T., *Loving with a Vengeance* (Hamden, Conn.: Shoe String Press, 1982).

Television You Can't See

Television You Can't See

Introduction

An analysis of the kinds of image not allowed to appear in television programmes can tell us a lot about the television medium. For cutting images involves assumptions about how audiences watch television, and how television images can be meaningful to us. The decision to cut an image out must be based on the ability to identify and determine what that image represents. So the act of seeing and making sense of the television image is the first precondition for censorship. Furthermore, the significance of what the image might mean for a viewer (for the person cutting it himself or herself, and for another hypothetical television viewer) draws on assumptions about the image's **effects**. Cutting out an image is motivated by a concern about how the image might provoke a response in the viewer who sees it. Television censorship, then, is a topic where questions of **ideology** (the political assumptions about right and wrong, good and bad), the **semiotics** of the television image (how images and sounds are meaningful as signs representing something) and pleasure and repulsion (what we enjoy seeing, and what we would prefer not to see) are fundamental. Paradoxically, looking at what we cannot see can tell us much about what seeing and understanding mean.

effects measurable outcomes produced by watching television, such as becoming more violent or adopting a certain opinion.

ideology the set of beliefs, attitudes and assumptions arising from the economic and class divisions in a culture, underlying the ways of life accepted as normal in that culture.

semiotics the study of signs and their meanings, initially developed for the study of spoken language, and now used also to study the visual and aural 'languages' of other media such as television.

Free speech and regulation

The American Constitution, largely because of the global power and influence of the United States, has been an influential statement on the right to free speech. The First Amendment (added in 1787) to the Constitution of the United States declares that 'Congress shall make no law . . . abridging the freedom of speech or of the press'. A similar statement was included in 1948 in the United Nations Universal Declaration of Human Rights, in the nineteenth Article: 'Everyone has the right to freedom of opinions without interference and to seek, receive and impart information and ideas through any media regardless of frontiers.' The European Convention on Human Rights seeks to protect freedom of speech in Article 10: 'Everyone has the right to freedom of expression. This right shall include freedom to hold opinions and to receive and impart information without interference by public authority and regardless of frontiers.' But this grand statement is soon subject to qualifications:

> The exercise of these freedoms, since it carries with it duties and responsibilities, may be subject to such formalities, conditions, restrictions or penalties as are prescribed by law and are necessary in a democratic society, in the interests of national security, territorial integrity or public safety, for the prevention of disorder or crime, for the protection of health and morals, for the protection

of the reputation or rights of others, for preventing the disclosure of information received in confidence, or for maintaining the authority and impartiality of the judiciary.

But the claim that restrictions will be those that are necessary in a democratic society is misleading. The obstacles to free speech are in fact normally determined not by a democratic process but instead by the interests of the elite groups, especially governments, that have the power to determine standards of conduct. These are the people who determine what 'the public interest' may be, for example. In media theory, members of the elite group that has the power to determine what information can be circulated are referred to as '**gatekeepers**'. These include, among others, the executives of television companies, the editors of television news programmes and the producers of television programmes in all genres. The gatekeepers make use both of published **regulations** and guidelines about programme content, and of their own internalised sense of what it is right and wrong to broadcast. Broadcasting organisations are ultimately dependent on government, since it controls the level of the BBC **licence fee** and the renewal of the **franchises** awarded to companies broadcasting on the ITV channels. So while direct censorship is uncommon in Britain, television companies are reluctant to bring themselves into confrontation with government.

ACTIVITY 10.1

Look up the current Producers' Guidelines on the BBC website or the ITC Programme Code on its website. What do these say about the reasons for not broadcasting some kinds of programme content, and in what ways might these restrictions be necessary 'in a democratic society'?

Broadcasting in Britain is largely self-regulated, on the basis of codes and guidelines drawn up and interpreted by bodies appointed by the government. The most important of these bodies are the **Independent Television Commission** (ITC) and the **Broadcasting Standards Commission** (BSC). The guidelines require broadcasters to treat controversial subjects accurately and impartially both in news and in other kinds of programme, and to refrain from expressing an editorial view of their own. Broadcasters must also not make programmes which include anything that could offend against good **taste** or **decency**, or that could encourage crime or lead to disorder. Although the regulators of British television do not have the power to censor programmes before they are broadcast, there are severe penalties such as fines or, in the case of ITV companies, the withdrawal of their licence to broadcast, that can be applied if broadcasters commit serious offences against regulation. The effect of this therefore is to introduce a culture of self-censorship among programme-makers, who know that regulators will review potentially controversial programmes and are required to investigate serious complaints made by viewers. **Terrestrial** broadcasters have for a long time agreed on a 9.00 p.m. '**watershed**', before which time programmes that could be offensive or disturbing to children will

gatekeepers the critical term used for the people and institutions (such as television commissioning producers, or regulatory bodies) who control access to television broadcasting.

regulation the control of television institutions by laws, codes of practice or guidelines.

licence fee an annual payment by all owners of television sets, which is the main source of income for the BBC.

franchise the right to broadcast in one of the terrestrial ITV regions for a set number of years, secured by paying a fee to government.

Broadcasting Standards Commission (BSC) the regulatory body set up by government to monitor the standards of BBC broadcasting services, superseded by Ofcom.

Independent Television Commission (ITC) the regulatory body set up by government to monitor the standards of commercial ITV broadcasting companies, superseded by Ofcom.

taste and decency conformity to the standards of good taste and acceptable language and behaviour represented on television, as required by regulations.

terrestrial broadcasting from a ground-based transmission system, as opposed to broadcasting via satellite.

watershed the time in the day (conventionally 9.00 p.m.) after which programmes with content that may disturb children can be shown.

Figure 10.1 An example of nudity on television. Joan Bakewell presenting *Taboo: 40 Years of Censorship*, 2001. Courtesy of BBC Photograph Library.

not be broadcast. The BSC oversees the activities of all broadcasters, and was set up by the Broadcasting Act of 1996. The Commission draws up a code on the portrayal of sex and violence and standards of taste and decency. It monitors these things, considers complaints and commissions research on the effects of violence and sex in television programmes. While the BSC has a largely negative role in that it determines what may not be shown, it also positively requires broadcasters to include in their schedules diverse programmes, programmes of 'quality', regional and educational programmes, and to maintain standards of political neutrality.

Programme-makers retain close links with regulators, and will often approach regulators at an early stage in the planning of a potentially sensitive programme to gain an opinion on whether it is likely to give rise to concerns over content or tone. It is not only written guidelines that are used by television companies to represent and disseminate standards of taste and decency. The internal culture of television production is involved in this since programme-makers use their experience and knowledge of industry histories, controversies and legal challenges to find rules-of-thumb that guide them as they plan and produce programmes. It can seem that high-profile cases of intervention by regulators are lamentable examples of programme-makers' creative freedom being attacked by distant, often ill-informed outsiders to the television production process. While this might occasionally be the case, it is more usual that problems with programmes could have been foreseen, either by the programme production team specifically or by the institutional culture within production organisations, which always provides a sense of the limits and sphere of freedom of action that programme-makers can expect. The contacts maintained between broadcasters and regulators are of course not just cosy ones, but they do form part of the day-to-day business of television executives and producers, who are aware that a good relationship between programme-makers and regulators smoothes the way for problems and challenges to be anticipated and avoided.

Although it is relatively rare for governments in Britain and other developed countries to legally prohibit television programmes from being shown, this does occasionally happen when matters of national security are involved. The mechanism is for the British government to issue a '**D Notice**' to a broadcaster, after a specific programme has been notified to, and considered by, the D Notice Committee. The D Notice Committee was set up in 1912 by the Admiralty and the War Office shortly after the passing of the Official Secrets Act during the build-up to the First World War. The secretary of the Committee in 2001 was Nick Wilkinson and among its eighteen members, four of whom have to be civil servants, were the ITV Controller of News Steve Anderson, the managing editor of *The Times* George Brock, the Editor in Chief of ITN Richard Tait and the BBC Director of Editorial Policy Stephen Whittle. The Committee is a liaison body between government and the media, and its purpose is to establish restrictions on the reporting of issues of national security such as domestic terrorism and nuclear weapons. But government is more likely to resort to the Official Secrets Act and injunctions against media organisations in order to restrict information more forcefully in most circumstances. Rather than prohibiting reporting, modern conflicts more often involve the channelling of information to the media by specially chosen spokespeople, for example in the 1990s during the Kosovo conflict and the 1991 Gulf War, the latter of which is discussed in the case study at the end of this chapter.

D Notice
an instruction to the media not to broadcast material that could undermine national security.

An issue which regularly gets a lot of coverage in the media itself, and which appears to be of concern to a substantial minority of television viewers, is the representation of sex and sexuality on British television. The representation of sexuality on television in Britain has been problematic because of the location of viewing. The fact that the television is physically located in the domestic environment leads to the fear that unsuitable material may be watched by children, and cause embarrassment to adults watching with them. The informal codes of behaviour governing family life that are imagined by the producers and regulators of television mean that bad language, sexual scenes and violence are considered to be outside the norms of behaviour expected in the family, and outside the norms of behaviour deemed good for the family audience. However, it is notable the degree to which attitudes to sex on television have liberalised over the decades of television's existence, and indeed the issue has itself been discussed on television. The Channel 4 documentary series *Sex on TV* (2002), for example, did not simply celebrate this liberalisation but noted the changing forces that have affected this history, and this chapter draws some of its material from this television source.

A brief history of sex on British television

1931: The statue of Ariel, a spirit representing broadcasting, situated on the front of the BBC Broadcasting House headquarters, had its penis shortened on the orders of Lord Reith, the first Director General.

BBC programme guidelines on radio broadcasting were very strict, and extended not only to programmes but also to their presenters. Newsreaders could be sacked if they were involved in a divorce. The BBC *Policy Guide* on **variety programmes** for 1948 contained strict rules on the subject of jokes that could be broadcast in BBC radio comedy. Prohibited subjects included:

variety programmes entertainment programmes containing a mix of material such as songs and comedy sketches.

- lavatories
- effeminacy in men, and
- honeymoon couples.

These subjects are understandable to us today as possibly offensive because of their connections with bodily functions, homosexuality and heterosexual sex. But we can see how what is offensive changes over time by noting the other subjects that were of concern to the BBC in the 1940s. Two other groups who were not allowed to be mentioned were chambermaids (stereotyped characters who were portrayed as sexually available in lewd jokes about hotels and aristocratic country houses) and travelling salesmen (who were supposedly free to engage in temporary sexual relationships while they moved around the country on business). Evidently, what is offensive to standards of taste and decency depends on the norms of a culture at a particular time, and in a particular location. Taste and decency are cultural concepts, not standards that arise by nature. They are the products of **ideology**, the system of beliefs and assumptions that shapes people's beliefs and attitudes, and which changes according to the social and political character of a given group or national population.

As we have seen in earlier chapters in this book, ideologies are always in conflict with each other, and in a state of change. Even though the BBC in the early days of television decreed that nothing could be broadcast that was in bad taste, or offensive to public feeling, there were challenges to this by television performers looking for ways of attracting large audiences. Successful comedians used innuendo to replace some of the more explicit material that they used in their music hall and theatre performances. The competition with ITV was important for the BBC, and the attraction of audiences not only by big-name performers but also by downmarket material was significant. Different forces were and are still involved in an often unconscious negotiation and conflict over what the standards of taste and decency should be, such as:

- television executives
- television performers
- audiences
- regulators
- the press.

1958: Sexuality was significant to teenage viewers, and was evident, for example, in the pop music programmes on which openly sexualised performers appeared.

As the category of the teenager became significant in Britain in the 1950s, television fulfilled its obligation to show society to itself partly by producing programmes for this audience. The gradual opening up of sexuality in British culture was marked by the paperback publication in 1960 of D. H. Lawrence's novel *Lady Chatterley's Lover*, banned since the 1920s, which included overtly sexual episodes between a high-class married woman and her gamekeeper. As so often in British culture, the subtext beneath this debate revolved around social **class**. Just as the novel depicted sex between an upper-class woman and a lower-class man, challenging the separation between classes, so the availability of representations of sexuality to ordinary working-class readers was the real problem behind the *Chatterley* case. The modification of the Obscene Publications Act to include a defence on the grounds of artistic merit allowed Penguin Books to argue successfully that Lawrence's novel, whether it was obscene or not, had artistic merit and could therefore be published. For television the key issue is that television is a mass medium, increasingly available to all classes, and a majority of British households began to own or rent television sets. It was in this context that the BBC satire programme *That Was the Week That Was* began in 1962. The programme was regarded as a primary offender in the loosening of national morals, and the Clean Up TV Campaign was initiated to combat it. Mary Whitehouse (author of the book *Cleaning Up TV*) was the leading figure in this movement. She objected, for example, to the BBC sketch comedy show *Between the Lines*, produced by BBC Scotland in 1964. It was broadcast at 6.35 p.m. on Thursday evenings, a time regarded as family viewing, and starred the actor Tom Conti in a sketch where his voice-over reveals his sexual curiosity in a young woman he meets at a dance. Mary Whitehouse's chief opponent was the Director General of the BBC in the early 1960s, Hugh Carlton Greene, portrayed by Whitehouse as a purveyor of pornography and a corrupter of society.

Just as the court ruled that *Lady Chatterley's Lover* could be published because of its artistic merit, so too in television, programmes claiming highbrow qualities were able to deal with sexual matters. Productions were able to depict sexuality, although no nudity or explicit sexual behaviour was shown on screen, as in the BBC

class a section of society defined by their relationship to economic activity, whether as workers (the working class) or possessors of economic power (the bourgoisie), for example.

adaptation of the play *In Camera* (*Huit Clos*) by Jean-Paul Sartre in 1964, and in 1965 the BBC adaptation *Bloomsday*, a version of James Joyce's 1922 novel *Ulysses*. This drama featured the sexual arousal of the character Gerty McDowell on the beach, depicted by cutting between the character's orgasmic expressions and shots of exploding fireworks. Documentary series such as *Man Alive* were also able to undertake serious investigations of contemporary sexual behaviour, recognising the effect of liberalisation of the laws on homosexuality, contraception, abortion and divorce.

1965: The BBC Wednesday Play Up the Junction *attempted to represent realistically the lives of young working-class women in London, including sexuality and a shocking scene depicting a back-street illegal abortion.*

realism the aim for representations to reproduce reality faithfully, and the ways this is done.

The aim for **realism**, coupled with a desire to compete with ITV for high ratings, led to unheard-of frankness about sex and its consequences. Perhaps the most significant aspect of this move was its focus on young women. Female desire seemed to have been newly discovered by television. It was particularly significant that working-class women were depicted in active sexual relationships, rather than a particular liberated sector of the middle class in programmes aimed at the middle class themselves. The BBC's high-profile drama slot The Wednesday Play attracted audiences of fifteen or eighteen million, so its depictions of sexuality were necessarily socially significant since they triggered public discussion and press coverage. Similarly, the immensely successful drama serial *The Forsyte Saga* on BBC in 1967 depicted rape within marriage for a mass audience, and brought this issue into public consciousness in a new way. After the episode which dealt with the rape of Irene Forsyte by her husband Soames, as an assertion of his power over her when she appeared to be unfaithful to him, the television review and commentary programme *Late Night Line-Up* conducted a poll of viewers asking whether the husband or the wife was in the right.

- Fifty-four per cent of viewers supported Soames.
- Thirty-nine per cent supported Irene.
- Seven per cent were indifferent.

The issue was not whether the BBC should have screened the scene of marital rape but about the morality which might enable Soames to feel justified in punishing his wife in this way for her waywardness. The play by Nigel Kneale from 1968, *The Year of the Sex Olympics*, depicted a society in which television was used to pacify its mass audiences by broadcasting a diet of explicit sex. By combining the **format**

format the blueprint for a programme, including its setting, main characters, genre, form and main themes.

of the game show with the expert evaluation and competitive qualities of television sports programmes, the play debated the future of television as a mass entertainment medium and the possibility of its manipulation as a form of social control.

The representation of sexual behaviour involving scantily clad young people has certainly been a feature of television history over the past forty years. Pan's People, the dancers on the BBC chart show *Top of the Pops* in the 1970s, were renowned at the time for their sexualised mode of dancing, and invited the viewer both to gaze **voyeuristically** and also to share an ethic of liberation and promiscuity that their dancing appeared to represent. Under the banner of art, Ken Russell's film for the BBC arts programme *Omnibus*, *The Dance of the Seven Veils*,

voyeurism gaining sexual pleasure from looking at someone or something that cannot look back.

was a **drama-documentary** on the life of Richard Strauss and included numerous scenes of simulated sex. The BBC drama *The Operation* in 1973 was the first programme to depict oral sex performed on a man, and the ITV drama *A Point in Time* depicted group sex using naked actors in an exterior location in the same year. The play also featured the first penis to be shown on television. Although the representation of homosexuality was most often in the camp humour of such television comedy personalities as Dick Emery and Larry Grayson, occasionally drama and documentary programmes represented it.

1974: The BBC drama Girl *depicted the first lesbian kiss on British television, some twenty-five years before the soap opera* Brookside *claimed to be breaking this boundary.*

Alastair Milne, later BBC Director General, objected personally to Dennis Potter's drama *Brimstone and Treacle*, due to be transmitted in the Play for Today slot in 1976. It not only suggested that good consequences could derive from evil actions, and thus challenged conventional morality, but also dealt with the rape of a severely disabled young woman in a suburban living room by a man who was clearly an incarnation of the devil. The play was never banned under broadcasting regulatory law, but was instead withdrawn from transmission by the internal self-censorship of BBC programme executives. Also in 1976, the BBC depicted numerous scenes of nudity and sexual activity in *I, Claudius*, a costume adaptation in which such scenes could be plausibly justified, and in the same year Andrea Newman's serial *Bouquet of Barbed Wire* was broadcast on ITV. This drama featured a suburban family and the numerous sexual relationships within it and beyond it, including the husband and his secretary, the wife and her son-in-law, the daughter and her many lovers, and the father's unrealised incestuous desire for his daughter. Clive James, a television critic of the time, described the drama as a 'The House of Atreus transferred to Peyton Place', in a reference to the extraordinary violence and sexual complication in the Greek tragedies of Oedipus and his family, and the popular contemporary American television **melodrama** serial *Peyton Place*.

The election of Margaret Thatcher as Prime Minister and the beginning of Conservative government in 1979 appeared to provide a political platform for conservative morality and censorship in broadcasting. Mrs Thatcher's espousal of 'Victorian values' seemed likely to lead to much tougher regulations on what could be depicted, and a return to repressive and infantile representations of sexuality such as the comedy programmes fronted by Dick Emery and Benny Hill. Both of these comedians had programmes in the top twenty highest rated shows of 1980, drawing on the working-class vulgarity of music hall and seaside postcards. In costume drama two major BBC productions, *The Borgias* of 1981 and *Cleopatra* of 1983, failed to gain audiences despite their combination of apparent historical seriousness with nudity. The arrival of Channel 4 into the British television landscape in 1982 changed the representation of sexuality, however. Since its remit was in part to cater for minority audiences, some of these audiences would necessarily be those with interests in alternative depictions of sexuality.

1982: The youth audience was one of the first audiences targeted by Channel 4, both in programmes conventionally displaying erotic imagery such as the pop videos on The Tube, *and also in programmes specifically targeting audiences defined by their sexuality such as the gay community in* One in Five *(1983).*

drama-documentary
a television form combining dramatised storytelling with the 'objective' informational techniques of documentary. Abbreviated as 'drama-doc' or 'docudrama'.

melodrama
a form of drama characterised by exaggerated performance, a focus on reversals of fortune and extreme emotional reactions to events.

GOVERNMENT INFORMATION 1987

Figure 10.2 Department of Health Aids information campaign, 1987. Courtesy of HMSO/the Medical Photographic Library, Wellcome Trust.

Paradoxically, Thatcher's free market policies and the value given to social groups with economic power led to the increased public visibility and visibility on television of groups such as gay people and British Asians, who were economically significant and whose interests and identity could in part depend on the representation of their sexual identities. Indeed the BBC drama *Oranges Are Not the Only Fruit* in 1990 dealt explicitly with the linkage between ideological repression expressed through religion and the liberation of its apparent opposite, lesbian sexuality. Channel 4's policy of screening 'art films' also increased the level of physical sexual activity on television under the rubric of culture. The screening in 1984 of Derek Jarman's film *Sebastiane*, for example, was problematic because the IBA refused to allow Channel 4 to include a scene depicting an erect penis. **Pan-and-scan** technology was used to shift the penis below the level of the frame. In 1986 Channel 4's film season included the use of red triangles at the top corner of the screen in order to alert viewers to potentially offensive content.

The realisation in the mid-1980s that Aids was likely to be a significant threat to the UK population led to a dramatic reversal in policy on the discussion and representation of sexual activity on television. In 1987 especially, the year in which a massive government information campaign was launched, television discussion of the varieties of sexual behaviour and the mechanics of sex was unprecedented. Ironically, the severity of British broadcasting regulations in earlier decades led to a worry that the television audience was severely underinformed and at risk from sexually transmitted diseases. Channel 4's programme *Sex with Paula* in 1987, which involved Paula Yates chatting to pop stars about their attitudes to sex, was withdrawn by Channel 4 and never broadcast because it appeared to promote promiscuity. Writers, producers and programme controllers in all British broadcasting organisations were very careful always to depict 'safe sex' in any television programme. The BBC transmitted Dennis Potter's serial drama *The Singing Detective* in 1986, at a time when the government had begun to give significant attention to Aids. The play's most controversial scene involved cross-cutting between the central character's mother having sex in the woods with her lover while her son observed them unseen from the undergrowth, and an elderly man dying of a heart attack in a hospital ward while a large hypodermic was pushed into his heart in an attempt to save him. Penetration, life and death were forcefully linked. Controversy followed in the tabloid newspapers, but the furore was deliberately provoked by the production team in order to boost the **ratings** of the third episode, in which the scene occurred, after the ratings of the first two episodes were lower than expected. When Potter's drama *Blackeyes* (BBC 1989) represented female nudity but in addition used deliberately voyeuristic camerawork combined with agonised discussion of its eroticism in the voice-over spoken by Potter himself, Potter as a writer, director and voice-over far exceeded the norms of representation of sexuality on British television in the 1980s. For although it had become common to discuss sexual activity in current affairs, documentary and other **public service** discussion genres, the dramatic representation of sexual activity had become increasingly self-censored by broadcasters as a result of the Aids crisis.

Changes to broadcasting regulations opened the way to satellite broadcasting and cable television in Britain during the 1980s, and during the 1990s the **audience shares** acquired by broadcasters such as Sky became a significant concern for terrestrial channels. Satellite and cable broadcasters had already been able to offer greater

pan-and-scan capturing a section of an image and enlarging it to fill the television frame, a technique used to fit wide film images into the square television screen.

ratings the number of viewers estimated to have watched certain programmes, as compared to the numbers watching other programmes.

public service in television, the provision of a mix of programmes that inform, educate and entertain in ways that encourage the betterment of audiences and society in general.

audience share the percentage of viewers estimated to have watched one channel as opposed to another channel broadcasting at the same time.

sexual content in programmes than their terrestrial competitors, by offering dedicated channels such as the Playboy Channel, and terrestrial broadcasters began to compete on the same terrain by increasing the degree of sexual content in their own programmes. Since the Conservative government of the 1980s had relaxed broadcasting regulations, the primary concern for broadcasters was market share, in other words the acquisition of valuable audience segments. This was significant not only in terms of total audiences, in which mainstream terrestrial channels succeeded in maintaining their dominance, but more importantly in terms of the acquisition of audience groups of high value to advertisers. The most valuable group was the young, whose high disposable income and willingness to spend on inessential and impulse purchases were especially attractive. Furthermore, while audiences in their thirties and over can be expected to watch television the most, audiences in the eighteen to twenty-five age range watch relatively little television. The youth audience is therefore simultaneously economically attractive yet also elusive.

1990: Channel 4's The Word, *in which hedonistic sexuality and the eroticisation of the talk-show and chart-show genres became highly controversial, was part of efforts on the part of television broadcasters to capture the youth audience.*

Yet in 1994 a television commercial for Neutralia shower gel in which a model briefly revealed a nipple was hastily shifted to after the 9.00 p.m. **watershed**. The depiction of sex was still controlled by powerful regulation and self-censorship, although discussion of sex, especially in a documentary or in ironic comedies on youth television, had become common. In 1997 the youth audience was offered, for example, *Ibiza Uncovered* by Sky, in which the relatively uninhibited desire of a group of young British holidaymakers to have as much sex as possible in their fortnight away was documented in some detail. The eroticised youthful body has become a commodity for the attraction of youth audiences, and also a source of titillation for the older viewer. The launch of Channel 5 depended on the depiction of sexuality since the channel had very small amounts of working capital, not all of the UK population could receive its signal and it had a very small budget to spend on programmes. In order to gain the 5 per cent audience share required for the channel to satisfy its backers, it concentrated on what its first chief executive, Dawn Airey, called 'films, fucking and football'.

ACTIVITY 10.2

On what days and at what times does Channel 5 schedule films that could be described (in listings publications, for example) as 'erotic dramas'? Who might the audience for these programmes be, and why are they scheduled on these days and at these times?

Taste and decency today

The force dominating the representation of sexuality on contemporary television is no longer the issue of what can or cannot be shown, or what can or cannot be discussed. Only two significant prohibitions remain in the television depiction of human sexuality:

- the representation of erect penises
- the representation of sexual behaviour involving children.

Erect penises remain impossible for broadcasters to show, and the Channel 4 documentary from 1993 *Hookers, Hustlers, Pimps and their Johns* was required to pixellate some scenes of unusual sexual behaviour, such as a man having his penis rubbed with a cheese grater, but there was no requirement for the film crew to stop filming or to edit out these sequences, which were portrayed in a neutral and unsensational way. The Channel 4 drama serial *Queer as Folk* (1999) represented the promiscuous and hedonistic lifestyles of a group of wealthy young gay men in Manchester with a degree of routine neutrality that had not hitherto been seen. Television soap operas routinely focus on the sexual relationships of their now predominantly youthful characters, even though sexual activity itself cannot be shown in the **prime-time** slots in which the soap episodes are broadcast. Instead, with a sense of weariness about the detail of sexual behaviour, the focus has shifted to the emotional and social significance of sexuality. In particular, the two driving forces of the medium seem to have become television programmes' ability to bear witness to the varieties of ordinary people's lives, and to become a forum for the public airing of confessions and revelations that seem unable to be shared with a person's intimate circle. **Reality TV** such as *Big Brother* is a notable example of this trend, in which well-honed youthful bodies are routinely paraded on screen (the presence of a Jacuzzi and cameras in the bedrooms of the contestants seem calculated to secure this), and where the question of how far the contestants will go in their intimate relationships with each other is a large part of their fascination for audiences.

But children's sexualities, and the possibility that children may be objects of sexual desire for adults, is the other significantly absent subject on British television. In July 2001 the current affairs comedy spoof *Brass Eye* screened a programme satirising hysteria over paedophiles which was much criticised in the press. Government ministers including Tessa Jowell (Head of the Department of Culture, Media and Sport) criticised the programme but refused to view it. The Independent Television Commission ruled that Channel 4 gave inadequate warnings to viewers but was not in breach of regulatory codes governing programme content. Much of the regulation of television is based on the perceived need to protect children from programme content that may be disturbing to them. Although this may seem to be a straightforward notion, it is worth considering how the idea of childhood is constituted. From a **semiotic** point of view, 'childhood' makes sense only in distinction to 'adulthood'. Of course it is adults who are responsible for broadcasting regulations, and who make decisions about what children should or should not see on television. For adults childhood is a time in their own lives and in the lives of other adults that is inaccessible to them except in memory or by imagining what it must be like to be

prime time the part of a day's television schedule when the greatest number of viewers may be watching, normally the mid-evening period.

reality TV programmes where the unscripted behaviour of 'ordinary people' is the focus of interest.

a child. In the developed nations of the Western world childhood is seen in two contrasting ways. Our current conceptions of childhood began to be developed around the beginning of the nineteenth century. On one hand, children have been regarded as:

- irrational
- immoral
- in need of adult guidance.

There have been high-profile incidents (such as the abduction and murder of the toddler James Bulger by two teenage boys) that seem to show that children can be dangerously violent, uncivilised and threatening. But on the other hand, children are also regarded as:

- innocent
- naturally predisposed to be good
- uncontaminated by adults' problems.

It is very common to see representations, including many representations on television, of children as cute, endearing and able to teach adults lessons about how to see the world more clearly. There is a continuing conflict between these two quite different meanings of childhood, and, when considering how television regulations protect children, it is important to remember that the meanings of childhood are both contradictory and the product of adult thinking.

ACTIVITY 10.3

List the ways in which children are represented on television as cute and innocent, and as uncivilised and threatening (don't forget to include advertisements). How are representations of childhood tied into the bigger issue of humankind as 'naturally' predisposed to goodness or to evil?

Frankfurt School a group of theorists in the mid twentieth century who worked on theories of contemporary culture from a Marxist perspective. Key members, notably Theodor Adorno and Max Horkheimer, left Nazi Germany in the 1930s to work abroad.

Protecting children from television content that could be disturbing or in some way bad for them is connected to assumptions about how other vulnerable groups in society can be adversely affected by television. Since television programmes and television regulations have been largely made by well-educated and socially powerful elite groups in society, the underlying ideology of television regulation has considered the less socially powerful and less well-educated mass audiences of television as vulnerable and prone to bad influences in the same way that children might be. Theodor Adorno and the **Frankfurt School** considered that the mass media perpetrated what we now call 'dumbing down' and encouraged the mass audience's fascination with trivia, immorality and indiscriminate consumption. There is a long tradition among commentators on television to consider mass audiences as 'them' in contrast to the more sophisticated 'us' represented by those commentators themselves. The mass audiences of television have been regarded as childlike and in need of protection. One of the ideological assumptions behind television regulation is that viewers (or at least some of them, who are not as sophisticated as the people who make programmes or frame television regulations) are not able to discriminate for themselves between programmes that have socially positive meanings and programmes that could encourage anti-social or dangerous behaviour. The way that broadcasting regulations refer to children or to vulnerable adults can be regarded as a way of justifying the ability of a small group in society to legislate for what the majority are able to understand.

Attitudes to the television viewer as a vulnerable person who needs to be protected tend to regard the viewer as an object, as a person separate and different from that small group of people who frame broadcasting regulations. The gradual liberalisation during the twentieth century of regulations on television programme content is partly the result of a recognition of this problem, and the granting to television viewers of greater agency and discrimination. Rather than thinking of the television viewer as a passive object that television programmes can directly affect, perhaps causing the viewer to imitate anti-social behaviour seen on the screen such as violent, sexually excessive or illegal behaviour, more recently television viewers have been thought of as people whose relationships with television are more complex. Rather than simply imitating what they see on the screen, viewers are now understood as aware of how television operates as a medium, and how the images and sounds on television are not just the same as real life but are representations. This issue of how the audience is considered increasingly as a subject rather than an object, and how television viewers understand what they see in diverse and complex ways, is the subject of later chapters of this book (Chapters 11 and 12) that consider television audiences and how they can be studied and understood.

Theories of regulation

Television programmes are **commodities**, offering pleasure to their viewers through the payment of money, whether via advertisements, subscription or a licence fee. When considered from a perspective informed by Karl **Marx**'s studies of economics, the real meaning of nudity, violence or sexual activity in television programmes is how programmes work within the exchange system of the **capitalist** economy. Viewers will pay money to see images of nudity or violence, for example by subscribing to 'adult' television satellite or cable channels. Television regulators largely support the position of television within the capitalist system, and are prepared to accept the exploitation of images of sexuality or violence as long as this is cloaked by an acceptable justification. This justification is the result of the discourses of **narration**, **genre** and form which contain images of sexual behaviour, violence or some other challenging content. Television representations mobilise the viewer's desire to see and hear these exciting or arousing images, and fix them in narratives. The question for regulators is how excessive the meanings and effects (such as sexual arousal or disposition to commit violent acts, for example) of programmes might be. But, as earlier chapters of this book have argued, the audio-visual representations on television never have only one meaning, but many. Since television texts are

commodity a raw material or product whose economic value is established by market price rather than the intrinsic qualities or usefulness of the material or product itself.

Marxism the political and economic theories associated with the German nineteenth-century theorist Karl Marx, who described and critiqued capitalist societies and proposed Communism as a revolutionary alternative.

capitalism the organisation of an economy around the private ownership of accumulated wealth, involving the exploitation of labour to produce profit that creates such wealth.

narration the process of telling a story through image and sound. Narration can also refer to the spoken text accompanying television images.

genre a kind or type of programme. Programmes of the same genre have shared characteristics.

polysemia the quality of having multiple meanings at the same time. Texts such as this are called 'polysemic'.

iconic sign in semiotics, a sign which resembles its referent. Photographs, for example, contain iconic signs resembling the objects they represent.

indexical sign in semiotics, a sign which is the result of what it signifies, in the way that smoke is the result of fire.

denotation in semiotics, the function of signs to portray or refer to something in the real world.

'**polysemic**', it is hard for television regulators or campaigners (and for academics and students) to find a secure set of rules to describe the images and sounds which should be cut out. The meaning of television representations can appear to be immediately readable because many of them are 'realistic' (in semiotic terminology, television signs are **iconic** and **indexical**). Television regulators, just like academics writing analyses of television programmes or students writing essays about them, try to decode the meanings of television programmes. Regulating television involves processes of 'translation' which aim to determine the meanings of programmes, and so this always leaves room for debate about whether a programme really means what a regulator thinks it does.

Meaning in a television programme, the way that different images are linked systematically together, depends on how each moment is contained and limited by the moments around it. In most television programmes all the various components of the programme are ordered by narrative (whether a fictional story, a non-fictional documentary treatment or a news story, for instance), with the aim that the programme will make sense for the viewer. Meanings are coded and systematised. Programme-makers aim for each moment to fit well with the next, and they avoid excessive stillness, too much movement, undecideable, meaningless images or images which are shocking and seem to leap right out of the programme's narrative flow. By setting up the regime in which programme-makers self-censor their programmes, regulators are taking further what programme-makers already do. They aim to cut what is excessive, while preserving the coherence, smoothness and comprehensibility which television culture already takes as the norm. The operation of television self-censorship at the programme planning stage or later in the editing suite depends on isolating particular images or sequences from the flow of the programme's narrative, identifying them as problematic and then removing them in a way which does not challenge the coherence of the programme as a whole. What is at stake in this is therefore the **denotation** of something which might be worthy of being cut out, and its relationship with the meanings of the programme.

Some of the laws which govern television regulation, in Britain as elsewhere, require that a television image must be cut out if it denotes something which is prohibited. Regulators make use of a list of acts and words that television programmes are not allowed to represent, and programme-makers know these rules and make changes during post-production, only occasionally requiring regulators to intervene. For example, obscene words are 'bleeped out' from *Big Brother* when it is shown in mid-evening, and in one programme from the salacious talk show *So Graham Norton* a webcam image of a woman playing the penny-whistle with her vagina was technically processed to blur the details of the whistle's relationship to her body. In these two examples programme-makers were following guidelines on taste and decency that do not in themselves have legal status. But some of the laws of the land in Britain can apply to television programmes. For example, the Protection of Children Act states that no image of a child in a sexual situation can be shown (on television, as well as in other media such as magazines or newspapers). So in programmes in the documentary series *The Hunt for Britain's Paedophiles*, videotapes and photographs that the police had seized as evidence had to be obscured by black bars or blurred patches so that television viewers could not see them in detail. It is important to recognise that the regulation of television depends on the ideological assumptions about what is acceptable and what is unacceptable in a given culture.

In other words, television regulation and censorship are a political matter that is potentially open to debate, and not self-evident or natural. At present television images of naked women's bodies have become more acceptable than images of naked men: television programmes cannot denote an erect penis, although they can denote female genitals in some non-sexual programme contexts (such as medical documentaries).

Television regulation is also affected by the **genre** that a programme occupies. Some laws, such as the Obscene Publications Act (1959), can be contested by arguing for the good intention of a programme, for example that it is in 'the public interest', or that it is artistically excellent. In other words, questions of **authorship** and **aesthetic** value are also significant. The Obscene Publications Act defines obscenity as something whose effect as a whole is to 'tend to deprave and corrupt persons who are likely, having regard to all relevant circumstances, to read, see or hear the matter contained or embodied therein'. For the Act a programme might be considered obscene because of what is represented, but it can be legal because the intention and effect of the whole work is artistically excellent or morally improving. It is for this reason that programmes claiming to be '**quality** television' can contain more graphic violence, more explicit sexual behaviour or more obscene language than programmes that cannot easily make a claim to be 'quality'. The Channel 4 drama serial *Queer as Folk* did not show explicit images of homosexual sex (it was after all performed by actors and therefore sex was simulated rather than real), but there were numerous scenes in which penetrative sex and other kinds of homosexual activity were represented. Because *Queer as Folk* was an authored drama, with high production values and a recognised 'artistic intention', its representation of homosexual sex was able to be much more graphic than in any previous British television drama.

> **authorship** the question of who an author is, the role of the author as creator, and the significance of the author's input into the material being studied.

> **aesthetic** a specific artistic form. Aesthetics means the study of art and beauty.

> **quality** in television, kinds of programme that are perceived as more expensively produced and, especially, more culturally worthwhile than other programmes.

ACTIVITY 10.4

Is it acceptable for adults subscribing to cable or satellite channels to see greater violence or sexual content in programmes than is currently seen in free-to-air terrestrial broadcasting? Could you draw up a list of images, actions or words that would be acceptable in subscription television but not in terrestrial television, and how would issues such as programme genre and format affect this?

Television regulation of taste and decency tells us a lot about how television is organised in society, and how our assumptions about the meanings of programmes and the interpretative activity of audiences work. Television regulation attempts to control the meanings the viewer can consume, and thus it is about the regulation of the viewer as much as the regulation of what the television set shows. Since television is a business and an industry, regulation predominantly follows the pattern of how society controls the channels of consumer culture more generally (in film, book publishing or advertising, for example). Regulation intervenes by naming, describing and prescribing ways of seeing and hearing. This rests on presumptions about how viewers perceive what they see and hear on television, how they identify with or are repulsed by the meanings of television programmes and how they might imitate what they see and hear or be prompted to adopt modes of behaviour that are represented. Inasmuch as television viewers' understandings and desires are not straightforwardly the product of television images and sounds, but are instead negotiated by viewers in complex ways involving images, sounds and the ideologies of culture in and around them, television regulation needs to be understood in this wider framework of social and political life.

ACTIVITY 10.5

How convincing is the argument that showing violence on television can persuade viewers to imitate the violent behaviour? Does the assumption by advertisers that watching commercials can stimulate viewers to purchase products affect your answer?

Case study: the 1991 Gulf War

The coverage of war and conflict in recent years has been dramatically affected by the ability of television news to convey very recently recorded moving images and sound both from battlefield sites themselves and also from locations behind the lines from where journalists can relay information. The largest recent war involving Britain and its Western allies was the Gulf War of 2003, but the conflict was still in its concluding stages when this book went into production, so that a critical discussion of its representation on television was not yet possible. This case study focuses on the war in the Gulf that took place in 1991, to provide a critical context in which the recent war can be considered. Television coverage had a dramatic effect on the perception of this conflict not only in Britain but also internationally. The topic of this case study is how television shaped the representation of the 1991 Gulf War, and how the television coverage of the conflict illuminates the technological, institutional and political organisation of television in such situations. As well as discussing the kinds of television images which were broadcast in the Gulf War, this section also considers the kinds of images that were not broadcast, and how the relationship between the visible and the invisible affects the meaning of world events of this kind.

According to the New York media monitoring group Fairness and Accuracy In Reporting (FAIR), in the months before the beginning of the Gulf War in 1991 the three major US television networks devoted less than 1 per cent of their airtime to organised popular opposition to President Bush's policy in the Gulf. Between 8 August 1990 and 3 January 1991 only twenty-nine minutes of coverage on ABC, NBC and CBS represented organised protest. In Britain BBC guidelines issued to producers stated: 'Programmes should make it known in general terms that some information will be held back for [Allied] military reasons and that reports out of Iraq are censored.' The guidelines also required producers to state that Iraq restricted Western reporters in the country to approved areas. However, the guidelines did not state that the **pool system** operated by the Allied forces imposed exactly the same restrictions. Many programmes were removed from the schedule if they consisted of actual or fictional representations of war, including:

pool system in journalism, grouping journalists together to share information so that not all of them need to be present at a news event.

- the film *Carry On Up the Khyber* (a British comedy set among soldiers in nineteenth-century Afghanistan)
- the sitcom *'Allo 'Allo* about the French resistance in the Second World War.
- about seventy pop songs withdrawn from BBC local radio and some commercial stations, including John Lennon's 'Give Peace a Chance' and 'Waterloo' by Abba.

ACTIVITY 10.6

In the 2003 Gulf War, reporters from Western nations were 'embedded' among Allied troops, and it was claimed that this made possible greater access to the action and greater understanding of the reality of the conflict. What are the gains and losses in arranging for television reports to be beamed live from Allied front lines, versus the reports mediated by military and political spokespeople in the 1991 Gulf War?

Media theorists have often noted that there were very few images in the 1991 Gulf War coverage either of soldiers in action on the ground or of the dead who were killed in the conflict. It has also been significant to the analysis of Gulf War coverage that the dominant sources of television images were those provided by Western journalists, and those images provided to them by the commanders of the alliance of nations fighting against Saddam Hussein, the Western allies' opponent. The predominant military forces in the conflict were those of the United States, assisted by British troops and allies closer to the scene of the conflict such as Saudi Arabia. The stated reason for the conflict was the invasion of Kuwait by the Iraqi armed forces commanded by the Iraqi leader Saddam Hussein. The Western allies aimed to eject Iraqi troops from Kuwait, and to safeguard the relationships between Western nations and countries in the Gulf area such as Kuwait and Saudi Arabia which supply oil to the developed world. Although the conflict was portrayed largely as a way of protecting Kuwait and other neighbouring nations from the aggression of Iraq, commentators both at the time and since have argued that the war was instead about the maintenance of Western (and especially American) influence over oil supplies, and the international authority of the United States as the world's only remaining superpower after the disintegration of the Soviet Union in 1989. The ways that television coverage focused on particular aspects of this complex situation and excluded others became the focus of widespread debate about the power and influence of television in the contemporary global media landscape.

For critics of the television coverage of the 1991 Gulf War, such as Douglas Kellner (1995), the function of television was not primarily to provide knowledge or information about the day-to-day events of the war or the experience of those who fought in it. Instead, Kellner and others have argued that television was manipulated as a largely passive instrument to reinforce the **hegemony** of the United States and to promote the effectiveness of its military technology. The Gulf War can be described as a 'television war' not only because television coverage in national broadcasting and in the international television sources such as **CNN** was so significant to the public's understanding of it. The war was also a television war because television technology was a component of the weapons used in the war itself. The 'smart bombs' used by the United States contained miniature video cameras in their nose cones, enabling on-board computer systems to guide to the bombs to their targets. American surveillance

hegemony a term deriving from Marxist theories of society, meaning a situation where different social classes or groups are persuaded to consent to a political order that may be contrary to their benefit.

CNN Cable News Network, the first international satellite news channel, operating from the United States.

continued

Figure 10.3 Norman Schwarzkopf demonstrating footage of a 'smart bomb' strike during a press briefing. Courtesy of Corbis Sygma.

satellites provided electronic images of the battlefield area, and enabled military leaders to develop their strategy. Surveillance aircraft equipped with both still cameras and video equipment also provided United States leaders with information, and the pilots of Western fighter jets were able to see video projections in real-time inside their cockpits that enabled them to launch computer-controlled missiles against Iraqi aeroplanes. The war was fought in part by using electronic video imaging, and was experienced by television audiences not only through the footage provided from news camera operators but also through video footage from the bombs and aircraft themselves. This footage was exhibited to journalists by the American General 'Stormin' Norman' Schwarzkopf and relayed to broadcasters' news studios.

The French theorist Jean Baudrillard wrote in 1991 (reprinted 1997), whom we have encountered earlier in this book in relation to theories of **postmodernism**, regarded the television representations of the war as much more accessible and important than the fighting itself. Because television imagery in the coverage of the war, and in the military technology used in it, was so dominant over the reality of the fighting and death which it involved, he wrote in 1991 that, in essence, the Gulf War did not take place. While the build-up to the war was escalating militarily and diplomatically, he argued that the non-declaration of war and the non-engagement of troops was a mechanism for deterring war itself, and that the escalation of media coverage of the conflict between the West and Iraq was in effect a substitute for military action. When the war had begun, he argued in a similar way that the media representation of the conflict had taken the place of the reality of the fighting, and that the media commentators arguing about the significance of what was occurring were experienced as more real disputes than the conflict on the ground: 'The true belligerents are those who thrive on the ideology of the truth of this war, despite the fact that the war itself exerts its ravages on another level, . . . through all those strategies of psychological deterrence that make play with facts and images . . . and the inexorable confusion between the two' (Baudrillard, quoted by Norris

postmodernism the most recent phase of capitalist culture, the aesthetic forms and styles associated with it and the theoretical approaches developed to understand it.

1997: 169). In opposition to Baudrillard's view, critics including Christopher Norris (1997) were shocked by his apparent disregard for the death and destruction actually occurring, and responded by detailing the statistics of the casualties. However, this misses Baudrillard's point that the extraordinary proliferation of television representations of the war so much overwhelmed the distant reality of conflict that the war came to seem a media event rather than a real one for the millions of television viewers whose only access to it was through television pictures.

During the conflict television coverage made much use of the medium's ability to broadcast either live or almost live, and key parts of the coverage included:

- reports from the press rooms of the Allied generals
- live discussions among experts about how the war was progressing
- live coverage in the Iraqi capital Baghdad by journalists working for CNN.

Scheduled programmes were occasionally dropped or shifted in order to bring live coverage to the television audience. As Chapter 7 on postmodernism has argued, the saturation coverage of the Gulf War was most striking in the developed Western nations of Europe and the United States. The international reach of news organisations such as BBC and CNN was one precondition for it to happen. Another precondition was the advanced satellite news-gathering technology available to journalists representing these television institutions. The unreality of the Gulf War that Baudrillard was describing is a specifically Western phenomenon, and is part of the media **globalisation** that has been discussed as part of postmodernism. In highly developed Western societies where most people gain their information from television, and where only a tiny number of people have direct experience of warfare and the horror of death and destruction that was occurring in the Gulf, it does make some sense to argue that the war was more of a battle between representations than a reality directly engaging with the audience's lives.

The distance between the television audience and the war was increased by the careful control over the media that was exercised by the Allied military authorities. Based on surveys conducted in the United States after the Vietnam War of the 1960s and 1970s, in which it was widely believed that television pictures of dead and dying American soldiers caused the American public to withdraw their support for the conflict, the military strategy for handling the media in the Gulf War was not to allow journalists and television camera operators access to images that could undermine public support for the military action. It was claimed by the Allies that 10,000 casualties (2 per cent of the total number of US troops) would render the war unacceptable to the US public (Freedman and Karsh 1993: 52). In view of this, Allied military authorities prevented television reporters from gaining access to the battlefield itself, and instead released to them footage of battles shot by military personnel themselves under the control of the military leaders. Aware of this, Iraqi authorities invited Western television reporters to the scene of missile attacks by the United States in which civilians were killed. Both sides were attempting to influence public opinion by manipulating television coverage, in a situation that led Mark Poster (1995:160) to claim that '"information" was the leading character and support for the war the discursive effect'.

The British writer on media sociology Marie Gillespie (1997) undertook some work in London on British Asian teenagers' use of the media in order to see how a specific group in the television audience understood the television coverage of the 1991 Gulf War. The results of her study make it much more difficult to understand the Gulf War in terms of simple oppositions between, for instance:

globalisation the process whereby ownership of television institutions in different nations and regions is concentrated in the hands of international corporations, and whereby programmes and formats are traded between institutions around the world.

continued

- the United States versus Iraq
- Christians versus Muslims
- West versus East
- Allies versus Arabs
- white versus black.

British Asian Muslims were upset by the fact that Allied troops continued fighting during the festival of Ramadan, traditionally a time of truce, and by the desecration of Muslim holy places in Iraq during the war. Some of the teenagers whom Gillespie interviewed supported Saddam Hussein because, like them, he was a Muslim, even though, at school and in other environments where these Asian teenagers were in a minority, they were immersed in a much more pro-Allied environment. The Asian teenagers' fear of racist violence against them by white Britons made them reluctant to admit this identification with Saddam Hussein, yet on the other hand more willing to see themselves as an oppressed group within British society for whom Saddam could be a positive figurehead.

ACTIVITY 10.7

If different groups within Britain could interpret news about the Gulf War in different ways, does this mean that researching the 'dominant reading' of the war coverage by doing close analysis is unimportant? How do your responses to this question depend on an assumption that media representations of the war are the 'reality' of the war?

preferred reading
an interpretation of a text that seems to be the one most encouraged by the text, the 'correct' interpretation.

Research such as this shows how it is important not to read off the meanings of television images too easily, to assume that the **preferred reading** of television coverage will be assimilated by everyone in the television audience. Some groups in the audience, like the British Asian teenagers, will have backgrounds and allegiances that predispose them to understand television coverage quite differently from the preferred reading, such as:

- gender
- race
- cultural environment
- family history.

Television viewers negotiate their relationship with television coverage both consciously and unconsciously, as a result of numerous factors. Furthermore, television viewers, like everyone else in society, are perpetually negotiating their identity and identifying themselves either in conformity or in contrast with the meanings of television at different times and in different places. Television viewers also use their understanding of the forms and genres of television in order to interpret the meanings of programmes. During her research Gillespie talked to groups of both boys and girls in the British Asian community that she studied. She found that some of the boys compared the coverage of bombing raids and missile attacks that they saw during the Gulf War television coverage with computer-game imagery. Some of the girls tended to identify either with the nurses involved in the conflict or with the female war reporters, and were bored by the boys' fascination with the technology and spectacle of the war. It is these issues of how different audiences respond to television in different ways, and how the meanings of television programmes can be interpreted differently, that are the subject of the following chapters on television audiences.

SUMMARY OF KEY POINTS

- Preventing audiences from seeing something on television relies on an often unacknowledged theory of how audiences might be affected by what they see. It has been impossible for researchers to prove that what television viewers see has a definite effect on their behaviour.
- The ways in which the censorship and regulation of television happen in any society depend on the ideologies of that society, and change as the norms of society change over time.
- Conflicting ideas about freedom of speech, versus the protection of vulnerable viewers, have marked the ways that censorship and regulation happen in Western societies.
- Institutions such as the Broadcasting Standards Commission and the Independent Television Commission in Britain, superseded in 2003 by Ofcom, lay down guidelines and rules about what can be shown on television.
- In times of war and other political crises, television regulation is much more evident than at other times in Western societies, and reveals the significance that television is thought to have on its audiences' understanding of events.
- But research in Television Studies on how audiences respond to television shows that different audiences respond to what they see in different ways.

Further reading

Badsey, S., 'The influence of the media on recent British military operations', in I. Stewart and S. Carruthers (eds), *War, Culture and the Media: Representations of the Military in Twentieth-century Britain* (Trowbridge: Flicks Books 1993), pp. 5–21.

Baudrillard, J., 'The reality gulf', *Guardian*, 11 January 1991, reprinted in P. Brooker and W. Brooker (eds), *Postmodern After-images: A Reader in Film, Television and Video* (London: Arnold, 1997), pp. 165–7.

BBC, *Producers' Guidelines* (London: BBC, 1993).

Bignell, J., 'Writing the child in media theory', *Yearbook of English Studies*, 32 (2002), pp. 127–39.

Broadcasting Standards Commission, *Codes of Guidance* (London: BSC, 1998).

Buckingham, D., *Moving Images: Understanding Children's Emotional Responses to Television* (Manchester: Manchester University Press, 1996).

Freedman, L. and E. Karsh, *The Gulf Conflict 1990–1991: Diplomacy and War in the New World Order* (London: Faber, 1993).

Gillespie, M., 'Ambivalent positionings: the Gulf War', in P. Brooker and W. Brooker (eds), *Postmodern After-images: A Reader in Film, Television and Video* (London: Arnold, 1997), pp. 172–81.

Goodwin, P., 'The role of the state', in J. Stokes and A. Reading (eds), *The Media in Britain: Current Debates and Developments* (Basingstoke: Macmillan 1999), pp. 130–42.

Independent Television Commission, *The ITC Programme Code* (London: ITC, 1998).

Kellner, D., *Media Culture: Cultural Studies, Identity and Politics Between the Modern and the Postmodern* (London: Routledge, 1995).

Norris, C., '"Postscript": Baudrillard's second Gulf War article', in P. Brooker and W. Brooker (eds), *Postmodern After-images: A Reader in Film, Television and Video* (London: Arnold, 1997), pp. 168–71.

Petley, J., 'The regulation of media content', in J. Stokes and A. Reading (eds), *The Media in Britain: Current Debates and Developments* (Basingstoke: Macmillan, 1999), pp. 143–57.

Poster, M., *The Second Media Age* (Cambridge: Polity, 1995).

Walker, I., 'Desert stories or faith in facts?', in M. Lister (ed.), *The Photographic Image in Digital Culture* (London: Routledge, 1995), pp. 236–52.

Shaping Audiences

Shaping Audiences

Introduction

In the decades when television was a new medium, viewing it was an event and an experience in itself. But now television viewers are very familiar with the medium, and television is available twenty-four hours a day and is provided on numerous channels delivered by conventional **terrestrial** broadcasting, through **cable** and **satellite** transmission and increasingly through **interactive** digital services. This increase in the quantity of television and the increase in the number of choices of what to view have made it increasingly difficult for broadcasters to gain reliable information about what audiences watch. This chapter discusses the largely numerical means by which broadcasters gain information about audience sizes, and why this information is important to them. An important matter to bear in mind when reading this chapter is that numerical, quantitative information does not reveal answers to the questions about why and how people watch. But since the measurement of audiences in terms of numbers of viewers is crucial to the economics and organisation of television, this chapter is devoted to ways of studying this. The Dutch television theorist Ien Ang (1991) has analysed the practices of audience measurement, and showed that broadcasters have an insistent desire to find ways of measuring audiences. But audience measurement techniques set limits to the kind of conclusions that can be drawn from them. Audience measurement:

- is statistical
- is based on samples of viewers, and
- results in generalisations about what viewers find pleasurable.

Another very significant issue is why audiences watch television programmes, whether they enjoy them and what role in their lives television programmes play. These are qualitative questions, questions that require information about the value people attribute to television, rather than statistical information, and are addressed in the next chapter.

The competition between television channels and methods of delivering television by terrestrial or non-terrestrial means has made competition for audiences more and more significant. The total television audience has become increasingly fragmented, although the number of hours per week that the average viewer watches has remained at about twenty-seven hours. Broadcasters aim to capture a significant share of the available audience for their own programmes, especially if their source of funding is advertising. Clearly, broadcasters can charge advertisers substantial amounts of money to put advertisements on their channel only if a large or valuable audience group is watching that channel when the advertisement is shown. The same concerns are also important to broadcasters that are not funded by advertising. The

---

terrestrial broadcasting from a ground-based transmission system, as opposed to broadcasting via satellite.

cable television originally called Community Antenna Television (CATV). Transmission of television signals along cables in the ground.

satellite television television signals beamed from a ground transmitter to a stationary satellite that broadcasts the signal to a specific area (called the 'footprint') below it.

interactive offering the opportunity for viewers to respond to what is broadcast, by sending signals back to the broadcaster (along a cable or phone line, for example).

BBC gains its income not through advertising but through the payment of the **licence fee**. But the government is unlikely to keep increasing the cost of a licence fee, and might even abolish the licence fee altogether, if the BBC is not gaining audiences comparable to those of the commercial channels. Broadcasters compete against each other to achieve large audience sizes for their programmes (**ratings**) and to encourage viewing of their own programmes rather than the competing programmes on other channels that are shown at the same time (**audience share**).

> ## ACTIVITY 11.1
>
> Which activites might compete for the time of the valuable eighteen to thirty-five age group and persuade them to watch less television? What connections might there be between time spent watching television and economic prosperity, rates of employment, other media in the household and leisure provisions?

The economics of watching television

Television programme-making has to be paid for. While cinema audiences pay for films by buying tickets to see them (and buying products associated with films), television viewers pay indirectly either by buying the television licence or by buying products that are advertised in television advertisements. Commercial broadcasters sell audiences to advertisers by estimating the size of audience expected to view a particular programme and estimating the composition of the audience (in terms of its age, gender and economic power). According to the size and composition of the audience, the broadcaster charges advertisers a particular sum of money per thousand viewers that it expects to view a certain programme. At the end of 2000 ITV charged advertisers £7.65 per thousand adults expected to be watching a programme in which the advertiser's commercial would be shown. The assumption behind this is that viewers are economically active in making purchases during the time that they are not watching television. The possibility that they will buy something advertised on television is assumed by broadcasters and the advertisers. So although it may seem that watching television is a respite from the activities of earning money and spending it, the viewer's economic activity is the precondition that enables television programmes on commercial channels to be made.

Jhally and Livant (1986) establish parallels between the nineteenth-century economist and political theorist Karl **Marx**'s theory of labour and watching television. For part of the time people are at work they are engaged in socially necessary labour. This is the time spent doing the work which generates the money that pays for people's wages. For the remaining hours spent at work people are engaged in surplus labour, which makes the money that generates profit for the **capitalist** (the owner of the business). In the hours people are not at work they are engaged in the reproduction of labour: sleeping, eating, recuperating in order to be ready to go to work the next day and do the same things all over again. The same model can be applied to commercial television broadcasting. Television networks make their

licence fee an annual payment by all owners of television sets, which is the main source of income for the BBC.

ratings the number of viewers estimated to have watched certain programmes, as compared to the numbers watching other programmes.

audience share the percentage of viewers estimated to have watched one channel as opposed to another channel broadcasting at the same time.

Marxism the political and economic theories associated with the German nineteenth-century theorist Karl Marx, who described and critiqued capitalist societies and proposed Communism as a revolutionary alternative.

capitalism the organisation of an economy around the private ownership of accumulated wealth, involving the exploitation of labour to produce profit that creates such wealth.

money by selling advertising time. The commodity which is sold by the network is audience time. In a parallel with Marx's concept of labour power, 'watching power' is the cost of reproduction, in other words the cost of the programme. During socially necessary viewing time, audiences watch the advertisements equivalent to the amount of money the programmes have cost the network to produce. In surplus viewing time audiences are watching advertisements solely for the profit of the networks, since the production of programmes has already been covered during socially necessary viewing time. For example, a programme might cost £400,000, which is the amount paid by the network to the television producers who made it. This programme might last twenty-four minutes, with another six minutes filled with advertisements. One thirty-second advertisement might bring in £100,000 in payments to the network by advertisers. Six minutes would allow twelve of these thirty-second advertisements, bringing into the network £1,200,000. So for this thirty-minute slot:

- the network income is £1,200,000
- the costs of broadcasting are £400,000
- making a surplus for the network of £800,000.

Once the operating costs of the network have been deducted from this figure, the rest is profit, for which Marx used the term surplus value. From the audience point of view, four of the advertisements during the six-minute break are socially necessary labour time which generate the £400,000 needed to cover the cost of the programme. The other eight advertisements watched by the audience in the six-minute commercial break are required to generate profit for the network.

The maximisation of profit by television networks depends on decreasing socially necessary viewing time and increasing surplus viewing time. This can be done by:

- selling shorter commercials which have proportionately higher cost per second
- reducing the cost of programmes
- reducing the amount of non-income-generating time by making programmes shorter and including more commercials.

people meter
a device resembling a television remote control, used in sample households to monitor what viewers watch. Viewers record which channels they watch and for how long.

Since advertisers pay for audiences' viewing time, they need to know that audiences are watching the commercials. The '**people meter**' is a mechanism for monitoring this, in which people in a household punch in their personal identification number when they begin to watch television, and punch out the number when they leave. This is very similar to punching in to work in a factory, and punching out at the end of the day. While it might seem strange to equate watching television with doing paid work, the analogy is actually very close. It is just that we are accustomed to thinking of television viewing as leisure (the opposite of work), and separating it from the harsh calculations of profit and loss that govern life in highly developed societies such as Britain. But television is a business and an industry, in which television viewers are increasingly regarded as a market, and could also be understood as participants.

ACTIVITY 11.2

If people watching television are generating income for television broadcasters by allowing them to charge advertisers to place commercials, why are viewers not paid by broadcasters to watch (viewers are, in a sense, 'working' for the broadcaster)? How does your answer illuminate the role of television as a 'leisure activity'?

Ratings: measuring audiences

BARB, the television audience research body, introduced a new audience panel on 1 January 2002, covering 5,100 households. The results are crucially important to programme **schedulers** and channel controllers, who make decisions each week based on the overnight viewing figures provided by BARB. About £3 billion a year in advertising revenue is traded on the basis of BARB figures, and, as Bob Mullan (1997: 16) notes, 'Counting the numbers of viewers allegedly watching television at certain times of day or night is essential to the requirements of advertisers as they attempt to target "audiences" and maximise their promotional messages.' Difficulties in making the early figures available from the new household sample are thought to have added to problems in early 2002 for ITV advertising revenue (exacerbated by an economic downturn). BARB's new household panel is the first entirely new panel to be recruited in more than thirty years. BARB selects its group of households so that it is as representative as possible of the whole British television audience. It chooses households from various regions of the country, comprising different combinations of household types, some with children, some without, across a range of ages and economic backgrounds. Complex statistical methods are used to ensure that the whole sample is representative, and that the results of the audience research information can be reliably multiplied up to give national figures.

Opportunities to commission, continue or cancel a television programme are significantly determined by BARB research. Although new forms of programme such as non-fictional **docusoaps** have been very popular with British audiences in recent years, fiction programmes have always attracted the largest audiences, and programmes in the long-established **genres** of the sitcom, the soap opera and the police drama, for example, are still the most popular according to BARB ratings. Across the whole of 1999 the highest-rated programme was an episode of the soap opera *Coronation Street* (ITV, 7 March) with 19.8 million viewers, and BBC1's rival soap *EastEnders* was the fifth most popular (7 January) with 15.7 million viewers. Episodes of popular genre fiction gained very large audiences that year and put them in the top twenty programmes, such as

- *Heartbeat* (ITV police drama, 28 February, 17 million)
- *A Touch of Frost* (ITV police drama, 21 March, 16.8 million)
- *Casualty* (BBC1 hospital drama, 13 February, 13.1 million)
- *The Vicar of Dibley* (BBC1 sitcom, 27 December, 14.4 million).

BARB (Broadcasters Audience Research Bureau) the independent body that gathers and reports viewing statistics on behalf of UK television institutions.

schedule the arrangement of programmes, advertisements and other material into a sequential order within a certain period of time, such as an evening, day or week.

docusoap a television form combining documentary's depiction of non-actors in ordinary situations with soap opera's continuing narratives about selected characters.

genre a kind or type of programme. Programmes of the same genre have shared characteristics.

The top twenty programmes of 1999 were all on terrestrial television rather than satellite or cable, and all were shown by either BBC1 or ITV. There were two American cinema films on television in the top twenty (*GoldenEye* and *Mission Impossible*), but all the most popular television programmes were British-made.

ACTIVITY 11.3

Why do you think that films on television are not more popular with audiences? Since British television fiction in genres such as soap opera and police and hospital drama are the most popular programmes, why do television channels bother to show films at all?

Audiences in the multi-channel environment

Figures released by BARB in February 2002 reveal that 50 per cent of the UK television audience have access to multi-channel television. Mark Sharman (2002: 8), director of broadcasting and production at BSkyB, wrote: 'Are Film Four and E4 a distraction from its [Channel 4's] remit or, worse, a cannibalisation of the audience for the parent channel, where E4's first year saw C4's 16–34 share fall by a staggering 38%?' But overall he regards the future optimistically, not surprisingly given his own position: 'According to government figures, the total size of the television broadcasting industry was estimated to be around £6.7bn in 1999. This represented a growth of 50% since 1994/95 – much of it reflecting the growth in multi-channel.' Sky Television now produces Channel 4's breakfast programme, Sky News is simultaneously broadcast on Channel 5, and Sky One's morning programme is produced by the terrestrial GMTV company. The interactions between terrestrial and satellite broadcasters seem likely to become more common, and it seems certain that non-terrestrial broadcasting will become more significant in the industry and to audiences.

In May 2002 British Sky Broadcasting (BSkyB) reported an annual increase in profits of 33 per cent, to £129 million. The channel had six million subscribers, paying an average of £341 per year, and the collapse of the ITV Digital channel will enable it to gain about another 300,000 households of the 800,000 that were left without programmes when the company collapsed. BSkyB is a '**vertically integrated**' company, owning the digital satellite platform on which its channels are broadcast. It also controls the technology used in **set-top boxes** to receive satellite programmes and sets the prices paid by rival channels to gain access to the digital platform through its subsidiary Sky Subscriber Services Ltd (SSS). The electronic programme guide that allows viewers to navigate between the channels broadcast by the Astra satellite system is also controlled by BSkyB, which charges £28,000 a year for a listing on the electronic programme guide. While this book was in production, the British government was considering how the new regulator, Ofcom, will deal with the virtual monopoly that BSkyB has over non-terrestrial broadcasting. BSkyB is one of numerous television businesses controlled by the

vertical integration the control by media institutions of all levels of a business, from the production of products to their distribution and means of reception.

set-top box the electronic decoding equipment connected to home television sets that allows access to digital television signals.

media entrepreneur Rupert Murdoch. Rupert Murdoch's media interests include film, television, newspapers, book publishing and magazines, and also financial stakes in major sports teams whose games are covered in the media. Restricting the list to television only, Murdoch owns controlling interests in the following television businesses:

- *United States cable television*: Fox News Channel, Fox Sports Enterprises, Fox News Net, FX, National Geographic Channel, and the Los Angeles Dodgers Channel.
- *United States network television*: Fox Broadcasting Company, Fox Television stations. It is also worth mentioning that he owns *TV Guide*, the dominant television listings publication.
- *Britain*: British Sky Broadcasting.
- *Italy*: Stream Television.
- *India, China and other Asian nations*: Channel Television and Star Television.
- *Japan*: Sky PerfecTV!
- *Australia*: Fox Sports Australia, FOXTEL and Channel television.

So there is powerful competition for audiences, and the struggle by established British broadcasters such as the BBC to develop strategies to survive in the contemporary environment must be seen in this international context. If the BBC gains large audiences, critics accuse it of being low quality, yet higher ratings are required by the BBC to justify its licence fee. In February 2002 the BBC launched its two new digital channels for children: CBBC and CBeebies, respectively for six- to thirteen-year-olds and for pre-school children. BBC4, an arts and culture channel, was launched later in the same year. Ninety per cent of CBeebies programmes and 75 per cent of CBBC programmes will be either British- or European-made (a considerably greater proportion than their competitors such as the Cartoon Network or the Disney Channel). Schedules are stripped into four-hour blocks, rotating three times a day. There are fourteen other channels competing for the child audience. John Ellis (2000: 28), considering the changing significance of audience ratings and targeted niche audiences, explains:

> Numbers still matter in that they provide the bench-mark for the performance of the channel as a whole. But overall audience numbers can only be increased by a subtle strategy of targeting particular sections of the audience on competing channels and providing something that will appeal to or satisfy them more . . . audiences can be specified according to age, class, gender, region, pattern of viewing and even by their degree of appreciation of the programme.

The BBC has built on its well-known brand, with its values of 'quality' and trustworthiness, to introduce channels that address **niche audiences** and particular **demographic** groups and rival the companies currently dominating the new multi-channel landscape.

niche audiences particular groups of viewers defined by age group, gender or economic status, for example, who may be the target audience for a programme.

demography the study of population, and the groupings of people (demographic groups) within the whole population.

> ## ACTIVITY 11.4
>
> How has the history of the BBC enabled it to claim the status of a 'quality brand'? Look for evidence of this branding (on the BBC's website, or in print advertisements for programmes, for instance) and analyse the 'brand values' that the BBC claims for itself.

Competing for valuable audiences

Spending on British programming in the last five years of the twentieth century rose from £3 billion to £8 billion. But ITV income from advertising was £1,966 million in 2000, and is now falling. The downturn in advertising income is likely to affect the ITV spend on programmes, which for all genres cost ITV £747 million in 2001. The proportion of soap and other drama on ITV rose 150 per cent in twenty-five years. ITV screens about 650 hours of drama per year, including soaps, at a cost in 2001 of £270 million. ITV has invested in drama partly by contracting six or seven major television stars such as Robson Green and Sarah Lancashire who are paid between £1 million and £2 million each for their exclusive services. In 2001 *EastEnders* began broadcasting four episodes per week, and ITV competed by beginning screenings of Premiership football matches at 7.00 p.m. on Saturdays. The cost of buying rights to screen sport cost ITV £160 million in 2001, more than the money spent on entertainment programmes (£110 million). Costume **adaptations**, long regarded as the province of the BBC, were deprioritised by the BBC in favour of adaptations of modern classics. By contrast ITV's effort in drama for the Christmas schedule included *Micawber*, a 'prequel' to Charles Dickens's nineteenth-century novel *David Copperfield*, and an adaptation in modern dress of Shakespeare's *Othello*. As channels compete by attempting to challenge a competitor's superiority in one programme genre or **format**, the values associated with each channel's brand can gradually shift. Indeed, it is notable the extent to which, in the early years of the twenty-first century, ITV (now branded as ITV1) is aiming to present itself differently to its current audience, and trying to attract newer audiences.

When certain genres of programme are recognised as attracting large or valuable audiences, broadcasting executives are quick to imitate these popular formats for their own channel. The popularity of Simon Schama's television series *A History of Britain* has encouraged television channels to switch funds from documentary and current affairs to history programmes presented by charismatic figures, often using reconstruction and dramatisation. Average ratings for these programmes have been impressive, considering that they address the relatively small and wealthy adult ABC1 audience group:

- *The Time of our Lives* (ITV) 4.4 million
- *The Six Wives of Henry VIII* (Channel 4) 4 million
- *A History of Britain by Simon Schama* (BBC2) 3.3 million
- *Battlefields* (BBC2) 3.3 million
- *What the Victorians Did for Us* (BBC2) 3.1 million.

adaptation transferring a novel, theatre play, poem, etc. from its original medium into another medium such as television.

format the blueprint for a programme, including its setting, main characters, genre, form and main themes.

In programmes aimed at younger audiences the success story of 2001 was the ITV talent show *Popstars*. Its success led to a string of 'copycat' programmes such as *Soapstars* and *Pop Idol*. Especially among young adult viewers, programmes featuring 'ordinary people' in competitive '**reality TV**' formats are the flavour of the moment in British television. In 2001 Channel 4 launched its **interactive** cable and satellite channel E4, whose most successful programme was not the expensive imported first-run showings (normally on its terrestrial channel) of the hospital drama *ER* or the long-running sitcom *Friends* but instead continuous footage of *Big Brother*.

reality TV
programmes where
the unscripted
behaviour of 'ordinary
people' is the focus
of interest.

ACTIVITY 11.5

Why are talent competions such as *Pop Idol* attractive to young adult viewers? In what ways do programmes such as this have relationships to 'reality TV' programmes in which 'ordinary people' become the focus of attention?

As the section above on the economics of television explained, the profitability of television programmes depends on the cost of making the programme, and the value of the audience that it attracts. One way of maximising profit is to gain the largest audience for the lowest production cost. A notable success in these terms is the ITV1 quiz *Who Wants to Be a Millionaire?*, which achieved a peak audience of 19.2 million viewers in 1999, as large as the most popular soap operas. Indeed ITV1 scheduled the programme against high-rated BBC soap *EastEnders*, and the BBC hospital dramas *Holby City* and *Casualty*. As the programme's title implies, the cost of paying out prizes to contestants in *Who Wants to Be a Millionaire?* can be very high. By November 2000 the programme had paid out £5.35 million in prize money, but this cost was covered by telephone call charges to people telephoning special phone-lines in order to put themselves forward as contestants. *Who Wants to Be a Millionaire?* has the relatively low production cost of about £200,000 per episode, and, with an average audience of 11.7 million viewers, takes a significant share of the available audience for its time slot. By covering its production costs through the income generated by telephone call charges, a very large proportion of the income generated by the programme is profit. With such large audiences ITV1 can charge significant sums to advertisers wishing to place their advertisements in the commercial breaks between the segments of the programme. Most of the money paid by advertisers is straightforward profit for its production company and the ITV channel.

But audience size is not the only consideration for broadcasters. The most valuable audience is young viewers, who have plenty of money to spend but do not watch very much television (because they go out more, spending money on the products and services advertised on television). *Who Wants to Be a Millionaire?* gains a 42 per cent share of eighteen- to thirty-four-year-olds, and *Blind Date* gets a 45 per cent share of this group. Channel 4 has scheduled a sequence of comedy programmes one after another on Friday evenings in the 1990s and into the 2000s, such as the US sitcoms *Friends* and *Frasier*, the light entertainment sketch show *Trigger Happy TV* and the comedy quiz programme *Whose Line Is it Anyway?*, and has attracted a high proportion of relatively prosperous young adult viewers for this time slot. Advertising agencies like Channel 4's Friday night comedy because it amounts to a 'brand' (a product with a familiar image such as Coca-Cola or Levi jeans) which viewers actively choose to watch. Channel 4's Friday night audience is not huge but it is desirable to advertisers. Costs to Channel 4 are not great compared to original drama, for instance, since the mainly imported American programmes in its Friday night schedule are generally cheaper to buy than original British drama.

The audience for ITV's terrestrial programmes has been getting older for many years, and has a typically lower average income than the BBC's audience. ITV1 has made various attempts to attract younger viewers, and viewers with the higher disposable incomes that are attractive to advertisers. Paul Marquess, a television producer who had formerly worked as a story editor on *Coronation Street*, a producer of *Brookside* and the creator of the successful drama about the British football scene *Footballers' Wives*, was recruited by Thames Television and ITV to turn the police drama series *The Bill* into a serial:

> ITV and Thames had decided the serial bits were very successful and the audience research supported that. I arrived with a clear brief – to turn *The Bill* into a serial. They'd have serial elements, but they were mixed with stand-alone episodes, so you'd watch the story of Page and Quinnan's affair for six hours and then that six-parter would finish and the next time you saw them in a scene together, there'd be no eye-contact, no acknowledgement they'd ever had an affair. That dissatisfied me as a viewer.
>
> (quoted in McLean 2002: 8)

soap opera
a continuing drama serial involving a large number of characters in a specific location, focusing on relationships, emotions and reversals of fortune.

In the episodes produced by Marquess seven regular characters were swiftly killed off, to be replaced by actors with track records in **soap opera** such as *EastEnders* and *Coronation Street*. Marquess's aim was to address a younger and more valuable audience for ITV: 'It still gets 7 million viewers as it is, but if you look at *The Bill*'s core demographic, it is white men over 50.' The aim was not to increase the audience for *The Bill* but to change its composition to make it more valuable as a commodity that could be sold to advertisers.

BARB and the broadcasters themselves use a standard breakdown of the population into groups according to their economic and social position. Highly paid professionals make up the 'A' group, lower-management and clerical workers form the 'B' group, while the 'C1' group consists of skilled manual workers. Less attractive groups to advertisers, such as people in temporary employment, people living on pensions and the unemployed are the least attractive groups in the population, represented by the codes 'C2', 'D' and 'E'. It is evidently very important for broadcasters that their audience contains a high proportion of the most economically and socially powerful people in the national audience. In 2001 the percentages of ABC1 viewers on four terrestrial channels (M. Brown 2001: 8–9) were:

- BBC1: 46
- Channel 4: 45
- BBC2: 44
- ITV: 38.

Figure 11.1 *The Bill*, one of ITV's longest running dramas. Courtesy of PA Picselect, © Thames Television

Watching television is important to ABC1s, and 22 per cent of the members of the elite AB social group relax by watching television, compared to 13 per cent who read and 8 per cent who listen to music. So the fact that 45 per cent of *EastEnders'* audience is ABC1 partly explains BBC1's decision to increase showings of the soap opera to four episodes per week, while ITV's police drama series *A Touch of Frost* gained a welcome 48 per cent share of ABC1s watching television in its time slot. Channel 4 has addressed this audience by buying American 'quality' programmes such as *ER* and *The West Wing*, and has commissioned original British drama addressed to the ABC1 audience such as the serials *Queer as Folk* and *Never Never*.

Attitudes to the audience

We have seen in this chapter how the television audience is conceived by broadcasters as a market and a **commodity**. The situation is made more complex by the requirement in British television for the audience to be informed and educated, as well as entertained. For the media theorist John Hartley (1992) this conflict can be understood by analysing how broadcasters consider audiences in a way that is parallel to adults' control of children. Hartley (1992: 17) argues that 'there's a struggle between what are presumed to be *paedocratic* audience practices on the one hand (governed *by* childlike qualities), and *pedagogic* discourses on the other (government *over* childish tendencies)'. Although television viewers can be addressed in a range of ways, for example as citizens, as working people or as members of ethnic, gender or class groups, Hartley argues that television in developed societies such as Britain

commodity a raw material or product whose economic value is established by market price rather than the intrinsic qualities or usefulness of the material or product itself.

is understood primarily as an entertainment medium. In this respect television focuses on the delivery of pleasure to its audience. Despite the fact that there are some genres of programme, such as news, that address the audience with information, and genres such as some children's programmes that aim to educate the audience, the majority of programmes either are entertainment or use entertainment forms in order to attract viewers, retain them on a channel and encourage viewing of future programmes. Hartley (1992: 111) claims that broadcasters 'appeal to the playful, imaginative, fantasy, irresponsible aspects of adult behaviour. They seek the common personal ground that unites diverse and often directly antagonistic groupings in a given population. What better, then, than a fictional version of everyone's supposed childlike tendencies which might be understood as predating such social groupings?' The argument is that treating the audience as children is a strategy of control. It is based on an assumption that television viewers, seeking pleasure and entertainment, unconsciously wish to regress to a childlike state.

The other side of Hartley's view is that television also aims to instruct television viewers, in parallel to the ways in which adults seek to instruct and train children. He is not referring only to programmes that have an explicit educational aim but also to a much broader address to the audience. For example, the promotion of television programmes, trailers and reviews of programmes instruct the audience about what is available for them to watch, and how they might choose to watch it. The regulation of television both within the industry and by the official regulatory bodies can also be regarded as instructional in this way. The activities of regulatory bodies in controlling what viewers can and cannot see (see Chapter 10), and devising regulations about, for example, what kind of programme content can be viewed by children or at certain times of day are, for Hartley, means of controlling and instructing the audience in the way in which adults seek to control the behaviour of children.

By discussing the television audience in this way Hartley draws our attention to the contradictory status of the audience in television culture. On one hand, the audience is very valuable to broadcasters. It is the group that they address, and the source of their income. Like the love that adults have for their children, broadcasters show care and interest in the audience. On the other hand, audiences can be hard to understand and difficult to communicate with, and it is difficult for broadcasters and regulators to gain control of viewers' attitudes and behaviour. Like children again, audiences can be unruly and undisciplined. Hartley draws attention to the way in which the institutions of television address an audience on which they depend, but whom they can also patronise and seek to control. He notes that the Annan Report on Broadcasting in Britain (1977: 25) stated a child-centred view of television viewing, in which the identities of viewers are those of family members, defined in terms of their relation to children: 'The audience for a programme may total millions: but people watch and listen in the family circle, in their homes, so that violations of the taboos of language and behaviour, which exist in every society, are witnessed by the whole family – parents, children and grandparents – in each other's presence.' In this context it is worth remembering the arguments in the preceding chapter of this book about television regulation. Regulators very often draw on their anxiety about what children might see on television in order to frame the guidelines used by programme-makers. Although it is certainly the case that regulators do worry about the influence of television on children, Hartley's argument can also remind us that this may be an ideological strategy unconsciously concealing assumptions about the audience as a whole, both adults and children. In television culture audiences are always nebulous, distant and hard to understand.

In Television Studies, approaches to audiences have followed a broadly similar pattern of differences of approach. Audiences can be regarded as distant and unknowable, as objects rather than subjects or agents who act on their own initiative. The alternative view to this is that television audiences have an active agency and are not simply passive objects who are positioned by television texts so that they lap up a single '**preferred reading**'. By considering audiences as active, it is possible to take account of the complex social and cultural contexts in which television viewing takes place, and in which television programmes are made. As Bob Mullan (1997: 18) has argued,

> Viewers often, but not always, engage in meaning-making: they do not always sit there empty-minded awaiting edification. When a viewer watches television they do not leave their histories at the living-room door: neither do they abandon their cultural, class, racial, economic or sexual identities, nor do they forget either their media knowledge of comparable programmes, information in newspapers, and other aspects of the infrastructure of television viewing.

From this '**active audience**' perspective, audiences are not regarded as masses, crowds or mobs whose behaviour appears from the outside to be irrational and uncontrollable.

Interactivity

Although interactive television, where viewers can respond directly to programme content through their remote-control handset, is a decisive and important development in contemporary television, viewers have always interacted with television. There are many genres of programme that invite the viewer to become involved and to participate remotely. For example, television coverage of sport routinely addresses the viewer as a witness watching the sport along with television commentators and spectators at the event. The spoken discourse of sports commentators also routinely invites viewers to make judgements about the performance of the sportspeople and to evaluate their success. The positioning of cameras in television coverage of sport provides a much closer view of the action than is normally available to spectators at the event itself, and cutting between camera shots allows the television viewer to identify with the efforts and emotions of the competitors. The production and editing of television sport are designed to promote viewer involvement and to stimulate viewers' interaction with the event as it is taking place.

In a similar way television talk shows address the viewer as someone taking part in the discussion. Expert commentators, often professionals such as psychologists, therapists or lawyers, appear in television talk shows and provide specialist opinion, while studio audiences engage either by individual audience members making comments of their own to the host or the guests, or simply by cheering, booing or laughing, for example. Television viewers are invited to identify at various points in the programme with the experts, their guests or the studio audience. Occasionally

preferred reading an interpretation of a text that seems to be the one most encouraged by the text, the 'correct' interpretation.

active audience television audiences regarded not as passive consumers of meanings, but as negotiating meanings for themselves that are often resistant to those meanings that are intended or that are discovered by close analysis.

talk shows also include opportunities for viewers to phone in and speak directly to the host and to ask questions or make comments. Although most of the time viewers of talk shows are involved only virtually, by responding to the programme only within their own viewing space in the home, nevertheless, as with sport's progress on television, the **format** and staging of the programme address the viewer as someone interested and involved in an ongoing discussion. A space is 'hollowed out' for the viewer to occupy, in which an active response and involvement is required.

Strategies such as these are intended to stimulate active viewing of television programmes, where viewers give their full attention to what they are seeing and hearing, and where there may be opportunities for action by the viewer. It is generally supposed by advertisers that the greater the attention given by television viewers to programmes, the more chance there is that viewers will also give their attention to advertisements. From an advertiser's point of view, of course, it is very important that viewers watch and remember the advertisements they have seen on television. Advertisements often include opportunities for viewer activity. These may simply be invitations for the viewer to get a joke, to solve a puzzle or simply to figure out what product an advertisement is selling. Being intrigued by a visually interesting advertisement, and enjoying its wit, are in themselves kinds of activity that make the advertisement and its product more memorable. But there are further strategies that advertisers can use, such as providing telephone numbers and Internet addresses that invite viewers to seek further information immediately about a product or service. A particular case in which the strategies of advertisements and programmes merge together is in television shopping channels. These of course address the viewer as a potential buyer of the products that are displayed, and the presenters of shopping programmes address the viewer directly in describing and recommending products. Displays of prices, availability and special offers appear in windows on the screen, along with the telephone number that the viewer can use to purchase a particular product. Shopping channels also sometimes use short segments in which viewers who have rung in to buy a product are interviewed briefly by the presenter about why they found a product attractive, and whether they would recommend a product having used it before.

But true interactive television goes much further than this. Cable television systems can allow television viewers to choose to watch a film from a menu available on an on-screen programme guide. Viewers can also call up additional information about programmes, and access brief television segments that support the programme they are watching. Wildlife programmes, for example, may have supporting material giving further information about the animals seen in the programme, or providing further footage that was not included in the eventual edited version. The technology of picture in picture allows this material to appear in smaller windows within the television screen, or for the viewer to see what is being broadcast on another channel. It has been suggested for a long time that it will also be possible for viewers to see alternative endings of drama programmes, or to change the relationship between narrative sequences, in a way that is already possible in retail DVD systems. The technological development that allows all of these opportunities to exist is **digital television**. By pressing buttons on a remote-control handset, viewers can control which stream of signals appears as picture and sound on their screen, and shift easily from one stream of digital information to another.

digital television television pictures and sound encoded into the ones and zeros of electronic data. Digital signals can also be sent back down cables by viewers, enabling interaction with television programmes.

With a range of available channels that may be up to 200 simultaneously, conventional television listings publications are difficult to use for viewers of inter-active television. Instead, electronic programme guides are available on the television screen. These look similar to the grids that are already common in listings publi-cations such as *TV Guide* in the United States. They are in effect lists of time slots where for a particular time period all of the programmes available on all channels are shown. Interactive television viewers can then scroll up and down through these lists, and view information about particular programmes. Electronic programme guides are easiest to use when programmes are of standard lengths, such as thirty minutes, one hour or two hours for programmes such as films or football matches. In the multi-channel environment of the United States, even in terrestrial broad-casting the use of standard programme lengths makes it easier for viewers to hop between channels. It is likely that the introduction of interactive television more widely in Britain will produce greater standardisation of programme lengths for this reason. It is also likely that the broadcast of digital interactive programmes will disrupt the conventional pattern of television schedules. Because interactive television makes it easy to choose to view a programme at a variety of different starting times (because the same programme is being streamed by perhaps three or four different channels, starting at, for example, 7.30 p.m., 8.00 p.m., or 8.30 p.m.) the viewer's chance to catch a programme is greatly increased. The power of tele-vision schedulers to control when audiences watch programmes is correspondingly diminished, and, in effect, television viewers become schedulers themselves.

Paying for interactive television

Six million households in Britain had access to digital television in the year 2000, and thus the ability to watch interactive television. Certain genres of programme have led the penetration of digital television in Britain. The most significant of these is sport. Around 40 per cent of the subscribers to the Sky Sports Active channel watch football games interactively. Digital technology allows them to select text information relevant to the game, and to choose the camera angle from which the game is presented on their television screen, for example. The Sky News Active channel also allows its users access to text and images that support news bulletins and particular news stories. From the perspective of the television broadcaster, interactive television is a 'premium service' that viewers can be charged additional money to use. But because of the slow development of interactive television tech-nology in Britain, for every new subscriber some other subscribers discontinue their payment for these services. Digital television broadcasters aim to reduce the **churn rate** by finding new ways of enhancing television coverage by providing interactive services. Eventually it is hoped that television viewers will become so accustomed to these enriched television programmes that they will consider them essential, and the number of non-renewals of subscriptions will fall to a low figure. It has been difficult, however, to find ways of making money from digital television in Britain. Shopping and online betting can also be provided through interactive television services, and the converged email and phone services on digital mean that viewers can enter phone competitions (on premium rate phone-lines) and post reviews of films. Digital television also allows games to be played over the line: for example

churn rate a ratio setting the numbers of new subscribers to a paid-for television service against the number of subscribers cancelling their subscription.

Sky offers *Tetris*, which can be played at a cost of about 25p per game. Interactive shopping through the television set has attracted relatively small numbers of users, and it currently seems that only online betting is a profitable use of the interactive technology for the companies that have invested in it.

So far it has not been profitable for television programme-makers to invest in interactivity in fiction programmes. The telecommunications and cable television company NTL announced in March 2000 that it had allocated a fund of £5 million that would be spent over five years to develop interactive television drama programmes. This was planned to be a joint venture with Channel 5, whereby Channel 5 would screen this interactive drama and thereby persuade more viewers to purchase the hardware such as digital television receivers and set-top boxes manufactured by NTL that are necessary to view such programmes. The pilot programme that Channel 5 commissioned from the independent production company Leisure Time was to be a crime drama. But knowing that the only currently profitable use of interactive television is in betting, Channel 5 adjusted the specifications for the programme to include an element of competition. It would therefore be possible for viewers to make bets about the fates of the characters and increase the element of suspense in the narrative. However, in 2001 the project was abandoned as being too complex and expensive. Making a drama programme that has multiple simultaneous plot lines, each of them accessible to viewers making choices through their remote-control handsets and thus composing different programmes according to the choices they have made, is an extremely expensive and complicated business. The programme-makers would be asked in effect to write and produce the equivalent of several different conventional programmes, and find ways of linking up narrative segments, plot events and character development so that the choices made by the viewer would continue to result in a meaningful and enjoyable programme.

In the digital television environment there are more broadcasting channels, and therefore smaller amounts of money per channel and per programme to spend because the audience sizes for particular programmes are correspondingly smaller than those of conventional terrestrial television. The costs of making programmes are therefore more difficult to recoup from advertisers, and need to be generated from the subscriptions paid by the viewers of interactive digital television channels, or from one-off payments made by viewers to see a particular programme. So far, subscription and **pay-per-view** are not economically significant in Britain, though it seems likely that these modes of viewing will increase in importance. Interactivity is bound to change the forms and formats of television programmes. If interactive betting becomes the primary way of generating revenue, programmes will be structured to include opportunities for competition among the people appearing in them, and the possibility of a range of different outcomes within programmes and at their conclusion, so that viewers are able to gamble on the results. The ways that audiences view programmes, identify with and relate to people appearing on television, and follow storylines, would also change.

Some of these changes can already be seen in programmes broadcast on terrestrial television and on cable and satellite in Britain. This is because new developments in technology of any kind are more likely to be adopted when they enhance a service that already exists, or offer services that are linked to an established brand or property. As John Storey (1999: 125) has argued, people's media use is strongly influenced

pay-per-view specific television programmes (such as sports events, or films) offered to subscribers on payment of a fixed one-off fee.

by their habits and routines, since 'cultural consumption is a practice of everyday life. Cultural commodities are not appropriated or used in a social vacuum; such usage and appropriation takes place in the context of other forms of appropriation and use, themselves connected to the other routines, which together form the fabric of everyday life.' When Channel 4 planned its second series of *Big Brother* in 2001, it introduced interactive services accessible through its digital television channel E4, as well as on the World Wide Web. Since the programme already had established **brand recognition**, and viewers of the first series had already been able to interact with the programme on the Internet, Channel 4 was able to enhance the second series in ways that audiences already understood. *Big Brother* has a large audience among the eighteen to thirty-four audience, and this group is more likely than others in the British population to have access to interactive television technology (and also to the Internet). Viewers of *Big Brother* were able to take part in interactive games using their remote-control handsets, and could also vote for the exclusion of contestants, take part in quizzes and gain access to additional information and video coverage. So *Big Brother 2* and *3* had numerous benefits for Channel 4 in attracting and maintaining a valuable youth audience, stimulating the use of and demand for digital interactive services, and promoting the brand identity of a programme closely identified with the channel.

The prominence of betting as a means of gathering revenue for interactive television has important consequences for audiences' relationships with television, and more generally as an index of shifts in the **ideology** of television culture. As this section has argued, betting is used in order to stimulate the involvement of the viewer in programmes, since putting the viewer's own money on the line produces a tangible reason for him or her to focus exclusively on what he or she is watching. There are significant differences between this kind of involvement with television and the conventional ways in which Television Studies has discussed the viewer's relationship with programmes. Conventionally, the viewer's relationship to programmes has been thought of in terms of identification with the patterns and rhythms of narrative and identifications with characters and people represented in programmes, and in terms of an ebb and flow of attention across the flow of a period of watching time. If interactive viewers have sums of money at stake in programmes, then that sum of money is a representation of the viewer himself or herself. The transaction of making a bet forms a link between the space of viewing and the represented space in the television programme. Indeed, the bigger the bet that the viewer makes, the more, perhaps, the viewer is involved and interested in the programme that he or she is watching and the more connected is the viewer's space with the represented space of television. It is also important to remember that betting is about risk and probability. If interactive betting becomes widespread and socially significant, there is likely to be a change in the ways that people conceive of their reality. Society could be considered primarily in terms of success and failure, winners and losers, and the ability of individuals to take risks in order to succeed. In such a society it is necessary to speculate in order to accumulate, but there will always be risk factors that cannot be predicted. The forces of chance and fate, rather than planning, effort and consistency of action, may acquire increasing importance. The sense that society is a collective community may reduce in importance compared to individualism and competition. Ideological assumptions such as these give support to the increased short-term thinking, acceptance of risk and unpredictability and diminished social

brand recognition the ability of audiences to recognise the distinctive identity of a product, service or institution and the values and meanings associated with it.

ideology the set of beliefs, attitudes and assumptions arising from the economic and class divisions in a culture, underlying the ways of life accepted as normal in that culture.

cohesion that are currently found in more capitalist societies such as the United States, as compared to Western European nations.

ACTIVITY 11.6

If you were trying to 'pitch' an interactive programme to a broadcaster, which programme format and genre might you choose in order to include plenty of opportunities for viewer interaction? How would you respond to the broadcaster's concerns about the profitability of your programme (the balance between programme cost and potential income)?

Case study: television scheduling

John Ellis (2000: 25) has argued that the composition of a television schedule is parallel to the operations involved in editing during the programme-making process: 'Instead of combining shots and sounds into a sequence and sequences into a programme, as an editor does, the scheduler combines whole programme units into an evening's flow, whole evenings into a week, whole weeks into a season, and whole seasons into a year.' Scheduling is therefore an activity of selection and combination, just as editing is, and schedulers aim to offer audiences a variety of programmes that have relationships between them of a similar kind to the relationships between the moments and sequences of an individual programme. Some programmes will have connections between them (in the same way that a current affairs programme may be scheduled after the news), while others will be placed next to programmes that have a quite different genre and format (a Hollywood film might follow Premiership football). Although in the early years of television production the lengths of programmes and their interrelationships with each other were subject to little overall planning, by the 1980s standard programme lengths such as thirty minutes and one hour had produced grids of time slots such as were already common in broadcasting in the United States.

Schedules are planned on the basis of assumptions about the nature of the television audience and the ways in which audiences watch. Television schedules have for a long time been planned around the ways that hypothetical family audiences organise their time. Children come home from school at the end of the afternoon, meals are usually eaten in the early or mid-evening, children are expected to go to bed at around 9.00 p.m. In general, the early evening contains shorter and more diverse programmes, while the later evening offers adult viewers longer and more complex forms and formats. At the level of the year as a whole, new programmes are traditionally introduced around September, when the holiday season has finished and family routines get back to normal as school time begins. In the summer people watch less television because they are more likely to be outside in the warmer weather, so the summer period contains more repeated programmes and fewer programmes that broadcasters have invested significant money in or attach greater importance to. At a particular point during the year, expected events such as the football Cup Final, the Eurovision Song Contest or Christmas celebrations will require the schedule to be rearranged and specially planned.

Of course the schedulers for one channel will need to take account of what its competitors have planned. There are several possible responses to competition. The purpose of scheduling is to gain **audience share** and audience **ratings**. Schedulers are working in the interests of the broadcasting channel for which they work, and not for the producers of individual programmes. Therefore, an individual programme which might seem to be worthy of a prominent place in the schedule might be moved to a much less attractive spot because of a strategic decision about the programming which a competing channel is offering at the same time. The schedulers for one channel might go 'head to head' with the competition and place a programme likely to attract large audiences against a high-rating programme on a competing channel. Or alternatively, the scheduler might accept that the ratings battle is lost in that time slot, and schedule a programme that was never likely to be a ratings winner, thus conceding the ratings battle to a strong competitor. British schedulers keep in contact with their competitors at other channels, under regulations which require them to exchange information about each other's programming one week beforehand. The power to commission new programmes is in the hands of the executives at broadcasting channels, but schedulers have an important role to play in identifying programmes which are likely to gain audiences, based on information schedulers have about what audiences have watched in the past. So schedulers provide recommendations to commissioning executives and thus have an important influence on which programmes are made. John Ellis (2000: 26) goes as far as to say that the schedule is 'the locus of power in television, the mechanism whereby demographic speculations are turned into a viewing experience. And it is more than that as well, for any schedule contains the distillation of the past history of a channel, of national broadcasting as a whole, and of the particular habits of national life.'

The scheduling of *Big Brother* in the summer has been successful for Channel 4, since television programming in summer is usually made at lower cost per hour and involves numerous repeats, because people are expected to be outdoors and going out more than at other times of year. *Big Brother* was initially shown in the late evening, but was shifted to an earlier time slot once the audience had sampled it and word of mouth began to increase the numbers of people interested in the programme. However, the critically acclaimed American drama series about a fictional US President and his staff, *The West Wing*, was shifted from a 10.00 p.m. start to an 11.00 p.m. start after a few weeks, because of initially small audiences, although the programme had built a significant audience of ABC1 viewers and gathered vocal support in broadsheet newspapers. Many objections to the shift in *The West Wing*'s start time were made, further increasing the prominence of the programme and emphasising what was perceived as a scheduling error. While the scheduling of *Big Brother* across the summer turned out to be a risk that paid off for Channel 4, its schedulers did not succeed in guessing correctly in the case of *The West Wing*. The problem arises in part from a vicious circle that affects schedulers' use of audience data:

> The success or failure of a particular scheduling strategy is measured by the same methodology that suggested it in the first place. A problem with audience size or composition produced by a particular programming policy is identified through using the BARB figures. This leads to changes in that policy, whose success is measured by using the same BARB data.
>
> (Ellis 2000: 35)

continued

public service in television, the provision of a mix of programmes that inform, educate and entertain in ways that encourage the betterment of audiences and society in general.

In 2001 the BBC had higher ratings per twenty-four-hour period than ITV for the first time in many years. The BBC needs to attract audiences large enough to justify the levying of the licence fee, and at the same time to provide **public service** programmes. The factors affecting ITV scheduling are somewhat different: decisions have commercial implications in terms of ITV's income from advertisers, which is based on the size and composition of audiences available to watch advertisements during programmes. Screening the third and last series of the popular drama serial *Cold Feet* on ITV on both Sunday night and Monday night was a strategy to hold large audiences on Monday, which is a difficult scheduling problem. New cars are registered in July and August, so ITV seeks to schedule programmes in the middle of the summer months which might appeal to the predominantly male buyers of new cars. Programmes about home improvement are likely to be shown at times when people are considering doing work on their houses, for example on Fridays and Saturdays when major DIY superstores will be open for people to purchase materials: ITV is unlikely to show DIY programmes on Sundays, when viewers will already have completed their shopping for such items. This British situation is different from that in the USA, where programmes are generally scheduled in **strips**, for example soap operas in the afternoon, sitcoms in **prime time**, drama in the late evening. Each American network channel's schedule is similar to those of its competitors, with much less variety and unexpectedness then we find in Britain.

stripping in television scheduling, placing a programme or genre of programme at the same time on several days of each week.

prime time the part of a day's television schedule when the greatest number of viewers may be watching, normally the mid-evening period.

By re-evaluating audience figures, channel controllers and schedulers identify patterns of audience movement. For example, a 'pre-echo' is an audience group intending to watch a programme starting shortly, thus increasing the audience for the programme scheduled just before the one they are interested in. 'Echoes' are audiences inherited from a programme that has just been broadcast. Now that British programmes tend to fit into the grid of half-hour and hour-long slots, there are more 'junction points' at which large numbers of viewers may switch from one channel to another. For example, at 10.00 p.m. news has been broadcast on both BBC1 and ITV1, and the 9.00 p.m. watershed is a point at which programmes aimed at a more adult audience can begin, resulting in a tendency for all channels to change the kinds of programme available at 9.00 p.m. or 10.00 p.m., thus producing a junction where audiences may choose to move to one channel or another. 'Tent pole' programmes are those that can be relied on to gain a large audience, thus lifting up the trend line showing audience size, like the ridge pole of a tent. Schedulers might also position a programme with a relatively low audience between two popular ones, hoping to inherit audiences from the preceding programme and to pick up audiences expecting to see the following one, producing 'hammocking', whereby a less popular programme is held up by those on either side.

ACTIVITY 11.7

Using information about programme ratings (which can be found in the weekly television newspaper *Broadcast*, for example), look for examples of relationships between programmes on the same channel in the current television schedules that seem to represent 'tent-poling' and 'hammocking'. How significant is it for broadcasters to 'protect' less popular programmes by trying to inherit audiences for them, by scheduling them next to more popular programmes? Why is this?

News programmes fulfil the regulatory requirement for broadcasters to inform their audience about contemporary events, but can also be used to control the audience's patterns of viewing because they occur at junction points. An early-evening news programme may encourage viewers to remain watching that channel for subsequent entertainment programmes in mid-evening prime time, while late-evening news occurs when adult-oriented programmes are shown. After the 9.00 p.m. 'watershed', when children are presumed not to be watching, the long late-evening news can hold viewers to remain on the same channel for the programmes that follow. ITV's late-evening news, which had been broadcast at 10.00 p.m. for many years, was broadcast even later in the evening for nearly two years under the name *ITN Nightly News*, after ITV executives had campaigned for more than five years to shift its schedule slot. ITV executives wanted to move the news later in the evening to make room for relatively long-duration programmes, especially films and football matches, that could take up the whole mid-evening period and deny prime-time audiences to the other competing channels. However, in July 2000, the Independent Television Commission required ITV to return *News at Ten* to the 10.00 p.m. slot from early 2001 onwards. *ITV News at Ten* can be moved to a later slot on Fridays and on one other day during the week, but is always named *News at Ten* because of viewers' high brand recognition for this name. The new *News at Ten* is shorter than before (at about twenty minutes), thus allowing ITV to add two-and-a-half minutes of advertising time to the 10.00 p.m. to 10.30 p.m. slot, and twenty seconds of extra trails for forthcoming programmes. This increase in advertising and trailer time is economically important because news is watched by comparatively high numbers of viewers in the ABC1 social categories (professional, managerial and skilled workers). It is these viewers whom advertisers prefer to target with advertisements for 'big-ticket items' that are both expensive and aspirational, such as cars. ITV gained about £70 million a year from moving its news to 11.00 p.m. and thus being able to schedule programmes with large audiences such as football matches that advertisers would pay large sums to advertise in. But with a shorter news programme in the traditional 10.00 p.m. *News at Ten* slot and more room for advertisements around it, the loss incurred from shifting the news back to its traditional time slot can be largely offset.

Scheduling is still hugely significant in British television, though some of the changes occurring in broadcasting in the present and near future may well change the ways in which it is done. This chapter has briefly discussed some of these changes, such as interactive digital television, the proliferation of channels and the threats to conventional terrestrial television from falling advertising revenues. The introduction of personal video recorders, such as TiVo, will also have an effect on scheduling, since viewers will in effect become schedulers themselves (see Chapter 2). The TiVo system or personal video recorder offers a fourteen-day searchable programme guide from which the viewer can choose up to thirty-five hours of programmes which will be stored digitally in the hard drive. Since all the programmes stored on the machine are there to be watched whenever the viewer wishes, and in any order, if this technology is widely adopted it will render much of the scheduling effort that currently takes place potentially redundant. Nevertheless, for the moment it seems likely that viewers will still want to see the free terrestrial programmes which are available simply by switching on the television when the daily routines of life in British households allow them the opportunity to do so. Scheduling remains a crucial activity in shaping audiences.

SUMMARY OF KEY POINTS

● The measurement of audiences and prediction of how they respond to television are important to television institutions' economic success and the planning of programmes.

● Not only audience size but also the composition of the audience is measured on behalf of British television institutions by independent researchers.

● The increasing number of television channels, broadcasting hours and systems of delivery (such as cable and satellite) has fractured television audiences into smaller niche groups.

● Some audience groups are more sought-after than others, usually because of their economic or social status.

● To address and hold particular audiences, television producers change programmes, create new programmes, mix the genre conventions used in programmes and look for opportunities to increase viewers' involvement in programmes.

● Television schedules are designed to attract and hold audiences, and studying schedules reveals how television channels conceive of their audiences.

Further reading

Allen, R., 'Audience-oriented criticism and television', in R. Allen (ed.), *Channels of Discourse, Reassembled: Television and Contemporary Criticism* (London: Routledge, 1992), pp. 101–37.

Ang, I., *Living Room Wars: Rethinking Audiences for a Postmodern World* (London: Routledge, 1996.

—— *Desperately Seeking the Audience* (London: Routledge, 1991).

Annan Committee, The, *Report of the Committee on the Future of Broadcasting* (London: HMSO, 1977).

Corner, J., *Critical Ideas in Television Studies* (Oxford: Clarendon, 1999).

—— *Television Form and Public Address* (London: Edward Arnold, 1995).

Dickinson, R., R. Harindranath and O. Linné (eds), *Approaches to Audiences: A Reader* (London: Arnold, 1998).

Drummond, P. and R. Patterson (eds), *Television and its Audience: International Research Perspectives* (London: BFI, 1988).

Ellis, J., 'Scheduling: the last creative act in television', *Media, Culture & Society*, 22:1 (2000), pp. 25–38.

—— *Visible Fictions: Cinema, Television, Video* (London: Routledge & Kegan Paul, 1982).

Hartley, J., *Tele-Ology: Studies in Television* (London: Routledge, 1992).

Jhally, S. and B. Livant, 'Watching as working: the valorization of audience consciousness', *Journal of Communication*, 36:2 (1986), pp. 124–43.

Lewis, J., *The Ideological Octopus: An Exploration of Television and its Audience* (London: Routledge, 1991).

Livingston, S. and P. Lunt, *Talk on Television: Audience Participation and Public Debate* (London: Routledge, 1994).

Ruddock, A., *Understanding Audiences: Theory and Method* (London: Sage, 2001).

Seiter, E., H. Borchers, G. Kreutzner and E.-M. Warth (eds), *Remote Control: Television, Audiences and Cultural Power* (London: Routledge, 1989).

Storey, J. *Cultural Consumption and Everyday Life* (London: Arnold, 1999).

Tulloch, J., *Watching Television Audiences: Cultural Theories and Methods* (London: Arnold, 2000).

Television in Everyday Life

Television in Everyday Life

code in semiotics, a system or set of rules that shapes how signs can be used, and therefore how meanings can be made and understood.

ideology the set of beliefs, attitudes and assumptions arising from the economic and class divisions in a culture, underlying the ways of life accepted as normal in that culture.

discourse in television, a particular usage of television's audio-visual 'language' (news programme discourse, or nature documentary discourse, for instance).

polysemia the quality of having multiple meanings at the same time. Texts like this are called 'polysemic'.

preferred reading an interpretation of a text that seems to be the one most encouraged by the text, the 'correct' interpretation.

negotiated reading a viewer interpretation of a television text where the viewer understands meaning in relation to his or her own knowledge and experience, rather than simply accepting the meaning proposed by the text.

resistance the ways in which audiences make meaning from television programmes that is counter to the meanings thought to be intended, or that are discovered by close analysis.

Introduction

In Chapter 4 a way of understanding how audiences understand the **codes** of television programmes, called the 'encoding–decoding' model, was discussed. This work by the media academic Stuart Hall (1980) argued that programmes contain dominant **ideological discourses**. These are encoded in programmes through the production practices of programme-makers that result in conventional forms of narrative structure, invitations to the audience to identify with particular characters and the telling of stories that reflect taken-for-granted social meanings. Hall was interested in the factors that might affect the encoding of these meanings and also how audiences might decode them. Since the images and sounds of television are **polysemic**, it can never be guaranteed that audiences will make sense of the programme in a way that is consistent with the meanings encoded in it. Hall argued that television programmes contain a 'dominant' or '**preferred**' **reading**, and thus limit the range of ways in which audiences can interpret the programme. However, the encoding–decoding model is subject to three important criticisms. First, it is easier to determine preferred meanings in programmes that are primarily intended to convey information, such as news programmes. Drama and other kinds of fiction tend to offer more alternative understandings of the action represented in them, and therefore a greater range of possible interpretations. Secondly, the encoding–decoding model does not make it clear whether preferred meanings are part of the television programme itself or whether they are something that can be identified after analysis by a media theorist, or whether they are actually in the minds of audiences. The third criticism is that the ideological values encoded in television programmes seem to be so powerful according to this model that they cannot be challenged. It is clear that some programme-makers produce radical and alternative programmes, so it remains to be explained how the conventions of communicating meaning in television leave a space for change.

In a study of how different audience groups made sense of *Nationwide*, a current affairs magazine programme shown in the 1970s, David Morley (1980) selected groups according to their social and economic background. He asked the different groups to watch selections from *Nationwide*, and tested Stuart Hall's encoding–decoding model against their responses. He found that many of their comments did not seem to justify the model. These actual viewers did not understand *Nationwide* primarily in the categories of 'dominant', '**negotiated**' and '**resistant**' readings. There were two main reasons for this:

● Characteristics of the groups that were not directly related to their social and economic position were affecting his results. The gender and ethnic background of people seemed to be just as important as their economic status.

● Many of the viewers in Morley's groups found *Nationwide* irrelevant to them, or were not able to make much sense of the programmes they had seen.

The conclusion that Morley drew from this was that audience research should pay much more attention to the knowledge and experience that viewers brought with them to watching television. This knowledge and experience are termed the viewer's 'cultural competence' or 'cultural capital'. On the basis of what viewers already know and understand, they have reactions to television that are as much to do with pleasure and frustration as they are to do with the issues of social and political position that Morley had focused on. Much of the audience research that is discussed in this chapter takes off from the two problems that Morley identified in these earlier studies. It is crucially concerned with gender and ethnicity, and with cultural competence.

Attention and involvement

Aiming to provide a way of distinguishing between the different levels of attention that television viewers give to the programmes they watch, Jeremy Tunstall (1983) distinguished between primary, secondary and tertiary involvement with media. The most concentrated kind of attention he refers to as 'primary involvement'. This is where the viewer concentrates closely on what he or she sees and hears on television, to the exclusion of any other activity. Of course many television viewers are also doing something else while they are watching television. The kind of attention where viewers are sometimes distracted is categorised as 'secondary involvement'. In a situation like this, the viewer is paying attention to the television screen some of the time, and listening to most of the sound, but might also be doing something else like flicking through a magazine, darning socks or keeping an eye on the children. The lowest level of attention is called 'tertiary involvement'. Here the television viewer is paying only momentary attention to television while being engaged in another activity that demands concentration. For instance, the viewer might be cooking a meal while a television set in the kitchen is switched on, so that he or she scarcely sees any of the images on the screen and tunes in only occasionally to the sound. Clearly the level of involvement in television makes a lot of difference to the meanings that viewers can make of what they see and hear. Television in contemporary culture is so deeply embedded in the routines of everyday life that the viewer's involvement with it can vary enormously. When studying television it is important to remember that there will be a whole spectrum of ways in which actual viewers engage with programmes.

ACTIVITY 12.1

Think about your own television viewing in relation to concepts of primary, secondary and tertiary involvement. How is the range of ways that you watch television affected by your daily routines? What kinds of programmes succeed in gaining primary involvement from you, and why?

Some television programmes are constructed in order to attract viewers to engage with them at the level of primary involvement. This is the case, for example, with news programmes. Main evening news bulletins are scheduled at fixed points such as 9.00 p.m. or 10.00 p.m. Their **scheduling** already carries the connotation that news programmes are important, and that viewers could and should make an appointment to view them. News programmes begin with loud and dramatic opening music, calling the viewer's attention to the television set and announcing that something important is about to be broadcast. The implication is that viewers should stop what they are doing and pay attention, granting primary involvement to the programme. Once the programme begins, the opening shot is normally a head-on address to the viewer by the presenter, who welcomes the viewer by saying 'good evening'. A situation of dialogue is constructed by this address to the viewer, and the viewer is invited to take up the position of someone being spoken to directly, someone who is paying attention to what is being said. News programmes are complex television texts, in which a large number of segments are linked together. There are likely to be:

- sequences in which the news presenter is speaking directly to the viewer
- sequences of news reportage
- dialogue between the presenter and experts in the studio or reporters live in a location where a news story is occurring
- displays on the screen of graphics, maps, statistics and diagrams.

News is a very rich **semiotic** text that is constructed to demand attention from the viewer. That attention is rewarded by allowing the viewer to gain information from a variety of viewpoints and by means of a variety of semiotic codes that convey meanings in different ways.

Some of the time, it is likely that the complex television texts of news programmes succeed in attracting and rewarding primary involvement from their viewers. But it is also likely that the density of news programmes often passes the viewer by. A few hours after watching the news, or even a few minutes after watching it, many viewers will find it very difficult to remember each of the news stories presented, let alone the nuances of the different points of view and fragments of information that the programme has offered. Instead viewers will construct for themselves a sense of what is important in the news, often based as much on their pre-existing knowledge of ongoing news stories, and on other information sources such as newspapers and gossip, as on a particular news programme itself. Some of this cultural knowledge of news must be shared among large numbers of people, since it is this shared but specific news knowledge which enables news quizzes, for instance, such as *Have I Got News for You* (a **satirical** television programme based on current news stories), or phone-in radio programmes to be both comprehensible and entertaining. The embedding of programmes in a **flow** of television over a period of time, and the distractions present during viewing, as well as the whole complex of factors that predispose viewers to be interested in some news items and not others, are all factors that tend to dissolve the detail of what is seen on television into the diffuse fabric of everyday life. This could be seen as a failing, in that television has to struggle so hard against the other aspects of people's lives that it has in many ways a relatively weak power to shape and inform. Yet, on the other hand, this criticism is based on the

schedule the arrangement of programmes, advertisements and other material into a sequential order within a certain period of time, such as an evening, day or week.

semiotics the study of signs and their meanings, initially developed for the study of spoken language, and now used also to study the visual and aural 'languages' of other media such as television.

satire a mode of critical commentary about society or an aspect of it, using humour to attack people or ideas.

flow the ways that programmes, advertisements, etc. follow one another in an unbroken sequence across the day or part of the day, and the experience of watching the sequence of programmes, advertisements, trailers, etc.

assumption that television should indeed shape and affect its audiences in this dramatic way. Audience researchers have been more sceptical about the role of television in society. They have argued instead that television should be regarded as only one of the very many ways in which people make sense of their reality. Although television is important, it needs to be understood as part of everyday life.

Broadcasters' audience research

Television programme-makers devise new programmes not simply on the basis of ideas that they are interested in but in order to target and attract particular audiences. The information provided to them about existing programmes by **BARB** gives them some basis for understanding that particular kinds of **format** are attractive to certain audiences (for example that significant numbers of young adult viewers enjoy **observational documentary** programmes with strong continuing characters, leading to a wave of **docusoap** programmes). But this information is not always reliable, so single pilot programmes of new formats are routinely made and shown to **focus groups** comprising carefully selected individuals of a certain age, gender and social background. Moderators are employed to lead the discussions in the focus group, in a similar way to how teachers ask questions and lead the discussion in a class. Drama programmes are an exception to this practice, since making a single programme from an intended series is expensive and may not provide a representative sample for the focus group to discuss. But even drama programmes are shown to focus groups once they have been completed. The results of the focus group discussions give the broadcasters a sense of the elements of a programme that can be emphasised in trailers and in advertising, and suggest how and when a new programme might be scheduled.

The aim of a focus group discussion conducted for a broadcaster is not only to find out whether audiences might enjoy a planned programme. It is important for the broadcaster to fit the programme into the existing habits and routines of audiences' television viewing. For example, participants might be asked whether they would prefer to watch the new programme at 7.00 p.m. or 8.00 p.m., and whether it would be best placed on a weekday or at the weekend. Finding out whether viewers might prefer the new programme to a competitor on another channel can enable schedulers to make decisions about whether the new programme should aim to inherit the same audience as a similar competing programme, and whether to place the new programme directly against its competitor. Since the majority of viewers watch television accompanied by other members of their household, participants in the focus group might also be asked whether they would be embarrassed to watch the new programme with their children, with their parents or with their spouse. Or, by contrast, participants might be asked whether this would be a programme that would attract the whole family to watch at the same time, perhaps around a mealtime. Clearly, focus groups represent very small samples of the total viewing audience, and the results derived from such studies can be unreliable. A further difficulty with using this methodology is that viewers tend to make judgements based on what they already know. It is very difficult for people to give an opinion on something that is really new, without comparing and contrasting it unfavourably with programmes they already like. It is for this reason that television

BARB (Broadcasters Audience Research Bureau) the independent body that gathers and reports viewing statistics on behalf of UK television institutions.

format the blueprint for a programme, including its setting, main characters, genre, form and main themes.

observational documentary a documentary form in which the programme-maker aims to observe neutrally what would have happened even if he or she had not been present.

docusoap a television form combining documentary's depiction of non-actors in ordinary situations with soap opera's continuing narratives about selected characters.

focus groups small groups of selected people, representing larger social groupings such as people of a certain age group, gender or economic status, who take part in discussions about a topic chosen for investigation.

genre a kind or type of programme. Programmes of the same genre have shared characteristics.

broadcasters are criticised for producing a diet of television that seems always the same. Once a particular **genre** or format has been successful (such as docusoap, police or hospital drama) there is a tendency for programme-makers to keep delivering more of the same, since they know it works.

Because of the difficulty of obtaining reliable information from focus groups, consultancy companies have begun to undertake what they call 'reality research'. This involves a researcher living full-time with, and filming, a selected family or household, and employing several researchers doing this simultaneously with different households such as a group of young professionals sharing a house, a family with several children or a retired couple. This is 'participant research', in which the researcher aims to become embedded in the lives of the subjects and thus understand how media use fits into the context of their lives. Research reveals that people use media technology in ways which had not been envisaged by its creators, such as leaving a television set on all day as a deterrent to burglars when all the occupants of the house are out, and that, because most households have only one **digital** television, collective family viewing is more likely in digital households than in **analogue** households. The procedures of focus group discussion and participant observation are commonly used by researchers in academic Television Studies, and the remainder of this chapter discusses the methods, findings and problems in audience research carried out by Television Studies researchers rather than the television industry.

digital television television pictures and sound encoded into the ones and zeros of electronic data. Digital signals can also be sent back down cables by viewers, making possible interaction with television programmes.

analogue broadcasting signals in waves of varying frequency. Analogue signals require greater space or 'bandwidth' than digital signals, and do not allow interactive response from viewers.

> ### ACTIVITY 12.2
>
> Think about the trailers you have seen for new programmes recently, and, if you can, videotape two or three so you can analyse them in detail. What aspects of the trailers (their visual and aural signifiers, signs of genre and their placing between particular current programmes) seem calculated to address a certain audience, and a certain mode of viewing?

Audience power

postmodernism the most recent phase of capitalist culture, the aesthetic forms and styles associated with it, and the theoretical approaches developed to understand it.

The rise of audience research in Television Studies, beginning around the end of the 1970s, has some connections with the theories of **postmodernism** that were discussed earlier in this book (see Chapter 7). Television Studies theorists began to regard the television audience not as a relatively uniform mass but instead as a complex set of overlapping groups with different allegiances, backgrounds and interests. The effect of this was to shift the object of study from the television programme, as a text, to the television audience responding to this text. The key concepts in the discourse of Television Studies of plurality and difference were still in use, but now applied not to the many meanings of programme texts themselves but to the many different ways in which audiences might interpret programmes. It could be argued that earlier critical methodologies focusing on the text privileged the role of the critic himself or herself in determining the correct meaning of television programmes, assuming that the meanings discovered through analysis were those that the audience were taking from programmes. By focusing on the audience, often by setting up situations in which the researcher listens in person to the talk of actual viewers, Television Studies granted more power and authority to ordinary viewers and undercut, to some extent, the mastery of academic discourse over the subject that it aimed to discuss. In undertaking these new methods of research, Television Studies also paid much more attention than it had done previously to groups of people excluded from study. In particular, television viewers belonging to ethnic subcultures, women viewers, children and the elderly began to be the subject of research, and their responses to television were taken seriously. As in theories of postmodernism, marginalised groups and marginalised forms of popular culture became central to the debate. Because the researchers working in Television Studies are generally critical of the power relationships operating in contemporary society, audience studies also provided an opportunity to find new sources of potential **resistance** to the ways that the television business is organised, and to the conventional and ideological meanings that are discovered in the majority of programmes by close **textual analysis**. Rather than looking for instances of television programmes that could be held up as examples of resistant texts, researchers looked for groups among the television audience that could be characterised as resistant viewers.

The case study at the end of this chapter discusses audience research on soap opera. Landmark studies often conducted by **feminist** Television Studies academics showed how programmes often regarded as of low quality (such as soap opera) could be central to the everyday experience of women viewers, who themselves were in a position of relatively low social power in comparison to men. The results of these studies were important for redirecting attention from television texts to television audiences, and making approaches to the decoding of the meaning of television much more sophisticated. It became possible to see how the **polysemic** range of meanings in a television text might be actualised in practice by viewers constructing a wide range of meanings from the television programmes they watch. The political context of this issue is connected to the feminist political agenda which states that 'the personal is political': in other words, that the everyday experiences of ordinary people can both reveal much about how society is organised and also suggest possibilities for change and models of resistance. The primary emphasis of research on soap opera, and of much audience research by Television Studies academics in general, has been on the viewer's pleasure in television. But it is worth considering the alternatives to pleasure as well, such as boredom, frustration and denigration.

The case study at the end of this chapter discusses the results of work by Ien Ang (1989) on viewers who wrote to her about their pleasure in the 1980s American soap opera *Dallas*. But some of the women who wrote to Ang expressed their dislike of *Dallas*, and for various reasons. Some of them criticised the programme because it was American (Ang's research was carried out in the Netherlands), since a number of viewers associated American television with a 'lowest common denominator' of culture. Other viewers criticised the programme because it seemed to reinforce the subordinate position of women because of its representation of female characters. Yet other respondents drew on the academic language of 'quality', 'realism' or other evaluative terms to argue that *Dallas* was poorly made. Indeed, many of the women who wrote to Ang about their pleasure in *Dallas* were aware that these criticisms

textual analysis a critical approach which seeks to understand a television text's meanings by undertaking detailed analysis of its image and sound components, and the relationships between those components.

feminism the political and theoretical thinking which in different ways considers the roles of women and femininity in society and culture, often with the aim of critiquing current roles and changing them for the better.

might be made of the programme. Their response was to negotiate with these criticisms by adopting an ironic attitude to themselves. They claimed that although they were aware that *Dallas* was a trashy and trivial programme, nevertheless they took a self-conscious pleasure in watching it despite its faults. A later study by Ann Gray (1992) analysed what women said about their viewing of rented video films. She found that some of her respondents, notably those with higher educational attainment, wanted to distance themselves from the films that they enjoyed by drawing attention to the fact that they were aware of the flaws in the films according to the evaluative procedures of academic criticism. It is so much a routine part of people's response to culture, including television programmes, to make judgements of what is good and bad, worthy and worthless, that audience researchers have to find ways of understanding not only pleasure but also the ways that pleasure can conform to or conflict with dominant standards of judgement. Furthermore, audience researchers are particularly keen to find out why television viewers feel the need to negotiate with standards of value, because this illuminates the ways in which values are themselves socially constructed and derive from ideological assumptions about culture.

ACTIVITY 12.3

Make a list of five programmes that you think are low in quality: programmes that you might not admit to liking, or even watching at all. Are there any common threads linking the programmes on your list (are they daytime television, programmes of a certain format or genre or programmes aimed at a certain audience)? Are the programmes on your list addressed by academic writing about television you have read, and if so how?

Cultures are of course located specifically in time and space, and although much of the research discussed in this chapter has taken place in relation to programmes made in Britain and the United States, based on research on audiences living in these countries, it is important to note how the findings of audience research can change remarkably even when the same programme is studied. In a programme of work which lasted several years, Elihu Katz and Tamar Liebes (1985) talked to viewers of *Dallas* from different ethnic and cultural groups in several countries. They found that not only were there differences in the ways that people belonging to the same ethnic and cultural group interpreted the soap opera but there were also differences between the range of interpretations made by different ethnic and cultural groups in different countries. They found that television viewers perceived programmes selectively, finding different narrative emphases, significant moments and cultural significance in the same programme. Viewers interpreted and evaluated *Dallas* by placing it in relation to their cultural competence: the ideological assumptions, base of knowledge and individual personal history and experience that each of them had gained. Of course this cultural competence is highly local in character, and Katz and Leibes found that viewers used television programmes as part of the repertoire of ways in which they made sense of their lives and assimilated new experiences by connecting them with what they already knew.

For example, in one episode of *Dallas* the character Sue Ellen ran away from her husband J. R. Ewing's house with her baby after a particularly dramatic dispute between them. When Katz and Leibes interviewed one member of a group of Arab viewers, this particular viewer had added an element to that part of the story: that Sue Ellen returned to her father's house after the argument. This decoding of the episode of *Dallas* is 'aberrant' or incorrect, meaning that it is contrary to the events as represented in the programme. There was no indication in the episode that Sue Ellen had returned to her father's house. But in the context of Arab culture, and the significance of daughters' relationships with their parents, together with the importance of marriage and family in that culture, it made sense to the viewer to explain Sue Ellen's behaviour in this way. Local ethnic understandings of the behaviour that could be expected from people were being introduced into this viewer's decoding of the episode in order to make sense of it in the terms of the culture in which the episode was screened. Another of the respondents in Katz and Liebes' study was a Jew living in Morocco. On the basis of the trials and tribulations of the Ewing family represented in *Dallas*, this viewer argued that the programme proved that Jewish cultural values were superior to those of the United States. Once again, television viewers' interpretation of programmes is carried out within the framework of their own cultural competence, and the meanings of programmes are given significance in relation to those norms and may help to justify them. In cultures where family relationships were significant, for Israeli Arabs and Moroccan Jews for example, kinship ties between the characters in *Dallas* were the most significant features of the programme. For viewers in the Soviet Union, living in a culture subject to a high degree of control by a distant bureaucratic government, respondents who talked to Katz and Leibes frequently discussed the ways in which the characters in *Dallas* were manipulated by the writers and producers who created them. Indeed, the researchers argued that viewers use television in order to work through problems that they are consciously or unconsciously concerned with. The cross-cultural study of *Dallas* showed that people were discussing and evaluating not only the issues in the Ewing family but those in their own lives.

ACTIVITY 12.4

How does the cross-cultural research discussed above affect the concept of 'preferred meaning': if the meanings of television are so different in different cultures, what are the reasons for continuing to do studies of television programmes as texts?

Limitations of ethnography

Ethnographic studies of television audiences take their methodology from the academic discipline of **anthropology**. Anthropology began in the nineteenth century, and means the study of humankind. It was part of the expansion of the methods of the experimental physical sciences (such as biology or chemistry) into the arena of human activity, and initially focused on the study of 'primitive' peoples

ethnography the detailed study of how people live, conducted by observing behaviour and talking to selected individuals about their attitudes and activities.

anthropology the study of humankind, including the evolution of humans and the different kinds of human society existing in different times and places.

living in the underdeveloped territories controlled by the empires of Western European nations. The ideology underlying these early anthropological studies was a belief in the possibility of human progress, from tribal cultures to the industrial and technologically developed societies from which the anthropological researchers themselves came. It was assumed by anthropologists that over time all human societies would evolve in more or less the same way, into industrial, democratic and bureaucratic cultures. However, anthropology has questioned some of these assumptions, and argued that there is no necessary forward movement of human societies towards a particular form. The underdeveloped non-technological societies that still exist in some parts of the world are no longer regarded as in some way 'behind the times' or as throwbacks to an earlier phase in the development of the human race. But anthropologists still seek to understand how different cultures function, and whether there are consistent structures that underlie human culture, family relationships and ways of organising work, leisure and identity. Research on television audiences asks some of the same questions, by seeking to understand how television functions in relationships between people, and affects the ways in which people's daily lives and understandings of themselves are formed. Yet one of the legacies that remains from the history of the discipline of anthropology is that the researcher has normally been in a much more socially powerful position than the respondents that he or she interviews and studies. Ordinary television viewers are interesting to researchers because they are different, even exotic, rather

Figure 12.1 Engraving showing the 'Principal Varieties of Mankind' by John Emslie, 1850. Courtesy of the Science Museum, Science & Society Picture Library.

like the 'primitive' tribal people who were the subjects for early anthropological projects.

Television audience researchers aim for what the anthropologist Clifford Geertz (1967) called a 'thick description' of audience behaviour. This involves discovering 'a stratified hierarchy of meaningful structures in terms of which [social behaviours] are produced, perceived and interpreted, and without which they would not . . . in fact exist' (Geertz 1967: 7). The observation must be interpreted in relation to the cultural frameworks which make it meaningful, so that the ethnographer can interpret what he or she observes. The television ethnographer's results are therefore interpretations of the subjects' interpretations of his or her own actions and thoughts, and often those of other people too. Ethnography is a form of textual analysis, and Geertz (1967: 10) stated that 'Doing ethnography is like trying to read (in the sense of "construct a reading of") a manuscript – foreign, faded, full of ellipses, incoherencies, suspicious emendations, and tendentious commentaries, but written . . . in transient examples of shaped behaviour'.

Interpreting audiences reveals the intricate, singular and different ways in which people make interpretations of their world and think about their own cultural behaviours. Layer on layer of interpretation is produced, and the best kinds of audience research explore not only the results obtained from the research but also the constructed quality of the ethnographer's text. Ethnographic researchers are writers, and the observing, transcribing and interpreting functions involved in their work are not as separate as the 'scientific' history of the discipline might imply, and in fact the different functions that researchers perform contaminate each other. Doing audience research requires the ethnographer to adopt several identities at different times, or at once, being:

- participant
- observer
- recorder
- author
- interpreter
- theorist.

Commonly, researchers reflect on their agendas but try to present viewers as sharing either the same enthusiasms or the same political views as themselves. But television audience researchers, who often say that they themselves belong to the subcultures they study, have to remember that what they do is a cultural practice itself which will inevitably alter and affect the behaviour which they observe.

Academic studies of television audiences using ethnographic methods are difficult to evaluate. They are most often carried out by talking to respondents who have voluntarily put themselves forward as research subjects, and who are therefore likely to have something they want to say about television. The methods used to find respondents can give rise to a number of problems in the design of audience research studies. Some researchers have used the method called 'snowballing', in which one person takes on the responsibility to find another who will participate in the study, then that person finds another volunteer, and so on. While this methodology is less artificial than trying to select a panel of respondents who are representative in some way, it inevitably produces a self-selected group. Other researchers have placed advertisements in magazines, for example, and reviewed the responses they receive. Here, of course, those people who respond have something that they wish to communicate, and they also communicate in writing. The formalities of writing letters, such as the need to organise material, to be polite and to choose a language that may distort information by formalising it, are all problems that this methodology has to address. When writing down their reactions, viewers may consciously or unconsciously modify their responses by putting them into the disciplined forms that are conventional in letters to people whom we do not know personally. Talking can present some of the same problems, when respondents can tailor what they say in order to give the answers that they think may be most interesting to the researcher, or that present them in the most interesting light, for example. Ethnographic research on television viewers is still relatively recent in the discipline of Television Studies, and few of the academics who have carried it out have been trained in the methodologies of anthropology or sociology from which ethnography derives. But researchers have become increasingly conscious of these problems, and books and articles presenting their findings now almost always contain explanations of their methodology and draw attention to the limitations of their results.

ACTIVITY 12.5

If you wanted to design an ethnographic study of how elderly viewers respond to daytime drama programmes, how would you go about selecting a sample of viewers, deciding on the questions you wanted to ask, and analysing your results? What problems might you encounter in conducting your study, and how could you minimise or solve these problems?

Specific cultural groups, such as the resistant television audience groups studied in media audience research, are imaginary communities. While some media audience cultures can claim a degree of cultural unity, this unity is sustained in distinction to national and global media cultures that they cannot change. The theorist of fan cultures Henry Jenkins (Tulloch and Jenkins 1995) conducted studies of the attitudes to *Star Trek* of a range of different groups, including science students at the Massachusetts Institute of Technology (MIT) and members of the gay *Star Trek* fan group the Gaylaxians. Jenkins points out that MIT students largely share the ideological values of the programme, such as faith in human progress, the ability of science to solve social problems, and value attributed to the technology represented in *Star Trek* and the technology used to represent it in special effects. Members of this group are hardly a resistant audience because they are highly educated middle-class males who are destined to be among the professionals who wield social power. In his study of the Gaylaxians, Jenkins (Tulloch and Jenkins 1995: 264) notes that

> Resistant reading can sustain the Gaylaxians' own activism, can become a source of collective identity and mutual support, but precisely because it is a subcultural activity which is denied public visibility, resistant reading cannot change the political agenda, cannot challenge other constructions of gay identity, and

cannot have an impact on the ways people outside the group think about the issues which matter to the Gaylaxians.

The more that an audience is identified by researchers as an emblem of resistance to the dominant norms of television and contemporary society, the less likely it is that this audience group will be able to exert any actual power to create change in either television or society.

But some of the television audiences studied by ethnographic researchers do not have a constituted identity at all except when an identity is attributed to them by the researcher doing the ethnographic work. In a discussion of some of the many studies of women viewers of soap opera, for example, Ien Ang and Joke Hermes (1996) have pointed out that researchers have a tendency to assume that the responses of particular research respondents are representative of the larger group made up of women viewers in general. The results of talking to one small sample of women can be made to stand for all women (often restricted to those of a certain social class or race) in order to make an argument about how this entire group is likely to understand and enjoy television. The impetus behind much audience research is to value the voices of viewers in a dominant television broadcasting culture which largely excludes them, and thus to claim the agency of the audience, and also to claim that audience research itself can have political agency as a way of intervening in the discussion of the politics of contemporary culture. The British television academics Julia Hallam and Margaret Marshment (1995) made a study of women viewers of the British three-part BBC television serial *Oranges Are Not the Only Fruit* (1989, based on a novel of the same name by Jeanette Winterson). After completing interviews with their sample of viewers, Hallam and Marshment (1995: 14) concluded that the diversity of viewers' responses 'remained within a recognizable "we" of common experiences and pleasures which seemed to owe much to our common positions as women'. The researchers claimed (1995: 3) that

> we were not "looking for" negotiated or resistant readings among the respondents . . . but our feminist standpoint does need to be taken into account. We hoped to find that they did like [the serial] and did interpret it in line with the preferred reading because . . . it would . . . thus constitute a significant feminist anti-homophobic intervention in popular culture.

Since research is always carried out with an explicit or implicit research agenda, or set of research questions, there is a tendency for academic publication of audience research to find the answers that it has already aimed to find. After all, it is much more interesting to read about research findings where positive results have been obtained, rather than studies where the research subjects had little coherent to say, or where the design and methodology of the research were found to be flawed.

Fan audiences

Viewers who regard themselves as fans of particular programmes are a special sub-group of television audiences who reveal some of the strengths and weaknesses of ethnographic audience research. As with the other research discussed in this chapter, the main emphasis has been on how fans gain pleasure from their close relationship with television programmes, and how their relationships with television provide fans with kinds of social identity that are desirable to them. The way that fans actively appropriate television culture can be regarded as an unusually extreme but revealing instance of how all television viewers take possession of the programmes they watch, and assimilate the meanings of programmes into their own lives. Fan communities are self-selected, groups of people who have decided to identify themselves closely with programmes and with fellow television viewers who also devote special attention to the same programme. Prominent programmes whose fan cultures have been investigated by television researchers include *Star Trek* and its sequels, *The X Files*, *Doctor Who* and *Buffy the Vampire Slayer*. It is notable that these programmes fall into the category of science fiction or fantasy television, since one of the arguments of audience research on their fan communities is that being a fan is itself crucially tied up with constructing fantasies that provide the scenario for fans to re-imagine themselves differently and to experiment with the possibilities and limits of their interests and desires.

The range of ways in which fans take possession of a television programme for themselves, and redirect its components and meanings for themselves, has been described by the media theorist Henry Jenkins (1992) as a 'textual poaching'. Drawing the analogy with poachers who illegally capture fish or animals to eat from land or rivers that are owned by someone else, Jenkins argues that fans invade the territory of television programmes that are created, controlled and owned by the 'official' television culture of professional programme-makers. Rather than viewing programmes according to the preferred readings encoded by their creators, fans pick out the elements that are of interest to them and make them function in new ways. For some audience researchers there is a heroic aspect to this, whereby fans are considered as a **resistant** audience that refuses to adopt the conventional position laid out for it by a television programme, and instead reappropriates programmes in ways that contradict the aims of their creators and owners.

Indeed, fans operate in similar ways to the creators of television programmes, producing alternative products that supplement or take the place of industrially produced television programmes. For example, fans:

- create websites about their favourite programme
- set up and distribute magazines and newsletters
- organise collective cultural events such as conventions.

These activities can be regarded as resistant, in that they promote ways of viewing, talking about and restaging programmes that take possession of the original and change it in interesting ways. But on the other hand, fan culture reproduces many of the ways in which 'official' television production culture works. Fans discriminate between insiders (who belong to the world of fan culture) and outsiders (who do not belong), just as television professionals seek to preserve their elite position within the industry and normally deny access to members of the audience. Fans produce and circulate texts and products, in parallel with the ways that programme-makers produce and circulate texts and products. The cultural competence that fans seek to possess (such as detailed knowledge about their favourite programme) is a form of capital that gives them status within their community. In a similar way television programme-makers accumulate insider knowledge about their business and also accumulate financial capital and profit for themselves and the broadcasting organisations for which they work.

The growth of the Internet has provided television fans with extensive possibilities for communicating with each other, and, for a minority, the ability to make available short films that fans have made for downloading by fellow devotees. To take the example of *Doctor Who*, the British science fiction adventure series that began in 1963 and whose last television production was broadcast in 1996, there were more than forty newsgroups and chat forums running on the Internet in 2002. These Web resources consist of fictional stories written by fans, websites devoted to actors appearing in the programme, fan magazines and sites offering non-professional films of *Doctor Who* made by fans. John Tulloch (Tulloch and Jenkins 1995: 145) describes the central fan activity as 'the power to gloss', meaning the power of television fans to interpret and reinterpret programmes for themselves and to engage in dialogue and debate with each other around questions of interpretation. Henry Jenkins (1992: 86) argues that 'Organised fandom is, perhaps first and foremost, an institution of theory and criticism, a semistructured space where competing interpretations and evaluations of common texts are proposed, debated and negotiated and where readers speculate about the nature of the mass media and their own relationship to it'. By engaging in such debates, fans are able to display their cultural capital of knowledge about the programme, and the debates and discussions themselves constitute a fan community. The possibility of potentially endless debate about interpretation enables the fan community and its activities to continue indefinitely, even when (as in the case of *Doctor Who*) there are no new programmes to discuss.

In fan culture there are powerful notions of what constitutes good and bad examples of a favourite programme, and debates over the boundaries of what constitutes the object of fans' affections. For example, among *Doctor Who* fans some regard the original BBC television serials as 'genuine' *Doctor Who*, and perhaps also the paperback novels authorised by the BBC, but not **spin-off merchandising** products, reconstructed lost episodes made by fans or the two cinema films that were produced at the height of the series' popularity. Even among fans who regard the BBC *Doctor Who* episodes as the 'genuine' *Doctor Who*, there are fans who regard some of these stories as not 'genuine'. For example, when the actor Sylvester McCoy portrayed Doctor Who in the final three years of the series, the slapstick performance style that he adopted, perhaps to draw younger children into the audience, made some fans repudiate these episodes as not part of the *Doctor Who* canon. Since television programmes are not coherent texts, it is possible to draw boundaries around episodes and groups of episodes that fans wish to include in or reject from the corpus. Series television, such as the long-running programmes that have tended to be the focus of fan interest, is normally written by a wide range of writers, may feature different actors who join and leave the series over the period of its run, and the narrative structure, thematic concerns and settings (the components of the programme format) may change. These discontinuities allow broad scope for fan interpretation, and for making value judgements about the success or failure, genuineness or inauthenticity, of particular episodes or groups of episodes.

The overwhelming majority of comments posted to newsgroups on television programmes consist of comments on the broadcast episodes, rather than

spin-off
a product, television programme, book, etc. that is created to exploit the reputation, meaning or commercial success of a previous one, often in a different medium from the original.

merchandising
the sale of products associated with a television programme, such as toys, books or clothing.

Figure 12.2 Tom Baker as Doctor Who and Lalla Ward as Romana outside the Tardis in *Doctor Who.* Courtesy of BBC Photograph Library.

participation in fan activities such as the making of amateur films. The majority of fans are interested in the official productions associated with television programmes, and the products produced under licence that are connected to them. So although the Internet provides a virtual community for television fans, only a very small proportion of fan activity has to do with media production itself, and instead it is concerned with consumption. As John Fiske (1992a: 44) notes, 'the emphasis is not so much on acquiring a few good (and thus expensive) objects as accumulating as many as possible'. Being a fan means acquiring the cultural capital of knowledge about television programmes, and also amassing the commercial objects such as videos and DVDs that make possible possession of the programmes. Being a fan is a means not only of resisting the dominant interpretations shaped by programme-makers and taking possession of the meanings of television programmes for oneself but also of positioning oneself as a consumer of the commodities that programme producers now increasingly use as valuable streams of income to fund further programme-making. Knowing that fans are likely already to have amassed videotape copies of programmes, it is currently common for the owners of franchises such as *Star Trek* and *Doctor Who* to re-release programmes on DVD with tempting extras such as interviews with cast members or producers, so that fans will buy the original programmes all over again. The desire for a complete collection of programmes in the highest possible quality stimulates the desire to amass commercial objects among the fan community. So although television fans are in a sense the heroes of audience research in Television Studies, since they are the viewers who most actively respond to television programmes and engage most consciously in alternative and resistant practices prompted by television programmes, fans are also complicit with the television industry and the structures and assumptions that underlie it. Indeed, fan culture is a response to a cultural disempowerment that derives from being a member of the audience rather than a producer of programmes. No matter how active, resistant, knowledgeable or interested a television fan may be, his or her activities and those of the fan community have little effect on the ways that the television industry works or on the television programmes that are produced.

Fans with access to film-making equipment are now increasingly common, since the prices of high-quality digital video cameras, editing systems based on home computers and a distribution network over the Internet through which films can be distributed have made it much easier to make low-budget productions. The films that fans make are produced for many different reasons, but primarily for the enjoyment of planning and producing the production itself, sometimes also as a way of obtaining an identity and a high profile among the fan community, and always as a way of activating the cultural capital about the television programme possessed by the fan film-maker himself or herself. The films that fans produce are not only circulated on the Internet but also shown at fan conventions (especially in the United States, where fan video production is taken more seriously than in Britain). By advertising the intention to make a fan video production, fans are able to draw on suggestions and advice from other members of the fan community on the Internet, and to find volunteers wishing to take part in a production as actors or as technical crew. Since the audience for fan video productions is fellow fans, the requirements of exposition, scene-setting and production values that conform to the expectations of broadcast television can be bypassed. But although fan videos are necessarily amateur works, they are produced with the intention of conforming to a sense of the essence of the programme, and thus take on the knowledge and expectations of their intended fan audience. This base of knowledge makes the production of spoof versions of cult programmes common. Jokes included in fan video productions work only in relation to the cultural capital of knowledge that their audience can be assumed to possess, and are an index of the significance of that knowledge for their producers as well as their viewers. It is also the case that spoof versions of television programmes are much easier to produce, since flaws in performance, structure and the lack of funds for equipment and special effects can in themselves be part of the appeal of the production.

Children and television

Television Studies academics have worked on how television viewing relates to wider social behaviour. As this chapter has shown, this includes how different kinds of audience watch different kinds of programmes, and how social groups of different age and status watch different programmes. Children watching television have been a focus of study for several decades. In the 1950s and 1960s, for example, researchers in the United States attempted to devise experiments in which the **effects** of television on children could be discovered (Bandura 1977 and Himmelwhite et al. 1958, for example). Working in specially designed university laboratories, they showed sequences either of broadcast programmes or of specially made videotapes showing aggressive behaviour, for instance, and then devised interview techniques or opportunities for play in which children could be monitored to see whether the television they had viewed made them behave differently. This kind of research has been heavily criticised, since the settings in which it took place, the kinds of television shown to children and the kinds of play laboratory set up by the researchers were very artificial and distant from the ways in which children normally watch television. Despite the flaws in the research, there were in any case very few increases in aggressive or anti-social behaviour that could be observed in the children the researchers studied. Nevertheless, work such as this provided sufficient material to support campaigns for the regulation of children's television in order to protect what were seen as vulnerable audiences from programmes that might turn children into anti-social adults (see Chapter 10). Another result of this research was to campaign for the teaching of '**media literacy**' in schools, with the aim that if children understood how television representations were constructed, and were equipped with study skills to analyse narrative and character, for example, children would be better able to negotiate the meanings of television for themselves. More recently, the developing strands of work described in this chapter, in which more sophisticated methods of studying audiences were devised using interviews conducted at home or in more real-world settings, have been used to attempt to find out how children make meanings from their television viewing, and how their television experience fits into their broader social lives.

Several books have been published by the media academic David Buckingham (1993a, 1993b, 1996), who draws on the range of audience research techniques discussed in this chapter to explore both parents' and children's reactions to television. Some of this work focuses on cognitive issues, in other words what adults and children understand from television consciously, while other strands of the research

effects measurable outcomes produced by watching television, such as becoming more violent or adopting a certain opinion.

media literacy the skills and competence that viewers learn in order to understand easily the audio-visual 'languages' of media texts.

focus on children's emotional and unconscious responses to television. The results show that both watching television and talking about television programmes play a significant role in the process by which children learn to understand themselves, other people and society. Some of children's interaction with television involves learning and using knowledge of television codes and conventions (media literacy), such as the differences between television genres, narrative forms and placing programmes in context by deploying knowledge about the production processes involved in the making of programmes. It appears that the more children know about television codes and conventions and production processes, the more they are able to control the emotional reactions that are provoked by programmes. This seems to support the arguments made by academics and educators that the teaching of television and media in schools performs a useful social function. But, interestingly, some of the more controversial aspects of children's viewing of television seemed also to be both useful and important to them.

It is known that children sometimes consciously seek out disturbing programmes containing violence or sex, and programmes in the genres of horror or action adventure that broadcasting regulations seek to protect them from. Buckingham (1996) found that the function of watching these programmes for children was to test their own maturity in coping with troubling emotions. In other words, watching programmes that could be disturbing was part of children's effort to grow up, to understand the adult world and to anticipate being part of it. A key concept in understanding this process is **modality**. Adults use the recognition of modality in order to judge whether representations are realistic, or whether they are fantastic or comic, for example. Children watch violent, sexual or otherwise potentially disturbing programmes in order to learn how to deploy an understanding of modality, and thus to share the viewing practices of adults. Indeed, children's television programmes commonly feature central characters who are childlike even though they may be adults, thus representing the negotiations that real children in the audience make about their difference or similarity to adults and their place in the adult world. Characters in children's television programmes who are actually children are also commonly active in the narrative because adults fail to deal with a problem, or are incompetent. Academic research on child viewers seems to confirm that for children the most important aspect of watching television is that it provides a resource for working through conscious and unconscious understandings of their identity, and their social position in relation to adults. Watching television is pleasurable for children, but it is also an essential part of their gradual integration into society as a whole.

> modality the fit between a fictional representation and the conventional understanding of reality. High modality describes a close fit, and weak modality a distant one.

ACTIVITY 12.6

To what extent do adults (like children) watch television not only in order to enjoy it but also to test their reactions to disturbing issues such as violence or sex? How might modality be useful in explaining adults' use of the concept of realism as a standard against which to judge and evaluate programmes?

Case study: soap opera audiences

In 1982 Dorothy Hobson produced an important study of women's relationship to television soap opera. Hobson's work focused on the original incarnation (1964–88) of ITV's soap opera *Crossroads*, in which the main characters worked in a motel in the Midlands, and which was screened in the early evenings in competition with the current affairs magazine *Nationwide* that Morley had studied (see above). Her concern was that the family environment could be regarded from a feminist point of view as a place in which women were subordinate. She wanted to know about how watching television fitted into the patterns of behaviour in the household, in particular how watching television might provide a space of pleasure and resistance for women at home. For women at home, television provides a contact with the outside world, and watching television, Hobson found, was not a spare-time activity but instead an important part of women's daily routines. She found that women did not watch programmes that had connotations of masculinity, such as:

- news
- current affairs
- documentary
- sport.

Instead, they watched:

- comedy series
- soap opera
- light entertainment
- quiz programmes.

feminine having characteristics associated with the cultural role of women and not men.

masculine having characteristics associated with the cultural role of men and not women.

Television was perceived in gendered terms, with some formats and genres regarded as **feminine**, and others as **masculine**. The programmes perceived as feminine were those that had connections with the personal and emotional concerns of everyday family life, or offered an escape in fantasy from the dreary routine of everyday life. Of course, these are precisely the programmes that are conventionally criticised as being trivial, trashy and lightweight. Hobson's research aimed to give value to these programmes and to the experiences of the women who watched them. In this respect her research is part of a larger tradition of **feminist** work on television which seeks to redress the balance of power in society that tends to render women's experience less significant than that of men.

   Much of the work carried out in the 1980s on the domestic context of ordinary viewing focused on women viewers, and on programmes attractive to female audiences. Indeed, the genre of soap opera in particular became a focus of attention because the textual characteristics of the genre were argued to map closely on to traits recognised in society as feminine. The narrative structure of the soap opera is multi-layered and open-ended. It is constructed in short segments, following a range of storylines, and does not come to an end. Whereas it might seem that nothing happens in soap opera, this is the result of attention being directed to the wrong things. Soap opera works primarily through dialogue, both between the characters in the programme and between members of the audience, who are invited to speculate about what will happen and to make judgements about the moral and emotional problems experienced by the characters. Talk and gossip are recognised by sociologists as an important component of women's lives, as ways of constructing community and shared experience. Soap operas provide both a representation of this community and material that actual women can discuss with each other. Furthermore, since narrative information is conveyed largely through dialogue in soap opera, it is possible to watch soaps with what Tunstall (1983) called secondary involvement, getting on with other tasks and looking occasionally at the screen, while following the action by listening to the television sound. Hobson reported (1982: 112), 'the woman with whom I had gone to watch the programme [*Crossroads*] was serving the evening meal, feeding her five and three year old daughters and attempting to watch . . . on a black-and-white television situated on top of the freezer opposite the kitchen table'. *Crossroads* was constructed in the segmented form and with information conveyed primarily by dialogue that are characteristic of soap opera. Despite being scheduled at a time when women were often very busy, it could be watched by the distracted viewer. Commenting on Hobson's research, Storey (1999: 109) noted:

> Television is usually watched in the midst of other everyday activities. As Hobson discovered, domestic routines and responsibilities and the expectations of other family members ensured that most of the women with whom she watched *Crossroads* were not allowed the luxury of the detailed concentration expected and enjoyed by staff and students watching in darkened rooms on media-studies courses.

The American prime-time soap opera *Dallas* became the subject of important studies by television theorists in the 1980s. This hour-long drama was set among the families of the oil barons of Texas, and focused on the struggles for power among the executives of the oil companies, and the family disputes, romantic affairs and personal problems that preoccupied them. The central characters of *Dallas* are the members of the Ewing family, and the storyline focuses on the sudden reversals of fortune, emotional crises and the relationships between business deals and personal allegiances that make up the daily life of its characters. While male characters, including J. R. Ewing and his brother Bobby, are significant to the narratives, J. R.'s wife Sue Ellen and other women are also central. The programme gained extraordinary popularity in the United States, Britain and worldwide, and was shown in over ninety countries, including Turkey, Hong Kong, Australia and Morocco. It is still being repeated on cable and satellite channels today. The most significant study of *Dallas* was by the Dutch media theorist Ien Ang, who published a book on the programme in 1985 (revised in 1989). Ang's aim was to understand how the predominantly female audience of *Dallas* fitted the programme into the texture of their daily lives, and to research the kind of pleasure and displeasure that they gained from it. In her native Netherlands *Dallas* was watched in the early 1980s by half of the population. At the time of her research three-quarters of the audience for *Dallas* in Holland were women.

Ang placed an advertisement in the Dutch women's magazine *Viva*, asking people to write to her giving their reactions to the programme. She received forty-two replies, and her study analysed episodes of the programme but, more significantly, it analysed the discourses in the letters of the women who wrote to her. Since *Dallas* focuses largely on the emotional relationships between characters, Ang argued that the programme has a 'tragic' **structure of feeling**. She meant that *Dallas* is structured so that any temporary resolution to the characters' problems gives rise to further narrative complication and emotional suffering. Ang argued that in order to gain this understanding of *Dallas*, its viewers must possess a cultural competence that she called a 'melodramatic imagination' (1989: 78). This melodramatic imagination was

structure of feeling
the assumptions, attitudes and ideas prevalent in a society, arising from the ideologies underpinning that society.

continued

melodrama
a form of drama
characterised
by exaggerated
performance, a focus
on reversals of
fortune and extreme
emotional reactions
to events.

an orientation to everyday life in which ordinary problems could be granted the emotional significance and moral weight that are found in theatre **melodrama** or tragedy, thus giving enhanced value to events and experiences that could otherwise seem trivial. The characteristics of melodrama include the heightening of emotion and the measurement of events against moral principles, conveyed through larger-than-life characters and exaggerated modes of performance. Ang found these characteristics in the performance style of the actors in *Dallas*, and showed that the behaviour of characters formed a system of signs that communicated powerful inner feelings through external behaviour. For example, J. R. Ewing's wife Sue Ellen became an alcoholic, and her extreme behaviour functioned as a sign of her emotional disturbance provoked by the aggressive actions of her husband and his unfaithfulness to her.

The main conclusion of Ang's analysis was that its predominantly women viewers decoded and found pleasure in *Dallas* through a melodramatic imagination because of their ideological position in culture. Different decodings are produced by viewers who occupy different social positions in a particular society, as well as by viewers who live in different nations and cultures. Women in Western societies such as the Netherlands are expected to be emotional, caring and community-forming (as opposed to the masculine characteristics of adventurousness, aggression and individualism). The negotiation of the meanings of television programmes is affected not only by membership of a national culture but also by the social status of the viewer in that culture. Ang found that there was a fit between the conventional meanings of femininity among the audience and the fictional moral and emotional world of *Dallas*. As well as finding the emotional and communal values of femininity in the programme itself, Ang noted that viewers' pleasure in the programme also depended on the sharing of its meanings with fellow women viewers. Audience responses to *Dallas* were determined not only by the text but also by the social environment in which talk about the programme among women friends, workmates and family members took place. As in Hobson's analysis of *Crossroads*, Ang's semiotic analysis of *Dallas* showed that it conforms in its structure to the cultural competences that its female audience held. *Dallas* has few action sequences, and is primarily occupied with dialogue. The characters interacted extensively with each other, and the giving and withholding of information through gossip was significant to the story. Viewers wrote about the realism of *Dallas*, but Ang (1989: 45) interpreted this as meaning emotional realism: 'the realism experience of the *Dallas* fans quoted . . . is situated at the emotional level: what is recognized as real is not knowledge of the world, but a subjective experience of the world'. This emotional realism was conveyed by the performance style in which characters say what they do not mean, and mean what they do not say, so that it is not only dialogue that conveys meaning but also the relationship between, for example, close-up shots of characters' reactions to events, which show how to read the meanings of the action.

Ien Ang's study of *Dallas* is important in Television Studies for several reasons. It took seriously a very popular programme that had little credibility as 'quality television', suggesting that television theorists should direct their attention not only to prestigious programmes but also to popular drama. Her work was written from a feminist point of view, putting on the critical agenda questions of gender and the politics of everyday life that contrasted with the emphasis of earlier critics on economics, social class and occupation. By making extensive use of the words of actual viewers, Ang sought to combine the analysis of a television programme from a textual point of view with evidence about how the decoding of meaning was carried out in ordinary everyday circumstances.

ACTIVITY 12.7

How might the watching of certain television programmes cement relationships between, for example, parents and young children, a group of *X Files* fans or a group of teenage girls? Which programmes might be the most productive in cementing relationships, and what role would be played by talk among the viewers in these kinds of collective viewing situations?

Viewing context, such as watching television with other members of a family, or with your best friends, for instance, affects viewing experience. People watching with their families will often be persuaded to watch something they do not enjoy, whereas watching a favourite programme with a group of friends might help to confirm a person's shared relationships with members of that group. John Storey (1999: 114) summarises this social role of television viewing by arguing that:

> Watching television is always so much more than a series of acts of interpretation; it is above all else a social practice. That is, it can be a means to isolate oneself . . . or to make contact with other family members . . . In these ways, the cultural consumption of television is as much about social relationships as it is about interpretations of individual programmes.

While women watching television might use television as a reward for work done in the home, their reasons for watching and the pleasures they gain might be quite different from, for instance, those of teenage girls watching MTV with their friends. Audience researchers have also studied people's talk about television. Information about who talks about television, to whom, where and how (for example in the school playground, at work, in pubs, or when meeting other people for the first time) reveals the different roles television can play in making, breaking and maintaining social relationships. Researchers have looked at how 'television viewing is generally a somewhat busy activity, interrupted by many other activities and routinely accompanied by talk, much of it having nothing to do with the programme being watched' (Storey 1999: 16). For the discipline of Television Studies in general, the shift of interest on to viewers and audiences rather than on television programmes as texts has focused on 'active' rather than 'passive' viewing, and provided good reasons to value kinds of viewing and kinds of television programme which have been considered of low quality. Rather than being passively positioned by the semiotic **codes** of a television programme, viewers can now be understood as makers of meaning. Watching television requires viewers to draw on their personal histories and their cultural, class, racial, economic or sexual identities, and to use their cultural competence, gained from media knowledge of comparable programmes and the various information sources available to them, to construct a relationship with the television programme in the context of their cultural lives.

SUMMARY OF KEY POINTS

● Television Studies has developed ways of understanding how audiences make meanings from television, and debated the significance of television in everyday life.

● The television audience is considered not as a uniform mass but instead as a collection of diverse groups whose personal and social experiences shape their responses to television.

● Television Studies has taken a particular interest in audiences from groups with relatively little social power (such as children, fans of cult programmes and women at home), and their use of television to express their identities and form social networks.

● Studies of television audiences in different regions and countries have shown that television is understood differently in different social contexts.

● The methods used to study audiences range from the statistical methods used by television institutions to detailed and lengthy personal interviews with small groups of viewers in ordinary settings.

● Television Studies researchers have sought to reduce the distance between them and the ordinary viewers they study, in order to understand and value everyday television viewing.

Further reading

Allen, R., 'Audience-oriented criticism and television', in R. Allen (ed.), *Channels of Discourse, Reassembled: Television and Contemporary Criticism* (London: Routledge, 1992), pp. 101–37.

Ang, I., *Living Room Wars: Rethinking Audiences for a Postmodern World* (London: Routledge, 1996.

—— *Watching Dallas: Soap Operas and the Melodramatic Imagination*, trans. D. Couling, revised edition (London: Routledge, 1989).

Ang, I. and J. Hermes, 'Gender and/in media consumption', in I. Ang, *Living Room Wars: Rethinking Audiences for a Postmodern World* (London: Routledge, 1996), pp. 108–29.

Bruhn Jensen, K. (ed.), *News of the World: World Cultures Look at Television News* (London: Routledge, 1998).

Buckingham, D., *Moving Images: Understanding Children's Emotional Responses to Television* (Manchester: Manchester University Press, 1996).

—— *Reading Audiences: Young People and the Media* (Manchester: Manchester University Press, 1993b).

—— *Children Talking Television: The Making of Television Literacy* (London: Falmer, 1993a).

—— *Public Secrets: EastEnders and its Audience* (London: BFI, 1987).

Dickinson, R., R. Harindranath and O. Linné (eds), *Approaches to Audiences: A Reader* (London: Arnold, 1998).

Dovey, J., *Freakshow* (Cambridge: Polity, 2000).

Dowmunt, T. (ed.), *Channels of Resistance: Global Television and Local Empowerment* (London: BFI, 1993).

Drummond, P. and R. Patterson (eds), *Television and its Audience: International Research Perspectives* (London: BFI, 1988).

Geraghty, C., 'Audiences and "ethnography": questions of practice', in C. Geraghty and D. Lusted (eds), *The Television Studies Book* (London: Arnold, 1998), pp. 141–57.

—— *Women and Soap Opera: A Study of Prime Time Soaps* (Cambridge: Polity Press, 1991).

Gray, A., *Video Playtime: The Gendering of a Leisure Technology* (London: Routledge, 1992).

Hall, S., 'Encoding/decoding', in S. Hall, D. Hobson, A. Lowe and P. Willis (eds), *Culture, Media, Language* (London: Hutchinson, 1980), pp. 128–38.

Hallam, J. and M. Marshment, 'Framing experience: case studies in the reception of *Oranges Are Not the Only Fruit*', *Screen*, 36:1 (1995), pp. 1–15.

Hobson, D., *Crossroads: The Drama of a Soap Opera* (London: Methuen, 1982).

Jenkins, H., *Textual Poachers: Television Fans and Participatory Culture* (London: Routledge, 1992).

Lewis, L. (ed.), *The Adoring Audience: Fan Culture and Popular Media* (London: Routledge, 1991).

Liebes, T. and Katz, E., *The Export of Meaning: Cross-cultural Readings of 'Dallas'* (New York: Oxford University Press, 1990).

Lull, J. (ed.), *World Families Watch Television* (London: Sage, 1988).

Morley, D., *Television, Audiences and Cultural Studies* (London: Routledge, 1992).

Petrie, D. and J. Willis (eds), *Television and the Household: Reports from the BFI's Audience Tracking Study* (London: BFI, 1995).

Ruddock, A., *Understanding Audiences: Theory and Method* (London: Sage, 2001).

Storey, J. *Cultural Consumption and Everyday Life* (London: Arnold, 1999).

Tulloch, J., *Watching Television Audiences: Cultural Theories and Methods* (London: Arnold, 2000).

Tulloch, J. and H. Jenkins, *Science Fiction Audiences: Watching Doctor Who and Star Trek* (London: Routledge, 1995).

Glossary of key terms

180 degree rule the convention that cameras are positioned only on one side of an imaginary line drawn to connect two performers in a scene. This produces a coherent sense of space for the viewer.

active audience television audiences regarded not as passive consumers of meanings but as negotiating meanings for themselves that are often resistant to those meanings that are intended or that are discovered by close analysis.

actuality footage television pictures representing an event that was filmed live. The term usually refers to pictures of news events.

adaptation transferring a novel, theatre play, poem, etc. from its original medium into another medium such as television.

aesthetic a specific artistic form. Aesthetics means the study of art and beauty.

affiliates local television stations (normally in the USA) that have made agreements (affiliations) with a network to broadcast programmes offered by that network rather than another.

analogue broadcasting signals in waves of varying frequency. Analogue signals require greater space or 'bandwidth' than digital signals, and do not allow interactive response from viewers.

Annan Committee a committee reporting in 1977 to government on the future of broadcasting. It supported public service broadcasting, the funding of the BBC by licence fee, and the planned introduction of a fourth television channel.

anthology a series of separate unconnected programmes broadcast under a shared title.

anthropology the study of humankind, including the evolution of humans and the different kinds of human society existing in different times and places.

art video the use of video technology in artistic work intended for gallery exhibition.

audience share the percentage of viewers estimated to have watched one channel as opposed to another channel broadcasting at the same time.

authorship the question of who an author is, the role of the author as creator and the significance of the author's input into the material being studied.

avant-garde work aiming to challenge the norms and conventions of its medium, and the group of people making such work.

back lighting lighting the subject of a shot from behind to provide depth by separating the subject from the background.

balance the requirement in television news and current affairs to present both sides of an argument or issue.

BARB (Broadcasters Audience Research Bureau) the independent body that gathers and reports viewing statistics on behalf of UK television institutions.

binary opposition two contrasting terms, ideas or concepts, such as inside/outside, masculine/feminine or culture/nature.

blooper a mistake by a performer in a programme, or a technical error. The term often refers to humorous mistakes.

bourgeoisie the middle class, who are owners of property and businesses.

brand recognition the ability of audiences to recognise the distinctive identity of a product, service or institution and the values and meanings associated with it.

broadcasting the transmission of signals from a central source which can be received by dispersed receivers over a large geographical area.

Broadcasting Standards Commission (BSC) the regulatory body set up by government to monitor the standards of BBC broadcasting services, superseded by Ofcom.

budget the money allocated to the making of a particular programme or series of programmes, which is controlled by the producer.

cable television originally called Community Antenna Television (CATV). Transmission of television signals along cables in the ground.

capitalism the organisation of an economy around the private ownership of accumulated wealth, involving the exploitation of labour to produce profit that creates such wealth.

CEEFAX the text-based information service provided by BBC and carried by analogue television signals.

censorship the omission of sensitive, prohibited or disturbing material at any stage in the production process from the initial idea to its transmission.

churn rate a ratio setting the numbers of new subscribers to a paid-for television service against the number of subscribers cancelling their subscription.

class a section of society defined by their relationship to economic activity, whether as workers (the working class) or possessors of economic power (the bourgoisie), for example.

classic serial the dramatisation in serial form of literature written in the past, most often in the nineteenth and early twentieth centuries, where the literary source already has high cultural status.

close-up a camera shot where the frame is filled by the face of a person or a detail of a face. Close-ups may also show details of an object or place.

closed-circuit television a small-scale television system where the images and sound are not intended for broadcast, for example a network of security cameras.

CNN Cable News Network, the first international satellite news channel, operating from the United States.

code in semiotics, a system or set of rules that shapes how signs can be used, and therefore how meanings can be made and understood.

commercial television television funded by the sale of advertising time or sponsorship of programmes.

commissioning the process by which an idea for a programme is selected to go into production.

committed a term used in the study of the politics of culture, implying that a person or a text has a commitment to positive and progressive social change.

commodity a raw material or product whose economic value is established by market price rather than the intrinsic qualities or usefulness of the material or product itself.

computer generated imaging (CGI) the creation of images by programming computers with mathematical equations that can generate realistic two-dimensional pictures.

connotations the term used in semiotic analysis for the meanings that are associated with a particular sign or combination of signs.

consensus a shared and accepted opinion or attitude among a certain group of people.

conventions the frameworks and procedures used to make or interpret texts.

convergence the process whereby previously separate media technologies merge together. For example, computers can now send faxes, show DVD films and play music.

copyright the legal right of ownership over written, visual or aural material, including the prohibition on copying this material without permission from its owner.

couch potatoes a derogatory term for television viewers supposedly sitting motionless at home watching television passively and indiscriminately.

cultural imperialism the critical argument that powerful nations and regions (especially those of the Western world) dominate less developed nations and regions by exporting values and ideologies.

Cultural Studies the academic discipline devoted to studying culture, involving work on texts, institutions, audiences and economic contexts.

culture the shared attitudes, ways of life and assumptions of a group of people.

cut the moment at which one camera shot ceases and another begins, where no transitional visual effect (such as a fade or a dissolve) is used.

cutaway in fictional dialogue or interviews, shots that do not include people speaking. Cutaways often consist of details of the setting or of interviewees (such as hands).

D Notice a instruction to the media not to broadcast material that could undermine national security.

demography the study of population, and the groupings of people (demographic groups) within the whole population.

denotation in semiotics, the function of signs to portray or refer to something in the real world.

deregulation the removal of legal restrictions or guidelines that regulate the economics of the television industry or the standards which programmes must adhere to.

dialectic a term associated especially with Marxist theories, meaning a struggle between two opposing ideas.

diegesis the telling of events as narrative. Diegetic sound is sound emanating from the represented environment, and extra-diegetic sound comes from outside that environment.

digital television television pictures and sound encoded into the ones and zeros of electronic data. Digital signals can also be sent back down cables by viewers, making possible interaction with television programmes.

director the person responsible for the creative process of turning a script or idea into a finished programme, by working with a technical crew, performers and an editor.

discourse a particular use of language for a certain purpose in a certain context (such as academic discourse, or poetic discourse), and similarly in television, a particular usage of television's audio-visual 'language' (news programme discourse, or nature documentary discourse, for instance).

documentary a form aiming to record actual events, often with an explanatory purpose or to analyse and debate an issue.

docusoap a television form combining documentary's depiction of non-actors in ordinary situations with soap opera's continuing narratives about selected characters.

dolly a wheeled camera platform. A 'dolly shot' is a camera shot where the camera is moved forward or back using this platform.

drama-documentary a television form combining dramatised storytelling with the 'objective' informational techniques of documentary. Abbreviated as 'drama-doc' or 'docudrama'.

dubbing replacing the original speech in a programme, advertisement, etc. with speech added later, often to translate speech in a foreign language.

dumbing-down the notion that television has reduced in quality as compared to an earlier period, showing programmes that are more 'dumb' or stupid and addressing its audience as if they were stupid.

effects measurable outcomes produced by watching television, such as becoming more violent or adopting a certain opinion.

electronic newsgathering (ENG)   the use of lightweight cameras and digital technology such as portable satellite transmission dishes to record and transmit news pictures and sound.

ethnicity   membership of a group with a specific identity based on a sense of belonging, such as British Asian or Italian-American, for example.

ethnography   the detailed study of how people live, conducted by observing behaviour and talking to selected individuals about their attitudes and activities.

fan culture   the activities of groups of fans, as distinct from 'ordinary' viewers.

Federal Communications Commission (FCC)   the government body in the USA which regulates the operations and output of television companies and other broadcasters.

feminine   having characteristics associated with the cultural role of women and not men.

feminism   the political and theoretical thinking which in different ways considers the roles of women and femininity in society and culture, often with the aim of critiquing current roles and changing them for the better.

final cut   the final edited version of a programme that is delivered to the television institution for broadcast.

flashback   a television sequence marked as representing events that happened in a time previous to the programme's present.

flow   the ways in which programmes, advertisements, etc. follow one another in an unbroken sequence across the day or part of the day, and the experience of watching the sequence of programmes, advertisements, trailers, etc.

fly-on-the-wall   a documentary form where the subject is observed without the programme-maker's intervention.

focus groups   small groups of selected people representing larger social groupings such as people of a certain age group, gender or economic status, who take part in discussions about a topic chosen for investigation.

format   the blueprint for a programme, including its setting, main characters, genre, form and main themes.

found footage   television or film sequences 'found' in previously made programmes or films, and which can be incorporated unchanged into the programme being made.

franchise   the right to broadcast in one of the terrestrial ITV regions for a set number of years, secured by paying a fee to government.

Frankfurt School   a group of theorists in the mid twentieth century who worked on theories of contemporary culture from a Marxist perspective. Key members, notably Theodor Adorno and Max Horkheimer, left Nazi Germany in the 1930s to work abroad.

free market a television marketplace where factors such as quotas and regulations do not restrict the free operation of economic 'laws' of supply and demand.

free-to-air television programming for which viewers make no direct payment.

gallery the enclosed room in a television studio where production staff observe the shooting of a programme and control the activities of camera operators, sound technicians, performers and other personnel.

gatekeepers the critical term used for the people and institutions (such as television commissioning producers, or regulatory bodies) who control access to television broadcasting.

gender the social and cultural division of people into masculine or feminine individuals. This is different from sex, which refers to the biological difference between male and female bodies.

genre a kind or type of programme. Programmes of the same genre have shared characteristics.

globalisation the process whereby ownership of television institutions in different nations and regions is concentrated in the hands of international corporations, and whereby programmes and formats are traded between institutions around the world.

hegemony a term deriving from Marxist theories of society, meaning a situation where different social classes or groups are persuaded to consent to a political order that may be contrary to their benefit.

hype publicity and public relations effort aiming to raise interest in a television programme or an aspect of one.

iconic sign in semiotics, a sign which resembles its referent. Photographs, for example, contain iconic signs resembling the objects they represent.

identification a term deriving from psychoanalytic theories of cinema, which describes the viewer's conscious or unconscious wish to take the place of someone or something in a television text.

idents the symbols representing production companies, television channels, etc., often comprising graphics or animations.

ideology the set of beliefs, attitudes and assumptions arising from the economic and class divisions in a culture, underlying the ways of life accepted as normal in that culture.

independent production companies businesses making television programmes which can be sold to television networks that transmit and distribute them.

Independent Television Authority (ITA) the first official body set up to regulate commercial television in Britain.

Independent Television Commission (ITC) the regulatory body set up by government to monitor the standards of commercial ITV broadcasting companies, superseded by Ofcom.

indexical sign   in semiotics, a sign which is the result of what it signifies, in the way that smoke is the result of fire.

information society   a contemporary highly developed culture (especially Western culture) where the production and exchange of information is more significant than conventional industrial production.

interactive   offering the opportunity for viewers to respond to what is broadcast, by sending signals back to the broadcaster (along a cable or phone-line, for example).

intertextuality   how one text draws on the meanings of another by referring to it, by allusion, quotation or parody, for example.

licence fee   an annual payment by all owners of television sets, which is the main source of income for the BBC.

location   any place in which television images are shot, except inside a television studio.

long shot   a camera shot taking in the whole body of a performer, or more generally a shot with a wide field of vision.

long take   an imprecise term denoting a longer than usual uninterrupted camera shot.

market research   the collection of information about consumers and their preferences, used to identify products that can be advertised to consumers likely to buy them.

Marxism   the political and economic theories associated with the German nineteenth-century theorist Karl Marx, who described and critiqued capitalist societies and proposed Communism as a revolutionary alternative.

masculine   having characteristics associated with the cultural role of men and not women.

media imperialism   the critical argument that powerful nations and cultures (especially the USA) exert control over other nations and cultures through the media products they export.

media literacy   the skills and competence that viewers learn in order to understand easily the audio-visual 'languages' of media texts.

melodrama   a form of drama characterised by exaggerated performance, a focus on reversals of fortune and extreme emotional reactions to events.

merchandising   the sale of products associated with a television programme, such as toys, books or clothing.

metaphor   the carrying-over from something of some of its meanings on to another thing of an apparently different kind. For example, a television narrative about life aboard ship could be a metaphor for British social life (the ship as metaphor for society).

metonymy the substitution of one thing for another, either because one is part of the other or because one is connected with the other. For example, 'the Crown' can be a metonym for the British state.

microwave link the transmission across large distances of digital signals carried by high-frequency microwaves, to ground stations or to satellites.

mise-en-scène literally meaning 'putting on stage', all the elements of a shot or sequence that contribute to its meanings, such as lighting, camera position and setting.

modality the fit between a fictional representation and the conventional understanding of reality. High modality describes a close fit, and weak modality a distant one.

monopoly control over the provision of a service or product by one institution or business.

multi-accentuality the situation where meanings are able to be read in different ways by different groups of viewers because a text offers multiple meanings at the same time.

narration the process of telling a story through image and sound. Narration can also refer to the spoken text accompanying television images.

narrative an ordered sequence of images and sound that tells a fictional or factual story.

National Viewers' and Listeners' Association an organisation devoted to monitoring the activities of British broadcasters, with a special interest in upholding standards of taste and decency.

natural break a vague term meaning a point at which a programme can be interrupted without causing undue disruption to the ongoing flow of the programme.

naturalism originally having a very specific meaning in literature and drama, this term is now used more loosely to denote television fiction that adopts realistic conventions of character portrayal, linear cause and effect narrative, and a consistent and recognisable fictional world.

negotiated reading a viewer interpretation of a television text where the viewer understands meaning in relation to his or her own knowledge and experience, rather than simply accepting the meaning proposed by the text.

network a television institution that transmits programmes through local or regional broadcasting stations that are owned by or affiliated to that institution.

news agency a media institution that gathers news reports and distributes them to its customers (who include television news broadcasters).

news value the degree of significance attributed to a news story, where items with high news value are deemed most significant to the audience.

niche audiences particular groups of viewers defined by age group, gender or economic status, for example, who may be the target audience for a programme.

noddy shot   in television interviews, shots of the interviewer reacting silently (often by nodding) to the interviewee's responses to questions.

observational documentary   a documentary form in which the programme-maker aims to observe neutrally what would have happened even if he or she had not been present.

off-line editing   the first stage of editing a completed programme, where the sequence of shots, sounds and music is established.

online editing   the final stage of editing a completed programme, where effects are added and a high-quality version of the programme is produced.

ORACLE   the text-based information service provided by ITV and carried by analogue television signals.

outside broadcast   the television transmission of outdoor events such as sport or ceremonial occasions, using equipment set up in advance for the purpose. Abbreviated as OB.

outsourcing   obtaining services from an independent business rather than from within a television institution, usually as a means of cutting costs.

outtake   a shot or sequence which was omitted from a finished programme, because of a mistake during production or an artistic decision.

PAL   Phased Alternate Line transmission of television pictures, a German technical standard introduced in the 1960s making possible improved picture quality and colour pictures.

pan   a shot where the camera is turned to the left or turned to the right. The term derives from the word 'panorama', suggesting the wide visual field that a pan can reveal.

pan-and-scan   capturing a section of an image and enlarging it to fill the television frame, a technique used to fit wide film images into the square television screen.

pastiche   the imitation of forms or conventions in another text. The term can convey a negative view that the imitation is less effective or valuable than the original.

patriarchy   a social system in which power is held by men rather than women, and masculine values dominate.

pay-per-view   specific television programmes (such as sports events, or films) offered to subscribers on payment of a fixed one-off fee.

people meter   a device resembling a television remote control, used in sample households to monitor what viewers watch. Viewers record which channels they watch and for how long.

period drama   television fiction set in the past, most often the nineteenth or early twentieth centuries.

personalities   people appearing on television who are recognised by audiences as celebrities with a media image and public status beyond the role they play in a particular programme.

Pilkington Report the report of a government committee chaired by Lord Pilkington (1960) whose recommendations included the setting up of a second BBC television channel.

pitch a very short written or spoken outline for a programme, perhaps only a few sentences, often used to persuade a commissioning producer to commission the programme.

point of view shot a camera shot where the camera is placed in, or close to, the position from where a previously seen character might look.

polysemia the quality of having multiple meanings at the same time. Texts like this are called 'polysemic'.

pool system in journalism, grouping journalists together to share information so that not all of them need to be present at a news event.

popular culture the texts created by ordinary people (as opposed to an elite group) or created for them, and the ways these are used.

Postmaster General the person appointed by government to regulate communications institutions such as the Post Office, radio and television.

postmodernism the most recent phase of capitalist culture, the aesthetic forms and styles associated with it, and the theoretical approaches developed to understand it.

preferred reading an interpretation of a text that seems to be the one most encouraged by the text, the 'correct' interpretation.

prime time the part of a day's television schedule when the greatest number of viewers may be watching, normally the mid-evening period.

private sphere the domestic world of the home, family and personal life.

privatisation the policy of placing industries or institutions in the hands of privately owned businesses, rather than state ownership.

producer the person working for a television institution who is responsible for the budget, planning and making of a television programme or series of programmes.

production values the level of investment in a television production, such as the amount spent on costumes, props, effects and sets.

progressive encouraging positive change or progress, usually implying progress towards fairer and more equal ways of organising society.

psychoanalysis the study of human mental life, including not only conscious thoughts, wishes and fears but also unconscious ones. Psychoanalysis is an analytical and theoretical set of ideas as well as a therapeutic treatment.

public service in television, the provision of a mix of programmes that inform, educate and entertain in ways that encourage the betterment of audiences and society in general.

public sphere the world of politics, economic affairs and national and international events, as opposed to the 'private sphere' of domestic life.

public television television funded by government or by private supporters, rather than solely by advertising.

quality in television, kinds of programme that are perceived as more expensively produced and, especially, more culturally worthwhile than other programmes.

quota a proportion of television programming, such as a proportion of programmes made in a particular nation.

ratings the number of viewers estimated to have watched certain programmes, as compared to the numbers watching other programmes.

realism the aim for representations to reproduce reality faithfully, and the ways this is done.

reality TV programmes where the unscripted behaviour of 'ordinary people' is the focus of interest.

reflexivity a text's reflection on its own status as a text, for example drawing attention to generic conventions, or revealing the technologies used to make a programme.

register a term in the study of language for the kinds of speech or writing used to represent a particular kind of idea or to address a certain audience.

regulation the control of television institutions by laws, codes of practice or guidelines.

resistance the ways in which audiences make meaning from television programmes that is counter to the meanings thought to be intended, or that are discovered by close analysis.

satellite television television signals beamed from a ground transmitter to a stationary satellite that broadcasts the signal to a specific area (called the 'footprint') below it.

satire a mode of critical commentary about society or an aspect of it, using humour to attack people or ideas.

schedule the arrangement of programmes, advertisements and other material into a sequential order within a certain period of time, such as an evening, day or week.

semiotics the study of signs and their meanings, initially developed for the study of spoken language, and now used also to study the visual and aural 'languages' of other media such as television.

serial a television form where a developing narrative unfolds across a sequence of separate episodes.

series a television form where each programme in the series has a different story or topic, though settings, main characters or performers remain the same.

set-top box the electronic decoding equipment connected to home television sets that allows access to digital television signals.

shooting ratio the number of minutes of film used to film a scene or complete programme as compared to the screen-time of the finished scene or programme.

shot-reverse shot the convention of alternating a shot of one character and a shot of another character in a scene, producing a back-and-forth movement which represents their interaction visually.

sign in semiotics, something which communicates meaning, such as a word, an image or a sound.

simulation a representation that mirrors an aspect of reality so perfectly that it takes the place of the reality it aims to reproduce.

slot the position in a television schedule where a programme is shown.

soap opera a continuing drama serial involving a large number of characters in a specific location, focusing on relationships, emotions and reversals of fortune.

sociology the academic study of society, aiming to describe and explain aspects of life in that society.

spectacle a fascinating image which draws attention to its immediate surface meanings and offers visual pleasure for its own sake.

spin-off a product, television programme, book, etc. that is created to exploit the reputation, meaning or commercial success of a previous one, often in a different medium from the original.

sponsorship the funding of programmes or channels by businesses, whose name is usually prominently displayed in the programme or channel as a means of advertising.

status quo a Latin term meaning the ways that culture and society are currently organised.

storyboard a sequence of drawn images showing the shots to be used in a programme.

strand a linked series of programmes, sharing a common title.

stripping in television scheduling, placing a programme or genre of programme at the same time on several days of each week.

structure of feeling the assumptions, attitudes and ideas prevalent in a society, arising from the ideologies underpinning that society.

subject in psychoanalysis, the term for the individual self whose identity has both conscious and unconscious components.

subscription payment to a television broadcaster in exchange for the opportunity to view programmes on certain channels that are otherwise blocked.

subtitle written text appearing on the television screen, normally to translate speech in a foreign language.

symbol a representation which condenses many meanings together and can stand for those many meanings in a certain context. For example, a brand-new car could be a symbol of wealth, social status and masculine prowess.

symbolic sign in semiotics, a sign which is connected arbitrarily to its referent rather than because the sign resembles its referent. For example a photograph of a cat resembles it, whereas the word 'cat' does not: the word is a symbolic sign.

syndication the sale of programmes for regional television broadcasters to transmit within their territory.

syntagm in semiotics, a linked sequence of signs existing at a certain point in time. Written or spoken sentences, or television sequences, are examples of syntagms.

taste and decency conformity to the standards of good taste and acceptable language and behaviour represented on television, as required by regulations.

teaser a very short television sequence advertising a forthcoming programme, often puzzling or teasing to viewers because it contains little information and encourages curiosity and interest.

telenovela a fictional continuing melodrama on television that lasts for a specific number of episodes. Telenovelas are particularly associated with South American television.

terrestrial broadcasting from a ground-based transmission system, as opposed to broadcasting via satellite.

text an object such as a television programme, film or poem, considered as a network of meaningful signs that can be analysed and interpreted.

textual analysis a critical approach which seeks to understand a television text's meanings by undertaking detailed analysis of its image and sound components, and the relationships between those components.

title sequence the sequence at the opening of a television programme in which the programme title and performers' names may appear along with other information, accompanied by images, sound and music introducing the programme.

tracking shot a camera shot where the camera is moved along (often on a miniature railway track) parallel to a moving subject of the shot while photographing it.

trailer a short television sequence advertising a forthcoming programme, usually containing selected 'highlights' from the programme.

treatment a short written outline for a programme, usually written for a commissioning producer to read, specifying how the programme will tell its story or address its subject.

uplink the electronic system which beams television signals from the ground to a satellite for onward transmission to a television institution elsewhere.

uses and gratifications a theoretical approach that assumes people engage in an activity because it provides them with a benefit of some kind.

utopia an ideal society.

variety programmes entertainment programmes containing a mix of material such as songs and comedy sketches.

vertical integration the control by media institutions of all levels of a business, from the production of products to their distribution and means of reception.

voice-over speech accompanying visual images but not presumed to derive from the same place or time as the images.

vox pop literally meaning 'the voice of the people', short television interviews conducted with members of the public, usually in the street.

voyeurism gaining sexual pleasure from looking at someone or something that cannot look back.

watershed the time in the day (conventionally 9.00 p.m.) after which programmes with content that may disturb children can be shown.

whip-pan a very rapid panning shot from one point to another.

zapping hopping rapidly from channel to channel while watching television, using a remote control (a 'zapper').

Select bibliography

Allen, J., 'The social matrix of television: invention in the United States', in
E. A. Kaplan (ed.), *Regarding Television: Critical Approaches – An Anthology* (Los
Angeles: AFI, 1983), pp. 109–19.

Allen, R. (ed.), *Channels of Discourse, Reassembled: Television and Contemporary Criticism*
(London: Routledge, 1992a).

—— 'Audience-oriented criticism and television', in R. Allen (ed.), *Channels of
Discourse, Reassembled: Television and Contemporary Criticism* (London: Routledge,
1992b), pp. 101–37.

—— *Speaking of Soap Operas* (Chapel Hill, S.C.: University of South Carolina Press,
1985).

Allen, S., G. Branston and C. Carter (eds), *News, Gender and Power* (London:
Routledge, 1998).

Alleyne, M., *News Revolution: Political and Economic Decisions about Global Information*
(Basingstoke: Macmillan, 1997).

Althusser, L., 'Ideology and ideological state apparatuses: notes towards an investigation', in *Lenin and Philosophy* (London: New Left Books, 1971), pp. 121–73.

Alvarado, M. and J. Thompson (eds), *The Media Reader* (London: BFI, 1990).

Ang, I., 'Melodramatic identifications: television fiction and women's fantasy', in
C. Brunsdon, J. D'Acci and L. Spigel (eds), *Feminist Television Criticism: A Reader*
(Oxford: Oxford University Press, 1997), pp. 155–66.

—— *Living Room Wars: Rethinking Audiences for a Postmodern World* (London:
Routledge, 1996).

—— *Desperately Seeking the Audience* (London: Routledge, 1991).

—— *Watching Dallas: Soap Operas and the Melodramatic Imagination*, trans. D. Couling,
revised edition (London: Routledge, 1989).

Ang, I. and J. Hermes, 'Gender and/in media consumption', in I. Ang, *Living Room
Wars: Rethinking Audiences for a Postmodern World* (London: Routledge, 1996),
pp. 108–29.

Annan Committee, *Report of the Committee on the Future of Broadcasting* (London:
HMSO, 1977).

Badsey, S., 'The influence of the media on recent British military operations', in
I. Stewart and S. Carruthers (eds), *War, Culture and the Media: Representations of
the Military in Twentieth-century Britain* (Trowbridge: Flicks Books 1993), pp. 5–21.

Balnaves, M., J. Donald and S. Hemelryk Donald, *The Global Media Atlas* (London:
BFI, 2001).

Bandura, A., *Social Learning Theory* (London: Prentice Hall, 1977).

Barker, C., *Global Television: An Introduction* (Oxford: Blackwell, 1997).

Baudrillard, J., 'The reality gulf', *Guardian*, 11 January 1991, reprinted in
P. Brooker and W. Brooker (eds), *Postmodern After-images: A Reader in Film,
Television and Video* (London: Arnold, 1997), pp. 165–7.

—— *In the Shadow of the Silent Majorities*, trans. P. Foss, J. Johnson and P. Patton (New York: Semiotext(e), 1983a).

—— *Simulations* (New York: Semiotext(e), 1983b).

Bayes, S., *The Avid Handbook*, third edition (Woburn, Mass.: Butterworth-Heinemann, 2000).

Bazalgette, C. and D. Buckingham (eds), *In Front of the Children: Screen Entertainment and Young Audiences* (London: BFI, 1995).

BBC, *Producers' Guidelines* (London: BBC, 1993).

Benjamin, W., 'The work of art in the age of mechanical reproduction', in *Illuminations*, ed. H. Arendt, trans. H. Zohn (New York: Schocken Books, 1969), pp. 219–54.

Bertens, H., *The Idea of the Postmodern: A History* (London: Routledge, 1995).

Bignell, J., *Media Semiotics: An Introduction*, second edition (Manchester: Manchester University Press, 2002a).

—— 'Writing the child in media theory', *Yearbook of English Studies*, 32 (2002b), pp. 127–39.

—— *Postmodern Media Culture* (Edinburgh: Edinburgh University Press, 2000a).

—— 'Docudrama as melodrama: representing Princess Diana and Margaret Thatcher', in B. Carson and M. Llewellyn-Jones (eds), *Frames and Fictions on Television: The Politics of Identity within Drama* (Exeter: Intellect, 2000b), pp. 17–26.

Bignell, J., S. Lacey and M. Macmurraugh-Kavanagh (eds), *British Television Drama: Past, Present and Future* (Basingstoke: Palgrave, 2000).

Billingham, P., *Sensing the City through Television* (Exeter: Intellect, 2000).

Boyd-Barrett, O. and T. Rantanen, *The Globalization of News* (London: Sage, 1998).

Boyle, R. and R. Haynes, *Power Play: Sport, the Media and Popular Culture* (Harlow: Pearson, 2000).

Brandt, G. (ed.), *British Television Drama in the 1980s* (Cambridge: Cambridge University Press, 1993).

Branston, G. and R. Stafford, *The Media Student's Book*, second edition (London: Routledge, 1999).

Briggs, A. and P. Cobley (eds), *The Media: An Introduction* (Harlow: Addison Wesley Longman, 1998).

Broadcasting Standards Commission, *Codes of Guidance* (London: BSC, 1998).

Brooker, P. and W. Brooker (eds), *Postmodern After-images: A Reader in Film, Television and Video* (London: Arnold, 1997).

Brown, I., 'T.V. in the Englishman's castle', *BBC Year Book 1951* (London: BBC, 1951), pp. 17–19.

Brown, M., 'Vying for VIPs', *Guardian*, Media section, 5 March 2001, pp. 8–9.

Brown, M. and M. Wells, 'How did it rate?', *Guardian*, Media section, 27 August 2001, pp. 2–3.

Bruhn Jensen, K. (ed.), *News of the World: World Cultures Look at Television News* (London: Routledge, 1998).

Brunsdon, C., *The Feminist, the Housewife, and the Soap Opera* (Oxford: Oxford University Press, 2000).

—— 'Structure of anxiety: recent British television crime fiction', *Screen*, 39:3 (1998a), pp. 223–43.

—— 'What is the television of television studies?', in C. Geraghty and D. Lusted (eds), *The Television Studies Book* (London: Arnold, 1998b), pp. 95–113.

—— 'Problems with quality', *Screen*, 31:1 (1990), pp. 67–90.

—— 'Crossroads – notes on soap opera', *Screen*, 22:4. (1981), pp. 32–7.

Brunsdon, J., J. D'Acci and L. Spigel, 'Introduction', in C. Brunsdon, J. D'Acci, and L. Spigel (eds), *Feminist Television Criticism: A Reader* (Oxford: Oxford University Press, 1997), pp. 1–16.

Bruzzi, S., *The New Documentary: A Critical Introduction* (London: Routledge, 2000).

Bryant, S., *The Television Heritage: Television Archiving Now and in an Uncertain Future* (London: BFI, 1989).

Buckingham, D., *Moving Images: Understanding Children's Emotional Responses to Television* (Manchester: Manchester University Press, 1996).

—— *Children Talking Television: The Making of Television Literacy* (London: Falmer, 1993a).

—— *Reading Audiences: Young People and the Media* (Manchester: Manchester University Press, 1993b).

—— *Public Secrets: EastEnders and its Audience* (London: BFI, 1987).

Burton, G., *Talking Television: An Introduction to the Study of Television* (London: Arnold, 2000).

Carson, B. and M. Llewellyn-Jones (eds), *Frames and Fictions on Television: The Politics of Identity within Drama* (Exeter: Intellect, 2000).

Caughie, J., *Television Drama: Realism, Modernism, and British Culture* (Oxford: Oxford University Press, 2000).

—— 'Television criticism: a discourse in search of an object', *Screen*, 25:4–5 (1984), pp. 109–20.

—— 'Progressive television and documentary drama', *Screen*, 21:3 (1980) pp. 4–35.

Clarke, A., '"You're nicked!": television police series and the fictional representation of law and order', in D. Strinati and S. Wagg (eds), *Come on Down? Popular Media Culture in Post-war Britain* (London: Routledge, 1992), pp. 232–53.

Coles, G., 'Docusoap: actuality and the serial format', in B. Carson and M. Llewellyn-Jones (eds), *Frames and Fictions on Television: The Politics of Identity within Drama* (Exeter: Intellect, 2000), pp. 27–39.

Collins, J., 'Postmodernism and television', in R. Allen (ed.), *Channels of Discourse, Reassembled: Television and Contemporary Criticism* (London: Routledge, 1992), pp. 327–53.

Cook, G., *The Discourse of Advertising* (London: Routledge, 1992).

Corner, J., *Critical Ideas in Television Studies* (Oxford: Clarendon, 1999).

—— *Studying Media: Problems of Theory and Method* (London: Arnold, 1998).

—— *The Art of Record: A Critical Introduction to Documentary* (Manchester: Manchester University Press, 1996).

—— *Television Form and Public Address* (London: Edward Arnold, 1995).

—— *Popular Television in Britain* (London: BFI, 1991).

Corner, J. and S. Harvey (eds), *Television Times: A Reader* (London: Arnold, 1996).

Corrigan, P., 'On the difficulty of being sociological (historical materialist) in the study of television: the "moment" of English television, 1936–1939', in T. Syvertsen (ed.), *1992 and After: Nordic Television in Transition* (Bergen: University of Bergen, 1990), pp. 130–60.

Creeber, G. (ed.), *The Television Genre Book* (London: BFI, 2001).

Crisell, A., *An Introductory History of British Broadcasting* (London: Routledge, 1997).

Curran, J. and J. Seaton (eds), *Power without Responsibility: The Press and Broadcasting in Britain*, fifth edition (London: Routledge, 1997).

Dahlgren, P., *Television and the Public Sphere* (London: Sage, 1995).

Dickinson, R., R. Harindranath and O. Linné (eds), *Approaches to Audiences: A Reader* (London: Arnold, 1998).

Dominick, J., B. Sherman and G. Copeland, *Broadcasting/Cable and Beyond: An Introduction to Modern Electronic Media*, third edition (New York: McGraw-Hill, 1996).

Dovey, J., *Freakshow* (Cambridge: Polity, 2000).

Dowmunt, T. (ed.), *Channels of Resistance: Global Television and Local Empowerment* (London: BFI, 1993).

Drummond, P. and R. Patterson (eds), *Television and its Audience: International Research Perspectives* (London: BFI, 1988).

Dyer, R., *Light Entertainment* (London: BFI, 1973).

Dyer, R., C. Geraghty, M. Jordan, T. Lovell, R. Paterson and J. Stewart, *Coronation Street* (London: BFI, 1981).

Eco, U., 'Interpreting serials', in *The Limits of Interpretation* (Bloomington, Ind.: Indiana University Press, 1990), pp. 83–100.

—— 'A guide to the neo-television of the 1980s', *Framework*, 25 (1984), pp. 18–25.

Eldridge, J. (ed.), *Glasgow Media Reader Volume 1: News Content, Language and Visuals* (London: Routledge, 1995).

Ellis, J., 'Scheduling: the last creative act in television', *Media, Culture & Society*, 22:1 (2000), pp. 25–38.

—— *Visible Fictions: Cinema, Television, Video* (London: Routledge and Kegan Paul, 1982).

Fairclough, N., *Media Discourse* (London: Arnold, 1995).

Feuer, J., 'Genre study and television', in R. Allen (ed.), *Channels of Discourse, Reassembled* (London: Routledge, 1992), pp. 138–60.

Fiske, J., *Media Matters* (Minneapolis, Minn.: University of Minnesota Press, 1994).

—— *Television Culture* (London: Routledge, 1992).

—— 'The cultural economy of fandom', in L. Lewis (ed.), *The Adoring Audience: Fan Culture and Popular Media* (London: Routledge, 1992a), pp. 30–49.

—— 'British cultural studies and television', in R. Allen (ed.), *Channels of Discourse, Reassembled: Television and Contemporary Criticism* (London: Routledge, 1992b), pp. 284–326.

—— 'Postmodernism and television', in J. Curran and M. Gurevitch (eds), *Mass Media and Society* (London: Edward Arnold, 1991), pp. 55–67.

—— *Introduction to Communication Studies* (London: Routledge, 1990).

Fiske, J. and J. Hartley, *Reading Television* (London: Methuen, 1978).

Flitterman-Lewis, S., 'Psychoanalysis, film, and television', in R. Allen (ed.), *Channels of Discourse, Reassembled: Television and Contemporary Criticism* (London: Routledge, 1992), pp. 203–46.

Freedman, L. and E. Karsh, *The Gulf Conflict 1990–1991: Diplomacy and War in the New World Order* (London: Faber, 1993).

Galtung, J. and M. Ruge, 'Structuring and selecting news', in S. Cohen and J. Young (eds), *The Manufacture of News: Social Problems, Deviance and the Mass Media* (London: Constable, 1973), pp. 62–72.

Garber, M., J. Matlock and R. Walkowitz (eds), *Media Spectacles* (London: Routledge, 1993).

Garnett, T., 'Contexts', in J. Bignell, S. Lacey and M. Macmurraugh-Kavanagh (eds), *British Television Drama: Past, Present and Future* (Basingstoke: Palgrave, 2000), pp. 11–23.

Geertz, C., *The Interpretation of Cultures: Selected Essays* (London: Fontana, 1967).

Geraghty, C., 'Audiences and "ethnography": questions of practice', in C. Geraghty and D. Lusted (eds), *The Television Studies Book* (London: Arnold, 1998), pp. 141–57.

—— *Women and Soap Opera: A Study of Prime Time Soaps* (Cambridge: Polity Press, 1991).

Geraghty, C. and D. Lusted (eds), *The Television Studies Book* (London: Arnold, 1998).

Gibbs, J., *Mise-en-Scene: Film Style and Interpretation* (London: Wallflower, 2002).

Giddens, A. *The Consequences of Modernity* (Cambridge: Polity, 1990).

Gillespie, M., 'Ambivalent positionings: the Gulf War', in P. Brooker and W. Brooker (eds), *Postmodern After-images: A Reader in Film, Television and Video* (London: Arnold, 1997), pp. 172–81.

Glasgow Media Group, *War and Peace News* (Milton Keynes: Open University Press, 1986).

—— *More Bad News* (London: Routledge and Kegan Paul, 1980).

—— *Bad News* (London: Routledge and Kegan Paul, 1976).

Goodwin, A., 'MTV', in J. Corner and S. Harvey (eds), *Television Times: A Reader* (London: Arnold, 1996), pp. 75–87.

—— *Dancing in the Distraction Factory: Music, Television and Popular Culture* (London: Routledge, 1993).

Goodwin, A. and G. Whannel (eds), *Understanding Television* (London: Routledge, 1990).

Goodwin, P., 'The role of the state', in J. Stokes and A. Reading (eds), *The Media in Britain: Current Debates and Developments* (Basingstoke: Macmillan, 1999), pp. 130–42.

Gray, A., *Video Playtime: The Gendering of a Leisure Technology* (London: Routledge, 1992).

Gray, H., *Watching Race: Television and the Struggle for 'Blackness'* (Minneapolis, Minn.: University of Minnesota Press, 1995).

Gripsrud, J. 'Television, broadcasting, flow: key metaphors in TV theory', in C. Geraghty and D. Lusted (eds), *The Television Studies Book* (London: Arnold, 1998), pp. 17–32.

—— *The Dynasty Years: Hollywood Television and Critical Media Studies* (London: Routledge, 1995).

Grossberg, L., C. Nelson and P. Treichler, with L. Baughman and J. Macgregor Wise (eds), *Cultural Studies* (New York: Routledge, 1992).

Gurevitch, M., 'The globalization of electronic journalism', in J. Curran and M. Gurevitch (eds), *Mass Media and Society* (London: Edward Arnold, 1991), pp. 178–93.

Habermas, J., *The Theory of Communicative Action*, vol. 2: *Lifeworld and System: A Critique of Functionalist Reason* (Cambridge: Polity, 1987).

Hall, S. (ed.), *Representation: Cultural Representations and Signifying Practices* (London: Sage, 1997).

—— 'Black and white television', in D. Morley and K. Chen (eds), *Remote Control:*

Dilemmas of Black Intervention in British Film and TV (London: BFI, 1996), pp. 13–28.

—— 'Encoding/decoding', in S. Hall, D. Hobson, A. Lowe and P. Willis (eds), *Culture, Media, Language* (London: Hutchinson, 1980), pp. 128–38.

Hallam, J. and M. Marshment, 'Framing experience: case studies in the reception of *Oranges Are Not the Only Fruit*', *Screen*, 36:1 (1995), pp. 1–15.

Harbord, J. and J. Wright, *Forty Years of British Television* (London: Boxtree, 1992).

Harrison, J., *Terrestrial Television News in Britain: The Culture of Production* (Manchester: Manchester University Press, 2000).

Hart, C., *Television Program Making* (Oxford: Focal Press, 1999).

Hartley, J., *Tele-ology: Studies in Television* (London: Routledge, 1992).

—— *Understanding News* (London: Routledge, 1982).

Harvey, S., 'Channel 4 television from Annan to Grade', in S. Hood (ed.), *Behind the Screens* (London: Lawrence and Wishart, 1994), pp. 102–29.

Havens, T., '"The biggest show in the world": race and the global popularity of *The Cosby Show*', *Media Culture & Society*, 22:4 (2000), pp. 371–91.

Herman, E. and R. McChesney, *The Global Media: The New Missionaries of Global Capitalism* (London: Cassell, 1997).

Hill, J. and M. McLoone (eds), *Big Picture Small Screen: The Relations between Film and Television* (Luton: University of Luton Press, 1997).

Himmelwhite, H. T. et al. *Television and the Child: An Experimental Study of the Effect of Television on the Young* (London: Nuffield Foundation and Oxford University Press, 1958).

Hobson, D., *Crossroads: The Drama of a Soap Opera* (London: Methuen, 1982).

Hood, S. (ed.), *Behind the Screens: The Structure of British Television in the Nineties* (London: Lawrence and Wishart, 1994).

Hutcheon, L., 'The politics of postmodernism, parody, and history', *Cultural Critique*, 5 (1986–7), pp. 179–207.

Huyssen, A., *After the Great Divide: Modernism, Mass Culture and Postmodernism* (London: Macmillan, 1986).

Independent Television Commission, *The ITC Programme Code* (London: ITC, 1998).

Jacobson, R., *Television Research: A Directory of Conceptual Categories, Topic Suggestions and Selected Sources* (Jefferson: McFarland, 1995).

Jameson, F., 'Reading without interpretation: postmodernism and the video-text', in D. Attridge and N. Fabb (eds), *The Linguistics of Writing: Arguments between Language and Literature* (Manchester: Manchester University Press, 1987), pp. 199–233.

Jenkins, H., *Textual Poachers: Television Fans and Participatory Culture* (London: Routledge, 1992).

Jhally, S. and J. Lewis, *Enlightened Racism: The Cosby Show, Audiences, and the Myth of the American Dream* (San Francisco, Calif.: Westview, 1992).

Jhally, S. and B. Livant, 'Watching as working: the valorization of audience consciousness', *Journal of Communication*, 36:2 (1986), pp. 124–43.

Kaplan, E. A., *Rocking Around the Clock: Music Television, Postmodernism and Consumer Culture* (London: Methuen, 1987).

Katz, E. and Liebes, T. 'Mutual aid in the decoding of *Dallas*: preliminary notes from a cross-cultural study', in P. Drummond, *Television in Transition* (London: BFI, 1985), pp. 187–98.

—— 'Once upon a time in Dallas', *Intermedia*, 12:3 (1984), pp. 28–32.

Kauffmann, S., *Avid Editing* (Woburn, Mass.: Butterworth-Heinemann, 2000).

Kellner, D., *Media Culture: Cultural Studies, Identity and Politics Between the Modern and the Postmodern* (London: Routledge, 1995).

Kidd-Hewitt, D. and R. Osborne (eds), *Crime and the Media: The Postmodern Spectacle* (London: Pluto, 1995).

Kilborn, R. and J. Izod, *An Introduction to Television Documentary: Confronting Reality* (Manchester: Manchester University Press, 1997).

Kozloff, S., 'Narrative theory and television', in R. Allen (ed.), *Channels of Discourse, Reassembled: Television and Contemporary Criticism* (London: Routledge, 1992), pp. 67–100.

Lacan, J., 'The mirror stage', in *Ecrits: A Selection*, trans. A. Sheridan (London: Tavistock, 1977), pp. 1–7.

Lacey, N., *Narrative and Genre: Key Concepts in Media Studies* (Basingstoke: Macmillan, 2000).

Langer, J., *Tabloid Television: Popular Journalism and 'Other News'* (London: Routledge, 1998).

Leal, O., 'Popular taste and erudite repertoire: the place and space of television in Brazil', *Cultural Studies*, 4:1 (1990), pp. 19–29.

Lewis, J., *The Ideological Octopus: An Exploration of Television and its Audience* (London: Routledge, 1991).

—— 'Decoding television news', in P. Drummond and R. Paterson (eds), *Television in Transition* (London: BFI, 1985), pp. 205–34.

Lewis, L. (ed.), *The Adoring Audience: Fan Culture and Popular Media* (London: Routledge, 1991).

—— *Gender Politics and MTV: Voicing the Difference* (Philadelphia, Pa.: Temple University Press, 1990).

Liebes, T. and Katz, E., *The Export of Meaning: Cross-cultural Readings of 'Dallas'* (New York: Oxford University Press, 1990).

Lindof, T. (ed.), *Natural Audiences: Qualitative Research of Media Uses and Effects* (Norwood: Ablex, 1987).

Lister, M. (ed.), *The Photographic Image in Digital Culture* (London: Routledge, 1995).

Livingston, S. and P. Lunt, *Talk on Television: Audience Participation and Public Debate* (London: Routledge, 1994).

Lorimer, R., with P. Scannell, *Mass Communications: A Comparative Introduction* (Manchester: Manchester University Press, 1994).

Lull, J. (ed.), *World Families Watch Television* (London: Sage, 1988a).

—— 'Critical response: the audience as nuisance', *Critical Studies in Mass Communication* 5 (1988b), pp. 239–43.

Lusted, D., 'The popular culture debate and light entertainment on television', in C. Geraghty and D. Lusted (eds), *The Television Studies Book* (London: Arnold, 1998), pp. 175–90.

Lyotard, J.-F., 'Answering the question: what is postmodernism?', in T. Docherty (ed.), *Postmodernism: A Reader* (Hemel Hempstead: Harvester Wheatsheaf, 1993), pp. 38–46.

—— *The Postmodern Condition*, trans. G. Bennington and B. Massumi (Manchester: Manchester University Press, 1984).

McCracken, E., *Decoding Women's Magazines: From Mademoiselle to Ms.* (Basingstoke: Macmillan, 1993).

Macdonald, M., *Representing Women: Myths of Femininity in the Popular Media* (London: Arnold, 1995).

MacGregor, B., *Live, Direct and Biased? Making Television News in the Satellite Age* (London: HodderHeadline, 1997).

Mackay, H. and T. O'Sullivan (eds), *The Media Reader: Continuity and Transformation* (London: Sage, 1999).

McLean, G., 'Corner shop to cop shop', *Guardian*, Media section, 18 February 2002, pp. 8–9.

McLuhan, M., *Understanding Media: The Extensions of Man* (London: Ark, 1987).

McNair, B., *News and Journalism in the UK: A Textbook* (London: Routledge, 1994).

McQueen, D., *Television: A Media Student's Guide* (London: Arnold, 1998).

Mader, R., 'Globo village: television in Brazil', in T. Dowmunt (ed.), *Channels of Resistance: Global Television and Local Empowerment* (London: BFI, 1993), pp. 67–89.

Marris, P. and S. Thornham (eds), *Media Studies: A Reader* (Edinburgh: Edinburgh University Press, 1999).

Masterman, L., *Television Mythologies: Stars, Shows and Signs* (London: Comedia, 1984).

Meech, P., 'Advertising', in J. Stokes and A. Reading (eds), *The Media in Britain: Current Debates and Developments* (Basingstoke: Macmillan, 1999), pp. 25–40.

Millerson, G., *Video Production Handbook*, third edition (Oxford: Focal Press, 2001).

Modleski, T., *Loving with a Vengeance* (Hamden, Conn.: Shoe String Press, 1982).

Moores, S., *Interpreting Audiences* (London: Sage, 1993).

Morley, D., *Television, Audiences and Cultural Studies* (London: Routledge, 1992).

—— *The 'Nationwide' Audience* (London: BFI, 1980).

Morris, M., 'Feminism, reading, postmodernism', in T. Docherty (ed.), *Postmodernism: A Reader* (Hemel Hempstead: Harvester Wheatsheaf, 1993), pp. 368–89.

—— 'Banality in cultural studies', *Block*, 14 (1988), pp. 15–25.

Mort, F., *Cultures of Consumption: Masculinities and Social Space in Late Twentieth-century Britain* (London: Routledge, 1996).

Mosely, R., 'Makeover takover on British television', *Screen*, 41:3 (2000), pp. 299–314.

Moss, S., 'New kids on the block', *Guardian*, Media section, 28 January 2002, pp. 2–3.

Mullan, B., *Consuming Television* (Oxford: Blackwell, 1997).

Mundy, J., *Popular Music on Screen: From Hollywood Musical to Music Video* (Manchester: Manchester University Press, 1999).

Murdoch, G., 'Authorship and organization', *Screen Education*, 35 (1980), pp. 19–34.

Myers, G., *Ad Worlds: Brands, Media, Audiences* (London: Arnold, 1999).

Neale, S. and F. Krutnik, *Popular Film and Television Comedy* (London: Routledge, 1990).

Neale, S. and G. Turner, 'Introduction: what is genre?', in G. Creeber (ed.), *The Television Genre Book* (London: BFI, 2001), pp. 1–7.

Nelson, R., *TV Drama in Transition: Forms, Values and Cultural Change* (Basingstoke: Macmillan, 1997).

Newcomb, H., *TV: The Most Popular Art* (New York: Anchor, 1974).

Nichols, B., *Introduction to Documentary* (Bloomington, Ind.: Indiana University Press, 2001).

—— *Blurred Boundaries: Questions of Meaning in Contemporary Culture* (Bloomington, Ind.: Indiana University Press, 1994).

—— *Representing Reality: Issues and Concepts in Documentary* (Bloomington, Ind.: Indiana University Press, 1991).

Norris, C., '"Postscript": Baudrillard's second Gulf War article', in P. Brooker and W. Brooker (eds), *Postmodern After-images: A Reader in Film, Television and Video* (London: Arnold, 1997), pp. 168–71.

Orlebar, J., *Digital Television Production* (London: Arnold, 2002).

O'Sullivan, T., 'Television, memories and cultures of viewing 1950–65', in J. Corner (ed.), *Popular Television in Britain: Studies in Cultural History* (London: BFI, 1991), pp. 159–81.

O'Sullivan, T., B. Dutton and P. Rayner, *Studying the Media: An Introduction* (London: Edward Arnold, 1994).

Paget, D., *No Other Way to Tell It: Dramadoc/Docudrama on Television* (Manchester: Manchester University Press, 1998).

Petley, J., 'The regulation of media content', in J. Stokes and A. Reading (eds), *The Media in Britain: Current Debates and Developments* (Basingstoke: Macmillan, 1999), pp. 143–57.

Petrie, D. and J. Willis (eds), *Television and the Household: Reports from the BFI's Audience Tracking Study* (London: BFI, 1995).

Philips, D., 'Medicated soap: the woman doctor in television medical drama', in B. Carson and M. Llewellyn-Jones (eds), *Frames and Fictions on Television: The Politics of Identity within Drama* (Exeter: Intellect, 2000), pp. 50–61.

Philo, G., 'Missing in action', *Guardian*, Higher Education section, 16 April (2002), pp. 10–11.

—— (ed.), *Glasgow Media Reader, volume 2: Industry, War, Economy and Politics* (London: Routledge, 1995).

—— 'Whose news?', *Media, Culture & Society*, 9:4 (1987), pp. 397–406.

Poster, M., *The Second Media Age* (Cambridge: Polity, 1995).

Purser, P., 'Dennis Potter', in G. Brandt (ed.), *British Television Drama* (Cambridge: Cambridge University Press, 1981), pp. 168–93.

Rose, B. (ed.), *TV Genres: A Handbook and Reference Guide* (Westport, Conn.: Greenwood, 1985).

Ruddock, A., *Understanding Audiences: Theory and Method* (London: Sage, 2001).

Saussure, F. de, *Course in General Linguistics*, ed. C. Bally, A. Sechehaye and A. Riedlinger, trans. W. Baskin (London: Fontana, 1974).

Scannell, P., 'Public service broadcasting; the history of a concept', in A. Goodwin and G. Whannel (eds), *Understanding Television* (London: Routledge, 1990), pp. 11–29.

Schlesinger, P., *Putting 'Reality' Together: BBC News* (London: Constable, 1978).

Sears, J., '*Crimewatch* and the rhetoric of versimilitude', *Critical Survey*, 7:1 (1995), pp. 51–8.

Seiter, E., 'Semiotics, structuralism, and television', in R. Allen (ed.), *Channels of Discourse, Reassembled: Television and Contemporary Criticism* (London: Routledge, 1992), pp. 31–66.

Seiter, E., H. Borchers, G. Kreutzner and E.-M. Warth (eds), *Remote Control: Television, Audiences and Cultural Power* (London: Routledge, 1989).

Selby, K. and R. Cowdery, *How to Study Television* (Basingstoke: Macmillan, 1995).

Sharman, M., 'A nation tunes in', *Guardian*, Media section, 18 February 2002, pp. 8–9.

Shattuc, J., *The Talking Cure: TV Talk Shows and Women* (London: Routledge, 1997).

Sheen, E. and R. Giddings (eds), *The Classic Novel: From Page to Screen* (Manchester: Manchester University Press, 1999).

Shubik, I., *Play for Today: The Evolution of Television Drama* (London: Davis-Poynter, 1975).

Sinclair, J., E. Jacka and S. Cunningham, 'New patterns in global television', in P. Marris and S. Thornham (eds), *The Media Reader* (Edinburgh: Edinburgh University Press, 1999), pp. 170–90.

—— (eds), *Peripheral Vision: New Patterns in Global Television* (Oxford: Oxford University Press, 1996).

Smith, A., *Television: An International History*, second edition (Oxford: Oxford University Press, 1998).

Sobchack, V., 'Democratic franchise and the electronic frontier', in Z. Sardar and J. Ravetz (eds), *Cyberfutures* (London: Pluto, 1996), pp. 77–89.

Sparks, R., *Television and the Drama of Crime* (Buckingham: Open University Press, 1992).

Sreberny-Mohammadi, A. with K. Nordenstreng, R. Stevenson and F. Ugboajah (eds), *Foreign News in the Media: International Reporting in 29 Countries* (Paris: UNESCO, 1985).

Sreberny-Mohammadi, A., D. Winseck, J. McKenna and O. Boyd-Barrett (eds), *Media in Global Context: A Reader* (London: Arnold, 1997).

Stewart, I. and S. Carruthers (eds), *War, Culture and the Media: Representations of the Military in 20th Century Britain* (Trowbridge: Flicks Books, 1996).

Stokes, J. and A. Reading (eds), *The Media in Britain: Current Debates and Developments* (Basingstoke: Macmillan, 1999).

Storey, J. *Cultural Consumption and Everyday Life* (London: Arnold, 1999).

Thussu, K. D. (ed.), *Electronic Empires: Global Media and Local Resistance* (London: Arnold, 1998).

Tolson, A., *Mediations: Text and Discourse in Media Studies* (London: Arnold, 1996).

Tulloch, J., *Watching Television Audiences: Cultural Theories and Methods* (London: Arnold, 2000).

—— *Television Drama: Agency, Audience and Myth* (London: Routledge, 1990).

Tulloch, J. and H. Jenkins, *Science Fiction Audiences: Watching Doctor Who and Star Trek* (London: Routledge, 1995).

Tunstall, J. (ed.), *Media Occupations and Professions: A Reader* (Oxford: Oxford University Press, 2001).

—— *Television Producers* (London: Routledge, 1993).

—— *The Media in Britain* (London: Constable, 1983).

Uricchio, W., 'Rituals of reception, patterns of neglect: Nazi television and its postwar representation', *Wide Angle*, 11:1 (1989), pp. 48–66.

Wagg, S. (ed.), *Because I Tell a Joke or Two: Comedy, Politics and Social Difference* (London: Routledge, 1998).

Walker, I., 'Desert stories or faith in facts?', in M. Lister (ed.), *The Photographic Image in Digital Culture* (London: Routledge 1995), pp. 236–52.

Webster, F., *Theories of the Information Society* (London: Routledge, 1995).

Whannel, G., *Fields in Vision: Television Sport and Cultural Transformation* (London: Routledge, 1992).

Wicke, J. and M. Ferguson, 'Introduction: feminism and postmodernism; or, The way we live now', in M. Ferguson and J. Wicke (eds), *Feminism and Postmodernism* (London: Duke University Press, 1994), pp. 1–9.

Williams, R., *Television, Technology and Cultural Form* (London: Collins, 1974).

—— *Drama in Performance* (London: C. A. Watts, 1968).

Winship, J., *Inside Women's Magazines* (London: Pandora, 1987).

Winston, B., *Media Technology and Society: A History* (London: Routledge, 1998).

—— *Claiming the Real: The Documentary Film Revisited* (London: BFI, 1995).

Woods, T., *Beginning Postmodernism* (Manchester: Manchester University Press, 1999).

Index

Note: Page numbers in *italics* denote references to illustrations.

slot 136, 314
So Graham Norton 244
soap opera 10, 19, 94, 114, 118–19,
    314; audience research 25, 296–9;
    Channel 4 audiences 46; close-ups
    90; demographics of audience
    262; director's skills 146; family
    relationships 174; feminist research
    25, 283–4; gender 215; *The Grove
    Family* 52; ITV 54; popularity 257;
    realism 56, 188–91; scheduling
    272; sexual activity 241; talk show
    comparison 125; telenovela contrast
    81; *Twin Peaks* 171; women 25, 283–4,
    289, 296–9; writers 141
Sobchack, Vivian 202
social change 17–18, 47
social class *see* class
social control 126–7, 236
social environment 4, 79, 299
social power 4, 16, 300
social responsibility 185, 189
social science research 20–1, 25, 211
sociology 2, 3, 15, 25, 314
Sony 69
Sopranos, The 139
sound 87–8, 153–4, 156, 158–9, 186
South Africa 224
Soviet Union 68, 73, 285
Spears, Britney 179
spectacle 76, 314
Spielberg, Steven 171, 172
spin-offs 124, 291, 314
sponsorship 4, 44, 314
sports television 103, 116, 196, 260, 265,
    296
Star Trek 27, 115, 165, 288, 290, 293
Star Trek: The Next Generation 90–2, 100
Star TV 45, 70, 74
Stars in Their Eyes 200–1
status quo 18, 47, 48, 314
stereotypes 8, 221, 222
Stewart, Alastair 131, 132
Storey, John 268–9, 297, 299
storyboards 136, 137, 143, 152, 314
storylines 141–2
strands 126, 195, 314
strips 272, 314
structure of feeling 23, 218–19, 297, 314
studio audiences 93, 97, 102, 103, 122,
    265
subcultures 21, 283, 288
subject 98, 102, 188, 191, 314
subjectivity 98, 164, 176, 177, 191

subscription 24, 243, 245, 268, 314
subtitles 14, 225, 315
suburbs 29, 30, 50
Sunday Night at the London Palladium 52
Survivor 100
Sweeney, The 89
symbolic signs 87, 315
symbols 315
syndication 223, 315
syntagms 88–9, 110, 315

Taboo: 40 Years of Censorship 232
Taiwan 74
talk shows 102–3, 123–5, 203, 265–6
Tarantino, Quentin 163
taste 9, 24, 231, 233–5, 241–3, 245, 315
teasers 117, 315
technology 30, 41–3, 46–7, 68; digital
    video recorders 6, 56–8, 273; editing
    7, 152, 154, 156–9; realism 186–8,
    207; *see also* digital technologies;
    Internet; satellite television
telenovelas 6, 69, 78, 80–2, 315
Teletubbies 63–4
Television Without Frontiers Directive
    79
Ten O'Clock News 89
terrestrial broadcasting 31, 45, 65, 231,
    240, 254, 315
texts 2, 6–7, 15–18, 86–112, 315; genre
    132; progressiveness 23; realism 188;
    reflexivity 56; *see also* narrative
textual analysis 5, 6–7, 15–18, 283, 315;
    Guinness 'Surfer' commercial 105–11;
    Mighty Morphin' Power Rangers 67–8;
    representation of groups 211, 226
Thailand 78
That Was the Week That Was 47, 235
Thatcher, Margaret 237, 239
Thaw, John 89, 114
themed channels 24, 117
Third World 168, 193; *see also* developing
    countries
This Life 148
Thompson, E. P. 47
Time of Our Lives, The 260
Time Team 100
Time-Warner 70, 219
title sequences 88–9, 100, 115, 315
TiVo 56, 273
Top of the Pops 236
Touch of Frost, A 63, 257, 263
tracking shot 315
trailers 5, 16, 117, 282, 315